The Politics of Immigration Beyond Liberal States

Immigration presents a fundamental challenge to the nation-state and is a top political priority for governments worldwide. Yet, knowledge on the politics of immigration remains largely limited to liberal states of the Global North. This book systematically compares immigration policymaking in authoritarian Morocco and democratizing Tunisia to theorize the role of political regimes in immigration politics. Drawing on extensive fieldwork and archival research, the study shows that immigration politics – how a state deals with 'the other' – offers a privileged lens into the inner workings of political regimes: It demonstrates that in Tunisia, restrictive policy continuity functioned as a safeguard for democratization, while in Morocco, liberal immigration reform was central to the monarchy's authoritarian consolidation. The study also reveals that most policymaking dynamics around immigration do not depend on the type of political regime in place, but are inherent to the issues raised by immigration or to public policymaking in modern states. Connecting comparative politics, international relations and political sociology scholarship on migration across the Global North and Global South, the book seeks to provide scholars, students and practitioners with food for thought on the fascinating interplay between immigration, political regimes and modern statehood around the world.

Dr Katharina Natter is Assistant Professor in Political Science at Leiden University. In her research, she explores modern statehood through the lens of migration politics. Natter holds a PhD in political sociology from the University of Amsterdam, and a Research Masters in comparative politics from Sciences Po Paris. She previously worked at the International Migration Institute, University of Oxford and also serves on the board of the NGO Asylos.

The Politics of Immigration Beyond Liberal States

Morocco and Tunisia in Comparative Perspective

Katharina Natter
University of Leiden

CAMBRIDGE
UNIVERSITY PRESS

Shaftesbury Road, Cambridge CB2 8EA, United Kingdom

One Liberty Plaza, 20th Floor, New York, NY 10006, USA

477 Williamstown Road, Port Melbourne, VIC 3207, Australia

314–321, 3rd Floor, Plot 3, Splendor Forum, Jasola District Centre, New Delhi – 110025, India

103 Penang Road, #05–06/07, Visioncrest Commercial, Singapore 238467

Cambridge University Press is part of Cambridge University Press & Assessment, a department of the University of Cambridge.

We share the University's mission to contribute to society through the pursuit of education, learning and research at the highest international levels of excellence.

www.cambridge.org
Information on this title: www.cambridge.org/9781009262620

DOI: 10.1017/9781009262668

© Katharina Natter 2023

This publication is in copyright. Subject to statutory exception and to the provisions of relevant collective licensing agreements, no reproduction of any part may take place without the written permission of Cambridge University Press & Assessment.

First published 2023

A catalogue record for this publication is available from the British Library.

Library of Congress Cataloging-in-Publication Data
Names: Natter, Katharina, author.
Title: The politics of immigration beyond liberal states : Morocco and Tunisia in comparative perspective / Katharina Natter.
Description: Cambridge ; New York, NY : Cambridge University Press, 2022. | Includes bibliographical references and index.
Identifiers: LCCN 2022030479 (print) | LCCN 2022030480 (ebook) | ISBN 9781009262620 (hardback) | ISBN 9781009262613 (paperback) | ISBN 9781009262668 (epub)
Subjects: LCSH: Morocco–Emigration and immigration–Government policy. | Morocco–Emigration and immigration–Political aspects. | Tunisia–Emigration and immigration–Government policy. | Tunisia–Emigration and immigration–Political aspects. | Morocco–Politics and government–1999– | Tunisia–Politics and government–2011–
Classification: LCC JV8978 .N38 2022 (print) | LCC JV8978 (ebook) | DDC 325/.264–dc23/eng/20220830
LC record available at https://lccn.loc.gov/2022030479
LC ebook record available at https://lccn.loc.gov/2022030480

ISBN 978-1-009-26262-0 Hardback

Cambridge University Press & Assessment has no responsibility for the persistence or accuracy of URLs for external or third-party internet websites referred to in this publication and does not guarantee that any content on such websites is, or will remain, accurate or appropriate.

To the little bird I met in the courtyard of the house where I stayed during my first fieldwork visit in the Oudayas, Rabat, in January 2012.

And to all those little moments that never make it into a book but that are essential to fill life with meaning and joy.

Contents

List of Figures	*page* viii
List of Tables	ix
Acknowledgements	x
Note on the Text	xii
List of Abbreviations	xiii
1 Introduction	1
2 Theories on the Move	20
3 The Contrasting Cases of Morocco and Tunisia	44
4 Regime Continuity and Immigration Policy Change in Morocco	79
5 The Illiberal Paradox of Autocratic Policymaking	109
6 Regime Change and Immigration Policy Continuity in Tunisia	140
7 The Ambiguous Effects of Democratization	165
8 Immigration Politics and State Transformation	198
9 Conclusion	220
Appendices	229
Notes	257
References	265
Index	296

Figures

1.1	Polity, politics, policy	*page* 5
3.1	Annual Moroccan emigration to main destinations, 1965–2010	58
3.2	Annual Tunisian emigration to main destinations, 1965–2010	59
3.3	Recorded number of foreigners according to Moroccan census data, 1935–2014	65
3.4	Recorded number of foreigners according to Tunisian census data, 1906–2014	65
4.1	Format of work contract in 1949 (top) and 1965 (bottom)	80
5.1	ODTI flyer from 2014 encouraging migrants to regularize	116
A.1	Evolution of real GDP per capita, 1950–2017	233
A.2	International tourism, number of arrivals, 1995–2018	234
A.3	Foreign direct investment (net inflows, current USD), 1970–2019	234
A.4	Export volume index (2000 = 100), 1980–2018	235
A.5	Personal remittances received, 1975–2019	235
A.6	Changes in political systems, 1956–2018	236
A.7	Changes in electoral and liberal components of democracy, Morocco, 1956–2019	236
A.8	Changes in electoral and liberal components of democracy, Tunisia, 1956–2019	237

Tables

1.1	Morocco and Tunisia, a puzzling contrast	page 3
2.1	Categorizing immigration policymaking theories	23
3.1	Geographic distribution of Moroccan and Tunisian emigrants, 2012–2018, in per cent	61
3.2	Number of immigrants living in Morocco, by country of citizenship, 2004 and 2014	67
3.3	Number of immigrants living in Tunisia, by country of citizenship, 2004 and 2014	69
4.1	Budget of Moroccan ministries, 2011–2016 (selection), in billions of dirham	101
A.1	List of interviewed actors	230
A.2	Key socio-political developments and events related to immigration in Morocco	238
A.3	Morocco's main legal and informal policy changes on immigration	240
A.4	National institutional changes related to immigration in Morocco	242
A.5	International activities and diplomatic developments around immigration in Morocco	243
A.6	Civil society developments on immigration in Morocco	245
A.7	Key socio-political developments and events related to immigration in Tunisia	247
A.8	Tunisia's main legal and informal policy changes on immigration	249
A.9	National institutional changes related to immigration in Tunisia	252
A.10	International activities and diplomatic developments around immigration in Tunisia	253
A.11	Civil society developments on immigration in Tunisia	255

Acknowledgements

This book is the fruit of an intellectual and personal journey that started over a decade ago, back in 2009. At the time, I was spending one year in Cairo as part of my undergraduate degree at Sciences Po. My conversations with young Egyptians confronted me with my Western worldview and the biases I had so naturally incorporated while growing up and studying in Europe. As a nineteen-year-old, I also for the first time experienced the privileges of my Austrian passport and realized the obstacles to freedom of movement my Egyptian friends were facing. This prompted my initial interest in migration and the politics around it.

Living in France, where immigration from North Africa was constantly debated in politics and in private, I wanted to learn more about the other side of the coin: how immigration was talked about and dealt with on the southern Mediterranean shore. In my master's thesis, I therefore researched on the domestic politics around immigration in Morocco over the 2000s, which laid the ground for the theoretical questions investigated in this book.

Fast-forward to spring 2015. At that time, my position in the Determinants of International Migration (DEMIG) project of Hein de Haas at the International Migration Institute in Oxford came to an end, and I decided to join him for my PhD in his new project Migration as Development (MADE) at the University of Amsterdam.

The four years I worked on my thesis expanded not only my intellectual but also my life horizons: I tried to settle in Amsterdam and to create a 'home' after having moved around for so many years. I immersed myself in social and political life in Rabat and Tunis during intense fieldwork stays. And I was offered the unexpected chance to discover Brazil, a fascinating country that played an important yet intangible role in my family history and now became central to my life. What brought this exciting but also exhausting journey to life were the many wonderful people I met along the way.

First of all, I am deeply grateful to my many respondents in Morocco and Tunisia, particularly those who opened their address and telephone books for me, and without whom this research would not have been possible. You remain anonymous, but I hope you know how grateful

Acknowledgements

I am. The insights, knowledge and experiences of my respondents build the foundation for this book on political regimes and immigration policymaking in Morocco and Tunisia, through which I hope to contribute to a collective academic effort of rethinking migration politics.

Over the years, I had the chance to pursue this research endeavour as part of a dynamic community of scholars whom I greatly admire. First and foremost, I am indebted to my mentors and PhD supervisors Hein de Haas, Hélène Thiollet and Rainer Bauböck for pushing me to think bold while always seeking depth and precision. This book would also not be the same without the brilliant Natalie Welfens and Lea Müller-Funk, who never ceased to share their wisdom with me and whose friendships I cherish so much. My thinking and research was also shaped and inspired by Feline Freier, Gerasimos Tsourapas, Samuel Schmidt, Luicy Pedroza, Saskia Bonjour, Fiona Adamson, Darshan Vigneswaran, Lorena Gazzotti, Federica Infantino and David Fitzgerald, whom I admire not only for pushing scholarly thinking on migration politics but also for creating a research field that is supportive, collegial and fun.

I am also grateful for the close friendships I made and wonderful colleagues I met in Amsterdam and now in Leiden, who shared this intellectual journey with me and made me feel at home in the Netherlands. Thank you Simona, Keri, Sonja, Flor, Ju, Sophie, Mijail, Tom, Corinna, Sander and Julia! *Shukran* also to Fede, Theo, Lorena, Tarik and all those who made my fieldwork interesting and fun! And *muito obrigada* to those who cheered me up every week without knowing – my jazz dance teachers, forró partners and samba drumming folks.

But what would this last decade have been like without my childhood and university friends – in order of appearance in my life: Paula, Julie, Yumi, Laura, Flo, Selina, Vero, Benni, Vincent, Magdi, Anca, Johanna, Johannes, Solveig, Maher, Marion, Jasper, Mariana, Leila, Franziska and Amr – who are spread across the world but have accompanied me from afar in my moments of euphoria as well as frustration, from Vienna, Frankfurt, London, Singapore, Stockholm, Brussels, Damascus, Florence, Vancouver, Berlin, Zürich and elsewhere!

Finally, I could not have sustained the energy for this project without my family – Barbara, Ehrenfried, Kornelia and Fernando. Thank you for loving me unconditionally, listening to me, giving me the right advice when I need it and always making me feel at home, be it in Vienna, Amsterdam or Recife.

And Fernando, thank you for making my life lighter when it feels heavy, for leading by example in living a life guided by kindness, respect and curiosity, and most of all for not being afraid to take the risks that spending our lives together entails.

Note on the Text

This book brings together my insights from a decade of research on migration policies and political change in North Africa and beyond. It is based on my PhD thesis, which was written as part of the Migration as Development (MADE) project at the University of Amsterdam and funded by the European Community's Horizon 2020 Program under ERC Grant Agreement 648496. The book draws on extensive fieldwork I conducted in Morocco and Tunisia during 2011–2012 and 2016–2017, as well as on archival, policy and media analysis up until the end of 2020. French or Arabic quotes from primary or secondary sources have been translated into English by myself. All errors are mine.

Abbreviations

ADESGUIM	Association for the Development and Sensitization of Guineans in Morocco
ADRA	Adventist Development and Relief Agency
AESAT	Association of African Students and Trainees in Tunisia
AfDB	African Development Bank
AFVIC	Friends and Families of Victims of Clandestine Migration
AI	Amnesty International
ALECMA	Association Light on Irregular Emigration in the Maghreb
AMAPPE	Moroccan Association for the Support and Promotion of Small Enterprises
AMDH	Moroccan Association of Human Rights
AMERM	Moroccan Association for Studies and Research on Migrations
ANAPEC	National Agency for the Promotion of Employment and Competences
ANETI	National Agency for Employment and Independent Work
ASTT	Association of Sub-Saharan Workers in Tunisia
ATFD	Tunisian Association of Democratic Women
ATMF	Association of Maghreb Workers in France
BRA	Bureau of Refugees and Stateless People
CCDH	Consultative Council on Human Rights
CCSM	Collective of Sub-Saharan Communities in Morocco
CEJJ	Centre for Legal and Judicial Studies
CGEM	General Confederation of Enterprises in Morocco
CGTT	General Confederation of Tunisian Workers
CMSM	Council of Sub-Saharan Migrants in Morocco
CNDH	National Council on Human Rights
CSO	Civil Society Organization

CTMM	Collective of Migrant Workers in Morocco
CTR	Tunisian Council for Refugees
DGCIM	General Directorate for International Co-operation on Migration
DIDH	Interministerial Delegation for Human Rights
EU	European Union
FIDH	International Human Rights Federation
FOO	Orient-Occident Foundation
FTDES	Tunisian Forum for Economic and Social Rights
GADEM	Anti-Racist Defense and Support Group of Foreigners and Migrants
GIZ	German Development Agency
IADH	Arab Institute for Human Rights
ICMPD	International Centre for Migration Policy Development
ILO	International Labour Organization
IO	International Organization
IOM	International Organization for Migration
LTDH	Tunisian League for Human Rights
MCMREAM	Ministry for the Moroccan Community Abroad and Migration Affairs
MdM-B	Doctors of the World Belgium
MoE	Ministry of Education
MoEPF	Ministry of Employment and Professional Training
MoF	Ministry of Finance
MoFA	Ministry of Foreign Affairs
MoH	Ministry of Health
MoHE	Ministry of Higher Education
MoI	Ministry of Interior
MoJ	Ministry of Justice
MoL	Ministry of Labour
MoSA	Ministry of Social Affairs
MP	Member of Parliament
MRE	Moroccans Residing Abroad
MSF	Doctors Without Borders
NCA	National Constituent Assembly
NGO	Non-Governmental Organization
ODT/ODTI	Democratic Organization of (Immigrant) Labour
OMDH	Moroccan Organization of Human Rights
ONM	National Migration Observatory
OTE	Office for Tunisians Abroad

List of Abbreviations

PJD	Justice and Development Party
RAMED	Medical Assistance Regime in Morocco
SDC	Swiss Development Cooperation Agency
SEMTE	State Secretariat for Migration and Tunisians Abroad
SNIA	National Strategy on Immigration and Asylum
SNM	National Migration Strategy
TAT	Terre d'Asile Tunisie
TRE	Tunisians Residing Abroad
UGTT	General Union of Tunisian Workers
ULA	Union of African Leaders
UNHCR	United Nations High Commissariat for Refugees
UTICA	Tunisian Union of Industry, Trade and Crafts

1 Introduction

> Tell me how you treat your minorities, your immigrants and your refugees, I will tell you what is the state of your democracy!
> —Geisser (2019: 4)

An Empirical Puzzle

In November 2016, a high-level civil servant within the Tunisian State Secretariat for Migration and Tunisians Abroad (SEMTE) confessed during an interview, 'I won't hide it from you, the protection of immigrants is not the biggest priority.' Our conversation took place in Tunis, only a few kilometres north of Habib Bourguiba Avenue, where large-scale protests by Tunisian citizens successfully ousted dictator Ben Ali almost six years earlier. Over weeks, Tunisians across the country had demanded the end of systemic corruption and political repression – and freedom of movement had been a core demand for more dignity and human rights. But while the democratic transition kick-started in January 2011 expanded Tunisians' civil and political rights, immigrants' rights remained essentially unchanged in the first decade of democratization.

In March 2017, only a few months later, I was in Rabat and interviewed an official from the Ministry for the Moroccan Community Abroad and Migration Affairs (MCMREAM). My respondent was in charge of implementing the liberal immigration reform that King Mohammed VI had launched in September 2013. He explained, 'The royal declaration based on shared responsibility, migrants' access to rights and respect for migrants' dignity provides a very positive general framework' for immigration policy, adding, 'This is the first time that a public policy has been planned around the orientations of a human rights report.' Such rights-based framing of immigration policy not only markedly differs from that of my Tunisian respondent; it is also surprising given Morocco's political developments over the 2010s, characterized by the monarchy's authoritarian consolidation.

These two anecdotes from my fieldwork illustrate the immigration policy dynamics that have unfolded over the past decade in democratizing Tunisia and autocratizing Morocco. In Tunisia, democratization reshuffled domestic political processes and set an end to the decade-long systematic repression under Ben Ali's one-party regime. However, although Tunisians in 2011 actively claimed 'the right to mobility as a revolutionary right' (Giusa 2018), citizens' increased political freedoms did not spill over into more liberal migration policies. In fact, the restrictive immigration policies inherited from the authoritarian era were largely continued – such as a 2004 law criminalizing irregular migration or informal detention and expulsion practices. Overall, immigration has remained surprisingly un-politicized since 2011, despite the fact that Tunisia has transformed into a destination country that hosts not only the 53,500 immigrants recorded in the 2014 census (INS 2015) and several thousand irregular migrants from across Western and Central Africa, the Middle East and Europe but also a large community of Libyan citizens, which is estimated at around half a million people – or 5 per cent of the Tunisian population.

In contrast to Tunisia, Morocco has experienced much more modest immigration growth over the twenty-first century: census data recorded 86,200 immigrants in 2014, representing only 0.25 per cent of the Moroccan population (HCP 2009, 2015); but also higher estimates of about 250,000 migrants do not substantially change the fact that immigration in Morocco is relatively small scale. Nonetheless, immigration – particularly from 'sub-Saharan Africa'[*] – has become intensely politicized in Morocco since the mid-2000s. In this context, Moroccan immigration policies have shifted over time: in 2003, a restrictive immigration law was introduced, criminalizing irregular migrants and those supporting them; but one decade later, in September 2013, King Mohammed VI launched a liberal immigration reform that included two regularization campaigns and a series of migrant integration measures (CNDH 2015). These immigration liberalizations were surprising, as they seemed

---

[*] In Morocco and Tunisia, migrants coming from Western and Central Africa (and more rarely from Eastern Africa) are generally referred to as 'sub-Saharan' migrants in public, political and also academic discourse. However, this term is fundamentally problematic due to its colonial and racist origins (Gazzotti 2021a; Merolla 2017; Mohamed 2010). In fact, 'sub-Sahara Africa' replaced the expression 'Black Africa' (or Afrique Noire) at the end of colonialism, which was a racist, essentializing construction that served the European colonial project by disconnecting it from North Africa, often referred to as 'European Africa' at the time (Zeleza 2006). Given the term's problematic legacy, I do not use it in my own writing and instead refer to the geographical denomination Western and Central Africa. However, I do keep the term whenever it is part of a quote, an institutional designation or a policy document.

An Empirical Puzzle

Table 1.1. *Morocco and Tunisia, a puzzling contrast*

	Morocco	**Tunisia**
Immigration policy dynamics	Liberal policy reform	Restrictive policy continuity
Political regime dynamics[*]	Authoritarian consolidation	Democratic transition

intuitively at odds with the increasingly repressive national political context. Indeed, Moroccan authoritarianism was strengthened over the 2010s as the monarchy's promises for more political freedoms – made to contain dynamics of regional 'revolutionary diffusion' after 2011 (Weyland 2009, 2012) – gradually waned.

The developments sketched in Morocco and Tunisia – where an autocratizing regime enacted a liberal immigration reform, while restrictive policies prevailed throughout a democratic transition (see Table 1.1) – go against baseline expectations that democracy has an inbuilt tendency to liberalize immigration policy and that autocracies tend to curtail human and thus also immigrants' rights. Such expectation that 'the link between migration reform and democratic reform is obvious' (M16-I6) was also common among my respondents: Moroccan respondents explained that 'if there is progress on human rights, there will be progress on migrants' rights, if there is a backlash, this will also impact migrants' (M17-I21). And in Tunisia, respondents highlighted that 'the democratic process will be incomplete' (T17-I22) without reforming the restrictive immigration regime, and that enacting an asylum law would have significant symbolic power, as 'talking about foreigners receiving asylum in Tunisia means that we are committed to democracy' (T17-I9).

Yet observations of policy developments on the ground do not match these baseline expectations on how political regimes shape immigration policy, raising a set of questions: what obstructed immigration policy liberalization in Tunisia after the democratic transition? Why did the Moroccan monarchy enact a liberal reform after a decade of policy restrictiveness? Or, more generally, to what extent do political regimes

---

[*] In this book, I use 'democratic transition' as synonym of 'democratization', and 'authoritarian consolidation' as synonym of 'autocratization'. Although democratic transition and authoritarian consolidation are, in fact, two specific processes within the broader phenomena of democratization and autocratization (see Cassani and Tomini 2020; Maerz et al. 2021), using them as synonyms in the context of twenty-first-century Morocco and Tunisia is unproblematic, as there are no other types of democratization or autocratization at play.

shape immigration politics, and what does immigration policymaking reveal about the inner workings of democratic and autocratic systems? As most scholarship on Moroccan and Tunisian immigration policy focuses either on the role of EU migration externalization (Cassarino 2014; Gazzotti 2021a; Roman and Pastore 2018; Wunderlich 2010) or on transnational civil society activism (Alioua 2009; Bartels 2015; Bustos et al. 2011; Üstübici 2018), domestic policy processes and their link to political regime dynamics remain largely unexplored, with some notable exceptions for Morocco (Alioua, Ferrié and Reifeld 2018; Bensaâd 2015; Norman 2016a).

This book zooms into the complex power dynamics on immigration within and among state, societal and international actors to understand how Tunisia's democratization and Morocco's authoritarian consolidation shaped their immigration policies in the twenty-first century. This systematic comparison of immigration policymaking in the context of contrasting regime dynamics hopes to provide critical food for thought for the scholarly debate on the 'regime effect' in immigration politics, which initially emerged in studies on Western liberal democracies and has recently been revived in the context of growing research on migration to the Global South.

The 'Regime Effect' in Immigration Politics

The scholarly discussion on how immigration policymaking – that is, the political processes underpinning decisions of how to govern and regulate the volume and rights of immigrants – is shaped by political regimes has been kick-started in the 1990s. At that time, migration scholars sought to explain why liberal democracies in Europe and North America consistently enacted liberal immigration policies despite popular demands for restriction. Freeman (1995), for instance, argued that immigration policymaking in democracies is dominated by 'client politics' that favour the interests of employers or human rights advocates who benefit from immigration. Sassen (1996) and Soysal (1994) pointed at how international human rights regimes and global liberal norms of individual freedom limit liberal democracies in restraining migrant rights. And Joppke (1998) stressed dynamics inside the liberal state that restrain attempts by executive and legislative powers to restrict immigration laws, particularly the role of national courts and judges in enshrining migrants' rights.

These explanations all emphasize the role of liberal democracy in creating internal and external constraints that limit states' possibilities to restrict immigration. Migration scholars have even suggested that

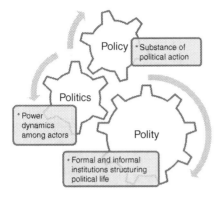

Figure 1.1 Polity, politics, policy.
Inspired by Leca (2012: 61–63)

'accepting unwanted immigration is inherent in the liberalness of liberal states' (Joppke 1998: 292) and that it is the 'features of liberal democracy itself that affect the way such regimes process migration issues' (Freeman 1995: 882). Also political theory work has highlighted how safeguarding foreigners' rights is the ultimate litmus test for liberal democracy (Abizadeh 2008; Carens 2013; Cole 2000, 2012). By assuming such a tight imbrication between polity, politics and policy on immigration (see Figure 1.1) – that is, between the institutions structuring political life, the power dynamics among actors involved in policymaking and the ultimate substance of political action – scholarship has introduced the idea of a 'regime effect'. According to this 'regime effect', liberal democracy gives rise to specific immigration policy processes – involving the role of courts, international norms, societal interest groups or inter-ministerial dynamics – that ultimately produce expansive immigration policy outcomes.

Since the 2000s, critical migration and securitization scholars have cast doubt on such claims of an inherent link between democracy and liberal immigration policy by showcasing how consolidated democracies in Europe and elsewhere have enacted increasingly illiberal, rights-denying policies towards foreigners (Adamson, Triadafilopoulos and Zolberg 2011; Guild, Groenendijk and Carrera 2009; Huysmans 2009; Skleparis 2016). Also political theorists and post-colonial scholars have questioned the fundaments of the 'regime effect' by highlighting that exclusion is inherent to the democratic project (Miller 2016; Song 2019) and that, historically, the consolidation of Western liberal democracy has been built on the oppression of 'underserving' populations – be they colonial subjects, women, Black people or migrants (Bhambra et al.

2020; Dahl 2018; Taylor 1998). While this has challenged the direct link between democracy and liberal approaches towards immigration – that is, between polity and policy – the question of how political regimes shape immigration *politics* remains underexplored and undertheorized, particularly when moving the gaze beyond the liberal state.

In fact, debates on the 'regime effect' in immigration politics have long focused on Western liberal democracies only. This can be partly explained by the political economy of migration research, where most resources are concentrated in Europe and North America. But it also stems from a tendency in scholarly and policy debates to associate the Global North with immigration and liberal-democratic rule, and the Global South with emigration or transit migration and autocratic or illiberal rule. Such binary world (di)visions disregard the fact that 44 per cent of international migrants and 86 per cent of refugees live in countries of the Global South, and that these countries have devised various immigration policies to regulate such flows (UNDESA 2019; UNHCR 2021). Also, while most of the countries classified as autocracies today are situated in the Global South (Marshall and Gurr 2020), systematically associating the Global North with liberal-democratic rule overlooks the fact that many European countries only democratized a few decades ago – such as Greece, Spain or countries in Central and Eastern Europe – and that autocratic tendencies are also gaining ground in the Global North, such as in Poland, Hungary or the United States under the Trump administration (V-Dem 2021).

Despite such limitation, binary (di)visions of the world into Global North/South, destination/origin country and democracy/autocracy have analytical power and structure theorizing of immigration politics. In particular, they have long limited scientific insight into the role of political regimes, as studies that would systematically investigate immigration policymaking beyond Western liberal democracies were largely missing. Fortunately, since the late 2000s, a dynamic research field has emerged that defies the Western- and democracy-centrism of earlier scholarship by putting the Global South centre stage, dissecting inter-actor dynamics and power plays in 'Southern' states and historicizing immigration politics in the broader context of (often post-colonial) state formation (Adamson and Tsourapas 2020; Fiddian-Qasmiyeh 2020; Gazzotti, Mouthaan and Natter 2022; Natter and Thiollet 2022).

This burgeoning scholarship on the Global South has also revived the 'regime effect' debate. On the one hand, scholars have demonstrated how population controls – and thus migration restrictions – are vital to autocratic regime survival: from Brazil to Saudi Arabia and Egypt to Russia, arbitrary emigration and immigration restrictions, large-scale expulsions or extreme curtailments of basic human rights for immigrants and emigrants have been identified as authoritarian regime survival tools throughout history (Alemán and Woods 2014; Filomeno and Vicino 2020; de Haas and Vezzoli 2011; Natter 2018a; Thiollet 2021; Tsourapas 2018, 2020). On the other hand, quantitative studies have explained migration policy openness or restrictiveness through countries' categorization as either autocratic or democratic (Miller and Peters 2020; Mirilovic 2010; Ruhs 2011; Shin 2017).

While these studies have significantly advanced migration research beyond the liberal state, they have (often implicitly) continued to analytically separate theorizing on the Global South from theorizing on Western liberal democracies (notable exceptions are Abdelaaty 2021; Adamson and Tsourapas 2020; Garcés-Mascareñas 2012; Stel 2021). This has reinforced the initial assumption that immigration policy processes are fundamentally different across the Global South/North and democracy/autocracy divides, requiring different sets of theories to be understood. However, immigration policy processes in autocratic and democratic contexts have not been systematically compared as of yet. By investigating immigration politics in the contrasting cases of Morocco and Tunisia, this book provides fruitful ground to start delineating the boundaries of the 'regime effect' and to explore commonalities in immigration policy processes across political regimes.

A Typology of Immigration Policy Processes

This book seeks to bridge immigration policy scholarship on the Global North and Global South with broader political sociology, comparative politics and international relations research on power, politics and modern statehood to systematically examine how political regimes shape immigration policymaking. The analysis of policy processes in twenty-first-century Morocco and Tunisia shows that while specific aspects of immigration policymaking are heavily influenced by how decision-making is concentrated or dispersed in a particular power system, there are in fact significant similarities in the functioning of immigration politics across political regimes. In particular, while the decision-making leverage of the executive and the weight of domestic political and civil society actors were closely intertwined with political regime dynamics in Morocco and Tunisia, the internal workings of the state apparatus as well as the influence of foreign policy interests or international norms in national policymaking remained largely unaffected by autocratization or democratization trends.

To initiate a more systematic discussion of the 'regime effect', this book advances a three-fold typology of immigration policy processes that distinguishes between generic, issue-specific and regime-specific processes.[1] This typology is meant to provide analytical building blocks to stimulate future research in view of consolidating and refining immigration policy theory across political regimes.

First, the typology identifies a set of *generic policy processes* that emerge out of the very essence of policymaking in modern states. Although the social sciences have tended to focus on the differences between states regarding their political regimes, institutional capacities or state–society relations, there are some fundamental commonalities in the nature of modern statehood (Tilly 1992). For instance, modern state bureaucracies are organized in strikingly similar ways – structured around ministries with distinct portfolios, separate executive, legislative and judicial institutions (even if only on paper) as well as a bureaucratic apparatus that links central decision-makers to local implementers. Also, despite wide variations in how states work on the ground, territory and population control are always central to national sovereignty, and regimes along the entire democracy–autocracy spectrum have to accommodate various societal, economic and international actors to legitimize their decision-making. Although the sources of legitimacy and means of preserving control vary across countries, 'no political regime or authority wishes to appear illegitimate' (Mazepus et al. 2016: 350). Such fundamental dynamics in the workings of modern states create theoretical ground for expecting more commonalities in policymaking across political regimes than dichotomous theorizations of democratic and autocratic politics would suggest. As I develop in this book, the gap between political discourses, policies on paper and policy implementation or the role of crisis in creating a window of opportunity for change are examples of such generic policy processes that are at play regardless of the political regime in place or the policy area at stake.

Second, the typology identifies *issue-specific policy processes*, which are inherent to the policy area of immigration and therefore at play across political regimes. In fact, these policy dynamics arise because immigration poses fundamental questions to state sovereignty that result in specific interest alignments of actors both within domestic and international policy spheres. By definition, immigration challenges the efforts of nation-states to maintain their sovereignty through control over people, borders and national identity narratives – be they democracies or autocracies. Scholars have therefore suggested that the modern nation-state is, in fact, a 'migration state' (Hollifield 2004), where attempts to control individual mobility through passports, visas and border controls 'contribute to constituting the very "state-ness" of states' (Torpey 1997: 240). Given the centrality of immigration control for modern statehood, the analysis in this book suggests that state formation trajectories and national identity conceptions structure immigration policymaking in every state, regardless of the political regime in place. Another issue-specific dynamic explored in this book is that immigration policy triggers specific inter-institutional conflicts within state bureaucracies worldwide – for instance, between Ministries of Interior and Foreign Affairs. And, as immigration is an intrinsically transnational issue, policies regulating the entry and stay of foreigners seem to offer unique opportunities for states across the globe to instrumentalize them in diplomatic relations.

Lastly, in contrast to policy processes that are at play across political regimes – either because they are tied to the nature of modern nation-states or because they are intrinsic to immigration as a policy field – the typology identifies *regime-specific policy processes* that are fundamentally shaped by a country's position on the democracy–autocracy spectrum. The empirical analysis of Morocco and Tunisia in this book shows that three aspects of immigration policymaking are particularly sensitive to a 'regime effect': the centrality of the executive, the weight of legal actors and the role of domestic socio-political actors, such as political parties and civil society. In particular, my analysis suggests that although autocratic leaders also have to reconcile diverging interests in their immigration policy decisions, they are less constrained by electoral processes or by courts that are central in democracies or countries with a strong rule of law. This implies that the executive has more leverage to enact rapid and fundamental policy shifts and that, paradoxically, autocracies can more easily enact liberal immigration reforms compared to democracies if it fits their broader economic agenda, foreign policy priorities or nation-building goals.

I call this dynamic in autocracies 'the illiberal paradox'[*] – as a counterpart to the liberal paradox Hollifield (1992a) introduced to capture the conflicting drivers that democracies are confronted with when developing their immigration policies. Hollifield argued that while the dominant ideology of liberalism pushes liberal states to globalize their labour markets, to enshrine international human rights in national law and thus to liberalize immigration, the political logic of democratic nation-states is

---

[*] In this book and earlier publications where I introduce and investigate this hypothesis in depth (Natter 2018a, 2021b), the illiberal paradox refers to immigration policymaking. Tsourapas (2018, 2020) has developed the idea of an illiberal paradox in relation to autocracies' emigration policies, whereby states' political and security imperatives drive them to restrict and surveil emigration, while economic and developmental interests push them to encourage emigration and secure good relations with the diaspora to attract remittances, alleviate unemployment and reduce political discontent through emigration.

dominated by electoral objectives and national identity claims and thus pushes states to restrict immigration (see also Hampshire 2013). In this view, immigration restrictions are attributed to the democratic dynamics of elections, party politics and public opinion – which are less prevalent in autocratic contexts. By introducing the illiberal paradox, I do not want to suggest that autocracies *do* enact more liberal policies than democracies. There are numerous examples where autocracies have drastically restricted immigration and violated immigrants' rights. Instead, I argue based on the Moroccan and Tunisian case studies that autocracies *can* open their immigration regimes more easily than democracies *if* they wish to do so because of their relative freedom from legal constraints and restrictive domestic demands.

Immigration Policy, a Lens into Modern Statehood and its Transformations

My typology of generic, issue-specific and regime-specific immigration policy processes provides a first attempt at systematizing insights on the commonalities and differences in immigration politics across political regimes. What stands out from this exercise is the range of issue-specific processes that showcase the centrality of immigration policy for modern statehood. As Hassenteufel (2008: 13) suggests, 'the state constructs itself through the production of public policies'. This is particularly valid when it comes to immigration. For Abdelmalek Sayad (1999: 6–7), 'immigration – and this is probably why it disturbs – forces us to unveil the state, to unveil the way we conceive of the state and the way it conceives of itself'. To systematically explore the imbrication of political regimes and immigration politics, we therefore need not only to examine how immigration policymaking is influenced by the type of regime that regulates political life in a certain country. We also need to analyse what immigration politics reveals about the functioning of democratic and autocratic structures, and of modern statehood more broadly.

Examining Tunisia, this book demonstrates that the depoliticization of immigration and the restrictive immigration policy continuity after 2011 in fact reflects the imperative of Tunisian political actors to preserve the democratic transition. In the wake of the revolution, immigration was set on the political agenda because large numbers of refugees and migrants arrived from neighbouring Libya and societal actors used their newly gained freedom of expression to voice their demands and concerns. However, the democratization of political processes did ultimately not spill over into more open policies towards foreigners, as security concerns overshadowed efforts by civil society organizations (CSOs) and international organizations (IOs) to initiate liberal immigration reform. Moreover, conflicting domestic demands – for and against immigration liberalization – cancelled each other out and compelled policymakers to reactivate a national unity narrative, to put 'Tunisians first' and to ignore immigration altogether because of its potential to polarize Tunisian society. In addition, the proliferation of state actors involved on immigration propelled institution-specific interests, such as future political and economic cooperation with Libya, to the foreground. Ultimately, as democratization required political leaders to legitimize policies before an electorate, strategic depoliticization and restrictive policy continuity seemed the safest option for Tunisian political elites.

While the absence of immigration reform in Tunisia provides central insights into the intricate dynamics of democratization, the liberal immigration reform in Morocco is exemplary of the inner workings of the monarchy and ongoing dynamics of authoritarian consolidation. As I show, the top-down politicization of immigration and the liberal immigration reform were, in fact, part and parcel of the monarchy's strategy to consolidate its power at home and abroad. Diplomatically, immigration was turned into political capital towards both Europe and Africa, principally to advance Morocco's foreign policy goals to rejoin the African Union, to strengthen its position as regional leader against its historical rival Algeria and to increase its bargaining power towards the European Union (EU). Domestically, the immigration reform bolstered the regime's legitimacy in front of liberal, progressive parts of Moroccan society who saw migrants' rights as intrinsic to Morocco's democratization agenda. The analysis in this book shows how the room for manoeuvre of pro-migrant CSOs was strategically increased and how relations between the monarchical institution and the Moroccan administration were instrumentalized to foster a progressive image of King Mohammed VI. The depth and speed of the liberal reform were thus driven first and foremost by the royal agenda to promote Morocco as a 'liberal monarchy' at home and abroad.[2]

In both Morocco and Tunisia, the analysis of immigration policymaking therefore offers a privileged lens to revisit political regime dynamics from the inside and to examine how trends of autocratization and democratization play out in practice. This showcases how, ultimately, studying immigration policymaking is always a study of the essence and transformation of the modern state.

Researching Immigration Politics in Morocco and Tunisia

The book's contribution to rethinking immigration politics across political regimes draws on one decade of empirical research on immigration policy, and in particular on the paired comparison of Morocco and

12   Introduction

Tunisia. Paired comparisons are widely used in social science for theory-building (Tarrow 2010: 243). Also called 'controlled case comparison' (George and Bennett 2005), they have the advantage of providing intimacy and depth of analysis similar to a single-case study, but with more analytical power to identify mechanisms or processes that connect contextual differences to particular outcomes, in my case political regime dynamics to immigration policymaking.

Of course, Morocco and Tunisia are not representative of the variety of political regimes that make up the world. On a spectrum between liberal democracy and closed autocracy, Morocco's hereditary monarchy and Tunisia's presidential one-party autocracy have shifted back and forth over time according to levels of repression and political freedoms, with Tunisia experiencing a qualitative jump towards democratization in 2011 (see Figures A.6 to A.8 in Appendix 2). However, Morocco and Tunisia are particularly fruitful cases to explore the role of political regimes in immigration policymaking because each country can be classified as a 'deviant' case (George and Bennett 2005; Seawright and Gerring 2008) in light of dominant theoretical expectations: in Morocco, authoritarianism drove immigration policy liberalization; in Tunisia, democratization drove restrictive policy continuity, while common sense and existing theories would have expected the contrary. At the same time, while Morocco and Tunisia differ on the outcome (immigration policy) and one crucial dimension (political regime dynamics), they are similar with regards to other potentially important immigration policy drivers: human and economic development trajectories, colonial histories or the position within regional migration systems (see Appendix 2).*

The resulting most similar systems design (Seawright and Gerring 2008) allows to almost isolate the role of political regime dynamics on immigration policy and to develop hypotheses on the boundaries of the 'regime effect' in immigration policy. Needless to say, the paired comparison of Morocco and Tunisia does not in itself offer generalizable conclusions on the role of political regimes in immigration politics. However, the typology of immigration policy processes advanced in this

---

* It would have been interesting to also include Algeria in this comparison: In Algeria, immigration is subject to negative politicization (compared to depoliticization in Tunisia and positive politicization in Morocco), and political regime dynamics differ from those in Morocco and Tunisia, with a socialist republic in the post-independence decades, a civil war opposing Algerian security services and Islamists in the 1990s, and a military regime since then that has been challenged by the country's youth in 2019 and 2020. However, fieldwork access to civil servants and civil society representatives is almost impossible in Algeria's closed political context. To guarantee the quality and comparability of insights across the in-depth case studies, I decided to focus on Morocco and Tunisia.

book hopes to serve as an intermediate step in a 'building-block strategy' (Becker 1968) that moves from exploratory, hypothesis-generating single-case studies towards more systematic theory-testing in view of generalizability.

To trace immigration policy processes in Morocco and Tunisia, I combine insights from 144 semi-structured interviews and 48 informal conversations conducted in Morocco and Tunisia in 2011–2012 and 2016–2017 with rigorous policy, legal and media analysis covering the period until the end of 2020. I interviewed three categories of actors involved in immigration policymaking:[*] first, high-level civil servants within Morocco's and Tunisia's Ministries of Interior, Foreign Affairs, Migration, Labour, Higher Education and Health, and within local administrations in Rabat and Tunis, as well as representatives of political parties and Morocco's National Council on Human Rights (CNDH). Second, civil society actors, such as representatives of migrant-led collectives, local migrant and human rights associations, labour and employer unions, as well as non-governmental organizations (NGOs) operating in Morocco and Tunisia. And third, international and diplomatic actors, such as representatives of the International Organization for Migration (IOM), the International Labour Organization (ILO), the United Nations High Commissariat for Refugees (UNHCR), local EU delegations and European embassies, as well as development aid organizations. Moreover, I attended workshops, seminars and roundtables on immigration policy in Rabat and Tunis, allowing me to observe inter-actor dynamics and conduct forty-eight additional informal conversations with a diverse range of respondents.

Access to most interviewees – especially at a high level – was surprisingly easy in Morocco and Tunisia. The main difficulty was to identify the right interlocutors in the first place and to get their contact details – at best a mobile phone number or private email address. But once contacted, most people were available for an interview – including the former head of the CNDH in Morocco as well as three former State Secretaries for Migration in Tunisia. Only two institutions proved difficult to access: Tunisia's Ministry of Interior (MoI) and Morocco's Ministry of Foreign Affairs (MoFA). In Tunisia, most respondents discouraged me even to try to get in touch with the MoI, as despite the revolution, the autocratic heritage is still palpable, and the MoI is said to 'function with the same mental configuration as before' (T17-I1). Although I did secure the contact of a key person in the MoI, I did not ultimately succeed in

---

[*] For a comprehensive list of interviewed actors, see Appendix 1.

arranging an interview. I experienced similarly closed doors at the Moroccan MoFA during my 2016/2017 fieldwork. While access had been relatively easy back in 2011/2012, respondents emphasized a change in the overall political climate, making access to the MoFA almost impossible for researchers at the time of my later fieldwork.

To complement my rich interview material, I also conducted systematic documentary research. Although this book is not historical per se, it integrates, whenever possible, the historical depth, roots and origins of contemporary developments (Bayart 1996; Migdal and Schlichte 2005). Indeed, understanding continuities has been as important to me as understanding change in immigration policy, and so it was crucial to gather archival data. I collected primary sources such as immigration laws, minutes of parliamentary discussions, action plans and reports of state institutions in Morocco's parliamentary archives and national library, as well as in Tunisia's national archives. I also analysed Morocco's and Tunisia's online databases of laws and decrees to search for changes in immigration policy since 1956.[3] On this basis, I built a comprehensive immigration policy chronology for Morocco and Tunisia spanning more than a century – from the early 1900s until the end of 2020 (see Appendices 3 and 4).

Moreover, I systematically screened six national and two regional news outlets for articles on immigration.[*] The analysis covers the entire period of these outlets' online archives, generally starting between 2005 and 2008, and going on until the end of 2020. Media analysis provided insights into the level of politicization of immigration in the public sphere and the core themes of interest. Finally, I collected secondary and grey literature, such as books and doctoral theses from Moroccan and Tunisian scholars, reports from associations and local institutions, as well as scholarly work on state formation, national identity and migration in Morocco and Tunisia. These sources' historical and descriptive depth allowed me to better evaluate actor motives and to contextualize the information gathered through interviews and primary documents.

Yet, doing fieldwork and tracing policymaking in (semi-)autocratic settings brings its own challenges (Art 2016; Glasius et al. 2018; Koch 2013; Shih 2015), as documents are not always openly accessible, the media biased, and people do not dare to speak up. Although Morocco's political context is more authoritarian than Tunisia's nowadays, Ben

---

[*] In Morocco, *Le Matin* functions as the mouthpiece of the state, *TelQuel* is more independent and critical, and *Yabiladi* more neutral in its reporting. In Tunisia, *BusinessNews* keeps to neutral and factual reporting; *Nawaat* and *Inkifaya* are investigative, online journalism platforms that have emerged after 2011. I also systematically screened *HuffPost Maghreb* and *Jeune Afrique* for regional coverage.

Ali's security state has left its marks, and so guaranteeing respondents' anonymity was crucial in both countries. Particularly on immigration, a topic closely linked to territorial integrity and national identity, the risk of crossing 'red lines' was high. While respondents were willing to talk to me, half of them did not want to be recorded. Also, because my respondents – activists, journalists, politicians and bureaucrats – represented antagonistic interests on immigration, I was alert in navigating 'reverse interviews' (Glasius et al. 2018: 61), whereby respondents would turn the interview situation around and question me about the people I talked to.

To not compromise my respondents' security, I therefore generally refrain from revealing their identity (names, job descriptions) throughout the book. Instead, I identify respondents through a code – the code M16-I1, for example, refers to Interview 1 in my 2016 Morocco fieldwork. I only reveal respondents' position within the cartography of actors when statements were made during public events or when it is imperative to contextualize the quote and does not in any way compromise the respondent's security. In these cases, I retract the number code to avoid cross-referencing.

Apart from the broader political context, the political salience (or non-salience) of immigration also shaped my fieldwork. In Morocco, many respondents seemed to have a set narrative on the 2013 policy change. The fact that immigration had been turned into a prestige project by the King meant that many respondents, especially within the state but also within civil society, took up the official policy framing. In contrast, in Tunisia I was in fact researching a 'no policy' (Rosenblum 2004b). I was often confronted with empty faces once interviewees realized I wanted to talk about Tunisia's approach towards immigrants, not about Tunisia's emigration and diaspora politics. Almost always, Tunisian respondents understood the word 'immigrant' as referring to Tunisians abroad, not to foreigners in Tunisia. While this non-politicization of immigration was at times challenging, as people felt they had nothing to say, it also provided an opportunity, as respondents were taken by surprise and did not have ready-made opinions or scripted responses.

Finally, my positionality inevitably shaped my fieldwork. Being a young woman, for instance, very likely played out to my advantage, facilitating my access to respondents given the (unfortunate) gendered assumptions that I would not be too inquisitive, too threatening or too politicized in my work. As Glasius et al. (2018: 64–66) write, 'Naivety is a commonly used interview strategy ..., typically more available to young women and foreigners. ... Women are considered less threatening, and may sometimes have greater access to officials precisely in authoritarian circumstances'.

I also sensed that being a White European facilitated my access to more high-level actors, as well as to workshops, receptions and seminars organized by Moroccan and Tunisian institutions. Back in 2011, when I was visiting the Mohammed V University in Rabat for the first time, a Moroccan student told me, 'Everything is easy access if you are a foreigner in Morocco. All doors are open'. This became particularly evident during my observation of the Moroccan regularization campaign in 2017 – had I been Black, I would likely not have been allowed to roam around the regularization office for several hours without being approached by local policemen. Such dynamics of White privilege that are at play in everyday life in Morocco and Tunisia (Hannoum 2020; Pouessel 2012b) have crucially affected my fieldwork.

Being a White European, however, also meant that some respondents probably perceived me as one of the numerous Western academics and journalists who arrived in Morocco and (to a lesser extent) Tunisia over the past years to investigate immigration politics, and thus as a vehicle to transmit specific messages to European publics, funders or politicians. While I remained alert to such dynamics in my interviews and analysis, ultimately, every researcher has to 'work with what [they] have' (Glasius et al. 2018: 64), and the question of 'what respondents would have told me was I Black, Moroccan or a man' will remain unanswered.

Altogether, the rich interview and archival material I gathered in Morocco and Tunisia over the past decade provide the backbone for this book. To empirically trace policymaking processes in Morocco and Tunisia and connect them to political regime dynamics, I focused the analysis on the shifting constellations of interests, ideas and institutions in Morocco's and Tunisia's immigration policy field (see Hall 1997; Palier and Surel 2005). I also paid particular attention to power relations between state, societal and international actors to understand how certain immigrant groups were turned into legitimate objects of political concern (or not). For this process tracing exercise (Hall 2006; Tansey 2007), I mobilized abductive data analysis, 'a qualitative data analysis approach aimed at theory construction' (Timmermans and Tavory 2012: 169) that focuses on the iterative process between data collection, data analysis and theory-building (Charmaz 2014). In practice, this meant that I built a back-and-forth between empirics and theory into my fieldwork set-up and coding strategy. Such 'duel process tracing' (Tarrow 2010), whereby I iteratively juxtaposed, contrasted and compared immigration policy processes in autocratizing Morocco and democratizing Tunisia provides the methodological foundation for examining immigration politics across political regimes.

The Book Outline

In this introductory *Chapter 1*, I made the case for rethinking the politics of immigration beyond the liberal state and for leveraging immigration policy as an analytical lens to explore the inner workings of political regimes. I introduced the empirical puzzle that motivated the book and sketched the research design and methods I adopted to trace immigration policy processes in Morocco and Tunisia. I also outlined the empirical and theoretical contributions of the book, particularly the three-fold typology of immigration policy processes that seeks to systematize insights into the boundaries of the 'regime effect'. Next, *Chapter 2* delves into the conceptual foundations of the book: by tying the vast immigration policy scholarship on the Global North and Global South to broader comparative politics, international relations and political sociology reflections on power, politics and modern statehood, I offer a first attempt at rethinking theories of immigration politics across political regimes.

The book then immerses the reader in the contrasting cases of Morocco and Tunisia. *Chapter 3* offers a concise account of Moroccan and Tunisian state formation and national identity trajectories, as well as focused overviews of immigration and emigration patterns and policies from the early twentieth century until the end of 2020, including Morocco's and Tunisia's treatment of migrants during the first year of COVID-19. The chapter hereby substantiates the empirical puzzle of the book, namely the contrast between liberal immigration reform in autocratizing Morocco and restrictive immigration policy continuity in democratizing Tunisia. The empirical analysis itself is structured as follows: Chapters 4 and 6 focus on the drivers of immigration policy in Morocco and Tunisia, respectively, and explore which institutions, interests and ideas have shaped policymaking since independence in 1956 and particularly since the turn of the twenty-first century, when immigration became increasingly salient in domestic and international policy spheres. Chapters 5 and 7, then, dissect how Morocco's 2013 policy change and Tunisia's 2011 revolution, respectively, affected the power dynamics on immigration among state, civil society and international actors.

Specifically, *Chapter 4* shows that Moroccan immigration policy is primarily driven by the monarchy's foreign policy and domestic regime legitimation goals. In the post-independence period, Morocco used selective immigration facilitations to strengthen diplomatic ties with European and African countries. In 2003, a restrictive immigration law successfully instrumentalized so-called 'sub-Saharan irregular transit migrants' for Moroccan diplomatic relations with the European Union

(EU) and for its domestic security goal of increasing control over population movements. And in 2013, enacting a liberal immigration reform has been instrumental in sustaining the regime's legitimacy at a moment of regional political turmoil after the 'Arab Spring' and in advancing Morocco's foreign policy interests in Africa. Even the inconsistent implementation that has mitigated the reform's impact on migrants' everyday lives has not jeopardized but only reinforced the King's power position at home and abroad.

Chapter 5, then, demonstrates how immigration policy liberalization not only emerged out of Morocco's autocratic political structures – a dynamic I call the illiberal paradox – but also consolidated them. In particular, it shows that the monarchy mobilized the expansion of migrants' rights, as well as its relations with the administration and an expanding civil society to portray King Mohammed VI as a 'liberal monarch'. In this process, legal actors and elected politicians have only played a subordinate role. However, the top-down, centralizing dynamic initiated by the King did not absorb resistances and diverging views within the administration and civil society, where actors kept their room for manoeuvre regarding agenda-setting and policy implementation.

Chapter 6 on Tunisia explores the drivers behind the continuity of restrictive immigration policy through the democratic transition. It shows that under Tunisia's autocratic leaders Bourguiba and Ben Ali, foreign policy priorities, sovereignty concerns and strategies for regime legitimation dominated immigration policy choices, leading to the generalized criminalization of immigration and an elaborate system of exceptions for particular migrant groups. While such foreign policy interests and state imperatives have remained powerful immigration policy drivers after 2011, the democratic transition increased the weight of domestic factors such as public opinion and civil society activism in policymaking. Despite initial attempts to translate democratic ideals into liberal immigration reform, however, conflicting popular demands have compelled policymakers to sideline liberal immigration reform. As the chapter demonstrates, the minor and mostly informal policy changes that were enacted after 2011 have ultimately not challenged the core of Tunisia's restrictive immigration regime in the first decade of democratization.

Chapter 7, then, dissects the power dynamics among state, societal and international actors on immigration in Tunisia and shows how democratization affected immigration policy processes in ambiguous ways. Under Ben Ali's authoritarian regime, the lack of real counterpowers reinforced the security-driven immigration policy of the Ministry of Interior. After 2011, the role of Tunisia's Parliament and civil society was strengthened as policy processes became more inclusive. However, democratization also brought to the fore inter-actor dynamics that put a break on immigration reform plans, such as turf wars within the administration, governmental volatility or competition within an expanding civil society. Ultimately, then, democratization has not delivered more rights for migrants in Tunisia.

Chapter 8 systematically compares immigration politics in Morocco and Tunisia and brings to the fore some striking continuities and parallels between democratic and autocratic contexts. The comparison shows that regime strategies to ensure political legitimation as well as territorial and institutional sovereignty provide the foundation for immigration governance. It also demonstrates the importance of national identity narratives and histories of state formation to understand contemporary immigration politics. Furthermore, the chapter teases out how Morocco's and Tunisia's political regime dynamics shaped immigration policymaking over the twenty-first century. It shows that while the decision-making leverage of the executive and the weight of domestic political and civil society actors were closely intertwined with political regime dynamics, the internal workings of the state apparatus as well as the influence of foreign policy interests or international norms in national policymaking remained largely unaffected by regime dynamics.

In the concluding *Chapter 9* I return to the key theoretical propositions of the book and summarize its contributions to research on Moroccan and Tunisian migration politics, to theories of immigration policy as well as to broader comparative politics, international relations and political sociology scholarship. I hereby showcase the value of immigration policy research as an analytical lens to study state transformations and political change. I end the book with a reflection on the most promising avenues for consolidating theory-building on immigration policy across the Global North/South and democracy/autocracy divides in the future.

2 Theories on the Move

Overcoming Binary World (Di)visions in Immigration Policy Research

Social theory is about detecting regularities and patterns to make sense of what is out there in the world. However, theory-building is in itself a social process and therefore tends to reflect global power structures. These shape the questions that are researched and the theoretical explanations that dominate (Acharya 2014; Connell 2018; Hobson 2012; Joseph Mbembe 2016; Mayblin and Turner 2020).

In classic political science, for instance, theorizing on modern statehood primarily focuses on the Western state, although nation-states are the dominant form of organizing power relations across the entire globe. Also in area studies and comparativist scholarship on the 'Arab state' (Anderson 1987; Ayubi 1995; Owen 2004; Salamé 2002) or the 'African state' (Bayart 2009; Bierschenk and de Sardan 2015; Herbst 2000; Jackson and Rosberg 1982; Young 1994), studies often tend to focus on identifying specificities compared to the Western state, such as dynamics of (neo)patrimonialism and rentierism or the dominance of kinship and ethnicity in politics. Scholars even highlight that the state concept itself has a different meaning in Latin, where 'state' refers to stability and continuity, compared to its Arabic counterpart 'dawla', which indicates circulation and changes in power (Ayubi 1995: 15). Such emphasis on difference and on the cultural determinants of statehood risks obstructing a systematic theoretical inquiry into the general nature of statehood. As Bierschenk and de Sardan (2015: 54) describe in the case of African states, it also leads to 'a tendency to exoticize states of the South by comparing actual practices in the South with an idealized notion of how things work in the North'.

In migration studies, the political economy of research, with most resources concentrated in Europe and North America, has led scholars to pay disproportionate attention to immigration policymaking in Western liberal democracies and, more recently, to emigration and so-called transit migration in neighbouring regions – North Africa, the

Middle East or Central America. As a consequence, theorizing of immigration policymaking is still dominated by the underlying assumption that there is a fundamental difference in how migration politics unfolds across political regimes and political geographies. In line with scholars who call for a more global social science (Bhambra 2014; Connell 2007), this book seeks to advance theory-building on immigration policymaking by bringing into dialogue research on democracies and autocracies in the Global North and Global South, and by critically interrogating the dichotomous categories that continue to structure thinking in immigration policy research (for a similar rationale, see Bakewell and Jónsson 2013; Haug, Braveboy-Wagner and Maihold 2021).

What does this imply? First, it requires breaking the unidirectional transfer of theory from 'North' to 'South' and fostering theoretical innovation through reciprocal comparisons that 'view both sides of the comparison as "deviations" when seen through the expectations of the other, rather than leaving one as always the norm' (Pomeranz 2000: 8; see also Austin 2007). Second, it invites us to open our eyes to similarities where we do not expect them. As Comaroff and Comaroff (2012: 114) suggest, 'the so-called "Global South" ... affords privileged insight into the workings of the world at large'. Third, such an approach entails embracing theoretical pluralism. As Timmermans and Tavory (2012: 169) highlight, 'if we wish to foster theory construction we must be neither theoretical atheists nor avowed monotheists, but informed theoretical agnostics'. In practice, this means that I approach immigration policy theories not as mutually exclusive but as building blocks whose complementarity and relevance need to be critically evaluated in light of empirical insights. Such an approach should allow migration scholarship to move beyond binary categories such as Global South/North or democracy/autocracy as default explanatory factors, which risk obscuring not only the diversity of immigration politics within each of these categories but also the fundamental similarities of immigration policymaking in modern nation-states worldwide.

In this vein, this chapter maps the main theoretical approaches that migration scholars have developed to explain immigration policymaking – namely political economy, institutionalist, historical-culturalist, globalization theory and international relations approaches – and reflects on their relevance for understanding immigration politics across political regimes. In doing so, I draw on the in-depth insights gained from the Moroccan and Tunisian cases, as well as on migration policy scholarship from around the globe. I also explore what consequences the fundamental structure and functioning of modern nation-states has for public policymaking across the world.

Mapping Immigration Policy Theories

Immigration policies are the set of formal rules, laws and regulations, informal administrative practices, as well as purposive laissez-faire that state authorities devise to govern the volume and rights of different categories of migrants: labour migrants, students, family migrants, irregular migrants, refugees and asylum seekers (see Zolberg 1978: 243). Immigration policy thus encompasses both immigration control policy – that is, the rules and practices governing the selection and admission of migrants, such as border control policies, visa requirements, regularizations, expulsion and return policies – as well as immigrant policy – that is, the rules and practices governing the conditions for migrants' stay and integration, such as socio-economic rights related to education, health or work (Hammar 1985: 7–9). Together, these diverse facets of immigration policy form a country's immigration regime. As Sciortino (2004: 32–33) writes,

> a country's migration regime is usually not the outcome of consistent planning. It is rather a mix of implicit conceptual frames, generations of turf wars among bureaucracies and waves after waves of 'quick fix' to emergencies, triggered by changing political constellations of actors.

Systematic theorizing of the 'factors that make and unmake migration policies' (Castles 2004: 852) emerged during the 1990s when social scientists sought to explain why European and North American states continued to enact liberal immigration policies despite popular demands for restriction. Back in 1985, Myron Weiner wrote that 'there is little systematic comparative and theoretical work on such issues as how and why states make their access rules, the interplay between domestic and international considerations, the relationship between regime type and access rules, and how the rules are affected by internal political transformations' (Weiner 1985: 446). This has changed. Over the past decades, scholars researching immigration in Western liberal democracies have theorized the drivers of immigration policymaking, developing five main sets of approaches:

(1) political economy approaches highlight the role of domestic societal interests on immigration that operate via interest groups, political parties and civil society;
(2) institutionalist approaches bring to the fore the importance of state institutions' potentially conflicting interests on immigration;
(3) historical-culturalist approaches pay particular attention to state formation histories and national identity conceptions to explain immigration policy;

(4) international relations approaches emphasize the role of foreign policy and diplomatic interests in bi- or multi-lateral cooperation on immigration; and
(5) globalization theory approaches highlight the importance of international norms and ideas in national policymaking.

As a starting point for the reflections in this chapter and to map this theoretical field,* I categorize these immigration policy theories along two dimensions: the factors of analysis they consider – that is, whether they emphasize the role of ideas, interests or institutions in immigration policymaking – and the level of analysis they adopt – that is, whether they localize the origin of immigration policy within society, the state or the international arena (see Table 2.1).[1]

Theory-building on migration politics *beyond* Western liberal democracies initially focused on emigration and diaspora policies (Adamson 2019; de Haas and Vezzoli 2011; FitzGerald 2006; Gamlen 2008; Liu and Van Dongen 2016; Miller and Peters 2014; Naujoks 2013; Tsourapas 2018), as well as on migration cooperation in the context of 'migration externalization' (Cuttitta 2020; Dini and Giusa 2020; El Qadim 2015; Karadağ 2019; Kimball 2007; Stock, Üstübici and Schultz 2019). Studies that investigate *immigration* politics across the Global South are more

Table 2.1. *Categorizing immigration policymaking theories*

	Factors of analysis			Levels of analysis		
	Interests	Ideas	Institutions	Society	State	International
(1) Political economy approaches	✓			✓		
(2) Institutionalist approaches	✓		✓		✓	
(3) Historical-culturalist approaches		✓	✓	✓	✓	
(4) International relations approaches	✓					✓
(5) Globalization theory approaches		✓	✓			✓

Source: *Adapted from Natter (2018b).*

---

* For comprehensive reviews, see (Boswell 2007b; Castles 2004; Massey 1999; Meyers 2000).

recent: since the 2010s, comparative politics, political sociology and international relations scholars have started to dissect domestic interests, inter-actor dynamics and power plays in 'Southern' states to historicize immigration politics in the broader context of (post-colonial) state formation and geopolitical relations, and to advance new concepts and typologies to theorize the dynamics around immigration policy across Asia, the Middle East, Latin America and Africa (see, for instance, Adamson and Tsourapas 2020; Fiddian-Qasmiyeh 2020; Gazzotti, Mouthaan and Natter 2022; Gisselquist and Tarp 2019; Natter and Thiollet 2022; Nawyn 2016; Sadiq and Tsourapas 2021).

These studies have been essential to overcome the dominant Western- and democracy-centrism in migration research. Yet, there is still surprisingly little cross-fertilization between research on immigration politics in the Global North and the Global South, as most studies continue to separate theorizing on democratic or Western policymaking from theorizing on non-democratic or non-Western policymaking (notable exceptions are Abdelaaty 2021; Garcés-Mascareñas 2012; Kemp and Kfir 2016; Stel 2021). Research that systematically examines to what extent the instrumentalization of immigration for foreign policy goals, the lobbying strategies of civil society and employer unions, or the conflicts around immigration within the state bureaucracy really differ across democracies and autocracies and thus remains relatively unchartered territory.

Rethinking Immigration Policy Theories Across Political Regimes

This book leverages the paired comparison of Morocco and Tunisia to critically interrogate the analytical power of political regimes to explain immigration policymaking. In this vein, this section puts into dialogue established immigration policy theories on Western liberal democracies – focusing on the role of domestic societal interests, the state as an actor, the weight of history, foreign policy interests and global norms – with my empirical insights on Morocco and Tunisia and the burgeoning research on migration politics in the Global South. This comparative exercise suggests that while there are specific aspects of immigration policy that seem heavily influenced by how decision-making is concentrated or dispersed in a particular power system, there also appear to be significant similarities in the functioning of immigration politics across political regimes. In particular, the 'regime effect' – that is, the fact that specific immigration policy dynamics are inherent to the type of political regime in place – seems to be restricted to political economy approaches and to institutional dynamics involving the legal domain and executive actors, while the core insights of international relations, historical-culturalist, bureaucratic politics and globalization theory approaches seem relevant to understand immigration politics across democratic and autocratic contexts. Such theoretical propositions, albeit tentative, seek to pave the way for more systematic, fine-grained theorizing of the politics of immigration beyond the liberal state and the role of political regimes therein.

Domestic Societal Interests

Political economy approaches locate the origin of immigration policy in liberal democracies within society and tend to reduce the state to a neutral arena captured by domestic economic and societal interests. They adopt a rational choice perspective that focuses on the interests of socio-economic actors such as the electorate, NGOs, employers or labour unions to understand which problems are set on the agenda and how decisions are taken. Within this tradition, Marxist approaches see the state as an instrument of domination by the capitalist class and explain liberal policies towards low-skilled workers and irregular migrants through employers' interests to create a large basis of dependent and vulnerable workers (Castells 1975; Castles and Kosack 1985). Pluralist or domestic politics approaches suggest that societal cleavages do not run along class lines but along societal interest groups. In this view, public policymaking is the outcome of the bargaining between societal groups with differential access to resources (see, for instance, Olson 1965). Most prominently, Freeman (1995, 2006) argued that immigration policymaking in liberal democracies is characterized by client politics, as the costs of immigration are diffused among the entire electorate, while its benefits are concentrated in the hands of specific groups such as employers and ethnic advocacy groups, which makes it easier for them to organize and lobby for their interests compared to the wider population.

Such domestic politics approaches have been instrumental in understanding how electoral considerations and party politics (Alonso and da Fonseca 2011; Bale 2008; Givens and Luedtke 2005; Perlmutter 1996) or the lobbying by employers and labour unions (Ellermann 2013; Marino, Roosblad and Penninx 2017; Peters 2017) shape immigration politicization and agenda-setting in Western liberal democracies. As the analysis of Morocco and Tunisia in this book suggests, societal dynamics around immigration policy involving the electorate, political parties or civil society fundamentally differ in more autocratic settings.

First of all, the mechanisms of civil society engagement and the channels used by CSOs to influence state actors differ across political regimes, with a focus on transnational lobbying networks in autocracies compared to more rights-based advocacy strategies in democracies (see also Henninger and Römer 2021; Kemp and Kfir 2016; Piper 2006).[*] As I show for Tunisia, the democratic transition in 2011 shifted the foundations of political life, with domestic societal actors becoming central to policymaking. In particular, Tunisian policymakers now need to ensure popular adherence to policy changes, parliamentarians became real actors in policymaking compared to the one-party regime under Ben Ali, and relations between state institutions and civil society organizations multiplied. More generally, studies on the consequences of democratization for immigration policy all emphasize that democracy puts domestic socio-political interests centre stage – even if findings on how democratization shapes immigration policy substance diverge (Acosta Arcarazo and Freier 2015; Chung 2010; FitzGerald and Cook-Martín 2014; Milner 2009; Whitaker 2005).[†]

In contrast, the analysis of Morocco shows that while domestic civil society can also play a crucial role in autocracies, the mechanisms through which CSOs succeed in influencing policymaking differ: to make their voice heard and increase pressure on the Moroccan state, CSOs in Morocco importantly rely on support from international civil society partners (see also Üstübici 2016). Similar dynamics have been observed across Asia, where trade unions have started to form transnational advocacy networks to defend migrants' rights more successfully at the national level (Hujo and Piper 2007; Piper 2006). In such an international advocacy loop, theorized as the 'boomerang effect' by Keck and Sikkink (1998), foreign civil society, media or governments strengthen the influence of domestic civil society on national policy

---

[*] Such studies of NGO lobbying in immigration policymaking are part of a broader research field that examines the strategies of civil society actors in more autocratic contexts (Bayat 2010; Bellin 1994; Harbeson, Rothchild and Chazan 1994; Lewis 2002), and which has gained momentum in the wake of the 2011 'Arab Spring' (Aarts and Cavatorta 2013; Cavatorta 2012; Lewis 2013).

[†] In some contexts, civil society groups that played a central role in democratic transitions were key in mobilizing for migrants' rights and initiating liberal migration reforms – such as in South Korea (Chung 2010; Mosler and Pedroza 2016), Ecuador, Argentina or Brazil (Acosta Arcarazo and Freier 2015; Álvarez Velasco 2020; Filomeno and Vicino 2020). However, in contexts where newly empowered voters showcased clear anti-migration preference, democratization provided an opportunity for restrictive migration reform, as work on asylum policy in Tanzania, Guinea and Kenya (Milner 2009), on xenophobia in Ghana, Côte d'Ivoire or Zambia (Brobbey 2018; Whitaker 2005) or on ethnic selection in historical immigration policy across North and South America (FitzGerald and Cook-Martín 2014) demonstrates.

processes by simultaneously challenging the legitimation of the regime at home and abroad. However, this overt reliance on international support also showcases the limits to societal input in autocratic contexts.

Next to civil society, political economy approaches pay particular attention to the electorate as a driver of immigration policy. So far, however, we have little insights into the role of partisan politics or public opinion in immigration politics in more autocratic contexts (for an exception, see Zhou and Grossman 2021).[*] The comparison of Morocco and Tunisia suggests that the electorate indeed plays a more central role in democratic contexts: in Tunisia, policy elites often referred to the divided public opinion on immigration to justify why restrictive policies inherited from the authoritarian era have not been reformed. Also, actors who lobby for immigrants' rights in Tunisia focus on raising awareness within the Tunisian population and among parliamentarians, as they believe that a change in public opinion is key for driving policy change. This contrasts with the situation in Morocco, where lacking democratic or parliamentary adherence to the liberal immigration reform has never been mentioned by respondents as a potential obstacle for policymaking and policy implementation.

Yet, this does not mean that autocratic leaders are entirely immune to public pressures, as they also have to secure their domestic legitimacy (Bueno de Mesquita et al. 2003; Keck and Sikkink 1998). In Ecuador, for instance, President Correa's competitive authoritarian regime had to give in to public pressure in 2008 and reintroduce visa requirements for certain nationalities only a few months after they were removed (Acosta Arcarazo and Freier 2015; Freier 2013). Even in Saudi Arabia, the chief example of autocratic immigration policymaking, increased popular opposition to large-scale immigration programs among the country's unemployed youth led the Saudi government in 2011 to enact a series of restrictive measures towards immigrants, including highly symbolic measures such as mass deportations, to prevent potential social unrest (Thiollet 2015). Ultimately, immigration seems to inevitably create social dynamics that – in the long term and regardless of the regime in place – politicize immigration in the public sphere and risk jeopardizing policymaking behind closed doors.

Lastly, political economy approaches highlight not only political parties and civil society as key societal actors but also employer interests.

---

[*] Existing research focuses mainly on the voting behaviour of emigrants or on autocracies' strategic use of dual citizenship and extra-territorial voting rights to maintain their power (Brand 2014; Jaulin and Nilsson 2015; Just 2019; Mirilovic 2015; Umpierrez de Reguero, Yener-Roderburg and Cartagena 2021).

As my empirical analysis shows, in both Morocco and Tunisia, employers are not politically invested in the issue of immigration given the imbrication of political and economic elites in both countries and the large pool of informal domestic and foreign labour that they can tap into. In fact, in an economy where every second worker is employed informally, incentives for employers to advocate for more legal immigration are minimal, and lobbying for migrants' rights would only weaken the power position of employers. Such dynamic has also been evidenced in Malaysia and Thailand, where large-scale irregular labour immigration is in fact in line with the interests of large employers (Anderson 2021; Garcés-Mascareñas 2012; Kaur 2014; Sadiq 2005; Vigneswaran 2020). Furthermore, in contexts characterized by clientelism and patronage, employers' need for active lobbying on immigration is low, given that their interests are directly integrated into the state. While such imbrication between economic and political actors has been highlighted in many autocracies – where domestic rule might be based on power arrangements between ruling and merchant families, and markets are sometimes conceptualized as an 'appendix to the state' (Hertog 2013: 175) – clientelism and systems of patronage also thrive in democracies (Hicken 2011; Roniger 2004) and affect how business interests are channelled into policymaking.

Thus, when it comes to the role of domestic societal interests in immigration policy, it seems that while the advocacy strategies of civil society and the role played by the electorate differ across political regimes, business interests in immigration policymaking are rather influenced by the structure of the labour market and the relationship between political and economic elites.

The State as an Actor

In contrast to political economy approaches that zoom into societal interests on immigration, political sociology explanations such as institutionalism grant the state (partial) freedom from socio-economic demands and put dynamics within the state apparatus centre stage. Bureaucratic politics approaches highlight how visions and interests on immigration diverge within a state's administrative apparatus and how state actors strategically use immigration to expand their own fields of power. For instance, Bonjour (2011) shows how – when it comes to labour migrants' family reunification rights – the vision of Dutch civil servants in the Ministry of Social Affairs clashes with that in the Ministry of Justice; and Calavita (1992) demonstrates in her groundbreaking study of the US Immigration and Naturalization Service (INS) how internal conflicts and power dynamics around the everyday implementation of the Bracero program turned the INS into one of the most powerful actors within the American state.

Such bureaucratic politics approaches seem not only relevant to understand immigration policy processes in democracies but also in autocracies. As I show for Morocco, the stepping up of immigration control in the early 2000s was partly the initiative of a new generation of civil servants within the Ministry of Interior, who saw immigration control as a tool to expand their power and to access resources at a moment in time when the centrality of the Interior Ministry in the state apparatus was at stake. More generally, the comparison of policy dynamics within the Moroccan and Tunisian state suggests that ministerial interests on immigration are determined by the intrinsic questions that immigration poses to each specific institutional actor rather than by the broader political structures within which these actors operate. For example, Ministries of Interior in both countries followed a security-driven agenda, privileging an approach that maximizes control over human mobility; whereas Ministries of Foreign Affairs used migration as a diplomatic tool – ready to sacrifice policy coherence over time if required by circumstances; and Ministries of Health were more sympathetic to opening services to foreigners given the imperative of securing public health. This inevitably triggered turf wars among these ministries. Such insights on the institution-specific interests on immigration suggest that ministerial positions might be strikingly similar across countries and political regimes, and that turf wars – for instance, between Ministries of Interior and Foreign Affairs – are almost programmed into any immigration policy dossier.

Beyond Morocco and Tunisia, other studies have showcase the importance of bureaucratic dynamics to understand immigration policy in more autocratic contexts: Russell (1989), for instance, zooms into the complex power dynamics among state institutions – particularly the Ministry of Interior, Ministry of Social Affairs and Labour, as well as Arab and Kuwaiti nationalists in the National Assembly – to explain why the Kuwaiti ruling family shifted between liberalization and securitization of labour immigration over time. Thiollet (2021) explores how immigration policy in Saudi Arabia is subject to the power politics among princes, who instrumentalize different parts of the state to advance their broader political interests via the issue of immigration. And Vigneswaran (2020) shows how, in Thailand, the independent actions of local police and immigration officials, who engaged in opportunistic raids of migrant workplaces, unexpectedly led to a massive migrant exodus that forced the Ministry of Labour and the military junta to reform Thailand's migrant protection regimes.

Taking such bureaucratic politics analyses one step further, the state interest approach not only grants the state partial freedom from societal interests and takes inter-actor dynamics within the state seriously but also argues that states themselves pursue interests, such as regime legitimation, national development goals or the maintenance of social peace (see, for instance, Krasner 1978; Stepan 1981; Trimberger 1978). Most prominently, Boswell (2007b: 77) argued that 'societal interests and institutional constraints are incorporated in migration policy only when conforming to the functional imperatives of the state', above all to secure its legitimacy and sovereignty.

As this book shows, state imperatives are a key immigration policy driver in Morocco and Tunisia: in Morocco, liberal immigration reform was a critical tool to foster the legitimacy of the monarchy at home and abroad by broadcasting a liberal, progressive image; and in Tunisia, political dynamics around immigration, namely depoliticization and restrictive policy continuity, were intimately tied to political elites' interest of safeguarding democratization. Furthermore, in both cases, the priority of state authorities to keep maximum leverage and control over immigration explains the preference for informal arrangements over legal changes and the limitations of reforms at the level of implementation.

Such insights resonate with broader findings on Africa and the Middle East, showing that migration governance is a vital tool for regimes to bolster their domestic and international sovereignty and legitimacy (Norman 2019; Tsourapas 2019a; Vigneswaran and Quirk 2015).[*] In particular, institutionalist scholars working on immigration policy in autocracies demonstrate how state actors strategically use policy informality and ambiguity to assure their power over immigration: Norman (2020b), for instance, shows that Morocco, Turkey and Egypt have consciously pursued a 'policy of ambivalence' towards migrants,

---

[*] The work of Tsourapas has been particularly important for efforts to theorize authoritarian state engagement with migration. Drawing from his research on Egypt, Tsourapas (2019a) develops a conceptual framework that explains labour emigration policies through their impact on authoritarian regime durability at domestic and international levels. He shows that the choice for restrictive or permissive labour emigration policies depends on a regime's broader tactics of repression, legitimation and co-optation. While his framework paves the way for a more systematic analysis of how *emigration* politics and authoritarianism co-create each other, it seems not directly transferable to the study of *immigration* politics that this book is concerned with. In fact, while the relationship between the state and its emigrants is inherently different under democratic or autocratic contexts, as Tsourapas and others show (Alemán and Woods 2014; de Haas and Vezzoli 2011; Miller and Peters 2020), the same is not necessarily the case for immigration politics. In fact, as this book shows, immigration poses similar challenges to the sovereignty and legitimacy of all nation-states, be they ruled by autocratic or democratic leaders.

preferring to grant migrants rights through ad-hoc policy decisions rather than through legal changes to ensure their ability to backtrack on these rights in the future. In Niger, narratives of temporariness and transit migration purposefully construct the image of a transit country to limit protection opportunities and maximize security interventions (Frowd 2020). And in Jordan and Lebanon, institutional ambiguity and uneven implementation are strategic components in the state's 'politics of uncertainty' aimed at reinforcing control over Syrian and Palestinian refugees (Nassar and Stel 2019; Sanyal 2018; Stel 2020).

Such concepts and insights, however, seem not only relevant to understand immigration policymaking in the Middle East and North Africa, as European democracies also increasingly mobilize ambiguity and informality to bolster migration control. The informalization of migration cooperation on return and readmission across Europe (Cassarino 2007; Slagter 2019), the instrumentalization of travel visas as a quick and effective migration policy tool (Czaika, de Haas and Villares-Varela 2018; Laube 2019), or the growing reliance on discretion in policy implementation to govern migrants' everyday lives in Europe (Bastien 2009; Lemaire 2019; Schultz 2020) are just some examples. Institutionalism thus seems to emerge as a critical theoretical frame to investigate immigration politics across political systems, with conceptual advances on the Global South also providing critical insights into the working of immigration politics at large (see Comaroff and Comaroff 2012).

Yet, within institutionalist approaches, there are also two policymaking dynamics that seem subject to a 'regime effect': the centrality of executive actors in initiating policy reform and the role of legal actors in safeguarding migrants' rights. As the empirical analysis shows, in Morocco and pre-2011 Tunisia, power is concentrated in the hands of the King and President, respectively, and their leverage to take strategic decisions that break with path dependency dynamics is high. The King's decision to engage in immigration reform in 2013 after a decade of restrictiveness and to frame immigration liberalization as necessary to achieve African regional integration and to consolidate Moroccan 'modernity' explains the extraordinary dynamism on immigration and the (at least discursive) adherence of state institutions to the new policy. In contrast, power in post-2011 Tunisia is diffused across various democratic institutions. This institutionalized plurality of positions and the inbuilt need for compromising slowed down decision-making and made politics prone to stalemate. Thus, while the 'royal will' has fostered administrative actors around a common agenda in Morocco, democratization in Tunisia has exacerbated the fragmentation and pluralism of voices. The executive's decision-making autonomy thus seems fundamentally higher in autocratic contexts.

Furthermore, autocratic contexts seem generally less prone to courts-based expansions of migrants' rights that characterize policy developments on family reunification, asylum or political rights for foreigners in liberal democracies (Hamlin 2014; Joppke 1998). The Tunisian case is exemplary in this regard: as I show, democratization has led Tunisian civil society actors to progressively and increasingly solicit courts to challenge migrant rights' violations. In contrast, although legal activism is also emerging in Morocco, court decisions on immigration remain incoherent, arbitrary and often protect the state interest (see also Khrouz 2016). Courts thus seem unlikely to act as reliable brakes for migrant rights' violations in regimes with a weak (or absent) rule of law. Indeed, as Kemp and Kfir (2016) show in the case of Singapore, juridical institutions are not even seen as a potential arena for advancing migrants' rights, given that CSOs cannot access courts in the first place. This does not mean that there is no role for legal actors in more autocratic contexts. In non-democracies, courts can also leverage their (limited) institutional autonomy to become islands of resistance and partners for domestic and international political activists, but only as long as they do not jeopardize the regimes' core strategies for maintaining political control (Moustafa and Ginsburg 2008; Solomon 2007).

Ultimately, while political regimes seem to significantly shape the margin of manoeuvre of courts, the cases of Morocco and Tunisia also show that opportunities for legal claims-making can remain limited regardless of the political regime in place, particularly when immigration regulations are enacted through governmental orders or dominated by informal policy practices. Indeed, in the context of growing informalization of migration control and in the absence of laws that can be contested in court, the power of legal actors to safeguard migrants' rights is reduced across the entire democracy–autocracy spectrum.

The Weight of History

Like institutionalism, historical-culturalist approaches to immigration policy are also part of a political sociology tradition to public policy research, but instead of focusing on dynamics within the state, they emphasize the national historical origins of immigration policy and the role of path dependency in structurally constraining policy choices. In studies on Europe and North America, the national identity approach has been widely used to show how a country's particular national history limits today's immigration policy options: Brubaker (1992), for instance, traces French and German immigration policies back to these countries' distinct histories of nationhood, Hansen (2002) explains French and British policies towards colonial migrants, as well as German asylum policies through path-dependent effects and policy feedbacks of these countries' own citizenship and constitutional regime, and Freeman (1995) identifies three distinct modes of immigration politics in Western liberal democracies depending on countries' immigration history and institutionalization of migration actors. Most forcefully, the work by Aristide Zolberg (1978, 2006) showcases how changing migration policies in Western Europe and North America reflect the emergence of modern states and global capitalism between the sixteenth and twentieth centuries, and how, since the colonial period, immigration policy has been a tool for nation-building in the United States.

In recent scholarship on immigration politics in the Global South, the link between immigration policy, state formation and national identity narratives is also central: Klotz (2012, 2013), for instance, shows how the contemporary immigration regime in South Africa is rooted in a century of racial exclusion and societal conflicts over national identity; and Manby (2018) demonstrates how across Africa, nationality laws after independence were central tools for political elites to shape national identity understandings. Work on India exemplifies how the initial introduction of migration regulations was intrinsically tied to the establishment of the modern nation-state under colonialism and how, since independence, the Indian state actively mobilizes immigration policies for nation-building – be it by expelling minorities or by strategically granting stay permits to particular religious groups such as Christians, Hindus or Sikh from Pakistan and Bangladesh as a counterweight to India's Muslim population (Mongia 2018; Naujoks 2018; Sadiq and Tsourapas 2021).

As I show, specific immigration policies in Morocco and Tunisia can indeed be understood through their fit with broader national identity narratives: in Tunisian history, authorities' approaches to refugees depended on whether the protection of that particular group would fit into the overall political narrative of the regime. While Algerian refugees were welcomed in Tunisia during the Algerian War of Independence in a spirit of brotherhood between two independence-seeking nations, those who arrived during Algeria's civil war in the 1990s were perceived as a security risk by Tunisian authorities who feared the rise of political Islam. Similar dynamics are at play in Morocco, where refugee politics have been significantly shaped by how origin states position themselves in the Western Sahara issue (Norman 2016b). Also the 2013 immigration reform can be partly understood through this lens, as it provided an unparalleled opportunity for the Moroccan state to showcase its liberal character and African belonging. A comparable dynamic has been highlighted in Iran, where the decision by revolutionary leaders to grant residence permits to Afghan refugees in 1979 was framed as part of Islamic fraternity and the importance of the *Ummah* (Moghadam 2018).

The attention to national historical processes in such historical-culturalist approaches showcases the power of path dependency and allows scholars to understand not only change but also continuities in immigration politics. As this book shows, the ways in which Moroccan and Tunisian states have historically consolidated power over their populations and dealt with ethnic or religious diversity shape the repertoire of actions that authorities tap into today when developing immigration policies. For instance, the dynamics underpinning the liberal immigration reform in 2013 in Morocco echo the strategies that the state successfully used in the past to appease leftist, Islamist or Amazigh critics, namely proactive politicization and co-optation of opponents. And in Tunisia, the depoliticization of immigration in the name of democratization recalls earlier strategies used by the authoritarian regime to silence opposition, namely referring to the need to preserve national unity in order to achieve overarching developmental goals. Such continuities in states' trusted strategies of population control are also visible in South Africa, where policy practices and institutions set up to enforce racial segregation among Black and White citizens in the past were redirected in recent years to police immigration (Klotz 2012, 2013; Vigneswaran 2018); and in China, where policies to control internal (rural to urban) migration, such as the 'hukou' registration system, were readapted to deal with international immigration (Haugen 2015; Van Dongen 2018).

Particularly in post-colonial contexts, colonial and imperial legacies of population control still inform immigration policies and practices until today. As I show, national authorities in Morocco and Tunisia largely took over French legal categories and administrative procedures on immigration upon independence in 1956. But also elsewhere, colonial practices continue to shape the ways in which immigration is governed – be it through path dependency or active institutional borrowing. For instance, the Kafala system that dominates labour immigration management in the Arab Gulf today was initially introduced by British colonial authorities in the early twentieth century to control foreign labour (AlShehabi 2021; Lori 2019). And in India, British colonialism left its traces on contemporary immigration control, as laws that were initially devised to regulate population movement within the British empire were reappropriated by the independent Indian state to regulate international migration (Mongia 2018; Sadiq and Tsourapas 2021). But colonial legacies are not set in stone, as Vezzoli and Flahaux (2017) show in the case of travel visa policies across the Caribbean, where countries gradually depart from mirroring the visa regimes of the former colonial state to more accurately reflect their own geopolitical alliances within the region.

A last state formation aspect that provides an important mould for contemporary debates on immigration is countries' historical experience with the emigration of their nationals. As I show, the large-scale emigration of Moroccan and Tunisian citizens since the mid-twentieth century informs current narratives and debates on immigration in both countries. In particular, diaspora groups, returnees and civil society associations have mobilized what I call the 'mirror effect' by using Morocco's and Tunisia's concern for their citizens in Europe as a tool to strengthen their advocacy of immigrants' rights in Morocco and Tunisia (see also Üstübici 2015). Similar feedback dynamics between past emigration and current immigration have been evidenced in historical countries of origin in Europe, such as Italy, Germany or Greece (Dinas, Fouka and Schläpfer 2021; Florio 2019). Historical-culturalist approaches that explore the particular legacies of nation-state formation thus seem to offer precious analytical tools to grasp the origins and drivers of immigration politics across political regimes and political geographies.

Foreign Policy Interests

While political economy, institutionalist and historical-culturalist approaches focus on the national arena as the primary locus of immigration politics, international relations approaches zoom into the interest structures dominating the supra-national realm: within the Marxist tradition, world systems' approaches and dependency theories posit that immigration policies reflect the global market structure, including the interests of large multinational companies (Portes and Walton 1981; Wallerstein 1974). Within the realist tradition, hegemonic stability approaches suggest that immigration policies reflect the security interests of geopolitically dominant states. In particular, analyses of the imbrications between migration and foreign policy (Mitchell 1989; Teitelbaum 1984; Weiner 1985) have helped explain the drivers behind the welcoming of Cold War refugees by Western liberal democracies until the late 1980s (Carruthers 2005), or the dynamics around the externalization of migration controls from European countries towards neighbouring regions since the 1990s (Boswell 2003; Reslow and Vink 2015).

In fact, such international relations approaches also dominate recent scholarship on immigration policy in the Global South. Research on West Africa, for instance, shows how governments balance electoral interests and international pressures when negotiating their immigration policy at the intersection of domestic and international policy spheres

36 Theories on the Move

(Adam et al. 2020; Mouthaan 2019). Scholarship exploring interactions with international organizations and donors demonstrates how states selectively assert their national sovereignty over migration and refugee politics, sometimes guarding and sometimes willingly delegating it for strategic reasons (Abdelaaty 2021; Hartigan 1992). And the wealth of studies of 'migration diplomacy' across the Middle East and North Africa shows how immigration control is instrumentalized to advance economic cooperation and foreign policy goals (Adamson and Tsourapas 2019; El Qadim 2015; Norman 2020a; Paoletti 2011; Thiollet 2011; Tsourapas 2017). Greenhill (2010: 262) even evidences the 'instrumental exploitation of engineered cross-border migrations' as a common tool in diplomatic relations across the globe.

Also in research on Morocco and Tunisia, explanations of immigration politics that highlight international interests dominate (Cassarino 2014; Cuttitta 2020; Gazzotti 2021a; Roman and Pastore 2018; Wunderlich 2010). While Moroccan and Tunisian immigration policy is sometimes wrongly portrayed as a simple reaction to European pressures, foreign policy interests have indeed crucially informed the selectivity of Morocco's and Tunisia's regional labour and refugee politics in the decades after independence, and immigration control has undeniably become central to diplomatic relations with European and increasingly also African actors since the turn of twenty-first-century. However, these international dynamics around immigration always exist alongside powerful domestic political interests – in both democratic Tunisia and autocratic Morocco.

In fact, the analysis of Moroccan and Tunisian immigration politics in this book suggests that the way in which states process international dynamics around immigration depends on a country's position in global migration systems and not primarily on the political regime in place (see also Adamson and Tsourapas 2019: 6–7). While destination countries in Europe and North America are said to elaborate their immigration policies in the context of a 'two-level game' (Putnam 1988; Rosenblum 2004a) between international and domestic spheres, the same can be expected for countries where primarily emigration is politicized, such as the Philippines, Egypt or Italy in the past. However, countries where immigration and emigration are politicized simultaneously – such as Morocco and Tunisia, but also Mexico, Ecuador, Turkey, Jordan, South Korea or Ukraine – seem to navigate a more complex three-level game in which vested interests in both origin and destination countries need to be reconciled with domestic demands.[*] In such a three-level game, one can expect foreign policy considerations to influence

---

[*] The three-level game concept has originally been developed in European studies to account for the level of EU decision-making in addition to the national domestic and

immigration politics more strongly compared to domestic concerns because of the need to satisfy origin and destination country interests simultaneously.

Furthermore, in these three-level games, immigration can be activated as a flexible foreign policy tool depending on the diplomatic vis-à-vis in question. On the one hand, states can capitalize on the presence of immigrants on their territory by using them as a 'weapon' (Greenhill 2010) or 'rent' (Bensaâd 2005; Tsourapas 2019b) in their geopolitical relations. Such dynamics are at play in Morocco (Brachet, Choplin and Pliez 2011; El Qadim 2015; Tyszler 2015), where authorities strategically relax border controls with Spain to bolster their bargaining power during negotiations on agricultural exports or fisheries agreements, as well as to put pressure on European countries to recognize Morocco's claim on Western Sahara. The use of migration in a 'blackmailing strategy' (Tsourapas 2019b) also dominates diplomatic relations on migration between the European Union and Libya or Turkey (Greenhill 2016; Paoletti 2011; Tsourapas 2017) or between the United States and Mexico or Cuba in the past (Greenhill 2010; Kimball 2007; Mitchell 1992).

On the other hand, states can also mobilize immigration on their territory for a policy linkage mechanism that Arrighi and Bauböck (2017: 631) call the 'demonstration effect'. In this dynamic, governments of countries where both immigration and emigration is politicized might enact liberal policies towards *immigration* to strengthen their *emigration* policy advocacy in diaspora host countries.[*] Such demonstration effect is particularly attractive when the number of immigrants is still relatively small. As I show, this is the case in autocratic Morocco, where liberal immigration reform has been effectively instrumentalized to advance Moroccan emigrants' rights in Europe, leading by example. Research on democracies such as Argentina, Ecuador or South Korea (Acosta Arcarazo and Freier 2015; Mosler and Pedroza 2016) also identifies such a demonstration effect as a driver of liberal immigration policies.

---

international diplomatic levels (Larsén 2007, Patterson 1997). Natasja Reslow has used this concept to analyse EU external migration policy – whereby the three levels are the European institutions, EU Member States and third countries (Reslow 2013; Reslow and Vink 2015). In the context of Morocco and Tunisia, the three levels refer to European, African and domestic policy arenas.

[*] As Arrighi and Bauböck (2017: 631) show in the case of foreigners' right to vote in Ecuador and South Korea, 'the enfranchisement of foreign residents was not the expression of a genuine desire to resolve a democratic deficit by encouraging the participation of a traditionally excluded group of residents. Instead, it was meant to produce a demonstration effect towards host states ... whom the government pressured to reciprocate'.

Ultimately, international relations approaches that put diplomatic dynamics and foreign policy interests centre stage seem critical to understanding immigration policymaking across the globe. Yet, the way in which such dynamics unfold seems not so much shaped by the political regime in place, but rather by a country's position in global migration systems – with international factors expected to weigh particularly heavily in countries facing a three-level game, where migration politics is made with regards to domestic, origin and destination country concerns.

Global Norms

Research inspired by globalization theories also zooms into the international drivers of immigration policy, but instead of focusing on interests, it highlights how global norms and institutions shape national immigration policymaking. Most prominently, Sassen (1996) argued that the rise of an international human rights regime constrains the leverage of national administrations in curtailing immigrants' rights (see also Guiraudon and Lahav 2000; Soysal 1994). Similarly, Hollifield (1992b: 577) suggested that the dominant norm in today's world – liberalism – 'constrain[s] the power and autonomy of states both in their treatment of individual migrants and in their relations to other states'. While much of the migration literature focuses on the dynamics surrounding international liberal norm constraints in the Global North (Gurowitz 1999; Hampshire 2013; Rosenblum and Salehyan 2004), in his initial formulation of the embedded liberalism hypothesis, Hollifield (1992b: 583) suggests that the constraining power of liberalism might also be at play beyond Western liberal democracies:

The liberal argument is relevant for other regions of the world such as the Middle East or South Asia. … the policies of nonliberal states are constrained by liberal norms and principles, expressed in the "court of world opinion" and international conventions.

As I show, international norm adherence has been an important driver of immigration politics in both Morocco and Tunisia: for instance, when migrant rights violations at the Moroccan–Spanish borders in 2005 triggered international outrage, Moroccan authorities reacted by shifting their policy strategy and actively promoting themselves as mediators on migration between Africa and Europe. Also in 2013, the ultimate trigger for the King to launch a liberal immigration reform was to alleviate the reputational damage created by the evaluation of Morocco's adherence to the *UN International Convention of the Protection of the Rights of All Migrant Workers and Members of Their*

Families. Thus, a core goal of the 2013 liberal immigration reform has been to react to civil society and international criticism of migrant rights' violations and to cast Morocco as a progressive state, a 'liberal monarchy'. Also in Tunisia, international norm adherence was instrumentalized by civil society actors, in particular to lobby for a law against racial discrimination in 2019 as well as for opening the education system to undocumented children. And in both Morocco and Tunisia, international norms and institutions were key factors behind the laws against human trafficking in 2016, which provided both countries with an opportunity to internationally showcase their adherence to a community of modern states. These findings rejoin FitzGerald and Cook-Martín (2014: 21), who state that 'one of the purposes of immigration and emigration policies is to make a country appear more modern and civilized. Migration policies are dramaturgical acts aimed at national and world audiences'.

The Moroccan and Tunisian cases thus suggest that adherence to international norms can be a key driver of immigration politics in both democratic and autocratic contexts. Indeed, autocratic regimes also seek economic and political cooperation with global and regional powers to secure international legitimacy for their rule at home and are therefore not immune to the pressure exerted by international norms (Cassarino 2014; Escribà-Folch and Wright 2015; Risse, Ropp and Sikkink 1999). However, international norms and standards do not affect national policymaking directly and need to be brought in by local actors to play out (see also Gurowitz 1999; Hartigan 1992).

The insights gained from Morocco and Tunisia suggest that while international norms can matter everywhere, the mechanisms through which they constrain immigration policy might differ depending on the regime in place. In particular, while democracies might be more vulnerable to international normative pressure exerted by national judicial and civil society actors, autocracies might be mainly affected through reputational damage and international shaming, especially when they seek to broadcast a progressive image of themselves. In those autocracies, displaying liberal norm adherence through immigration policy might be more urgent compared to democracies that can already point at national political processes to showcase their liberalness. This suggests that countries with a robust civil society and an independent judiciary might be more exposed to direct norm adherence through the enforcement of international human rights standards and conventions by courts, while liberal norm adherence might play out more indirectly, through symbolic politics, in countries that seek to portray themselves as progressive on the international scene.

Yet, the global liberal norm that provides the fundament for these dynamics might not be set in stone. As Thiollet (2016, 2019) suggests in her work on Arab Gulf countries, a new norm of illiberal migration governance is diffusing and challenging assumptions of transnationalism as an inherently cosmopolitan, liberal phenomenon. Not only in the Gulf monarchies, but also across Europe, North America and Australia, policy trends suggest that international normative dynamics on immigration politics might not be limited to liberalism but increasingly encompass illiberal policy convergence (Adamson, Triadafilopoulos and Zolberg 2011; FitzGerald and Hirsch 2022; Guild, Groenendijk and Carrera 2009; Skleparis 2016). How this diffusion of illiberal norms might affect insights from globalization theory approaches on immigration policymaking deserves to be studied in a systematic way.

Exploring the Fundamentals of Public Policymaking in Modern Nation-States

This first attempt at rethinking immigration policy theories across political regimes suggests that political economy approaches such as domestic politics, as well as institutionalist approaches that emphacize the role of legal or executive actors are subject to a 'regime effect'. At the same time, the dynamics highlighted by international relations approaches, historical culturalism, bureaucratic politics and globalization theories seem to be relevant accross the political regime spectrum and rather shaped by factors such as a country's colonial legacy, labour market structure or geopolitical embedding. As a consequence, the theoretical tools required to understand immigration politics might not be as fundamentally different across political regimes and political geographies as often assumed. This is even more so the case because immigration policymaking is also subject to generic dynamics of public policymaking that emerge out of the fundamental structure and functioning of modern nation-states.

Across the globe, states are fragmented into different actors with potentially diverging interests that clash with their image as a unitary and coherent actor (Migdal 2001; Migdal and Schlichte 2005; Pierson and Skocpol 2002; Skocpol 1985). Although executive powers usually have higher decision-making leverage in autocracies compared to liberal democracies, more than one actor is involved in developing, taking or implementing policy decisions regardless of the political regime in place. Autocratic policymaking is thus often wrongly assumed to be so centralized as to not leave any room for contestation, negotiation and lobbying. As Castles (2004: 865) writes, 'political systems are complex and contradictory in themselves ... even less democratic receiving states find that migration control comes up against competing interests'. Indeed, non-democratic regimes also have to reconcile interests, negotiate decisions with economic and political actors, and garner political support to sustain their legitimacy – be it among the citizenry, the international community, patronage networks or specific interests groups (Brooker 2014; Bueno de Mesquita et al. 2003). This rejoins the conclusion of Moustafa and Ginsburg (2008: 12) that 'when we expand the focus from a simple electoral model to a broader one of state fragmentation, authoritarian and democratic regimes may not be as dissimilar as first appears'.

As a result of such state fragmentation, policy intentions announced in public discourses often end up being watered-down in policy decisions or not enacted at all because the policymaking process in between requires the reconciliation different societal and institutional interests – regardless of the political regime in place. Concerning immigration, research on Europe suggests that such a 'discursive gap' between what politicians say and what they do generally comes in the form of restrictive rhetoric and permissive policies (Bonjour 2011; Cornelius et al. 2004; Geddes 2003). Also in the case of Japan and South Korea, Chung (2010) shows that governments have maintained the official discourse of closed-door immigration policy while responding to business interests by filling needs for migrant labour through 'side doors' such as temporary worker schemes or trainee programs. In contrast, the main dynamic at play in Morocco and Tunisia has been a gap between liberal discourse and restrictive policy continuity: in Morocco, many of the integration measures announced by King Mohammed VI in 2013 have not been effectively enacted because of institutional resistances, and in Tunisia, initiatives by the Ministries of Social Affairs or Foreign Affairs that would have facilitated access to residence permits or travel visas have ultimately not been followed up. Similar dynamics of a 'reverse discursive gap' have also been evidenced across South America (Acosta Arcarazo and Freier 2015).

But even if they are enacted, policies developed in central-level institutions will inevitably be reinterpreted and adapted by local-level actors in the course of their implementation (Eule 2014; Infantino 2010; Lipsky 1980). This can work to migrants' advantage or disadvantage: in Morocco, for instance, migrants' access to social services or residence permits after 2013 varied strikingly across the national territory, with the situation in major Moroccan cities reportedly more favourable towards migrants compared to smaller cities in the north-east or the countryside (see also Diallo 2016). And in Tunisia, individual exemptions from irregular stay penalties could be negotiated informally with a particular civil servant at the Ministry of Finance. While such individual leverage can create more permissive environments than policies-on-paper might suggest, these policy openings are by definition fragile and subject to backlashes. Beyond Morocco and Tunisia, similar implementation dynamics have been evidenced. For instance, as Bakewell (2015) shows in the case of Zambia, local authorities in the Zambian–Angolan border subverted national refugee policy based on personal interpretations and local conventions by handing out Zambian national identity cards to Angolan refugees and their children. And in Mexico, attempts by the central government to control emigration are systematically undermined by municipal authorities because of their distinct local political interests (FitzGerald 2006). Thus, public policymaking across the democracy–autocracy spectrum seems inevitably characterized by gaps between policy discourses, policies-on-paper and policy implementation (Czaika and de Haas 2013).

Because public policy research tends to emphasize the role of institutions in the policy process, an often underestimated driver of policymaking in modern nation-states is the power of individuals making up these institutions. This not only concerns policy implementation, as just suggested, but also agenda-setting and decision-making. As I show, in Morocco, the personality of Driss El Yazami – a human rights activist who was exiled in France but later became head of the Council for Morocco's Community Abroad (CCME) and of the National Council on Human Rights (CNDH) – was central in setting immigration on the agenda of the Moroccan monarchy. And in Tunisia, political exiles who were appointed to high-level political positions after 2011, such as Radhouane Nouicer, Houcine Jaziri or Kamel Jendoubi, crucially shaped the discourses and policy decisions on migration in the immediate aftermath of the revolution. Although institutional identities and organizational cultures can strongly shape the behaviour of its members, the leverage of individuals in policymaking is thus crucial: for Kingdon (2003: 180), 'one can nearly always pinpoint a particular person, or at most a few persons, who were central in moving a subject up on the agenda'. In contrast to the ideal-type of a 'neutral' administration (see Weber 1922), then, it is often so-called political entrepreneurs or claims-makers (Becker 1963) who personally invest themselves in a policy issue and play a key role in framing policy issues, developing policy options and ultimately triggering policy change – regardless of the formal political regime in place.

Lastly, the analysis of policy processes in Morocco and Tunisia suggests that, to understand policy change, it is essential to distinguish between 'politics-as-usual' and 'moments of crisis' in both democratic and autocratic contexts, as 'crisis allows the state to take on more autonomy from societal actors and … to consider larger issues such as "the national interest"' (Grindle and Thomas 1991: 73). As I show, crisis reshuffled inter-actor dynamics on immigration in both Morocco and Tunisia: in Morocco, the migrant rights violations at the Spanish–Moroccan border in autumn 2005 allowed civil society and international actors to challenge the monopoly of the Moroccan state on the immigration issue; and in Tunisia, the 2011 revolution and large-scale immigration from neighbouring Libya opened up space for civil society activism and propelled immigration into the centre of socio-political debates. More generally, crises such as '9/11' in the United States or the 2015 'refugee crisis' in Europe have become keywords to signal shifts in political actors' priorities and discourses (Boswell 2007a; Golash-Boza 2012; Hagelund 2020; Reslow 2019). In both democracies and autocracies, crisis thus seems to open up a 'window of opportunity' (Kingdon 2003: 174) for new issues to be set on the agenda, new actors to enter the political field and new policy ideas to be heard.

In dissecting policymaking in Morocco and Tunisia, the book explores what consequences the fundamental structure and functioning of modern nation-states has on policy processes. It suggests that the gap between policy discourses, policies-on-paper and policy implementation, the leverage of individuals making up institutions, as well as the role of crises in reshuffling priorities and coalitions of actors characterize policy processes regardless of the issue at stake and the political regime in place. By developing such hypotheses on the commonalities in immigration policymaking across political regimes, this book is part of a broader scholarly effort that seeks to bridge theorizations of socio-political processes in the Global South and the Global North.

The following chapters now dive into the contrasting cases of Morocco and Tunisia. They examine in detail to what extent and how immigration policymaking has been shaped by the political regime dynamics that Morocco and Tunisia have undergone over the past decades, and hereby explore what immigration politics reveals about political change and the inner workings of modern states.

3 The Contrasting Cases of Morocco and Tunisia

Differing State Formation Trajectories

In both Morocco and Tunisia, migration patterns and policies have unfolded in the context of differing state transformations. In Morocco, apart from some controlled openings towards civil society, the monarchy remains a full-fledged autocracy that maintains its power through a combination of repression, divide-and-rule tactics and co-optation of elites and political opponents. In Tunisia, the 2011 revolution triggered a substantive leap towards liberal democracy, breaking with the single-party regimes of Bourguiba and Ben Ali, whose power was tied to a societal modernization and economic liberalization agenda coupled with population surveillance. Despite similarities in the ways in which authoritarianism has maintained itself in Morocco and Tunisia over the twentieth and early twenty-first centuries, diverging state formation trajectories provide distinct foundations for debates and policies on immigration.

The Resilience of the Moroccan 'Makhzen'

Over centuries, Moroccan state formation was structured by the constant struggle between 'lands of sovereignty' (*bilad al makhzen*), urban areas that would pay taxes to the Moroccan Sultans, and 'lands of dissidence' (*bilad al siba*), mountainous or rural areas inhabited by Amazigh groups[*] that did not recognize the sovereignty of Moroccan Sultans. As a result, the territorial spheres of influence of the Moroccan Sultanate (since 1667 in the hands of the current Alaouite dynasty) have shifted over time, and political power was 'itinerant', characterized by a moving court (Hibou and Tozy 2015). Only in 1934 would French and Spanish

---

[*] People who lived in North Africa before the Arabs arrived are often called 'Berber', an originally Roman appellation that refers to the absence of civilization (barbarism). In contrast to this depreciative term, 'Amazigh' (plural: Imazighen) originates from the local language of these communities (Tamazight) and means 'free men' (Vermeren 2002: 121). For this reason, this book adopts the term 'Amazigh'.

colonial armies crush the resistance in the Moroccan rural areas, establishing effective state power across the entire Moroccan territory (Anderson 1986: 42–43; Hart 2000; Vermeren 2002: 124–25). More generally, the establishment of the French and Spanish Protectorates in 1912 and the infrastructure projects, road constructions and bureaucratization of the Moroccan state apparatus that colonization brought with it accelerated the state's grip on territory and population (Berriane, de Haas and Natter 2021): stable national borders were drawn up and population registries introduced (de Haas 2003).

Yet, colonization did not signify a fundamental rupture in the way in which political power was organized in Morocco, as the monarchy was reaffirmed at independence in 1956: the composition of Morocco's independence movement, dominated by an alliance between Morocco's nationalist independence party, the Istiqlal, and the exiled King Mohammed V against the French colonizers, explains why Morocco's independence movement did not oust the monarchy at independence, as was the case in Tunisia. The main difference was that, now, the monarchy had a centralized state bureaucracy with effective control over national territory at its disposal. In the words of Waterbury (1970, in: Willis 2012: 22), colonial rule 'significantly disrupted the governmental and administrative continuity of Morocco, [but] it left the political style of Moroccans largely intact'. Political power in post-independence Morocco thus remained concentrated within the *Makhzen*,[*] the informal network of advisors, high-level civil servants and members of the economic elite around the King (Ayubi 1995; Hibou and Tozy 2015). The King retained absolute political authority, especially but not only in sensitive areas related to identity and the nation, such as foreign policy, defence, religious affairs and migration. Reflecting this, my respondents have often equated the royal will to the political will of the state: 'the State's will, in Morocco, is the monarchical institution' (M17-I16).

Since independence, Morocco's monarchy secured its power through a mix of repression, elite co-optation and a divide-and-rule strategy towards political opponents guaranteeing that those challenging the regime never got too powerful. At the same time, controlled liberalizations that extended political, civil society and women's rights since the 1990s were central tools in consolidating authoritarian power structures, with stark differences remaining between liberalizations on paper and the limited ways in which political rights and the rule of law are realized in

---

[*] With the development of administration and taxation, in particular, under Sultan Moulay Ismail (1672–1727), the term 'Makhzen' – literally 'storehouse' or 'treasury' – is progressively used to designate the Moroccan state apparatus (Vermeren 2002).

everyday life (Boukhars 2011; Cubertafond 2001; Vermeren 2011; Waterbury 1970).

Indeed, the decades after independence were marked by efforts to consolidate the Moroccan monarchy against political opponents, such as tribal leaders in the northern Rif, the nationalist Istiqlal party, the left-wing National Union of Popular Forces (UNFP) or nationalist and communist student unions. Systematic repression of strikes and urban riots, arbitrary arrests and execution of political opponents characterized the infamous 'Years of Lead' between the 1970s and the early 1990s. In 1990, Gilles Perrault's book 'Notre Ami le Roi' exposed the torture practices of the Moroccan state during the 'Years of Lead' and spurred accusations of human rights violations from outside (Vairel 2004; Willis 2012). In parallel, transnational support for Moroccan CSOs – such as the Moroccan Association of Human Rights (AMDH) created in 1979 or the Moroccan Organization of Human Rights (OMDH) created in 1988 – bolstered pressures on the Moroccan state from within (Gränzer 1999: 133).

To widen the domestic regime base before the throne succession and to improve Morocco's image abroad, King Hassan II engaged in a limited political liberalization (Cubertafond 2001; Monjib 2011; Waltz 1995): freedom of the press was increased, a Consultative Council on Human Rights (CCDH) was created in 1990, and constitutional revisions in September 1992 – although not touching royal powers – enshrined a reference to universal human rights in the preamble and granted more powers to Parliament. Most importantly, the controlled opening towards Moroccan civil society created negotiation spaces between state and society in ways that would consolidate the regime.[*]

In parallel to repression and controlled liberalization, the Moroccan monarchy co-opted rural notables and urban elites through neopatrimonialism by distributing political-administrative functions (Hibou 2005; Hinnebusch 2015; Vermeren 2002) and integrating opposition parties into power (Willis 2002; Zartman 1988): between 1998 and 2002, the two main opposition parties (the nationalist Istiqlal and the leftist USFP) renounced their traditional resistance to the monarchy by joining the 'alternation government' of Abderrahmane Youssoufi. Also, the strength of Islamism has remained limited in Morocco compared to Tunisia – not only because of the King's historical

---

[*] As Hibou (2005: 79) writes on Morocco's earlier regime stability strategies, 'in a context where central power is not able to permanently control all of Moroccan space, the sovereign encourages and often contributes to the construction of dissident spaces .... The "controlled dissidence" ... was thus part of state engineering'.

religious legitimacy as Commander of the Faithful (*amir al-mu'minin*) but also because, since 1997, the moderate PJD has been represented in Parliament and between 2011 and 2021 has participated in government (Hinnebusch 2015; Sater 2002; Willis 2012: 177–86). While often portrayed as an 'arbiter among the state's groups and institutions' (Ayubi 1995: 121), the monarchy in fact actively exacerbated rivalries between societal groups and political parties in a divide-and-rule strategy. For Brumberg (2002: 61), this is typical for 'rulers of liberalized autocracies [who] strive to pit one group against another in ways that maximize the ruler's room for manoeuvre and restrict the opposition's capacity to work together'.

When Mohammed VI became King in 1999, there was widespread optimism that liberalization would deepen. A 'new concept of authority' was introduced in 1999 to express his will for democratization and civil society inclusion in policymaking, and the 'civic monarchy' launched in 2007 underscored his goal to present himself as an enlightened, benevolent King eager to achieving progress and the respect of the rule of law (Vermeren 2011; Willis 2012: 221). And indeed, just after assuming the throne in 1999, Mohammed VI dismissed Interior Minister Driss Basri, a symbol of repression under his father, and invited former exiles to return to Morocco. In 2004, an Equity and Reconciliation Commission[*] was set up to investigate human rights abuses during the 'Years of Lead', and despite the widespread protest of conservative and religious parts of society, the reform of the family code (*mudawana*) that expanded women's rights was enacted (Vermeren 2011). Despite – or because – of such developments, in the spring of 2011, mass protests also erupted in Morocco: the '20 February movement', rallying Islamist and leftist parties, as well as secular human rights groups and Amazigh activists, called for more political freedoms and socio-economic equality but did not demand regime change, in contrast to Tunisia (Abdelmoumni 2013; Hinnebusch 2015). Within one month, Mohammed VI announced a constitutional reform, 'mimick[ing] a strategy long used by his father, Hassan II: offering small changes through constitutional amendments as a means of removing pressure for more thoroughgoing reforms' (Brand 2014: 59). Indeed, while the new constitution enacted in July 2011 consecrated human rights and a more diverse understanding of national identity, it only minimally widened

---

[*] The Commission was in charge of identifying and compensating victims of human rights abuses between 1956 and 1999. It ultimately compensated 9,779 victims. However, neither the decision-makers nor the executors of the human rights abuses have been pursued (Vermeren 2011: 21).

parliamentary and governmental powers and did not touch royal prerogatives.

However, trust in Morocco's political institutions has remained limited over the 2010s, electoral participation low and, in the absence of actual representation through political parties, cyclical riots and regular social unrest continue to channel public grievances into the political sphere. In October 2016, intensive protests for social justice and political freedoms erupted anew in the Rif region, led by the 'Hirak' movement, whose protests have been repressed by security forces and leaders imprisoned throughout 2017 and 2018 (Masbah 2017). In 2019, Amnesty International forcefully denounced Moroccan authorities' repeated attempts to restrict freedom of expression and assembly by intimidating Moroccan journalists and activists (AI 2020). As shown later, this interplay between authoritarian consolidation and repression on the one hand and civil society activism and controlled liberalization on the other is crucial to understanding Moroccan immigration policymaking.

Tunisia's Leap Towards Democratization

Tunisia has gone through a different set of colonial and modernization experiences than Morocco. At the turn of the nineteenth century, the local Husainid dynasty that ruled Tunisia as a quasi-independent Ottoman province pursued a forceful modernization agenda: a standing army of native Tunisians was established in 1831, and a taxation system was introduced in 1857. In 1846, Tunisia was one of the first countries in the world to abolish slavery, and in 1861, it promulgated the first written constitution in the Arab world that separated legislative, executive and judiciary powers and guaranteed equal rights to Muslims, Christians and Jews (Anderson 1986; Djebali 2005; Perkins 2004). Other reforms modernized property rights, access to justice, and education in Tunisia. For Ayubi (1995: 119), Tunisia was therefore 'the most integrated and centralized of the Maghrib countries' before colonization. Such state formation entailed significant financial investments that – although meant to protect Tunisia from foreign interference through 'defensive modernization' – ultimately accelerated colonization (Anderson 1986: 31, 85).

In May 1881, the Treaty of Bardo established the French protectorate over Tunisia.[*] Although some Tunisian tribes and parts of the

---

[*] Italy had shown interest in colonizing Tunisia – Italian emigrants outnumbered the French by 15:1 in the 1870s. At the 1878 Berlin Congress, however, Tunisia was

administration initially resisted occupation, within a year, French forces were in control of the Tunisian territory. As in Morocco, colonization ultimately consolidated state power over the entire Tunisian territory and strengthened the centralized bureaucracy through the restructuring of central and regional governments, the expansion of the public education system as well as the implementation of large-scale infrastructure and industrialization projects (Perkins 2004). It also expanded pre-existing practices of clientelism and patronage networks that would continue to shape politics in post-independence Tunisia (Anderson 1986: 32–3). Yet, in contrast to Morocco's King, the Tunisian Bey collaborated with the French colonial power – and at independence in 1956, he was disposed by the National Constituent Assembly, and Tunisia became a republic.

Post-independence politics centred around independence-hero Habib Bourguiba, who became President for life in 1974. In contrast to Moroccan Kings who emphasized the traditional legitimacy of the state after independence, Bourguiba pursued socio-political modernization: women were granted the right to vote in 1957, the Personal Status Code of 1958 established equality between men and women to an extent unseen in the Arab world, and universal primary education was introduced (Camau and Geisser 2003; Perkins 2004). These reforms challenged the role of tradition and religion and laid the ground for Tunisia's international image as a progressive country. Despite such a modern outlook, Bourguiba's leadership was authoritarian in nature, characterized by three pillars: the instrumentalization of the single party, neo-patrimonialism as well as open civil society repression.

Indeed, the Neo-Destour party (later renamed into Democratic Constitutional Rally (RDC) under Ben Ali) legitimized the regime by providing a patronage network to tap into and a rapid communication channel with Tunisia's population (Anderson 1986; Ayubi 1995: 120). This led to a dynamic in which the 'state [was] in the service of the party' and the 'party in the service of the president' (Perkins 2004: 130). Bourguiba also maintained his hegemonic power through clientelist links with the urban bourgeoisie and rural elites that had their roots in the pre-colonial and colonial period (Anderson 1986: 229). The economic liberalization agenda adopted in the 1970s not only crafted Tunisia's image as 'best student' within international financial institutions but also provided the regime with new resources to distribute to its allies, turning

---

attributed to France because of the economic difficulties faced by the young Italian state (only created in 1861) and because of European geopolitics, especially German and British interests in the Mediterranean Sea (Choate 2010; Perkins 2004: 36–37).

Tunisia into a prime example of neopatrimonialism (see also Hinnebusch 2015). Such economic liberalism, however, consolidated political illiberalism, as the emerging middle profited from clientelist structures instead of claiming political freedoms (Bellin 1995; Hibou 2006; King 2003). In this context, political freedoms were openly repressed: under Bourguiba, opposition leaders, trade unionists and human rights activists were arbitrarily arrested or forced into exile.

In November 1987, then-Prime Minister Ben Ali declared the ageing Bourguiba unfit for the presidency due to his deteriorating health and seized power in a bloodless coup d'état. To consolidate his power, Ben Ali initially opened up the political sphere to secular and religious opposition, as well as to civil society. In April 1988, the Tunisian branch of Amnesty International (AI) was legalized, and in 1989, the Arab Institute for Human Rights (IADH) was created. However, the opening was short-lived, as key members of opposition parties were arrested or forced into exile ahead of the 1989 elections. State repression grew again in the 1990s when up to 150,000 police officers were mobilized across the territory, and so-called 'neighbourhood committees' (*Lijan al-Ahya*) were created to ensure population surveillance and crack down on political opponents (Aleya-Sghaier 2012; Beau and Tuquoi 2011; Bellin 1995). Also, state authorities infiltrated human rights associations with loyal party members and persecuted their leaders, pushing Tunisian civil society to operate mainly from abroad throughout the 1990s and 2000s (Bellin 1995; Gränzer 1999: 116–29; Redissi 2007). The pillars of Bourguiba's autocratic survival were thus largely maintained by Ben Ali after 1987 (Beau and Tuquoi 2011; Camau and Geisser 2003; Hibou 2006; Perkins 2004).

Despite the failure of political liberalization, Tunisia continued to be internationally praised as a modernization model and – since the 'war on terror' in 2001 – as a stronghold against Islamism. Investors and diplomatic partners benevolently overlooked authoritarianism. Domestically, economic growth and the fear of Islamism trumped the political dissatisfaction of the growing middle classes (Beau and Tuquoi 2011; Bellin 1995). The fact that the political quietism rested upon Tunisia's economic growth, however, meant that as soon as economic prosperity collapsed, Ben Ali's regime was at risk. With the global economic crisis hitting Tunisia in 2008, the socio-economic disparities between Tunisia's industrialized coast and the interior that had been exacerbated by decades of economic liberalization came to the fore (Hibou 2015a; Perkins 2004; Willis 2012: 95). Worker strikes erupted in the Gafsa mining area in Tunisia's interior to protest structural unemployment and systemic corruption and, although crushed by Tunisian security forces, prepared the ground for 2011 (Allal and Bennafla 2011; Deane 2013; Hibou 2015b).

Ultimately, the growing divide between Tunisia's image as an economically prosperous and politically progressive country and the reality of political illiberalism and socio-economic inequalities sparked the 2011 revolution (Hibou 2015a): in contrast to 2008, the demonstrations by workers and trade unions following the self-immolation of street vendor Mohammed Bouazizi on 17 December 2010 in Sidi Bouzid, a small town in Tunisia's interior, spread to the capital. Tunisia's educated youth and urban middle class joined the protests, and social media allowed them to bypass state censorship and publicly expose Ben Ali's repressive, corrupt and nepotist regime. Within less than a month, by 14 January 2011, President Ben Ali was toppled and fled to Saudi Arabia after twenty-three years in power (Aleya-Sghaier 2012).

Tunisia's first free elections on 23 October 2011 brought the Islamist Ennahdha Party into power. Together with the Ettakatol Party and the Congress for the Republic (CPR), Ennahdha led the two 'Troika governments' between November 2011 and December 2013.* During 2013, however, the security situation deteriorated, with the assassinations of two leftist figures by Salafists epitomizing the political divisions between Islamists and nationalists. Increasingly large street protests denounced the Troika's loss of legitimacy and requested its demission (for a detailed account of the crisis, see: Gobe and Chouikha 2014). Ultimately, the *National Dialogue Quartet* – a joint effort by the UGTT, the Tunisian League of Human Rights (LTDH), the National Order of Lawyers (ONAT) and the Tunisian Union of Industry, Trade and Crafts (UTICA) to mediate between political fractions – brokered a compromise in the split political sphere, leading to the Troika's demission and the appointment of a technocratic government in January 2014.† Following the adoption of a new constitution on 26 January 2014 and new elections in the fall of 2014, the secular Nidaa Tounes replaced the Islamist Ennahdha as the largest party.

Since then, political volatility has exacerbated Tunisians' disaffection with political institutions (Schäfer 2017; Yardımcı-Geyikçi and Tür

---

* The Troika refers to a division of power between three parties, with the Head of Government from Ennahdha, the President from CPR and the President of the Constituent Assembly from Ettakatol.
† The national dialogue was initiated in October 2012. It initially failed, boycotted by Ennahdha. In August 2013, the national dialogue was revived as the 'National Quartet'. Ennahdha eventually agreed to participate in the national dialogue in mid-September 2013. In 2015, the National Quartet was awarded the Nobel Peace Prize for its mediation efforts.

2018): over the 2011–2020 decade, Tunisia saw nine successive governments and many more cabinet reshufflings, and political parties were constantly renamed, split or merged (Allal and Geisser 2011). The 2019 elections confirmed these trends: in presidential elections, Tunisian voters have expressed their disaffection with main parties' presidential candidates and their wish for stability and strong leadership, with independent, conservative candidate Kais Saied winning the second round against the populist media-mogul Nabil Karoui. And in the parliamentary elections, out of the 220 recognized parties, 31 were voted into Parliament, but only 14 had more than one seat and the two biggest parties, Ennahda and Heart of Tunisia, received only 24 per cent and 18 per cent of the seats, respectively (Yerkes 2020).

Such political instability has jeopardized Tunisian governments' capacity to deal with the socio-economic challenges facing the country: a lasting economic stagnation, with tourism and foreign investments remaining at pre-2011 levels or even declining (see Figures A.1 to Figure A.4 in Appendix 2), and ongoing security issues as a result of the conflict in neighbouring Libya. Since 24 November 2015, the Tunisian government has maintained a state of emergency in the country. In 2017 and 2018, demonstrations against the governments' economic and security policies erupted anew in both Tunis and the interior,[1] and every January, large-scale protests mark the revolution's anniversary (Yardımcı-Geyikçi and Tür 2018; Yerkes 2017). Over 2018–2020, irregular emigration was on the rise again, signalling Tunisians dire economic circumstances and lacking perspectives. The fact that, in 2020, Tunisia saw two governments within just six months only reinforced the political impasse amidst the public health crisis and unprecedented economic decline triggered by the COVID-19 pandemic.

Contrasting National Identity Narratives

Alongside such state formation dynamics, immigration debates are also shaped by official national identity narratives. In Morocco, apart from the immediate post-independence period that favoured a single national identity, the imperial understanding of the state has defined *marocanité* through pluralism, while in Tunisia, official discourses always sought to emphasize the unicity and homogeneity of *tunisianité*. This is also reflected in the countries' constitutions, which provide a 'window... into the nature of national selfhood' (Kommers 2012: 128): Morocco's 2011 Constitution diversified the Muslim and Arab referential framework set out in 1962 by adding references to Africa, Amazigh culture and the Mediterranean. In Tunisia's 2014 Constitution, the Islamic and Arab references central to the preamble of 1959 were subject to intense debates but ultimately not altered. These contrasting national identity understandings provide very distinct foundations for the countries' immigration policies.

Morocco's Affirmation of Pluralism

Until colonization, the idea of a nation was alien to the Moroccan Kingdom with its fluid borders and multi-ethnic and multi-confessional inhabitants (Hibou and Tozy 2015). Colonization introduced the modern concepts of nation and nation-state, and in the 1920s, Moroccan nationalists fighting for independence rallied around a shared national identity, with Islam serving as the central bond (Djebali 2005; Vermeren 2002: 239–40). This shaped Morocco's identification as a Muslim and Arab country after independence, with the monarchy as a religious symbol and unifying factor (Bensadoun 2007; Hassani-Idrissi 2015). The large-scale emigration of Moroccan Jews until the mid-1960s, the active suppression of Amazigh identity, as well as the Arabization of education after 1977 have only reinforced the homogeneity of Moroccan official national identity.

Within Morocco's post-independence identity as a Muslim, Arab country, the first popular claims for a more plural understanding of national identity came from Moroccan Amazigh activists. The historical division between Arab and Amazigh populations is one of the most potent myths of Moroccan national identity and largely a product of colonialism. Indeed, French colonial authorities tried to create an artificial ethnic division between Arab and Amazigh populations by introducing autonomy in customary law for Amazigh populations in the 1930 'Berber Dahir'. Yet, this divide-and-rule strategy backfired: it triggered widespread protests and ultimately bolstered the Moroccan nationalist movement, as rural, largely Tamazight-speaking populations fought together with urban nationalists against the French (Hart 2000). After independence, Amazigh leaders were integrated into the Moroccan state apparatus through the military as a counterweight to the nationalist and left political opposition (Djebali 2005; Vermeren 2002: 121–25). Yet, while they were allowed to form cultural associations, political activism was proscribed.

Political claims for the recognition of the Amazigh identity only emerged in the late 1980s (Willis 2012: 203–29). In 1991, Amazigh organizations published the 'Agadir Charter' to request the integration of Amazigh cultural heritage into Moroccan national identity. Because of increased domestic and regional pressure to democratize and a growing fear of Islamism in neighbouring Algeria, the monarchy made concessions, and King Hassan II promised to introduce the Tamazight language in schools and on national television. However, the implementation of royal promises on the ground was slow and partial. The arrival of King Mohammed VI in 1999 created new hopes for Amazigh activists who politicized their work by linking identity claims to broader issues of economic inequality and political oppression. The 'Berber Manifesto' of March 2000 called for the constitutional recognition of Amazigh as a national language, the economic development of Amazigh regions, and the revisiting of Moroccan historiography. Within two years, it reached two million Moroccan signatures (Vermeren 2011: 14). In October 2001, Mohammed VI recognized the Amazigh roots of Moroccan national identity and announced the creation of the Royal Institute for Amazigh Culture (IRCAM) (MVI 2001). A decade later, Amazigh groups were a key force in the '20 February movement' and were successful with their request to acknowledge Amazigh as an official Moroccan language in the 2011 Constitution.

In parallel to these bottom-up claims, Mohammed VI has actively promoted Morocco's African identity since the 2000s to foster economic and political cooperation with Africa and bolster Morocco's regional leadership, particularly in competition with Algeria (Barre 2012; Rousselet 2015). While geopolitical relations with African countries such as Senegal or DRC have always been key in Moroccan foreign policy (Bamba 2015; Barre 2003; El Hamel 2012; Lanza 2011), Morocco's Africa diplomacy has deeply suffered from the Western Sahara dispute for decades: since independence in 1956, Morocco has claimed sovereignty over Western Sahara, a southern region occupied by Spain since 1884. In November 1975, 350,000 unarmed Moroccans walked into the territory of Western Sahara (the so-called Green March), leading to Spain's withdrawal in February 1976 and to shared administrative control by Morocco and Mauritania over Western Sahara. Since then, the nationalist Sahrawi Polisario Front (created in 1973) and the Sahrawi Arab Democratic Republic (SADR, created in 1976) have resisted Moroccan sovereignty, backed militarily and diplomatically by Algeria in their claims for self-determination. In 1991, the Polisario and Morocco negotiated a ceasefire, but no agreement has been reached since on the status of Western Sahara; all UN mediation attempts have remained unsuccessful (Vermeren 2002: 213–18).[*]

---

[*] De facto, the 'southern provinces' – as they are called by Morocco – are fully integrated into the Moroccan state: they receive important financial transfers from Rabat, send deputies and students to the capital, and are central to Morocco's military activities, with around 150,000 Moroccan soldiers based there (Vermeren 2011: 31–33). Officially, however, the territory of Western Sahara is not recognized as part of the Moroccan state by the international community.

Western Sahara has been Morocco's number one foreign policy priority over decades – capable of disrupting diplomatic relations with the United Nations, the European Union, the African Union (AU) or individual states. Most strikingly, Morocco left the African Union in 1984 after it had recognized the SADR as a member state. Since 2000, Mohammed VI's has stepped up its efforts to knit ties with African partners: regular diplomatic tours to West and East Africa have allowed Moroccan firms to expand, especially in the telecommunications, banking and infrastructure sectors. It also strengthened Morocco's claims for reintegrating the African Union and for joining ECOWAS. Morocco's Africa policy culminated in 2017 with the re-accession to the AU in January and the creation of a new Delegate Ministry of African Affairs under the umbrella of the MoFA in October.

Ultimately, the monarchy has pluralized Moroccan national identity narratives over the past decades, co-opting Amazigh claims and integrating geopolitical considerations. Instead of Muslim and Arab referents only, the preamble of the 2011 Constitution now refers to eight influences of Moroccan national identity: Muslim, Arabo-Islamic, Amazigh, Saharo-Hassani, African, Andalusian, Hebraic and Mediterranean.[*] However, particularly the new affirmation of Morocco's African identity is not met with unanimous support among the Moroccan population. As discussed later, racism is deeply engrained in Moroccan society, and attitudes towards immigrants are shaped by the history of slave trade and the structural marginalization of Morocco's Black minority (El Hamel 2012). As a result, both Black Moroccans and migrants from Western and Central Africa are subjected to everyday racism in the Moroccan public sphere.

Tunisia's Struggle in the Quest for Unicity

In contrast to Morocco, Tunisian official identity discourses have emphasized the unity of the nation. Such discourses are rooted in Tunisia's independence struggle that insisted on the common interest and unity of the Tunisian people against French colonizers (Anderson 1986: 138–39). Yet, on the ground, Tunisia's national identity debate has always been structured by the opposition between Arab nationalism

---

[*] Last-minute changes of the draft have toned down some of the constitution's advances: while the first draft put Tamazight and Arabic on equal footing, the revised version strengthened the Arabic reference and ranked Tamazight second. Also, geopolitical belonging has been changed to the detriment of African references and in favour of Muslim and Middle Eastern countries. See Monde Diplomatique, *Maroc: trois projets de Constitution et des doutes*, 30 June 2011.

and tradition on the one hand and Mediterranean republicanism and modernity on the other – a debate that resurged after 2011.

After independence, Bourguiba's ideology of modernization and reformism put forward the unity and homogeneity of the Tunisian nation (Abbassi 2009; Hibou 2006, 2010; Zemni 2016: 142): 'Diversity is left in the shade; the official discourse on reformism shows a negation of differences, a refusal of pluralism, an impossibility of divisions and oppositions' (Hibou 2010: 10). Bourguiba also relegated Arab and Muslim identifiers to the second rank, as Tunisia's more conservative identity rooted in Arab nationalism was embodied by his primary political opponent, Salah Ben Youssef, and violently repressed by the regime (Bellin 1995).[*] After his 1987 coup, Ben Ali shifted official national identity discourses towards a more balanced position between Tunisian republican nationalism and Arab nationalism. Notwithstanding, official national identity discourse has continued to emphasize the unity of the Tunisian nation. In the name of Tunisian unity, plural identities were actively repressed and 'the authoritarian power in place ... turned the unity of the nation into a Leitmotif' (T16-I9).

This authoritarian heritage of cultural monolithism has been challenged since 2011, as the revolution created space for Tunisians to affirm their diversity and Black, Amazigh or Jewish minorities reclaimed their identities (Mrad Dali 2015; Pouessel 2012a): 'In 2011, Tunisians discovered themselves' (T16-I9). Such claims for pluralism, however, have also fuelled divisions, in particular between those adhering to a religious, Islamic identity and those adhering to secular, republican national identity, leading to an intense societal polarization on national identity in the 2011–2013 period. Throughout the three-year constitution-making process, these two main identity referentials clashed against each other in street protests and in National Constituent Assembly (NCA) debates (for an analysis of identity debates in the assembly, see Avon and Aschi 2014; Gobe and Chouikha 2014).

The adoption of the 2014 Constitution has at least temporarily settled the debates, with the discourse around a single national identity prevailing again (Zemni 2016). In fact, the pillars of Tunisian national identity outlined in the new constitution are strikingly similar to those in the 1959 Constitution, structured around Islam, the Maghreb and the Arab world.

---

[*] Salah Ben Youssouf was Bourguiba's main opponent after independence. Both were key figures of Tunisia's independence movement, but they represented two different conceptions of Tunisian nationalism: Bourguiba's vision was anchored in European nationalism and modernization, while Ben Youssef represented a more conservative, Arab nationalism. Ben Youssef ultimately went into exile and was assassinated in Germany in 1961 (Bellin 1995; Perkins 2004).

This continuity is not accidental: it symbolizes the lowest common denominator possible between republican secularists and Islamic conservatives. Ultimately, while Tunisian society continues to be polarized on national identity, Tunisia's political elite seems to have prioritized compromise and a depoliticization of identity debates (Gobe and Chouikha 2014; Marzouki 2016; Murphy 2013). As I show later, the inherited preference for a unitarian national identity was key in shaping Tunisian discussions on immigration, notably the reluctance to politicize issues such as racism or migration that could potentially seed divisions within society.

Tunisia's national identity has also been shaped by its geopolitical involvements – but less so than in Morocco: while Bourguiba sought to knit ties with African and other Third World leaders in the immediate post-independence period, Tunisia's diplomatic and economic relations with African neighbours have weakened over the decades to the extent that one of my respondents qualified Tunisia as an 'off-shore state' (T16-I16), set apart from the African landmass in its geopolitical belonging. Over the years, Tunisia adopted a 'neutral diplomacy' (T17-I31, T17-I25) or 'pragmatic neutrality' (Murphy 2014: 243) in foreign policy, characterized by the non-interference in other countries' internal politics and a more general avoidance of geopolitical positioning: 'Tunisia's foreign policy was always very passive, we didn't want to be involved in polarized contexts, we didn't want to be with or against this country, we are friends with all' (T17-I31), one respondent summarized.

Since 2011, Tunisia's political elite tacitly sought to revive political and economic cooperation with African countries: successive Tunisian Prime Ministers have gone on 'African tours' in 2014, 2016 and 2017. Tunisia has opened embassies in Burkina Faso and Kenya in 2016, and the Union of Industry, Trade and Crafts (UTICA), representing the Tunisian private sector, has started to send business delegations to French-speaking African countries. Yet, these developments have so far neither translated into immigration policy changes nor challenged the historical marginalization of Tunisia's Black minority, which is estimated at around 15 per cent of the population (Abdul Hamid 2013; Mrad Dali 2015). As in Morocco, Black Tunisians continue to be considered as 'inferior' and subject to socio-economic discrimination and racism (Mrad Dali 2009; Pouessel 2012b). As shown later, this history and treatment of Black Tunisians also shape current debates on immigration from Western and Central Africa to Tunisia.

Comparable Emigration Patterns and Policies

Emigration has played a crucial role in these political transformations and identity debates, used by regimes in power as a legitimation tool and by emigrants themselves as a means of protest from abroad (Brand 2006; Iskander 2010; Natter 2014a; Sahraoui 2015). Although not the main focus, Moroccan and Tunisian emigration patterns and policies, which have followed similar developments since the mid-twentieth century, are a key reference point for the immigration patterns and policies analysed in this book.

Two Prototypical Emigration Countries

Morocco and Tunisia are among the world's leading emigration countries: 12–13 per cent of their populations are estimated to live abroad – that is, 4.8 million Moroccans and 1.4 million Tunisians (HCP 2020: 3; ONM 2020).[*]

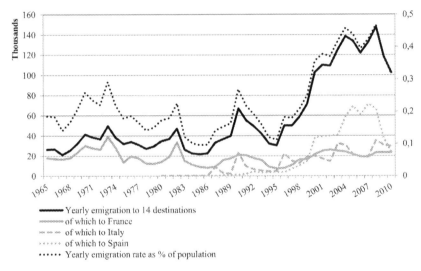

Figure 3.1 Annual Moroccan emigration to main destinations, 1965–2010.
Source: *DEMIG (2015)*[†], *adapted from Natter (2014a)*

---

[*] In both countries, These numbers are highly disputed given that origin and destination country statistics differ in terms of their inclusion or exclusion of second- and third-generation migrants, dual citizens and naturalized migrants. A more conservative estimate sets the number at 2.6 million Moroccans and 0.5 million Tunisians residing abroad in 2012 (Fargues 2013: 173, 231).

[†] As annual emigration flow data from Morocco is not available, emigration flows were reconstructed based on data of Moroccan immigration to fourteen prime destination countries (Austria, Belgium, Canada, Denmark, Finland, France, Germany, Italy, the Netherlands, Norway, Spain, Sweden, Switzerland and the United States). The figure only displays the top three destinations. Not included in these statistics is intra-Maghreb migration.

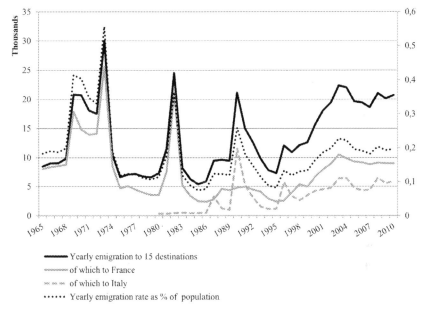

Figure 3.2 Annual Tunisian emigration to main destinations, 1965–2010.
Source: DEMIG (2015)*, adapted from Natter (2014a)

Moroccan emigration was kick-started with colonization in 1912, partly because France and Spain recruited around 200,000 Moroccans for their industries and armies during World Wars I and II, as well as the Spanish Civil War (1936–39). Although most of these migrants returned to Morocco, this trend sowed the seeds for future emigration. In contrast, Tunisia's colonization by France did not lead to comparable emigration levels, even if around 80,000 Tunisians served in the French army and 30,000 worked in industry during WWI (Perkins 2004: 75).

Significant labour emigration took off after Morocco's and Tunisia's independence in 1956, fuelled by European economic growth and shaped by bilateral labour recruitment agreements (see Figures 3.1 and 3.2).†

---

* As annual emigration flow data from Tunisia is not available, emigration flows were reconstructed based on Tunisian immigration to fifteen prime destination countries (Austria, Belgium, Canada, Denmark, Finland, France, Germany, Italy, Israel, the Netherlands, Norway, Spain, Sweden, Switzerland and the United States). The graph only displays the top two destinations. Not included in these statistics is intra-Maghreb migration.
† Most importantly, with Germany (1963 Morocco, 1965 Tunisia), France (1963 Morocco and Tunisia), Belgium (1964 Morocco, 1969 Tunisia) and the Netherlands (1969 Morocco, 1971 Tunisia).

The number of Moroccans living in Europe increased to 300,000 in 1972, and around 250,000 Tunisians emigrated in the first two decades after independence (Findlay 1980: 187). Also, almost the entire Jewish communities – around 270,000 in Morocco and 105,000 in Tunisia – left for Israel and to a lesser extent Europe and North America (Ben-Layashi and Maddy-Weitzman 2010; Ben Achour 2015).

After the 1973 Oil Crisis, and despite the recruitment stops for low-skilled workers enacted by European countries, emigration did not subside. Instead, it diversified: family migration became the main entry pathway to Europe, emigrants became more educated and female, and new migration corridors gained in popularity. For Morocco, Spain and Italy emerged as new destinations, receiving respectively 45 per cent and 18 per cent of total Moroccan emigration in the 2000s – due to the migrant labour demand in construction, care and agriculture. For Tunisian migrant workers, Libya and Italy became new destinations, prompted by the economic boom of the 1980s, as well as lax immigration regimes at that time. As Italy and Spain introduced visa requirements for North African nationals in 1990 and 1991, respectively, Moroccan and Tunisian emigration have shifted into irregularity. More recently, alongside the growing feminization of migration, soaring unemployment among tertiary-educated youth has increased student and high-skilled emigration, mainly to Germany and North America (Garelli and Tazzioli 2017). Today, 31 per cent of Moroccan migrants live in France, 23 per cent in Spain and 18 per cent in Italy. While the majority of Tunisian emigrants still reside in France (58 per cent), Italy and Germany consolidated their attractiveness, with respectively 15 per cent and 7 per cent of Tunisian migrants living there (see Table 3.1).

The paradox of Morocco's and Tunisia's emigration history is thus the growth of emigration in a context of restricted entry rules: reconstructed emigration flows show that Moroccan emigration increased from around 47,000 annually in the 1990s to 133,000 annually over the 2000s (Natter 2014a) (see also Figure 3.1). In Tunisia, emigration peaked in 2008 after months-long strikes in Tunisia's interior were violently crushed (Boubakri 2013: 2). This foreshadowed the developments in early 2011 when the revolution and effective absence of Tunisian border controls prompted an immediate surge in irregular emigration: over 20,000 Tunisian nationals arrived on Italy's shores in the first three months of 2011, compared to around 1,700 yearly over 2000–2010 (FRONTEX 2011: 29). Since then, irregular emigration

Table 3.1. *Geographic distribution of Moroccan and Tunisian emigrants, 2012–2018, in per cent*

	Morocco		Tunisia	
Country of residence	2012	2018	2012	2017
France	28.2	31.1	54.4	57.9
Spain	16.5	23.4	0.3	0.3
Italy	11.9	18.7	15.5	15.2
Germany	3.1	3.4	7.1	7.2
Netherlands	8.9	2.3	0.7	0.6
Belgium	7.3	3.8	2	n/a
Canada	1.3	3.8	1.6	2
USA	0.8	3.6	1.2	1.3
Arab countries	5.3	3.8	4.9	6.6
Other	16.7	6.1	21.3	8.8
Total, percentage	100	100	100	100
Total, millions of emigrants	4.1	4.8	1.2	1.4

Sources: Morocco (de Haas 2014a: 75; HCP 2020: 24), Tunisia (ONM 2020; OTE/DIRP 2012)

has again fluctuated depending on seasonal and economic cycles. However, the intrinsic link between political freedom, economic equality and freedom of movement persists, as the underlying causes of discontent continue to fuel Moroccans' and Tunisians' emigration aspirations.

A Dual Policy of 'Courting and Controlling' the Diaspora

Given its numerical and political importance, emigration developed into a prominent field of public policy in Morocco and Tunisia throughout the twentieth century. As scholars have highlighted, Morocco and Tunisia have oscillated 'between courting and controlling' citizens abroad (de Haas 2007a), encouraging emigration to stimulate the economy while at the same time monitoring emigrants to dissipate political engagement and regime criticism from abroad (Brand 2002; 2006; de Haas 2007a; Mzali 1997; Sahraoui 2015).

Since independence, emigration policies have been part and parcel of Moroccan regime legitimation strategies: in the 1960s, as the Moroccan monarchy was faced with political protests in the Rif area and urban revolts in Casablanca, Fez and Rabat, selective recruitment was actively used by the Moroccan state as a tool to relieve high domestic unemployment and political discontent in specific regions. This selection policy had repercussions in Europe: in the 1960s and 1970s, Moroccan workers actively opposed the Moroccan King from abroad through involvement in communist groups and labour unions. To control such migrant activism, Moroccan authorities created so-called 'amicales' (friendship societies), led by members of the intelligence services. Political activists and trade unionists abroad were openly intimidated, and emigrants risked being detained or having their passports seized upon return. These measures sought to attenuate the negative light that politicized emigrants shed on Morocco across Europe and to stop them from importing critical political ideas from abroad (Brand 2002; de Haas 2007a; Iskander 2010).

However, preventing emigrants' political engagement through repression was of limited success, so Moroccan authorities shifted towards co-optation in the mid-1980s. Administrative procedures for the delivery of Moroccan passports were eased at the beginning of the 1990s (de Haas 2007b), and new institutions were created to culturally bind emigrants to their homeland and to capitalize on their financial potential, such as a Ministry for Moroccans Residing Abroad and the Foundation Hassan II in 1990, or the Council for Morocco's Community Abroad (CCME) in 2007 (El Qadim 2015: 195–207). Radio and TV shows, as well as Islamic religion and language courses, were launched to engage Moroccans abroad in cultural activities, and the Al-Amal Bank was created in 1989 to facilitate money transfers to Morocco. This contributed to a major surge in remittances to $6.9 billion in 2012, representing about 7 per cent of Morocco's gross national product and roughly six times the amount of official development aid (de Haas 2014b) (see also Figure A.5 in Appendix 2). The magnitude of emigration and remittances showcases the crucial importance of Moroccans residing abroad (so-called MRE, Marocains Residents à l'Etranger) for the Moroccan state.

Also in Tunisia, national institutions such as the Office for Professional Training and Employment (OFPE) were set up in the 1960s and 1970s to organize labour recruitment (Brand 2002; Mzali 1997). In parallel, Tunisia also created 'amicales' in Europe to surveil and prevent emigrant communities' involvement in labour unions or political activities (Beau and Tuquoi 2011: 189–98; Bel Hadj Zekri 2009). As in Morocco, two main concerns motivated this external surveillance: to ensure that Tunisians residing abroad (TRE) would not stain Tunisia's positive image in Europe as a liberal and attractive tourist destination; and to avoid support from abroad for domestic political opponents. However, in contrast to Morocco, the amicales not only operated through top-down surveillance but also actively sought to co-opt TRE by appealing to their patriotism and rewarding their regime loyalty (Brand 2006). To bolster his legitimacy just after the coup d'état in 1987, Ben Ali extended formal voting rights to Tunisians abroad. However, de facto voting abroad was tightly controlled and, over time, developed into an act of allegiance to the regime (Brand 2006: 113–22). In the face of decreasing remittances (see Figure A.5 in Appendix 2), the (in)famous Office for Tunisians Abroad (OTE) – often called 'Ben Ali's eye abroad' (T17-I4) – diversified its activities beyond control in the 1990s by providing legal assistance to citizens abroad, facilitating investment and setting up cultural programs.

Since 2011, Tunisian emigrants are included as active subjects in the Tunisian polity (Brand 2014; Jaulin and Nilsson 2015), as they were attributed eighteen seats in the Parliament (out of 217). Other institutional changes, discussed more extensively later, include the creation of a State Secretary for Migration and Tunisians Abroad (SEMTE) in 2012, a National Migration Observatory (ONM) in 2014, and a National Council for Tunisians Abroad in 2016. In parallel, however, emigration controls were re-established, irregular migration cooperation with Italy continued, and since 2015, Tunisia has also stepped up its border controls towards Libya.[2] Although the goal of safeguarding Tunisians' rights abroad and creating legal emigration opportunities is still on the top of the political agenda, border controls and security-focused migration cooperation have continued throughout the revolution (Boubakri 2015; Natter 2021c).

Diverging Immigration Patterns and Policies

The dominant account of Morocco and Tunisia as prototypical emigration countries overshadows that, for centuries, they were in fact immigration countries. First, immigration regulations were introduced by colonial authorities in the early twentieth century, but immigration remained a side-topic for Moroccan and Tunisian authorities in the post-independence decades. While immigration gained political salience in Euro-African relations in the 1990s, Moroccan and Tunisian immigration patterns and policies however diverged over the late twentieth and early twenty-first centuries: in Morocco, immigration – particularly from Western and Central Africa – plays an increasingly important role in domestic and foreign politics despite remaining moderate in size. In contrast, immigration to Tunisia has grown significantly yet remains strikingly depoliticized.

Immigration Trends: Historical Roots and Continuing Diversification

While media and policy reports tend to pin down the beginning of immigration to Morocco and Tunisia in the 1990s, this disregards its historical roots and volume: Morocco has always been a destination for West African merchants and Sufi pilgrims (Berriane 2015), and in Tunisia, with its central place along Mediterranean commercial routes, migration of Jewish merchants, Maltese labourers and Italian artisans or farmers accelerated over the nineteenth century (Perkins 2004: 20–21). Furthermore, the slave trade between Northern, Western and Central Africa crucially shaped population movements between the sixteenth and twentieth centuries (Bensaâd 2002; Bredeloup and Pliez 2005; de Haas 2007c; Lanza 2011).

Immigration to Morocco and Tunisia further intensified with European colonization: although a French colony, Italians represented nearly 90 per cent of Tunisia's European population in 1900, leading Italian Prime Minister Francesco Crispi to call Tunisia an 'Italian colony occupied by France' (Choate 2010: 6). To entrench French rule, citizenship acquisition for non-French Europeans and their children was facilitated so that by 1930, French citizens outnumbered Italians (Choate 2010; Perkins 2004). In 1950, almost 300,000 French and 150,000 Spanish citizens lived in Morocco (see Figure 3.3) and nearly 350,000 foreigners lived in Tunisia, mainly from France, Italy, Libya and Algeria (see Figure 3.4). Within ten years of independence, however, most Europeans had left.

Over the second half of the twentieth and early twenty-first centuries, immigration towards Morocco continued on a smaller scale, dominated by three trends (Berriane, de Haas and Natter 2015): first, Morocco consolidated itself as a destination for students from Western and Central Africa. This trend had started in the 1960s as part of Morocco's strategy to strengthen economic and political ties with West Africa, in particular Mali, Zaire (after 1997, the DRC) and Senegal (Infantino 2011; Mazzella 2009). With the emergence of Moroccan private universities in the 2000s, student migration grew from 8,700 in 2006 to 15,600 in 2010 and 20,410 in 2017 (Laouali and Meyer 2012; Levantino 2015; MCMREAM 2018: 89).

Second, Morocco became a de facto place of residence for workers and refugees from Africa and the Middle East. Over the 1990s, in the wake of political crises in Western and Central Africa, increasing numbers of refugees from Sierra Leone, Nigeria, Côte d'Ivoire and the DRC arrived in Morocco. In parallel, labour immigration from Western and Central Africa to Morocco grew as an alternative to Libya and Europe, where

Diverging Immigration Patterns and Policies 65

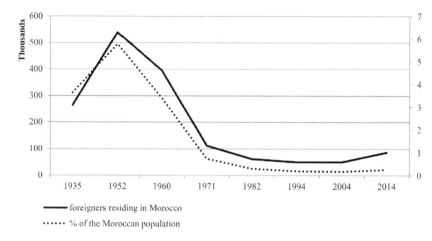

— foreigners residing in Morocco
······ % of the Moroccan population

Figure 3.3 Recorded number of foreigners according to Moroccan census data, 1935–2014.
Sources: Moroccan Census (RGPH), see HCP (2009: 15–16) and HCP (2015)

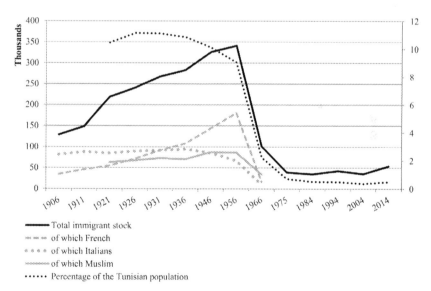

— Total immigrant stock
--- of which French
∗ ∗ ∗ ∗ of which Italians
~~~ of which Muslim
······ Percentage of the Tunisian population

Figure 3.4 Recorded number of foreigners according to Tunisian census data, 1906–2014.
Source: Tunisian Census, National Statistical Institute (INS) in Seklani (1974); Touhami (n.d.), adapted from Natter (2015b)

entrance became increasingly difficult (Boesen and Marfaing 2007; Brachet, Choplin and Pliez 2011). Since 2013, more and more Syrian refugees also have arrived in Morocco (Tyszler 2015). By September 2020, UNHCR had registered 11,960 asylum seekers and refugees in Morocco, nearly one in three from Syria, followed by refugees from Guinea, Yemen, Cameroon and Côte d'Ivoire (UNHCR 2020a).

The growth of immigration from Western and Central Africa is visible in census data, representing 33 per cent of all immigrants recorded in 2014 compared to only 15 per cent a decade earlier (see Table 3.2). Against the cliché of poverty migration, most migrants from Western and Central Africa in Morocco come from the middle class in their origin countries, have secondary or tertiary education and were employed before migrating (Bredeloup and Pliez 2005; de Haas 2007c; Mourji et al. 2016). They found (mostly informal) employment in agriculture and construction, the service and tourism industry, or French-speaking journalism and call centres (Mourji et al. 2016; Weyel 2015). Also, a majority of migrants indicate Morocco as the intended destination (AMERM 2008; Mourji et al. 2016), signalling the effective transformation of Morocco into a country of immigration not by default but by choice.

European migration also grew since the 1990s. In fact, Europeans have always been the numerically largest migrant group in Morocco, well ahead of migrants from Western and Central Africa. High-skilled workers, entrepreneurs, retirees but also graduates and, in the wake of the 2008 Global Economic Crisis, low-skilled workers have increasingly migrated from Europe to Morocco (de Haas 2014b; Hannoum 2020). As many Europeans live and work in Morocco irregularly or on a tourist visa, official numbers underestimate the size of Morocco's European community. For instance, the French Embassy in Morocco registered 46,995 French citizens in 2013, while the 2014 census recorded only 21,344 (Therrien and Pellegrini 2015). As discussed later, these European migrants are rarely subject to political discussions in Morocco.

Lastly, immigration from Asia, particularly of Chinese merchants and traders (Taing 2015) or Filipino female houseworkers, grew over the 2000s.[3] The 2014 and 2017 regularizations that granted legal status to migrants from more than 100 nationalities attest to this growing diversification of immigration. Yet, such diversification is often disregarded in public discourses that convey the image of a mainly poor, irregular migrant population from Western and Central Africa transiting through Morocco on their way to Europe.

Table 3.2. *Number of immigrants living in Morocco, by country of citizenship, 2004 and 2014*

Citizenship	2004	Percentage	2014	Percentage
North African / Middle Eastern countries	15,365	30.6	17,617	21
Algeria	*8,911*	*17.7*	*5,710*	*6.8*
Tunisia	*1,747*	*3.5*	*1,859*	*2.2*
Syria	*1,206*	*2.4*	*5,225*	*6.2*
Libya	*599*	*1.2*	*2,013*	*2.4*
European countries	23,063	45.9	33,615	40
France	*14,562*	*29*	*21,344*	*25.4*
Spain	*2,725*	*5.4*	*3,990*	*4.7*
Italy	*1,009*	*2*	*1,970*	*2.3*
African countries	7,717	15.4	27,397	32.6
Côte d'Ivoire	*334*	*0.7*	*2,271*	*2.7*
Guinea	*570*	*1.1*	*2,424*	*2.9*
Senegal	*810*	*1.6*	*6,066*	*7.2*
Congo-Brazzaville	*948*	*1.9*	*1,955*	*2.3*
Other countries	4,065	8.1	5,372	6.4
Total	**50,210**	**100**	**84,001**	**100**

Sources: 2004 and 2014 Moroccan Census (RGPH). Data received upon demand from the HCP.

In Tunisia, immigration in the post-independence decades was dominated by refugees and labour migrants from the Maghreb and the Middle East (Boubakri 2009): between 1954 and 1962, nearly 200,000 Algerians fled to Tunisia in the wake of the Algerian War of Independence (UNHCR 2000: 38–42), and in 1982, several thousand Palestinians arrived in Tunisia after the Israeli–Lebanese war. On the other hand, Tunisia's economic growth over the 1980s has attracted regional labour migrants, particularly Moroccans working in the caretaking and tourism sectors (Boubakri 2004).

Since the late 1990s, Tunisia has become a destination for African workers and students, although to a lesser extent than Morocco. Student immigration – in particular, from Senegal, Côte d'Ivoire and Mali – accelerated due to the mushrooming of private universities (Mazzella 2009): as a consequence, around 7,000 to 8,000 international students were recorded yearly in Tunisian universities between 2015 and 2020 (TAT 2016: 8),[4] compared to 2,500 to 3,000 over the 2000s (CARIM 2010). With Tunisia not requiring travel visas for many citizens from Western and Central Africa, migrants have also arrived in Tunisia as tourists and overstayed their visas to look for economic opportunities. Survey data shows that 71 per cent have no valid residence permit and 80 per cent work in the informal sector – in agriculture, on construction sites, in restaurants, or as domestic workers (Ben Sedrine 2018: 42–54; TAT 2016). In addition, several thousand highly qualified West African bank employees, as well as their lower-skilled support staff, migrated to Tunis during the temporary relocation of the African Development Bank (AfDB) from Côte d'Ivoire to Tunisia between 2003 and 2014. According to respondents, the presence of the AfDB partly shifted Tunisia's collective imaginary of Africa, challenging stereotypical images of poverty and misery and introducing a 'bourgeois Africa' (T17-I15).

Lastly, Tunisia has consolidated its role as a destination for Europeans. Over the 2009–2015 period, French and Italian citizens made up respectively around 25 per cent and 15 per cent of the 6,000–8,000 foreigners who received work permits in Tunisia every year (Labidi, Bennour and Jaidi 2017: 43), and census data recorded 15,000 European migrants in 2014 (see Table 3.3). However, as in Morocco, European immigration is underestimated, as most Europeans either live and work on a tourist visa or reside in Tunisia irregularly.

Against such historically small-scale immigration, the 2011 protests against the Gaddafi regime in neighbouring Libya and the ensuing civil war fundamentally reshuffled Tunisia's immigration profile: within less than a year, 345,000 people crossed into Tunisia, among which were Asian, Arab and African migrant workers; Libyan families, both pro- and anti-Gaddafi; and 137,000 Tunisian returnees. Although IOM evacuated 115,000 third-country nationals by December 2011 (IOM 2012) and UNHCR resettled more than 3,500 refugees by summer 2013 (Boubakri 2015: 21), many remained in the south-east of Tunisia, around the cities of Ben Guerdane and Medenine, or moved on towards the capital Tunis, seeking to rebuild their lives in Tunisia. As most are not registered as refugees, UNHCR recorded only 5,202 asylum seekers and refugees by September 2020, of which around half were from Syria and one-third from Côte d'Ivoire (UNHCR 2020b).[*]

Next to such immediate effects, the Libyan crisis led to the long-term settlement of a large number of Libyan citizens in Tunisia. While census data recorded only 8,772 Libyans in Tunisia in 2014 (compared to 1,738 in 2004, see Table 3.3), Tunisia's Head of Government Mehdi Jomâa suggested in 2014 that 1.2 million Libyans were living in Tunisia;[5] and in 2015, MoI estimates it even reached two million.[6] Official data thus by far underestimates the size of Tunisia's Libyan community, whose presence is clearly visible in Tunisian daily life – be it in schools, hospitals or on the streets of Tunis and the coastal towns of Djerba, Sfax and Sousse. A conservative estimate of the Libyan immigrant community thus hovers

---

[*] An estimated 9,000 to 12,000 Syrians reside in Tunisia (Garelli and Tazzioli 2017: 35). In general, few Syrians have sought refuge in Tunisia because the government introduced a visa requirement for Syrians in 2012.

Table 3.3. *Number of immigrants living in Tunisia, by country of citizenship, 2004 and 2014*

Citizenship	2004	Percentage	2014	Percentage
North African countries	21,200	60.2	28,500	53.3
Algeria	*9,600*	*27.3*	*10,000*	*18.7*
Morocco	*6,400*	*18.2*	*5,600*	*10.5*
Libya	*1,700*	*4.8*	*8,800*	*16.4*
European countries	9,700	27.6	15,000	28
France	*4,600*	*13*	*8,300*	*15.5*
Italy	*1,500*	*4.2*	*2,200*	*4.1*
Germany	*1,000*	*2.8*	*1,400*	*2.6*
African countries	3,000	8.5	7,500	14
Other countries	1,300	3.7	2,500	4.7
Total	**35,200**	**100**	**53,500**	**100**

Source: INS (2015), adapted from Natter (2015b)

around half a million, or 5 per cent of the Tunisian population. With over 80 per cent of Libyans planning to stay in Tunisia permanently if the Libyan political conflict persists and a quarter seeking to remain in Tunisia even if peace is restored (Mouley 2016: 19), the Libyan political crisis has transformed Tunisia overnight into an immigration country.

As I show next, however, in both Morocco and Tunisia, the scale of immigration on the ground is largely disconnected from its politicization: while Tunisia's immigrant community is estimated at around 600,000 (5.2 per cent of the population),[*] this is not reflected in the country's continued self-understanding as emigration country and non-policy towards immigration after 2011. In Morocco, even if migrants' presence is increasingly visible in urban areas, the fact that immigration remains a minor phenomenon statistically speaking – probably not exceeding 250,000 (0.75 per cent of the population)[†] – stands in striking contrast with the salience of immigration on Morocco's political agenda over the 2010s.

Immigration Policy Foundations: Generalized Securitization and Selective Openings

In pre-colonial times, immigration to Morocco and Tunisia was either not regulated or loosely organized through bilateral agreements with

---

[*] This includes an estimated 500,000 Libyan nationals, 53,000 recorded migrants in the census, and between 25,000 and 50,000 non-Libyan irregular migrants.

[†] This includes the 86,200 migrants recorded in the 2014 census, the roughly 50,000 migrants regularized in 2014 and 2017, and the estimated 50,000–100,000 foreigners who live in Morocco either irregularly or on a tourist visa.

origin countries. Religious minorities, in particular, Jews and Christians, were treated as *dhimmi* – a legal category in the Ottoman world denoting non-Muslims who were protected by the state in return for paying a capital tax.* Immigration regulations were first introduced by the colonial administrators in the early twentieth century, who transposed French immigration laws onto Moroccan and Tunisian territory, leaving a lasting imprint on the organization of migration control far beyond independence in 1956.

In the post-independence decades, and in contrast to emigration, immigration was not a field of extensive public policymaking: in Morocco, colonial immigration regulations were simply taken over in 1956 and throughout the years complemented by a set of administrative decisions or bilateral agreements with origin countries. In Tunisia, colonial immigration regulations were reformed in 1968 and 1975 through Laws 68–7 and 75–40, setting out criteria for foreigners' entry and stay, as well as sanctions for irregular border crossings or falsification of documents. However, both Morocco's and Tunisia's state engagement on immigration remained largely limited to select groups of immigrants whose preferential treatment could foster regional integration with Europe, the Maghreb or Western and Central Africa.

At the turn of the twenty-first century, a new regional context raised the political stakes associated with immigration and its control: in 2003, Morocco enacted *Law 02–03* – the first immigration law since independence. It sanctioned irregular migrants with a prison sentence of one to six months and a fine of 2,000 to 20,000 dirhams [around 200 to 2,000 USD at the time], as well as people assisting irregular migrants with a prison sentence of six months to three years and a fine of 50,000 to 500,000 dirhams [around 5,000 to 50,000 USD at the time] (B.O. 2003a). To step up migration control institutionally, a Directorate of Migrations and Border Surveillance (DMST) was created within the MoI in December 2003.† Although the new policy was implemented inconsistently over time and across the Moroccan territory (Khrouz 2016, 2019), it heralded a decade of restrictiveness towards so-called 'irregular transit migrants' from Western and Central Africa.

---

* In the pre-colonial period, religious groups in Morocco and Tunisia benefited from relative independence: although Islam was the majority religion, Jewish and Christian communities were allowed to administer and handle family law themselves under the *dhimmi* system (Vermeren 2002: 16; El Hamel 2012: 205).
† Documents also mention the creation of a Migration Observatory within the MoI – although respondents in 2012 have contested its actual existence. Following the 2013 reform, a (new) Migration Observatory has been created – indirectly admitting the non-existence of the one launched in 2003.

Migrants without legal status faced constant fears of crackdowns, detention or expulsion by Moroccan police forces, both in cities and in informal migrant settlements in northern Morocco (Cimade and AFVIC-PFM 2004; CMSM and GADEM 2012; MSF 2005; Valluy 2007). In parallel to this repression of immigrants from Western and Central Africa, however, Moroccan authorities turned a blind eye to the irregular residence and employment of European migrants. The years leading up to 2013 were characterized by non-linear policy developments: On the one hand, Morocco's officially restrictive stance towards immigration did not change, and police violence against migrants peaked in 2005 and 2012. On the other hand, there have been some tacit openings towards migrants and refugees in the areas of education and healthcare as local public authorities used their (limited) room for manoeuvre in response to growing pro-migrant activism within Morocco and from abroad.

Also in Tunisia, immigration control became central to regional politics, particularly to the international legitimacy of the Ben Ali regime. In the mid-1990s, the framework regulating irregular migration was stepped up: a 1994 decree by the Ministry of Finance (MoF) introduced a penalty of 10 dinars [around 10 USD at the time] for every week spent irregularly on the Tunisian territory, and two amendments to the Labour Code in 1994 and 1996 increased the penalties for the irregular employment of workers. This policy was complemented by a welcoming discourse for select categories of foreigners, as Tunisia sought to attract foreign competencies and investments in the context of its economic liberalization. In 2004, *Law 2004–06* legally cemented the securitization of irregular migration, sanctioning irregular migrants and their supporters with penalties ranging from 8,000 to 100,000 Tunisian dinars in fines [around 6,400 to 80,000 USD at the time] and/or three to twenty years of imprisonment. These sanctions could be applied to anyone failing to report contact with irregular migrants, including lawyers or doctors protected by professional secrecy. Although the law was applied inconsistently over the years and across the Tunisian territory (Meddeb 2012: 380–92), it was central in creating an overall climate of fear and suspicion towards migrants, in particular from Western and Central Africa. Yet, in contrast to Morocco, where civil society was vocal, immigration remained depoliticized until 2011: anything related to immigration was managed solely by the President and Tunisia's security apparatus; potential counterpowers, such as the Parliament, international organizations (IOs), or civil society were almost absent; and immigration was silenced in the public sphere: 'Under Ben Ali, no one talked about migration, ... it was part of the security field' (T17-I14).

Tunisia's Striking Policy Continuity Throughout the Democratic Transition

Against expectations, democratization did not lead to a reform of Tunisia's security-driven immigration policy. While the post-revolutionary euphoria on human rights led to an initial dynamism on immigration translating into some institutional and constitutional changes in 2011 and 2012, wider economic and political priorities over the 2013–2016 period eventually sidelined immigration and contributed to the persistent security framing and the fizzling out of legal and policy initiatives. Since 2017, relentless lobbying by CSOs and IOs has started to bear fruits on authorities' awareness and discourse, but legal and administrative changes remain small-scale and scattered.

The revolution could have reshaped Tunisia's approach to immigration, as exiled political leaders and activists who returned after the revolution were keen to integrate their migratory experiences into Tunisian politics, and the large-scale arrival of refugees and migrants from Libya broke with the previous silence on the topic. In the post-revolutionary euphoria, people fleeing from Libya were met with open arms by the local population in southern Tunisia (Boubakri and Potot 2012; Natter 2015b). CSOs such as the Tunisian Red Crescent, the Tunisian Forum for Economic and Social Rights (FTDES), Terre d'Asile Tunisie (TAT) or the Association of African Students and Trainees in Tunisia (AESAT) started to advocate for migrant protection. And IOs such as UNHCR, IOM or the World Health Organization (WHO) arrived in southern Tunisia to provide accommodation, healthcare and food for those arriving at the border. In parallel to such societal and international activities, in March 2011, Tunisia's transitional government relaxed the dispositions of the 2004 law that criminalized irregular migrants (Boubakri and Potot 2012: 136) and in 2012 created a State Secretariat for Migration and Tunisians Abroad (SEMTE) within the Ministry of Social Affairs (MoSA).[*] Shortly after its creation, the SEMTE started working on Tunisia's legal framework on immigration, elaborating a *National Migration Strategy* (SNM), as well as laws on asylum and human trafficking.

This initial dynamism, however, was cut short by Tunisia's political and economic crises. The political assassinations in 2013 and the continuously decreasing foreign investments in tourism and the economy

---

[*] The state secretary changed its name several times over the years, from State Secretariat for Migration and Tunisians Abroad (SEMTE) to State Secretariat for Migration and Social Integration (SEMIS) and State Secretariat in charge of Immigration and Tunisians Abroad (SEITE). For convenience, I always refer to it as SEMTE.

more generally, after 2011, pushed migration – and especially immigration – off the agenda. The continuous presence of foreigners strained Tunisians' welcoming attitude: after the first year, when the situation of immediate urgency had passed and security concerns in the border region grew, popular solidarity faded away (Boubakri and Potot 2012). Political lenience towards incoming migrants also diminished. In the face of renewed conflicts in Libya, the Tunisian government hardened the tone vis-à-vis foreigners because it feared a repetition of 2011. In August 2014, the government 'stresse[d] that this time, Tunisia will be only a "transit" country. ... non-Libyans can only enter the territory if they prove that they will leave it immediately'.[7] Only Libyan citizens continue to be tolerated by Tunisian authorities regardless of their legal status, as detailed later.

Policy continuity thus characterized the 2013–2016 period: security remained the central paradigm in Tunisian immigration politics, and the MoI the primary actor despite the creation of new institutions: 'There are lots of actors now, the debate is happening in the public sphere ... but the substance has not changed, the underlying logic remains a logic of control' (T17-I32). On the ground, the relationship between migrants and the administration deteriorated over the years, with migrants facing increasing bureaucratic hassling and the continuation of pre-2011 detention and expulsion practices (FTDES and Migreurop 2020; Garelli, Sossi and Tazzioli 2015). For instance, penalties for irregular stay were doubled in 2013 from 10 to 20 dinar per week [around 12.5 USD at the time], and their implementation was reinforced. In addition, policy and law-making initiatives have fizzled out. While work on the asylum law started already in October 2011, the finalized draft law was forwarded to the Council of Ministers only in 2018 and is since awaiting to be sent to the Parliament (FTDES and Migreurop 2020). Also, the *National Migration Strategy* (SNM) has been in elaboration since 2011, but repeated governmental reshufflings have prevented the political validation of successive drafts in 2013, 2015 and 2017. As a result, one of my respondents sarcastically called it 'the ghost strategy' (T17-I14). A fourth draft of the strategy was elaborated in 2020.

Within this restrictive policy environment, however, year-long, joint policy efforts by CSOs and IOs have started to bear fruits: projects on immigrants' access to healthcare and work, as well as discussions around their legal and socio-economic difficulties, are not taboo anymore. This discursive shift has led to incipient policy changes, such as exemptions from the irregular stay penalties introduced in 2017 and 2018 or improved access to healthcare and social security for refugees recognized by UNHCR in 2019 and 2020. Yet, such progressive changes often remain informal or are limited to specific migrant groups. Only on two issues has legal change been successful: Law 2016–61 against human trafficking, passed in August 2016, and Law 2018–50 against racial discrimination passed in October 2018. However, the centrepiece of Tunisian immigration policy, Law 2004–06, is still in force, and migrants continue to be excluded from democratic achievements and increased freedoms (Cassarini 2020; FTDES and Migreurop 2020; Geisser 2019). As Tunisian migration law expert Ben Achour (2019: 99) concluded in 2019,

> Tunisia's immigration law is closed, intolerant and inhospitable. … The democratic transition and the radical change in the political climate in Tunisia since 2011 have not had any effect on the rights of foreigners.

Morocco's Unexpected 2013 Immigration Policy Reform

In contrast to Tunisian authorities privileging restrictive policy continuity, the Moroccan King Mohammed VI launched a liberal migration agenda in September 2013 based on recommendations of the country's National Council on Human Rights (CNDH) and in response to sustained civil society and international criticism of migrant rights' violations (RC 2013).

Migrant regularizations were the centrepiece of reform, carried out in three parallel processes: first of all, two 'exceptional' regularization campaigns for irregular migrants were launched in 2014 and 2017. Six groups of irregular migrants were eligible for regularization (MoI and MCMREAM 2013).[*] Yet, given the difficulty migrants faced in meeting the requirements and thus the high number of rejected applications, these criteria were eased at the appeal stage – for women and children, as well as concerning the proof of work and residence. Back in 2013, the MoI had estimated Morocco's irregular migrant population between 25,000 and 40,000 (Karibi 2015: 167). Ultimately, 23,096 migrants from 116 nationalities were regularized in 2014 out of 27,649 submitted requests (MCMREAM 2016). Throughout 2017, 28,400 requests have been submitted by applicants from 113 nationalities, and more than 20,000 migrants have been regularized up to October 2018 (MCMREAM 2018: 72). With an approval rate of over 80 per cent, the regularization was a success in Morocco and abroad.

---

[*] The six groups were (1) foreigners married at least three years to Moroccan nationals, (2) foreigners married at least five years to other foreigners lawfully residing in Morocco, (3) the children of the two cases, (4) foreigners with an employment contract of at least two years, (5) foreigners with five years of continuous residence in Morocco, and (6) foreigners with serious illnesses.

The second type of regularization concerned refugees recognized by UNHCR. The Moroccan Bureau of Refugees and Apatrides (BRA), initially created in 1957 but closed in 2005, was reopened in October 2013, and an ad-hoc inter-ministerial Commission was set up to interview refugees and 'to confirm the decisions of UNHCR' (M16-I27). Lastly, the MoI legalized migrant associations and Moroccan migrant support CSOs – such as the Anti-Racist Defence and Support Group of Foreigners and Migrants (GADEM) or the Council of sub-Saharan Migrants in Morocco (CMSM) – that operated without authorization beforehand. This allowed civil society to play a more proactive role in the new immigration policy.

In parallel to these regularizations, institutional structures on immigration were upgraded: In October 2013, the Ministry in Charge of Moroccans Residing Abroad was renamed Ministry in Charge of Moroccans Residing Abroad and Migration Affairs (MCMREAM), and its portfolio broadened to include immigration. In April 2014, a Directorate for Migration Affairs was created within the MCMREAM and tasked with elaborating and implementing a *National Strategy on Immigration and Asylum* (SNIA) (MCMREAM 2014). The Government Council officially adopted the SNIA on 18 December 2014, the *International Migrants Day*. Its four strategic objectives were to integrate regularized immigrants in education, health, social services, and labour markets; upgrade the regulatory framework; establish an institutional framework; and manage migration flows with respect for human rights.[*] In line with this strategy, a range of integration measures was launched: In 2013, the Ministry of Education (MoE) opened public schools to migrant children regardless of their legal status (MoE 2013). In 2015, the Entraide Nationale (EN), Morocco's public provider of social support services, opened its centres to refugees and migrants regardless of their legal status, and the Ministry of Health (MoH) announced the creation of a health insurance for regularized migrants and refugees. The same year, the Ministry of Labour (MoL) exempted regularized migrants from the labour market test, the so-called 'ANAPEC procedure'.[†]

---

[*] These objectives are operationalized through eighty-one actions organized in eleven programs; seven sectoral programs (on education and culture; youth and leisure; health; housing; social and humanitarian assistance; vocational training; and employment) and four transversal programs (on managing migration flows; international cooperation and partnerships; regulatory and conventional frameworks; and governance and communication). See MCMREAM (2014: 8–9).

[†] The national employment office (ANAPEC) has to attest that there is no national with the required profile who would be available to take on this job (national preference procedure).

Next to such integration measures coordinated by the MCMREAM, the Moroccan Interministerial Delegation for Human Rights (DIDH) was tasked with enshrining the human-rights based approach into legislation. Although three draft laws on immigration, asylum, and human trafficking were elaborated by the end of 2014 (for details, see: Benjelloun 2018a: 78–95), only *Law 27-14* on human trafficking was enacted by the end of 2020. Generally speaking, legal reform on immigration is stuck at the political level.

Internationally, Morocco has excelled in its immigration diplomacy since 2013: In October 2013, Morocco launched the *African Alliance for Migration and Development* at the New York Migration Summit and has been in charge of the migration dossier within the African Union (AU) since spring 2017. In January 2018, King Mohammed VI presented Morocco's *African Migration Agenda* in front of the AU to promote 'a new afro-centred approach that reconciles realism, tolerance and the primacy of reason over fears' (MVI 2018). As part of this agenda, Rabat also hosts the *African Migration Observatory* of the AU since December 2020.[8] In 2017–2018, Morocco also co-presided the *Global Forum on Migration and Development* together with Germany and hosted the UN International Migration Conference in Marrakesh in December 2018, where the *Global Compact for Safe, Orderly and Regular Migration* was adopted.

These administrative and diplomatic developments since 2013 underscore Morocco's shift away from restriction and efforts to foster its position as a regional 'role model' on migration governance. However, integration measures remain scattered, and legal reform is still missing. As detailed later, the implementation of liberal reform is limited by the often symbolic character of announced measures and the preference of Moroccan authorities for ad-hoc decisions instead of legal reforms. On the ground, while migrants' physical security and access to services improved over the years, particularly in cities, the continued violence of state authorities in the border areas, particularly since mid-2018, continues to clash with liberal reform promises. Also, the downgrading of the MCMREAM into a Delegate Ministry in 2017 and its integration into the MoFA in 2019 has jeopardized the institutional capacity of those in charge of Morocco's immigration strategy.

'Have things changed?' one respondent asked. 'Of course. I think no one denies that. Do the changes translate into different practices? I'm not sure. In any case, there are many ambiguities, many grey areas in the implementation of the new migration policy' (M17-I21).

As the book shows, these ambiguities and the constant duality between restrictions and openings reflect the inherently contradictory interests on immigration within the Moroccan state.

Immigration in Times of COVID-19

In spring 2020, the COVID-19 pandemic also reached Morocco and Tunisia, requiring political leaders to devise effective public health strategies to protect their populations. Crises such as these provide unique insights into a state's self-understanding and core priorities. As both countries entered into roughly two-month lockdowns in late March 2020[*] and implemented emergency support programs for the country's socio-economically weakest, the hardship faced by migrants was initially ignored and – if at all – only partially and gradually addressed by authorities in Morocco and Tunisia. In fact, the ways in which state authorities and civil society organizations operated to include or exclude migrants from emergency support mechanisms reveal some of the broader dynamics on immigration that have unfolded in Morocco and Tunisia over the past decades.

In Tunisia, civil society mobilized rapidly in support of migrants, particularly in Tunis, Sousse and Monastir, with Caritas, the Red Crescent, FTDES and TAT coordinating citizen support. A Facebook initiative called 'Cellule Solidarité Africaine Covid-19 Tunisie' was launched in March by African migrant organizations to collect funds and support migrants' rent and daily food costs.[9] IOM has also offered support services to migrants across Tunisia. Partly responding to demands by CSOs and IOs, Tunisia's Ministers of Interior, Social Affairs and Human Rights announced targeted measures for migrants on 7 April 2020, which included delaying unpaid rents, access to COVID state support programs, as well as prolonging visas until the end of the crisis to prevent irregularization (MoI 2020). Yet, this state response did not meet civil society expectations: On 10 April, FTDES, together with sixty other associations and supported by twenty-three Tunisian deputies, called for more systematic state protection of migrants in COVID-19 times, including an exceptional regularization.[10] These dynamics showcase that while Tunisian civil society is highly mobilized in support of migrants, state responses remain largely ad-hoc and limited to emergency measures.

In Morocco, the COVID-19 pandemic revealed that the immigration liberalizations since 2013 were fragile and not set in stone. During the nationwide lockdown, migrants were not allowed to leave the house for necessary activities and were excluded from the Coronavirus Pandemic Fund set up in April 2020 – despite repeated requests of the National

---

[*] The lockdowns lasted in Morocco from 20 March to 20 May, and in Tunisia, from 22 March to 4 May, restrictions were only progressively lifted afterwards.

Council of Human Rights (CNDH) and Moroccan CSOs to include migrants (Boukhssass 2020).[11] Also, while crackdowns on migrant settlements stopped between mid-March and mid-April 2020, police activities were resumed on 15 April, and migrants whose houses were raided were forcibly tested for COVID-19 and detained if their test result was positive.[12] The sanitary crisis thus provided an opportunity for state authorities to increase population – and migration – control. At the same time, more protective measures were put in place at the regional level, as regional offices of the CNDH in northern and south-western Morocco organized basic medical and survival support structures for migrants. Also refugees and asylum seekers benefited from a more inclusive treatment when in May 2020, a Cooperation Agreement between the National Council of the Order of Physicians (CNOM) and UNHCR was signed to regulate refugees' access to healthcare.[13] However, key support for migrants throughout the pandemic came from Moroccan civil society, which launched support systems for migrants in distress, such as the weekly financial support scheme set up by GADEM and ALECMA for families in need,[14] or the distribution of food packages to migrants in Rabat and Casablanca by the National Institution of Solidarity with Women in Need (INSAF).

In both countries, civil society support for immigrants has thus been crucial in the early days of the COVID-19 pandemic. Yet, while it has been more extensive and institutionalized in Morocco than in Tunisia, state responses to bottom-up demands have ultimately been more accommodating in Tunisia, where migrants were included in state support programs, compared to Morocco, where state support has been limited to certain regional efforts or particular groups such as refugees. As the analysis in this book shows, the dynamics characterizing these state-civil society relations are illustrative of the broader developments characterizing the politics of immigration in Morocco and Tunisia over the twenty-first century. In this vein, the following chapters now dive into the core dynamics of Moroccan and Tunisian immigration politics. The detailed analysis of how political processes and inter-actor dynamics on immigration were affected (or not) by political regime dynamics showcases how immigration liberalization in Morocco was a strategy for authoritarian consolidation, while in Tunisia the continuity of immigration restrictions has been a safeguard for democratization.

4 Regime Continuity and Immigration Policy Change in Morocco

The Origins of Moroccan Immigration Policy: Imperialism, Colonial Heritage, and Diplomacy

Before colonization in 1912, Morocco's imperial understanding of statehood did not require a meticulous system of control over foreigners' entries and exits (Hibou and Tozy 2015). During the eighteenth and nineteenth centuries, foreigners in Morocco were subject to the consular jurisdictions of their countries of origin on the basis of bilateral agreements, and many benefited from preferential treatments (Khrouz 2016: 82–83). When French colonial administrators took control over the Moroccan state in 1912, Morocco therefore did not have clear-cut immigration regulations (Diallo 2016; Sefrioui 1973). As a result, France transferred French immigration law onto Moroccan territory in December 1915. After the 1929 Economic Crisis, the French administration further restricted labour migration to Morocco: in 1931, work permits and fines for irregular migrants were introduced. In 1934, work permits were conditioned to the labour market situation and sanctions were introduced for employers and carriers of irregular migrants. With World War II raging in Europe, French administrators also securitized immigration to Morocco; in 1940, a decree was issued to expel or detain anyone considered a national security risk.

European colonialism has left its marks on Moroccan immigration law and practice up until today. As Diallo (2016) details in his ethnographic study on local migration control in Morocco, 'after independence, the local bureaucracy has reconverted all the practices and know-how deployed in the colonial context and integrated it into their government of foreigners'. For instance, foreigners are still required to hand in health and housing certificates with their residence permit application, a practice introduced in the 1930s and 1940s. The work permit application form provides a striking visual example of this colonial heritage (see Figure 4.1), as the document used in 1965 by Moroccan authorities is exactly the same as the one used in 1949 by the French administration.

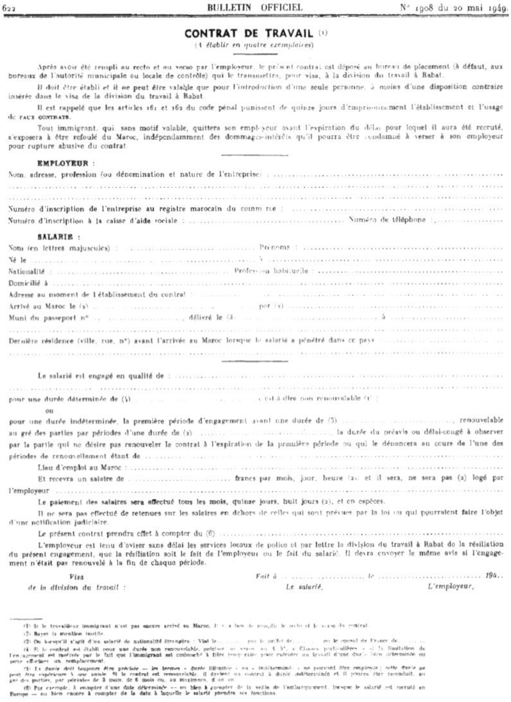

622 BULLETIN OFFICIEL N° 1908 du 20 mai 1949.

CONTRAT DE TRAVAIL (1)

(A établir en quatre exemplaires)

Après avoir été rempli au recto et au verso par l'employeur, le présent contrat est déposé au bureau de placement (à défaut, aux bureaux de l'autorité municipale ou locale de contrôle) qui le transmettra, pour visa, à la division du travail à Rabat.

Il doit être établi et il ne peut être valable que pour l'introduction d'une seule personne, à moins d'une disposition contraire insérée dans le visa de la division du travail à Rabat.

Il est rappelé que les articles 161 et 162 du code pénal punissent de quinze jours d'emprisonnement l'établissement et l'usage de FAUX CONTRATS.

Tout immigrant, qui, sans motif valable, quittera son employeur avant l'expiration du délai pour lequel il aura été recruté, s'exposera à être refoulé du Maroc, indépendamment des dommages-intérêts qu'il pourra être condamné à verser à son employeur pour rupture abusive du contrat.

EMPLOYEUR :

Nom, adresse, profession (ou dénomination et nature de l'entreprise) : ....

Numéro d'inscription de l'entreprise au registre marocain du commerce : ....

Numéro d'inscription à la caisse d'aide sociale : .... Numéro de téléphone : ....

SALARIE :

Nom (en lettres majuscules) : .... Prénoms : ....

Né le .... à ....

Nationalité : .... Profession habituelle : ....

Domicilié à ....

Adresse au moment de l'établissement du contrat : ....

Arrivé au Maroc le (2) .... par (2) ....

Muni du passeport n° ...., délivré le (3) .... à ....

Dernière résidence (ville, rue, n°) avant l'arrivée au Maroc lorsque le salarié a pénétré dans ce pays ....

Le salarié est engagé en qualité de : ....

pour une durée déterminée de (4) .... c'est-à-dire non renouvelable (1) ;

ou

pour une durée indéterminée, la première période d'engagement ayant une durée de (5) ...., renouvelable au gré des parties par périodes d'une durée de (2) .... la durée du préavis ou délai-congé à observer par la partie qui ne désire pas renouveler le contrat à l'expiration de la première période ou qui le dénoncera au cours de l'une des périodes de renouvellement étant de ....

Lieu d'emploi au Maroc : ....

Et recevra un salaire de .... francs par mois, jour, heure (2), et il sera, ne sera pas (2) logé par l'employeur ....

Le paiement des salaires sera effectué tous les mois, quinze jours, huit jours (2), et en espèces.

Il ne sera pas effectué de retenues sur les salaires en dehors de celles qui sont prévues par la loi ou qui pourraient faire l'objet d'une notification judiciaire.

Le présent contrat prendra effet à compter du (6) ....

L'employeur est tenu d'aviser sans délai les services locaux de police et par lettre la division du travail à Rabat de la résiliation du présent engagement, que la résiliation soit le fait de l'employeur ou le fait du salarié. Il devra envoyer le même avis si l'engagement n'était pas renouvelé à la fin de chaque période.

Visa de la division du travail :

Fait à .... le .... 194..

Le salarié, *L'employeur,*

(1) Si le travailleur immigrant n'est pas encore arrivé au Maroc, il y a lieu de remplir le recto et le verso du contrat.

(2) Rayer la mention inutile.

(3) Ou lorsqu'il s'agit d'un salarié de nationalité étrangère : Visé le .... par le préfet de .... ou le consul de France de ....

(4) Si le contrat est établi pour une durée non renouvelable, préciser au verso, au § 5°, « Clauses particulières », si la limitation de l'engagement est motivée par le fait que l'immigrant est embauché à titre temporaire pour exécuter un travail d'une durée bien déterminée ou pour effectuer un remplacement.

(5) La durée doit toujours être précisée — les termes « durée illimitée » ou « indéterminée » ne pouvant être employés ; cette durée ne peut être supérieure à une année. Si le contrat est renouvelable, il devient un contrat à durée indéterminée et il pourra être reconduit, au gré des parties, par périodes de 3 mois, de 6 mois ou, au maximum, d'un an.

(6) Par exemple, à compter d'une date déterminée — ou bien à compter de la veille de l'embarquement, lorsque le salarié est recruté en Europe — ou bien encore à compter de la date à laquelle le salarié prendra ses fonctions.

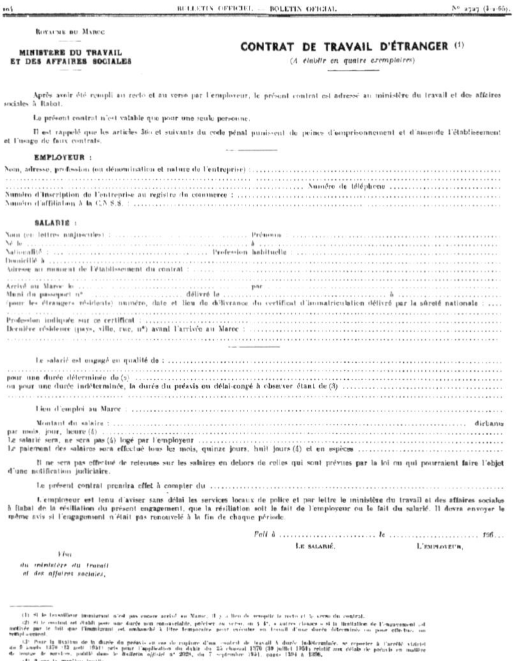

104 BULLETIN OFFICIEL — BOLETIN OFICIAL N° 2727 (3-2-65).

ROYAUME DU MAROC

MINISTERE DU TRAVAIL ET DES AFFAIRES SOCIALES

CONTRAT DE TRAVAIL D'ÉTRANGER (1)

(A établir en quatre exemplaires)

Après avoir été rempli au recto et au verso par l'employeur, le présent contrat est adressé au ministère du travail et des affaires sociales à Rabat.

Le présent contrat n'est valable que pour une seule personne.

Il est rappelé que les articles 360 et suivants du code pénal punissent de peines d'emprisonnement et d'amende l'établissement et l'usage de faux contrats.

EMPLOYEUR :

Nom, adresse, profession (ou dénomination et nature de l'entreprise) : ....

.... Numéro de téléphone ....

Numéro d'inscription de l'entreprise au registre du commerce : ....

Numéro d'affiliation à la C.N.S.S. : ....

SALARIE :

Nom (en lettres majuscules) : .... Prénoms : ....

Né le .... à ....

Nationalité : .... Profession habituelle : ....

Domicilié à ....

Adresse au moment de l'établissement du contrat : ....

Arrivé au Maroc le .... par ....

Muni du passeport n° .... délivré le .... à ....

(pour les étrangers résidents) numéro, date et lieu de délivrance du certificat d'immatriculation délivré par la sûreté nationale : ....

Profession indiquée sur ce certificat : ....

Dernière résidence (pays, ville, rue, n°) avant l'arrivée au Maroc : ....

Le salarié est engagé en qualité de : ....

pour une durée déterminée de (2) ....

ou pour une durée indéterminée, la durée du préavis ou délai-congé à observer étant de (3) ....

Lieu d'emploi au Maroc : ....

Montant du salaire : .... dirhams par mois, jour, heure (4) ....

Le salarié sera, ne sera pas (4) logé par l'employeur ....

Le paiement des salaires sera effectué tous les mois, quinze jours, huit jours (4) et en espèces ....

Il ne sera pas effectué de retenues sur les salaires en dehors de celles qui sont prévues par la loi ou qui pourraient faire l'objet d'une notification judiciaire.

Le présent contrat prendra effet à compter du ....

L'employeur est tenu d'aviser sans délai les services locaux de police et par lettre le ministère du travail et des affaires sociales à Rabat de la résiliation du présent engagement, que la résiliation soit le fait de l'employeur ou le fait du salarié. Il devra envoyer le même avis si l'engagement n'était pas renouvelé à la fin de chaque période.

Fait à .... le .... 196..

LE SALARIÉ, L'EMPLOYEUR,

Visa du ministère du travail et des affaires sociales,

(1) Si le travailleur immigrant n'est pas encore arrivé au Maroc, il y a lieu de remplir le recto et le verso du contrat.

(2) Si le contrat est établi pour une durée non renouvelable, préciser au verso, au § 4°, « autres clauses » si la limitation de l'engagement est motivée par le fait que l'immigrant est embauché à titre temporaire pour exécuter un travail d'une durée déterminée ou pour effectuer un remplacement.

(3) Pour la fixation de la durée du préavis en cas de rupture d'un contrat de travail à durée indéterminée, se reporter à l'arrêté viziriel du 9 kaada 1370 (13 août 1951) pris pour l'application du dahir du 25 chaoual 1370 (30 juillet 1951) relatif aux délais de préavis en matière de louage de services, publié dans le *Bulletin officiel* n° 2028, du 7 septembre 1951, pages 1394 à 1396.

(4) Rayer la mention inutile.

Figure 4.1 Format of work contract in 1949 (top) and 1965 (bottom).
Source: Bulletins Officiels (B.O. n° 1908 of 20 May 1949, p.622 and B.O. n° 2727 of 3 February 1965, p.104).

Only the name of the French authority in charge of granting work permits (the work division in Rabat) was replaced by that of the Moroccan authority (the Ministry for Labour and Social Affairs), and the currency of negotiated salaries was changed from French francs to Moroccan dirham. This illustration is exemplary for Morocco's immigration policy over the second half of the twentieth century, characterized by policy inactivity.

At independence in 1956, Moroccan authorities simply took over existing immigration regulations from the colonial administration. This concerned not only rules and regulations around entry, stay and travel documents, but also refugees: in fact, the last decree issued by the French administration with regards to foreigners in Morocco was the ratification of the Geneva Refugee Convention in 1955. And in one of its first decisions, the Moroccan post-independence administration confirmed its commitment to refugee protection, creating the Bureau of Refugees and Apatrides (BRA) within the Ministry of Foreign Affairs (MoFA) in August 1957. Morocco hereby became one of the first countries in Africa and the Middle East with an asylum institution. However, the BRA never established a legal procedure for national refugee determination, instead using discretion to 'grant refugee status to befriended states or offer protection to specific populations' (M16-I15). Refugees from Zaire (after 1997, the DRC), for instance, were granted protection because its former President Mobutu and Moroccan King Hassan II were personal friends and close political allies (Barre 2003; Goldschmidt 2004). In contrast, most of those arriving in the 1990s from Sierra Leone, Liberia or Côte d'Ivoire were not admitted as refugees but remained irregularly in Morocco.

Morocco's post-independence authorities also engaged in immigration politics in the realm of education cooperation: to deepen relations with francophone Africa, Morocco established public scholarships for African students and signed bilateral agreements on student exchanges with Mauritania in 1974, Zaire in 1975, and Guinea in 1977 (Goldschmidt 2004; Infantino 2011). By the 1980s, student migration was well established: in 1981, the Confederation of African Pupils, Students and Interns in Morocco (CESAM) was created, and in 1986, the MoFA created the Moroccan Agency for International Cooperation (AMCI) as an instrument of educational cooperation with Africa (Mazzella 2009).

To deepen post-independence regional integration, Morocco also signed Establishment Conventions with Senegal, Algeria and Tunisia in 1963–1964, whose citizens were granted the right to enter and reside in Morocco without a visa (and vice versa), to buy property, and to work without a labour market test. While these agreements are still in place today, their implementation is inconsistent. On the one hand, it is subject to the volatile political climate between these countries. For instance, tensions between Morocco and Algeria around the Western Sahara issue, as well as regular territorial border disputes that have culminated in the closure of the border since 1994, have impeded the implementation of the bilateral agreement. On the other hand, implementation is subject to the arbitrary leeway of implementing bureaucrats. The treatment of Senegalese migrants is exemplary in this regard: while they should automatically receive a stay permit with an employment contract, many Senegalese work and live irregularly in Morocco, as access to the stay permit is often difficult in practice. As a result, more than 4,800 Senegalese citizens were regularized in the 2014 regularization.

Generally speaking, the legislative framework on migration inherited from the colonial period remained untouched in the decades after independence. Within this colonial legacy, the central tools of Moroccan immigration politics over the second half of the twentieth century were bilateral agreements or informal administrative decisions that created selective openings for refugees, students and workers from select European, Maghrebi or West African countries.

The Constitution of an Immigration Policy Field over the 2000s

In 2003, Morocco enacted its first immigration law since independence and set up a Directorate of Migrations and Border Surveillance (DMST) within the MoI to institutionalize immigration governance. Law 02–03 heralded a decade of restrictions towards irregular migrants and those assisting them. Irregularity restricted migrants' possibilities to work, rent houses and access education and healthcare, subjecting them to dire living conditions and 'a quasi-generalized denial of rights' (Khrouz 2011: 49). One respondent remembered, 'You could not take a bus if you had no papers. You could not go outside out of fear to be arrested' (M16-I21). Arrested migrants were systematically expelled across the border to Algeria or Mauretania, where many made their way back into Morocco. Interviews showed that migrants were on average removed 1.73 times to the frontier near Oujda, some up to seven times (Collyer 2006: 23). Ultimately, by enacting Law 02–03, Moroccan authorities politicized immigration in political and public life, triggering two different reactions within Moroccan society: racist discrimination of so-called 'sub-Saharan African migrants' and civil society mobilization. At the same time, such politicization also generated increased international involvement in immigration and led to the tacit inclusion of migrants by certain local authorities, turning immigration into a veritable field of public policy in Morocco.

The Geopolitical and Domestic Drivers of Law 02-03[1]

Law 02–03 has often been framed as a by-product of European migration externalization efforts within the literature (see, for instance, Belguendouz 2003, 2009; Lahlou 2011; Perrin 2009; Valluy 2007). Indeed, since the 1990s, the European Union offensively engaged in a migration control agenda, with the 1999 Tampere Conclusions officially turning cooperation with third countries into an essential element of Europe's 'remote control' strategy to manage irregular migration. Morocco has been a key target for such migration control demands by the European Union (EU) and particularly Spain, and has oscillated between cooperation and obstructive behaviour depending on which position would more effectively advance Morocco's own interests (El Qadim 2015; Wunderlich 2010). Such external explanation of immigration policy is also present in many of my interviews: 'With this law, Morocco has obeyed and surrendered to the security policy of the European Union' (M12-I2), one civil society respondent concluded. Even Morocco's Interior Minister publicly framed the law in these terms back in 2003: 'Law 02–03 is part of the attempt ... to respect Morocco's commitments towards its partners in the fight against emigration.'[2] However, a purely Eurocentric approach ignores the multifaceted interests that Moroccan authorities pursued through this law and the fact that European pressures for restriction are only successful when they align with Moroccan authorities' interests. In the words of one respondent: 'Without domestic political will, nothing works' (M11-I7).

Most importantly, Law 02–03 allowed Morocco to 'play the migratory card' (M11-I4, M12-I5, M12-I4) and to capitalize on Europe's migration obsession to advance two foreign policy goals: to consolidate its position on Western Sahara vis-à-vis Algeria and to negotiate favourable terms for its economic cooperation with Europe. For example, Morocco regularly increases the migratory pressure on its northern borders by relaxing border controls at strategic moments in time to bolster its bargaining power during negotiations on agricultural exports or fisheries agreements, as well as to put pressure on European countries to recognize Morocco's claim on Western Sahara. The incidents in May 2020, when Morocco loosened its border controls and turned a blind eye to the over 8,000 migrants who crossed the fences into Ceuta in response to Spain's decision to give medical treatment to Brahim Ghali, leader of the Polisario Front fighting for the independence of Western Sahara, are just the most recent example of this dynamic.[3] In fact, it is not in Morocco's interest to seal off its northern borders, as 'it is important to sometimes show that the problem still exists' (M12-I4). The 2003 law thus symbolizes Morocco's ability to overstate the magnitude of 'transit' migration and turn it into diplomatic 'capital' (El Qadim 2010; Kimball 2007).

In addition to geopolitical interests, two domestic factors drove Law 02–03: on the one hand, it allowed Moroccan authorities to increase control over population movements (of Moroccans and foreigners alike) across its territory and hereby advance security interests. On the other hand, particular dynamics within the Moroccan administration favoured the politicization of irregular migration: when Mohammed VI dismissed the infamous Interior Minister Driss Basri in 1999, large parts of the MoI personnel was renewed. The new generation of MoI civil servants saw immigration control as a tool to expand their power and access resources at a moment in time when the centrality of the MoI in the state apparatus was at stake. Compared to the 1990s, when the MoI largely turned a blind eye to irregular migration, the early 2000s saw a systematic increase in police controls and expulsions of irregular migrants (El Qadim 2015: 216; Goldschmidt 2004: 164).

Yet, migration restrictions were highly unpopular among Moroccans who also relied on largely irregular migration to diversify family income. To create social adherence around Law 02–03, authorities framed it as 'modernizing' Morocco's immigration regime, securing the national interest, and controlling growing 'transit migration' from Western and Central Africa (Natter 2014b). First, the law was portrayed as necessary to decolonize Morocco's immigration regime. During parliamentary discussions in June 2003, 'the abrogation of all legal texts in place since the time of the protectorate and that served first and foremost the interests of the colonizer' (B.O. 2003b) was presented as key to safeguarding national sovereignty. A respondent from the MoI described the law as a necessary 'legislative upgrade' to replace old regulations with a 'modern' legal framework in line with international legal standards. Given this declared goal of decolonizing immigration policy, the parallels between Law 02–03 and France's restrictive Law 2003–1119 enacted in November 2003 seem quite ironic (see also Khrouz 2011).

Authorities also framed the law's border-control measures as a national security guarantee. Although the law was finalized in early 2003, state respondents retrospectively cast it as a reaction to the Casablanca terrorist attacks on 16 May 2003 that killed over forty-five people. The attacks provided a window of opportunity to silence public or political criticism of migration control and rapidly enact the law. For instance, a debate organized in May 2003 by the Moroccan Association of Studies and Research on Migration (AMERM) on the shortcomings of the law 'had no impact, it was taken over by the terrorist attacks'

(M12-I1). Also, criticism raised within the Parliament went unnoticed: all twenty-five amendments – eighteen put forward by the leftist USFP and seven by the Islamist PJD – were rejected (B.O. 2003b). Ultimately, the law was passed almost unanimously, with sixty votes to two. This blatantly contradicts the statement of an MoI civil servant who highlighted that 'the law has been the fruit of a large consultation. I assure you that the law has been finalized in concert with all concerned actors'.

Lastly, and most prominently, Moroccan authorities presented the 2003 law as a much-needed response to growing 'transit' migration from Western and Central Africa: 'We moved quickly from a country of emigration to a transit country in the 2000s. ... We had to legislate, to put things in order,' one respondent said (M12-I18). This official discourse, largely taken over by the media, deliberately framed nationals from Western and Central Africa as the main migrant group targeted by the law – disregarding the demographic reality on the ground, where 'transit' migration remained statistically insignificant compared to continuously high emigration (Feliu Martínez 2009; Gazzotti 2021a). This discourse, however, succeeded in shifting domestic and international attention away from the continued (irregular) emigration of Moroccans. Irregular migration was no longer associated with Morocco's failure to provide opportunities for the country's youth but with national security and foreign policy issues (Khrouz 2016: 352–54; Natter 2014b).

Polarized Societal Dynamics: Growing Racism Versus Transnational Civil Society Mobilization

This top-down politicization of immigration by Moroccan authorities triggered two different reactions within Moroccan society: racist discrimination and civil society mobilization. The growing political focus on migrants from Western and Central Africa and restrictive approach by the Moroccan state subjected them to increasing stigmatization in Moroccan newspapers and television (Belguendouz 2009; Feliu Martínez 2009; GADEM 2010: 12–14; Natter 2014b; Vignati 2009). Migrants from Western and Central Africa were often presented as an economic threat, as a public health hazard because of prostitution and AIDS, or as a security issue related to criminality, drug trafficking and terrorism (AMERM 2009; Mbolela 2011). Back in November 2012, the cover of the francophone weekly newspaper *Maroc Hebdo* was met with outrage as it referred to migrants from Western and Central Africa as 'the Black peril',[4] and in November 2019, the arabophone daily *Assabah* again triggered a wave of criticism by relaying the statements of a

Moroccan woman qualifying irregular migrants in Casablanca as 'cockroaches'.[5]

Such racism, however, is anything but new in Morocco. It is, in fact, deeply rooted in the country's history of slavery between the sixteenth and early twentieth centuries and the contemporary marginalization of its own Black minority.[6] Although not all Black Moroccans are descendants of slaves and, vice versa, not all slaves were Black, popular discourses in Morocco commonly relate Black Moroccans to the African slave trade (Badoual 2003): in Morocco, 'slavery was associated with Blackness' (El Hamel 2012: 238). Such perceptions of Black Moroccans, and the resulting societal marginalization of these communities, have more recently spilt over onto attitudes towards migrants from Western and Central Africa (Bahmad 2015: 153–54; Menin 2016): 'The "Black" population, Moroccan but even more so foreign, is considered by a part of the Moroccan population as descendants of slaves, as socially inferior' (GADEM 2010: 5). As a result, both Black Moroccans and migrants from Western and Central Africa are often called *'abid* (slave) or *aâzi* (literally 'tanned') on the streets – and this is regardless of their social class or legal status: 'The treatment is the same if you are a student or irregular; if you are Black, that's it. Even if you are a diplomat, they will treat you the same way' (M12-I3), one respondent recounted.

In parallel to such racist stigmatization, however, migrants' associations, religious institutions and human-rights CSOs have developed into a vibrant pro-immigrant activist sphere in Morocco since the late 1990s (AMERM 2009; Feliu Martínez 2009). Religious actors and (European and African) migrants themselves were the first to mobilize and organize emergency healthcare or psychological support for migrants: the Moroccan branch of Caritas started receiving migrants at its office as early as 1995, and the International Mutual Aid Committee (CEI), a humanitarian support network for irregular migrants from West Africa, was created in 2002 in Rabat by an evangelical pastor. In parallel, associations working with Moroccan irregular emigrants or on migrant deaths in the Mediterranean – such as the Friends and Families of Victims of Clandestine Migration (AFVIC) or the northern sections of Moroccan Association of Human Rights (AMDH) – started including Western and Central Africa migrants in their activities.

Morocco's own experience with emigration and migrant advocacy in Europe provided a mould for civil society activism on immigration in Morocco, and organizational support from abroad – by Moroccan diaspora organizations and European human rights associations such as Migreurop and La Cimade – was vital for making its voice heard (Lacroix 2004: 112–13; Üstübici 2016). As one respondent recalls, such transnational backing 'was the only way to exert some pressure on the Moroccan government' (M12-I12). In 2003, partly in reaction to Law 02–03, Moroccan and European CSOs founded the first Migrant Platform (PFM) to unite civil society work on immigration. These dynamics were in the making when a 'crisis' of international outreach reshuffled the actors on immigration in 2005.

In autumn 2005, approximately 1,400 migrants attempted to cross the barbed wire fences separating Morocco and the two Spanish enclaves Ceuta and Melilla cities in northern Morocco. At least twelve migrants were shot dead by border guards, and hundreds were severely injured (Migreurop 2006: 96–98). These events, and the international outrage it triggered, provided a window of opportunity for civil society to consolidate its transnational character and to shift from purely humanitarian, caritative support towards political, rights-based advocacy (Alioua 2009; AMERM 2009; Üstübici 2016): 'In October 2005, national civil society woke up' (M17-I3). Migrant associations were founded – such as the Council of Congolese Refugees and Asylum Seekers (ARCOM) or the Council of Sub-Saharan Migrants in Morocco (CMSM). In parallel, the Anti-Racist Defence and Support Group of Foreigners and Migrants (GADEM) was created in December 2006, and Moroccan human rights organizations such as the Moroccan Organization of Human Rights (OMDH) and the AMDH started to integrate immigration more systematically into their activities:

It was the right moment, a matter of chance. We had in front of us representatives of migrant communities who wanted to get organized. We started to find activists to join us. We had an international community that started to look more closely at what was happening in Morocco (M17-I12).

Two other developments strengthened civil society activism over the 2000s: on the one hand, irregular migrants started to move from the border regions towards Moroccan cities. Their increased visibility in Moroccan public space facilitated contacts with migrant support organizations. Second, the organization of the *Euro-African Conference on Migration and Development* by the Moroccan government in July 2006 provided momentum for civil society, as CSOs organized a parallel conference reuniting European, Moroccan and African civil society.[7] Although most of these CSOs were not legally recognized by the Moroccan state and operated in constant fear of a crackdown, they managed to carve out a role for themselves in the Moroccan public sphere. As developed later, this bottom-up mobilization for migrant rights gained more political clout after 2011.

International Norms and Institutions: The 2007 UNHCR Headquarters Agreement

The Ceuta and Melilla incidents not only affected domestic dynamics on immigration but also severely damaged Morocco's international reputation – journalists called it 'the dirtiest affair that Moroccan diplomacy ever had to face'.[8] Moroccan authorities realized that civil society criticism had an international audience and that 'Morocco's image in Europe and Africa was at stake' (M11-I10). In response, Morocco shifted strategy and started to actively promote itself as a mediator on migration between Africa and Europe. Morocco's new 'global' role was heralded through the organization of the first *Euro-African Ministerial Conference on Migration and Development* in Rabat in July 2006, which brought together European and African leaders for the first time to discuss migration. This regional dialogue was later institutionalized in the 'Rabat Process', bringing together fifty-seven states across Europe and Central, Western and Northern Africa. Paradoxically, although the 2005 incidents were a diplomatic disaster, they eventually allowed Morocco to serve both its African and European interests in an increasingly complex three-level game on migration. This tactic of turning a crisis into an opportunity is not specific to the migration dossier. For instance, when critical reports by Amnesty International (AI) and the International Human Rights Federation (FIDH) in November 2003 denounced ongoing torture in Morocco, the King launched the Equity and Reconciliation Commission to deal with human rights violations during his father's reign: 'From the rank of accused, Morocco becomes a world leader in reconciliation' (Vermeren 2011: 20).

Ceuta and Melilla also provided the springboard for International Organizations (IOs) and donors to step up their activities in Morocco. The Swiss Development Cooperation Agency (SDC) started funding humanitarian and advocacy work on immigration. IOM established its headquarters in Rabat in 2005, and in 2006, the UN created an interagency group on migration to develop a comprehensive international response to migration to, through and from Morocco. However, the most significant development concerned UNHCR: while Morocco was among the first countries outside Europe to host a UNCHR delegation back in 1968,[*] it was reluctant to grant UNHCR full representation and

---

[*] The UNHCR's honorary delegation in Casablanca was led for over forty years by Mohammed M'jid, a Moroccan businessman and president of the Royal Tennis Federation. With only a small group of local staff, UNHCR activities were minimal, limited to the support of selected refugees.

the right to conduct refugee status determination procedures on the governments' behalf. This was in part because of UNHCR's long-standing involvement in Western Sahara – not recognized by the UN as part of the Moroccan state – and its support of Sahrawi refugees in the Tindouf refugee camp in southern Algeria. In 2005, however, the blatant lack of refugee protection at the Ceuta and Melilla borders, as well as the official closure of Morocco's (dysfunctional) Bureau of Refugees and Stateless People (BRA), provided a window of opportunity for UNHCR to intensify its work in Morocco.

The path leading to the ratification of the Headquarters Agreement between UNHCR and Morocco in July 2007 was thorny. It was ultimately achieved by UNHCR through a two-fold strategy: forging alliances with key Moroccan actors and creating facts on the ground. On the one hand, and despite the prohibition to work with local actors, UNHCR started to cooperate with Moroccan CSOs – such as AMAPPE for socio-economic integration of refugees, the Orient-Occident Foundation (FOO) for their socio-cultural support, and OMDH for legal assistance – as well as with local authorities such as hospitals and educational authorities to build a support network for refugees and asylum seekers. UNHCR was also supported by progressive opinion leaders within the Moroccan political elite, such as Driss el Yazami, the then-head of the Council for Morocco's Community Abroad (CCME); Kamel Lahbib, the driving force behind the Maghreb Social Forum; and Amina Bouayach, then president of the OMDH. The cooperation with actors on the ground and the support of high-level Moroccan advocates increased pressure on the MoFA, the chief negotiator on the Moroccan side, from within and below.

On the other hand, UNHCR simply started to create facts by registering Ivorian, Congolese, Nigerian, and Sierra Leonean asylum seekers – over 2,000 until mid-2006. This alarmed the Moroccan MoFA, who 'noted the major risk of systematically granting the registration certificate to any applicant by the UNHCR office, which is synonymous with a strong incentive for the influx of illegal migrants' (MAEC 2005, in: Valluy 2007). To legitimize its activities in front of Moroccan authorities and showcase its professionalism, UNHCR adopting stricter procedures for unfounded claims. A high-level respondent from UNHCR recalls, 'We were very rigorous with screening, to make sure that those we screened in were really refugees. ... we kept it manageable and Morocco also saw that.'

Despite many obstacles throughout the negotiations, in particular because Morocco wanted UNHCR to also cover refugee registration in the Western Sahara territories, a demand that could not be satisfied, the headquarters agreement was ultimately signed on 20 July 2007.[*] In the words of a former UNHCR employee:

> All this together, ... showing how UNHCR is doing a serious job in determining quality decisions, showing Moroccan authorities that we made arrangements for refugee assistance, pressure from civil society, pressure from the donor community, also playing on Morocco's honour and pride – they want to be the first in the class, they want to be better than Algeria and Tunisia – they really should act. And that together brought them to sign the agreement.

Inside the State: Institutional Dynamics As Drivers of Informal Openings at the Local Level

Despite this victory of UNHCR in advancing refugee protection in Morocco, between 2003 and 2013, Morocco's official, restrictive stance towards immigration did not change. Yet, the state is not a unitary actor, and so policies devised by the central government become subject to a range of new dynamics at the stage of implementation. On the ground, therefore, Morocco's immigration policy oscillated between restrictions and selective openings towards migrants, a dynamic that showcases the room for manoeuvre of local public authorities and engaged individuals, even in an autocratic context.

First of all, the formal presence of UNHCR after 2007 slightly changed, implementing actors' practices towards refugees. Although the refugee papers handed out by UNHCR were still not officially recognized by Moroccan authorities, they provided refugees with protection from arbitrary police expulsion (Mbolela 2011; Perrin 2009: 264). According to a respondent, 'they [authorities] sent out an internal note that the documentation issued by UNHCR should be protecting people from expulsion' (M16-I31). Also, the local authority responsible for registering children in public schools in Rabat started to enrol refugee children without legal status. As one respondent from within the responsible institution related,

> It was the only [education authority] that did this, and it was thanks to the courage of the director; it was she who initiated all this. ... When a list of children was brought to me, I would not check the details, whether they ask for asylum or not, I did not care ... it was important to me that all children can go to school.

In 2011, this informal practice was widened to include children of all irregular migrants. According to respondents, around forty irregular or

---

[*] The international climate regarding Western Sahara and the question of Sahrawi refugees in Tindouf, Algeria, continued to impact UNHCR activities in Morocco even after the agreement was signed (see also Planes-Boissac 2012a: 19).

refugee children were eventually enrolled in Rabat every year between 2009 and 2013, although this was in fact forbidden. Health authorities also intensified their engagement with irregular migrants in the early 2000s, fearing that migrants' exclusion from healthcare would jeopardize Morocco's efforts to control certain diseases (Mourji et al. 2016: 75; Planes-Boissac 2012a). In 2003, a circular directed at the border police permitted healthcare access to irregular migrants. In 2008 and 2010, further circulars clarified that non-Moroccan patients should be admitted to hospitals independently of their legal status, even if healthcare often remained difficult to access for irregular migrants. Also in the area of employment, such dynamics were visible, as the public Office for Professional Training and Work Promotion (OFPPT) started to accept refugees in their professional training courses in 2011.

These small-scale advances in education, health and employment attest to some openings within the overall restrictive climate – not in policy but in practice. In other areas, however, the situation deteriorated: throughout 2012, civil society reports documented growing and systematic migrants' rights abuses by Moroccan police, such as raids of informal migrant settlements and the arbitrary detention and expulsion of irregular migrants (CMSM and GADEM 2012; HRW 2014). In October 2012, the former president of the migrant association CMSM was arrested and denied legal assistance (Planes-Boissac 2012a: 9). Also, while it was relatively easy to receive a work permit for specific sectors in the 2000s, the Ministry of Labour (MoL) tightened rules in November 2012 (Khrouz 2016: 221). Finally, the signature of the EU-Morocco Mobility Partnership in June 2013 – although largely symbolic and without real policy consequences – shattered activist hopes that migrants' rights would improve anytime soon: 'We were all pessimistic, we thought there would be more repression, more controls ... because 2012 was a tough period for migrants with a lot of violence and expulsions' (M16-I26).

Within this context, both civil society and state representatives interviewed back in 2012 categorically excluded the possibility of a liberal reform: 'There cannot be an open integration policy in Morocco', a high-level civil servant within the Ministry of Interior (MoI) exclaimed. 'Morocco does what all countries do: some regularizations, through a case by case policy, but no real regularization or integration policy.' Nonetheless, eighteen months later, Mohammed VI launched precisely such a liberal migration reform. This triggered one main reaction:

Everyone was taken by surprise, really! ... We did not know anything, and the administration did not know anything. It was a political decision taken by the top, a decision that opened all doors in a rather spectacular manner (M16-I29).

Crafting a 'Liberal Monarchy': The Drivers of the 2013 Liberalization[9]

A specific constellation of factors can explain the suddenness and liberal nature of Morocco's 2013 reform, as strategies from within the state, international pressures from outside, and domestic mobilization from below converged. Undoubtedly, the most important driver for immigration liberalization was King Mohammed VI's vision to cast Morocco as a 'modern', 'liberal monarchy'. The reform allowed the monarchy to bolster its legitimacy in front of liberal, progressive parts of society who saw migrants' rights as intrinsic to Morocco's democratization agenda and who had gained momentum since 2011. Closing the gap between Moroccan official human rights discourses and realities on the ground was particularly urgent in the context of the 'Arab Spring' and the monarchy's fear of regional 'revolutionary diffusion' (Weyland 2009, 2012). But the reform did not only satisfy domestic constituencies. It also simultaneously served Morocco's European and African diplomatic interests: gaining concessions from the European Union in terms of economic cooperation and the rights of Morocco's diaspora, as well as advancing economic cooperation and garnering political support for the Western Sahara question within Africa. For Bensaâd (2015: 250),

> even if it was a civil society demand, this decision to regularize sub-Saharan migrants, in fact, could only find its way to the decision-making centre of the state because there was a favourable alignment of geopolitical issues whereby it could serve the interests of the Moroccan state.

Despite its humanitarian outlook, the 2013 reform was first and foremost driven by Moroccan domestic regime legitimation and foreign policy priorities and a very effective policy tool within the context of a three-level game.

The Performative Dimension of Power: 'Geopolitical Rebordering' and African Leadership

Ostensibly, the chief purpose of the immigration reform was to portray the Moroccan regime – 'obsessed with maintaining and embellishing its image' (M17-I21) – as a 'liberal monarchy' and to hereby secure its legitimation and interests abroad. Indeed, the regularization and integration policies launched in 2013 were crucial tools to showcase the progressive character of the Moroccan state. As the royal press release announcing the 2013 reform reads, 'This Royal Initiative, which is part of the Kingdom's tradition of welcoming, illustrates the constant involvement of the Sovereign in favour of protection of human rights' (RC 2013).

In particular, the reform was instrumental in what I call 'geopolitical rebordering', the shifting of Morocco's position on the (imaginary and symbolic) map splitting the world into developing and developed, democratic and autocratic countries. Although such categories are analytically problematic, this does not obstruct their symbolic power, and the 2013 reform managed to place Morocco discursively in proximity with 'receiving countries': 'We offer migrants a regularization and integration in Morocco so that we can put ourselves on equal footing with Europe' (M17-I21), one respondent said. In the same vein, Anis Birou, Migration Minister between October 2013 and April 2017, highlighted at a public event:

We should not forget that migrants leave their countries first and foremost to live a life in dignity, and this is only possible in a country that offers security and opportunities to participate in development (M17-D5).

Although this framing undermines the fact that Morocco is still first and foremost an emigration country, it allowed Morocco to cast itself as part of the 'receiving country family', a group of countries that (at least in peoples' mindsets) is characterized by high levels of development, democracy and modernity. In the words of IOM Director General William Lacy-Swing back in 2017, 'Morocco is showing the way to a much better humanitarian and benevolent approach to migrants'.[10]

Within this larger goal of showcasing Morocco internationally as a progressive actor, 'the heart, the catalyst of the new migration policy is Morocco's new positioning towards Africa' (M17-I21). Indeed, systematic migrant rights' violations by police and border guards had jeopardized Morocco's political and economic interests in Africa over the 2000s, and so welcoming immigrants became key in Morocco's soft power strategy to strengthen its role as a regional leader in Africa. On the one hand, the regularization and integration measures allowed Moroccan media and interviewees to emphasize Morocco's achievements and progressiveness compared to the regional rival, Algeria, which regularly made headlines with its ill-treatment of migrants. In this vein, respondents stressed the exceptional character of Morocco's liberal reform in a regional context dominated by restrictive immigration policies: 'Morocco is the only African country that regularizes irregular migrants!' On the other hand, the symbolic weight of the immigration reform facilitated the expansion of Moroccan firms' markets and investments across West Africa, particularly in the financial, telecommunication and national resources sector (Cherti and Collyer 2015).

Ultimately, the 2013 reform – and the fact that King Mohammed VI announced the launch of Morocco's second regularization campaign in December 2016 – proved instrumental for Morocco's reintegration into the African Union in January 2017. At a public event in Rabat in February 2017, Ali Coulibaly, African Integration Minister in Côte d'Ivoire, exclaimed, 'Morocco is a pioneer on the migration issue ... show[ing] considerable leadership by making bold and innovative decisions' (M17-D5). As an African role model on immigration governance, Morocco is now in charge of the organization's migration portfolio and has been hosting the AU's *African Migration Observatory* since December 2020. (M17-I13).

Morocco's 2013 migration reform is part of a broader effort to transform Morocco into an example of democracy, the rule of law, and economic development in Africa.[11] Moroccan ministries have established cooperation programs with their African counterparts to provide strategic advice and training in the fields of religious diversity, education, employment policies, human rights and justice: 'Each department, in its own field, creates relations with Africa to reflect the global approach of the Moroccan state' (M17-I18). While this progressive image seems detached from Moroccan political realities, 'it always depends what you take as your referent' (M17-I12). In the past, Morocco's geopolitical focus on Europe meant that Europe was the referent to evaluate the progressiveness of Moroccan policies. By shifting the focus towards Africa – by whose standards Morocco scores relatively well on levels of economic development and political freedoms – Morocco can position *itself* as the reference. Instead of remaining 'Europe's student' in terms of human rights, Morocco is carving out its role as 'Africa's teacher', with migrants' rights becoming a tool in Morocco's Africa policy.

Societal, Bottom-Up Policy Drivers: Migrants Rights As Human Rights

But the new migration policy not only reflected a shift in Morocco's foreign policy strategy. It was also meant to bolster the regime's domestic legitimacy among liberal parts of Moroccan society at a moment when authoritarianism was weakened by regional political developments. Indeed, the 2013 reform was partly responding to intensified civil society claims for migrants' rights after the monarchy's limited political opening in 2011 and succeeded in fostering the King's image as a progressive actor on the domestic scene.

The pro-migrant, transnational civil society that had emerged since the early 1990s and regularly jeopardized Morocco's image over the 2000s gained political momentum in the context of the regional atmosphere of change after 2011: '2011 gave a lot of liberties, we could denounce what happened in Morocco with the migrants because of the changing socio-political context' (M16-I26). Civil society actors felt empowered to make their voice heard and to increase their presence in Moroccan public space. Most symbolically, on 1 May 2012, more than 160 migrants joined Moroccan labour unions on their Labour Day march in the centre of Rabat. They demanded the regularization of irregular migrants under the header: 'We love Morocco, we work in Morocco, regularize us.'[12] In addition, civil society capitalized on Morocco's new constitution, which gave primacy to international treaties over national law and laid down the constitutional right to political asylum in its Article 30, to advocate for migrants' rights: 'We can profit from the new constitution to ask for our rights ... Article 30, the Convention on migrant workers, the Convention on refugees. Suddenly we have tools that we can rely on' (M17-I3).

The most important development that emerged from the 2011 Constitution, however, was that it upgraded the existing Consultative Council on Human Rights (CCDH) into a more powerful National Council on Human Rights (CNDH). Driss el Yazami, a former refugee in France and prominent human rights activist, was appointed by King Mohammed VI as its president. Under his mandate, the CNDH set up a working group on discrimination in Morocco and started to expand its work on immigrants' rights: in August 2011, the CNDH asked for a revision of Morocco's asylum law, and in 2013, the CNDH's report entitled *Foreigners and human rights in Morocco: For a radically new immigration and asylum policy* (CNDH 2013) provided the impetus for the King's decision to launch the immigration reform, as outlined later.

The constitutional and institutional changes in 2011 thus increased the legitimacy and leverage of national civil society actors and the CNDH, allowing the immigration issue to take shape in the context of Morocco's wider human rights and democratization debate. Also migrant organizations such as ALECMA, CCSM or CMSM increased their political clout by portraying themselves as essential for Morocco's democratization: 'the link between migration reform and democratic reform is obvious ... We don't do [advocacy] only for migrants, but for change in Morocco'. As a result, foreigners' rights were as a testing ground for Morocco's promise of political liberalization, as a 'thermometer' to gauge the human rights situation in Morocco more generally.

Linking Emigration and Immigration Policies: Mirror and Demonstration Effects

The 2013 reform not only bolstered the image of Morocco's monarchy at home and abroad. It also allowed Moroccan authorities to align their emigration and immigration policies which had so far been incoherent, given that Morocco was lobbying for more migrant rights in Europe but denying basic human rights to immigrants on its own territory. Back in 2011, Ali El Baz from the Association of Maghreb Workers in France (ATMF) highlighted this inconsistency: 'We do not understand how we demand the regularization of hundreds of thousands of Moroccans abroad while Morocco does not even want to do it for a few thousand sub-Saharan immigrants.'[13]

Over the years, Moroccan civil society and progressive state actors have increasingly highlighted this discrepancy and mobilized what I call the 'mirror effect', namely the translation of Morocco's history of emigration and concern for its migrants in Europe into calls for immigrants' rights in Morocco. Mehdi Alioua, a founding member of the GADEM, writes in 2015, 'Because we are a nation of emigrants, of which many have lived in camps and shantytowns in Europe and have suffered and sometimes still experience racism, discrimination, and police violence, we owe it to ourselves to be exemplary.'[14] But also within state institutions, the concern about Moroccan migrants in Europe has translated into concern about foreigners in Morocco: 'We could not maintain this policy of double standards. If we ask the application of international human rights for our diaspora, we also need to apply it here.'

Such mirror effect has not only been at work on a societal level – reminding Moroccan leaders and citizens of the familiar experiences of emigration and racial discrimination. Also personal journeys, such as that of Driss el Yazami, president of the CNDH, have crucially informed civil society's and progressive state institutions' work on immigration in Morocco: 'He was himself a refugee in France, he fought for migrants' rights in France, so he wanted to avoid that Morocco makes the same errors as France' (M16-I30). Seen through the mirror effect, the 2013 reform is thus also partly the outcome of 'political remittances' (Lacroix, Levitt and Vari-Lavoisier 2016; Levitt 1998), as emigration experiences were fed back into the Moroccan polity.

Yet, actors have not only mobilized Morocco's emigration history to lobby for progressive immigration reform. Once enacted, Moroccan authorities have in turn mobilized the liberal reform to advance their diaspora policy objectives through what Arrighi and Bauböck (2017: 631) have called the 'demonstration effect'. Indeed, state respondents have used the 2013 reform to critique European immigration restrictions and to boost Morocco's claims for more migrants' rights in Europe: 'With the new policy, we did what we asked others to do,' a high-level civil servant told me. Even Mohammed VI said in August 2016, 'Those who criticize our approach would be better off ... offering immigrants at least a tiny part of what we have achieved in this area' (MVI 2016).

At the core of this demonstration effect stands the comparison between European restrictions and Moroccan liberalizations in recent years, with respondents juxtaposing the 'human and far-sighted' Moroccan approach and the 'radicalization of the European vision on immigration' (M17-I13): 'All countries in the world are closing their borders, talking about deportation, and Morocco says all illegal migrants can stay here and get a legal status' (M17-I4), one respondent concluded. As developed later, the small scale of immigration to Morocco makes the demonstration effect a particularly attractive strategy: 'One should not forget that they have 5 million migrants abroad compared to 24,000 on their territory' (M16-I16). Yet, regardless of their effectiveness, what such mirror and demonstration effects showcase is the tight imbrication of contemporary immigration policy debates with Morocco's history as an emigration country.

International Norms As a Window of Opportunity

Morocco's legacy of large-scale emigration set the scene, and strategies for regime legitimation both at home and abroad provided the drivers for reform. The immediate trigger for the King's decision in September 2013 to launch the reform, however, was the evaluation of Morocco's adherence to international norms. International norms came into play because of an unexpected turn in history: in 1993, Morocco was the third country worldwide to ratify the *UN International Convention of the Protection of the Rights of All Migrant Workers and Members of Their Families*, hoping it would pressure European countries to enhance migrant protection and thus improve Moroccans' rights abroad. The Convention only came into force in 2003 due to the limited interest it generated among receiving countries, but soon thereafter, a committee was created in Geneva to oversee its implementation.*

Morocco's evaluation by the committee in 2012 offered a window of opportunity for civil society to make its voice heard internationally and

---

* Morocco has participated in the committee from its inception until the present day through the nomination of Mr. Abdelhamid El Jamri, a Moroccan diplomat, who also presided over the commission during the Moroccan review process in 2012–2013.

denounce Morocco's migrant rights' violations. Doctors Without Borders (MSF), AMDH and GADEM handed in 'parallel reports' to the committee in Geneva to counter the government's official report that denied the arbitrary detentions and expulsions of migrants: 'During the whole process in Geneva, civil society attacked Morocco on what is happening, and Moroccan officials said the opposite: no it does not happen, everything is fine' (M17-I12). The particularly harsh report by MSF (2013) triggered broad international attention and 'made the Royal Court particularly nervous, as it made such a bad impression on the international arena' (M17-I4). The committee's conclusions, inspired by civil society reports, highlighted the alarming situation of migrants in Morocco and created a moment of cumulative internal and external pressure on the Moroccan government.

On 9 September 2013, in parallel to the final meeting of the committee in Geneva, the CNDH presented a set of recommendations to the Moroccan King, entitled *Foreigners and human rights in Morocco: For a radically new immigration and asylum policy* (CNDH 2013). The next day, Mohammed VI announced an immigration reform along the lines of the CNDH recommendations (RC 2013) – 'to calm things down a bit' (M16-I26). The CNDH report was key in legitimizing the 2013 reform as a home-grown initiative. As 'a legitimate voice coming from Moroccan society' (M16-I22), it created a window of opportunity for state authorities to close the gap between the official discourse and realities on the ground that was threatening Morocco's image at home and abroad, without losing face. Ultimately, the CNDH report allowed the bringing of international human rights norms into the national policy process while showcasing that the decision was a recommendation from within the Moroccan state, and not a result of international pressure or civil society advocacy: 'The CNDH had the legitimacy in front of civil society and authorities. When in 2013 the CNDH confirmed the civil society reports, it could be heard by the institutions' (M16-I26).

Despite Morocco's autocratic context, adherence to international human rights standards was ultimately key in triggering the adoption of a more liberal approach towards migrants. The bad publicity generated by civil society activism and the UN evaluation jeopardized Morocco's continued efforts to consolidate the regime as a 'liberal monarchy' at home, as well as in front of European and African partners. In this three-level game, liberal immigration reform was the most promising tool to relieve external and internal pressure and to pursue domestic and diplomatic priorities. As already outlined, the reform launched in September

2013 led to two regularization campaigns in 2014 and 2017 that granted legal status to over 50,000 migrants, introduced measures to integrate migrants into healthcare, education and labour markets, and kick-started legal work to reform the 2003 law and introduce new laws on asylum and human trafficking. It also stepped up Morocco's institutional capacity on immigration through the creation of a Directorate for Migration Affairs within the renamed Ministry in Charge of Moroccans Residing Abroad and Migration Affairs (MCMREAM). However, as shown next, the reform's progressive character is limited at the level of implementation, which has remained inconsistent and partial.

Inconsistent Implementation: The Power and Weakness of 'Royal Cards'

Given the discursive shift away from restriction and the administrative-legal decisions that accompanied the 2013 reform, what changed for migrants? On the one hand, respondents highlighted improvements on the ground: legal papers, also dubbed 'royal cards' (M16-D7), provided peace of mind and physical security to migrants in Moroccan cities. Round-ups of migrants and forced expulsions diminished in the years after 2013 (Norman 2016a; Tyszler 2015): 'There is no identity control anymore on the street, so you can circulate freely – with or without papers' (M16-I26). Access to basic services such as education or emergency healthcare improved. As a result, migrants have welcomed the reform: 'In churches where some members have benefited from the measure, one hears positive prayers for the host country: May Morocco be blessed! God bless the economy of Morocco! May He bless the King!' (Coyault 2015: 62–63).

On the other hand, respondents also emphasized that legal reform has remained incomplete and integration measures scattered. As one respondent summarized, 'Morocco has taken a step, but it is necessary that speeches and laws are now implemented, and this is not the reality for now. Morocco now needs to turn talk into action' (M17-D6). Indeed, the immigration reform is limited by the often symbolic character of announced measures, their limited applicability to regularized migrants, the preference of Moroccan authorities for ad-hoc administrative decisions, and the continued violence of state authorities in the border areas. These implementation dynamics are driven by Moroccan institutions' overarching goal of protecting the state interest and keeping maximum policymaking leverage within the executive power.

Symbolic Politics: Discourse over Action

First of all, while the 'royal cards' protected from expulsion, they did not necessarily facilitate migrants' access to employment or improved livelihoods, as many of the changes promised in 2013 had very limited effects. For instance, the exemption of regularized migrants from the labour market test, mediatized as a big step towards their labour market integration, only led to the validation of twenty-seven work contracts in 2015 and 2016 (MCMREAM 2016). In comparison, the accelerated procedure for foreign investors and rare competencies has benefited 277 people from October 2015 to March 2016 alone (MCMREAM 2016: 69–77). Also the short-term nature of the 'royal cards' – one-year immatriculation cards and not multi-annual residence permits – clashed with the promise of migrant integration, as it exposed regularized migrants to arbitrary renewal decisions by Moroccan street-level bureaucrats and increased their risk of falling back into irregularity after one year. In response to widespread criticism, and under civil society pressure, those regularized in 2017 were granted a three-year residence permit instead of a one-year one (Alioua, Ferrié and Reifeld 2018). However, access to permanent residency permits remains almost impossible for most migrants even after 2013. For Benjelloun (2018a: 96), the media coverage of the SNIA is thus 'disproportionate... given its content and its possible impact on the integration of migrants and refugees'.

Next to their limited effects, many of the changes promised in 2013 remained at the level of announcements, showcasing the importance of symbolic politics. Indeed, while specific policy proposals were highly mediatized, less attention was given to their follow-up and implementation. For instance, although healthcare coverage for regularized migrants was announced back in 2015, it has still not been implemented by the end of 2020: 'No migrant has benefited from the card. We are still waiting for the government to realize its promises' (M16-I11). In the same vein, while Moroccan Labour and Social Affairs Minister Abdeslam Seddiki announced in 2016 that all 'sub-Saharan' nationals are exempted from the ANAPEC procedure, my respondents could not confirm the implementation of this measure.[15]

A last indicator for the importance of symbolic politics is that the budget of the MCMREAM did not substantially increase after the launch of the migration reform (see Table 4.1). This means that the state has not allocated additional resources to implement the *National Strategy on Immigration and Asylum* (SNIA): 'The problem is that for the moment we work on our own funds, there are no additional funds for the SNIA' (M17-I1), one respondent said back in 2017.

Table 4.1. *Budget of Moroccan ministries, 2011–2016 (selection), in billions of dirham*

	2011	2012	2013	2014	2015	2016	2017	2018	2019
Ministry of Foreign Affairs	1.9	2	2.1	2.1	2.2	2.5	3.5	4.4	4
Ministry of Interior	20.2	21.5	22.2	21.2	21.8	23	26.8	28.2	31.3
Ministry of Justice	3.5	3.7	4	4.3	4.7	4.8	4.5	4.6	5
Ministry of Education and Higher Education	60.4	57.5	55.1	58.2	56.7	57	56.3	62.3	66.1
Ministry of Health	12.2	13.2	14	21.1	18.1	16.8	16.3	16.8	19.8
Ministry of Employment	1	1.3	1	0.35	0.5	0.5	0.5	0.5	0.6
Ministry for MRE (since 2014 also in charge of Migration Affairs)	0.401	0.439	0.391	0.426	0.482	0.544	-	-	-

Sources: National Finance Laws 2011–2019. The budget includes the operating budget and the investment budget.

With the downgrading of the MCMREAM into a Delegate Ministry in 2017 and its ultimate integration into the MoFA in 2019, this dynamic has only been exacerbated.

Policy Fragmentation and Migrant Categorization

A second limitation of the 2013 reform is that not all immigrants in Morocco could benefit from the integration measures, but that the creation of a new migrant category – the regularized migrant – fragmented legal frameworks. As one respondent criticized, '[the reform] targets only the 20,000 that have been regularized ... We were a bit disillusioned from the moment that the change was limited to one category' (M17-I17). As a result, different groups of migrants now have different sets of rights: while for some healthcare is free, for others, it remains a paid service; while some are subjected to a labour market test in their application for a work permit in Morocco, others are not.

This focus on regularized migrants has also shifted domestic and international attention away from irregular migrants and questions of rights violations towards regularized migrants and issues of migrant integration: 'No one is talking about irregular migrants anymore, all the focus is on those who got regularized' (M16-I23), one respondent lamented. This shift was not only discursive but has also affected the allocation of funding. While over the 2000s, CSOs were funded to provide support structures for migrants – such as the Caritas-run primary school, UNHCR-run legal assistance services, or healthcare projects of Doctors Without Borders (MSF) – the 2013 reform has reoriented parts of this funding towards state actors such as the MCMREAM, the MoH, or the Entraide Nationale (EN) in the expectation that state institutions would open their public services to migrants.

Such shift in priorities and funding has overshadowed the fact that other migrant groups, such as Syrian refugees, Filipino domestic workers, or Congolese irregular migrants, still face systematic rights violations: 'Now we are discouraged from talking about promoting migrants' rights, now we only talk about integration' (M16-I22). At the same time, this overt focus on regularized migrants did not dissolve but reinforced the informal privileges of European migrants in Morocco, as authorities continued to turn a blind eye to their irregular work and stay (see also Gazzotti 2021b). For instance, although not only European but also certain African countries are exempt from entry visa requirements by Morocco, different rights are attached to these visa exemptions in practice: 'Europeans can enter and exit without problems every three months and therefore work irregularly, stay irregularly. … But apart from businessmen, it's not easy for Africans to go back and forth' (M17-I17). Also access to permanent residency is racialized: 'In practice, a sub-Saharan migrant receives his residence permit after ten years, a European after five years. There is the law, and there is the practice' (M16-I26). Even more strikingly, when a Guinean citizen handed in his documents for a ten-year resident permit, 'an official of the Wilaya of Rabat replied that he could not qualify for it, as this permit was only intended for French' (GADEM 2010: 24). Testimonies such as these collected by the GADEM highlight the differential treatment of migrants according to race and nationality in Morocco.

Ad-Hoc Administrative Measures Over Legal Reform: A Choice for 'Pragmatism'[16]

A third dynamic limiting the impact of the 2013 reform is that Morocco's legal framework on immigration remains almost untouched by the time of writing, seven years after the reform was launched. The preference for ad-hoc administrative decisions rather than legal changes reveals

Moroccan authorities' intention to keep the migration reform as flexible – and thus as reversible – as possible.

A draft of Law 26-14 that would create a national asylum institution and refugee determination procedure was elaborated by the Interministerial Delegation for Human Rights (DIDH) in 2014. It was set on the governmental agenda in December 2015, but removed again after the government decided to postpone the decision: 'Officially, the government justified this decision in a statement by claiming there is a need to "deepen the study of this text due to its importance", sending back the draft law to the drawing board' (UNHCR 2015). Other sources suggest that the draft law was rewritten overnight by the Ministry of Interior (MoI) and is caught in inter-ministerial conflicts. Law 95-14 on immigration that was intended to reform the restrictive 2003 law has been even less in the spotlight. In nearly fifty sessions between January and July 2014, the inter-ministerial committee led by the DIDH elaborated a draft based on comparisons with immigration laws in Europe and Latin America. In 2017, work on both laws was taken up again. According to the MCMREAM, by October 2018, the law on asylum (now Law 66–17) has been finalized and awaits the initiation of the legislative process, while inter-ministerial consultations on the immigration law (now Law 72–17) are still ongoing (MCMREAM 2018: 92). However, there are no further details regarding the laws' content or timeline for enactment. Only *Law 27-14 relative to the fight against human trafficking* was enacted in 2016.

Discussing the reasons underlying these law-making dynamics, respondents pointed at the contradictory interests involved in the asylum and immigration laws, the political sensitivity of the issue, questions of regional security, and the fear of a 'pull effect': 'Morocco wants to be a model in the region, but they are also aware of the consequences if Morocco is the only country in the region with a functioning asylum system' (M16-I12). Interestingly, both state and civil society respondents emphasized the potential dangers of a functional asylum system:

> I asked friends within civil society why are you not saying anything so that they pass the asylum law, they said look we are civil society activists, but we feel that the asylum law is not in Morocco's national interest (M17-I5).

In contrast, respondents highlighted that the human trafficking law was successfully passed because it concerned not only foreigners but also Moroccans, raising its stakes for national policymakers. The law was also useful for Morocco's 'geopolitical rebordering': 'There is also a bit of marketing in it … all European countries have a law on trafficking, so Morocco also wanted to pass one' (M16-I15). Lastly, respondents emphasized that the victim/perpetrator framing central to the trafficking discourse has enabled advocates of the law to rally actors with different interests around it – those focusing on the protection of vulnerable people and those focusing on fighting organized crime and stepping up national security.

Given the deadlock on the asylum and immigration laws, the regularization procedure and expansion of migrants' rights were not enshrined in law. Instead, ministerial circulars created exemptions and privileges for specific migrant groups to advance socio-economic integration – selectively. For instance, only regularized migrants were exempt from the labour market test in their application for a work permit, and the enrolment of migrant children in Moroccan public schools initially targeted 'foreign children from sub-Saharan and Sahel countries'. Although the MCMREAM has de facto widened the circular's applicability to children of all nationalities – leading to the enrolment of around 5,000 to 7,000 migrant children every year (MCMREAM 2016: 31; MCMREAM 2018: 27) – the original circular has not been officially amended. Also, instead of reforming the law on associations that requires the president of an NGO to be a Moroccan citizen, an ad-hoc administrative decision permitted the legalization of migrant associations in 2014, an approach qualified by state respondents as 'pragmatic'.

By privileging administrative and informal solutions, authorities have opted for pragmatism, flexibility and ultimately arbitrariness in the new migration policy – what I have called 'policy ad-hocracy' elsewhere (Natter 2021a) and Norman (2016a) a 'policy of ambivalence'. This means that, as long as laws are not adopted, the 2013 reform remains vulnerable to restrictive backlashes. Talking about the regularizations, one respondent stressed, 'They occurred outside of the law, there is no legal basis for them. That's the fragility of it – it can be gone as quickly as it came' (M17-I4). In fact, the regularization of refugees was subject to such dynamics, as the BRA has suspended auditions and stopped granting refugee status between March 2017 and December 2018 without justification, leaving asylum seekers in an uncertain legal situation.[17] Also, the regularization of refugees excluded Syrians recognized by UNHCR, as Moroccan authorities decided not to rule on them for security reasons. Instead, 5,500 Syrians received residence permits through the 2014 regularization campaign (Bailleul 2015; Sidi Hida 2015), which offers them a much lower protection level than the one they would be entitled to as refugees. Thus, although the regularization of refugees showcases Morocco's efforts to 'nationalize the refugee status' (M17-D8), this also meant that 'people now have to deal with the Moroccan state' (M17-I10), with its arbitrariness and national security priorities. Fears of a more general backlash on migrant rights have also resurfaced in late 2018, when the renewal of residence permits became more difficult, according to civil society and migrant representatives.[18] The legal void surrounding liberal immigration policy measures is thus one of the biggest challenges to the sustainability of Morocco's migration reform.

Continued State Violence on the Ground

A consequence of symbolic politics, legal fragmentation and policy ad-hocracy is that although the regularizations and tacit integration measures developed since 2013 attest to a change in Morocco's approach to migrants, improvements on the ground are largely limited to Moroccan cities and overshadowed by continued violence towards migrants in border regions (Natter 2015a). On 10 February 2015, one day after the MoI officially closed its first-ever regularization campaign, Moroccan authorities launched their by then most extensive removal operation in the north of Morocco. Approximately 1,200 irregular migrants were arrested in the Gourougou forest near Nador and Melilla and transported to improvised detention facilities in the south and centre of Morocco. Civil society mobilization and the legal intervention by a judge from Casablanca ultimately led to the release of detained migrants after several weeks.[19] In a similar way, CSOs observed an increase in violence against migrants in the north of Morocco, as well as the start of a series of arbitrary detentions of migrants in the Casablanca airport waiting zone in parallel to the announcement of the second regularization campaign in December 2016 (GADEM and Anafé 2017: 24–40).

More generally, the 2013 reform did not end state agents' violence towards irregular migrants but shifted its focus (FIDH/GADEM 2015): 'The hot zone now is the Northern border, around Tangiers' (M16-I26).[20] In the past, migrants arrested in cities were expelled across the border to Algeria or Mauritania; since 2013, irregular migrants are detained in the border areas and brought to cities in the south and centre of Morocco: 'Another system has been put in place: expulsions have been replaced by internal displacements' (M17-I10). Police violence against migrants in border regions, such as destructions of migrant settlements and internal displacements, reached new momentum in summer 2018, when around 6,500 migrants, including some with regular residence permits, were rounded up and internally displaced from northern to southern Morocco, as harshly condemned by Moroccan and international human rights actors (GADEM 2018; UN-HRC 2019).[21]

Securitarian tendencies have also affected civil society activities in Morocco, even when they do not have a clear policy advocacy component. Most symbolically, in November 2018, local authorities in Tangiers forbid the ninth edition of the Migrant'scène festival – an annual cultural event celebrating multiculturalism through art – last-minute without justification. Abderrahman Tlemçani, president of GADEM and one of the organizers, asks, 'Is this in connection with the latest reports in which we pointed out what is happening in the police stations in Tangier? We don't know.'[22] More recently, detentions and expulsions have also targeted migrants in the south-west of Morocco around Laâyoune and Dakhla. Except during the COVID-19 lockdown in March–April 2020, such practices are still commonplace across Morocco.[23]

Morocco's immigration policy is thus neither characterized by linear progress, nor by a back-and-forth between restriction and liberalization, but by a constant duality, as one migrant leader I interviewed pointed out: 'The Migration Minister says that Morocco wants to be a model country on migration. But one week later, the security forces beat up migrants at the border.' Yet, this duality is not contradictory but complementary: on the one hand, Morocco mobilizes an open integration discourse towards migrants who show a willingness to settle in Morocco, comply with the rules, and integrate to satisfy domestic demands for human rights and advance its Africa policy. On the other hand, Morocco reinforces control activities at the borders and continues to frame irregular migrants as outlaws and criminals, keeping EU policy interests in mind. In the words of one of my respondents,

The Moroccan vision is simple: We will integrate those who are here, but we will make sure to arrest those that try to pass through. ... A human approach for those who choose Morocco, but those who want to profit from Morocco to transit, they are still cast as enemies (M17-I12).

Shifting Configurations of Immigration Policy Drivers in Morocco

This chapter has dissected the origins, drivers and implementation of the 2013 reform. It showed that the Moroccan monarchy has launched the 2013 immigration reform to portray itself as a 'liberal monarchy' and hereby satisfy potentially conflicting demands within a complex three-level game, in which immigration is both politicized domestically as a human rights issue and diplomatically in Morocco's relations with European and African partners. Indeed, the reform safeguarded the regime's domestic legitimacy in front of more progressive parts of

Moroccan society – who saw migrants' rights as intrinsic to Morocco's democratization agenda and whose voice was bolstered after 2011. At the same time, Morocco instrumentalized the reform in its diplomatic relations with Europe and Africa to advance economic cooperation and foreign policy priorities such as the Western Sahara question. Ultimately, the improvement of migrants' rights after 2013 has thus paradoxically been the outcome of an authoritarian consolidation strategy.

As the discussion on the colonial origins and post-colonial developments of Moroccan immigration policy showed, this is nothing new: be it selective migration facilitations in the 1960s, arbitrary refugee determination in the 1990s, the 2003 restrictive law or the 2013 reform, Morocco's immigration policy is, since its inception, driven by regime legitimation strategies, as well as foreign policy interests, rather than by national-electoral considerations. This does not mean that other factors have not played a role: in particular, Morocco's history as an emigration country has been a key component in pro-migrant advocacy both from civil society and from within the Moroccan state apparatus. Also, while the King's Africa strategy and overall modernization agenda, as well as domestic political developments since the 2000s, were long-term drivers, the necessity to adhere to international norms (in this case, the UN Convention on the Rights of Migrant Workers) created a window of opportunity for the King to launch the policy reform in September 2013.

These findings on the central role of geopolitics, international norms, state formation legacies and the state interest in driving policy change in Morocco showcase the relevance of international relations and historical-culturalist approaches, as well as institutionalist and globalization theories for making sense of Moroccan immigration policy developments. Yet, they also exemplify the limits of political economy or legalistic explanations that dominate accounts of liberal policy change in democracies.

Ultimately, despite the overall discourse of progress and change, many continuities with the pre-2013 immigration policy remain. While the 2013 reform fundamentally reshaped Morocco's immigration regime in terms of discourse and overall approach, with substantial changes for migrants' physical security and socio-economic opportunities, the declared humanist foundation of the policy has been jeopardized by continued violence towards irregular migrants in the border areas. Also, inconsistency and a lack of implementation, as well as a preference for ad-hoc measures instead of legal changes that would enshrine migrants' rights, limit the extent of the change and attest to the highly symbolic nature of the 2013 reform. The main change since the 2013 reform is thus a matter of focus: while Morocco's restrictive policy has been mitigated by informal, selective openings in the past, since 2013, Morocco's official, welcoming policy is jeopardized by selective state violence towards irregular migrants.

For Bensaâd (2015: 254), 'the persistence of police violence and arbitrary measures of expulsion probably reflect[s] the contradictory tendencies within Moroccan power on this issue [immigration] as well as on political openness in general'. These internal contradictions within the state stand at the centre of the next chapter, which dissects inter-actor dynamics within Morocco's immigration policy field. In particular, it showcases how institutional stickiness, organizational cultures, as well as overarching regime legitimation goals have shaped immigration policymaking at the intersection of state, civil society and the international sphere.

5 The Illiberal Paradox of Autocratic Policymaking

A Changing Cartography of Actors in Morocco's Immigration Policy Field

Over the years, Morocco's decision-making landscape on immigration and the power relations between institutional, international and civil society actors became increasingly complex. Before 2005, there was minimal involvement from Moroccan state actors on immigration, and the presence of civil society and international actors was limited: the central actor was the Ministry of Interior (MoI), who adopted a purely securitarian approach towards immigration in view of both satisfying European demands and advancing its interest of increasing population surveillance across the Moroccan territory. The Ministry of Foreign Affairs (MoFA), albeit nominally housing the Bureau of Refugees and Apatrides (BRA), was disengaged on the issue except for the immigration of students from Western and Central Africa. Civil society activism, emerging since the late 1990s and dominated by religious actors and Moroccan diaspora organizations, remained small-scale and humanitarian in outlook. They were supported by international civil society such as Migreurop, CIMADE or Amnesty International on an ad-hoc basis. UNHCR and IOM were present in Morocco but not active on immigration issues.

After the Ceuta and Melilla events in 2005, new actors entered the Moroccan immigration policy field: first, with the emergence of GADEM, migrant-led organizations and the growing interest for immigration from established Moroccan human rights organizations, local civil society efforts multiplied and shifted from humanitarian work towards political advocacy, supported by international NGOs. Second, international organizations stepped up their engagement in Morocco, with IOM and UNHCR establishing formal headquarters in Rabat in 2006 and 2007, respectively, becoming more vocal politically and expanding their cooperation with both Moroccan state and civil society actors. Geopolitically, while the European Union and European countries such as France and Spain remained central for discussions on immigration, the King's pro-active Africa policy meant that West African interests on immigration were introduced as a new variable in immigration politics. Lastly, within the Moroccan state, new actors and lines of division appeared: while the MoI remained dominant, local education and health authorities started to engage with immigrants and migrant support associations, mostly in Rabat, and the 2011 Constitution propelled the CNDH to the centre of immigration debates.

After 2013, the field has become more crowded at all levels, increasing complexity and ambiguity in immigration policymaking. Most importantly, the King has entered the picture, followed by the CNDH and its president Driss el Yazami as central figures of Morocco's immigration reform. Within the Moroccan administration, the monopoly of the MoI has not been fundamentally challenged, but the creation of the Migration Ministry (MCMREAM), the reactivation of the BRA within the MoFA, as well as the involvement of other ministries (Health, Education, Labour) and institutions (CNDH, DIDH, EN, ANAPEC) for the implementation of the SNIA have complicated power dynamics within the state and obstructed legal reform on immigration. In parallel, civil society work on immigration burgeoned in response to domestic and international funding opportunities – to the extent that an overview of actors became almost impossible. In particular, Moroccan civil society actors working on education, women's rights, youth or poverty have started to integrate immigrants into their work, as have Moroccan labour unions. This mushrooming civil society, however, is facing challenges such as fragmentation of interests, internal competition for funds or co-optation attempts by the state. Thus, while relations between civil society and Moroccan state actors multiplied, they often remain conflictual or dominated by mistrust. Finally, international organizations, European diplomatic representations or development agencies stepped up their activities after 2013, providing funding and capacity-building for Moroccan institutions aligned with their interests on immigration control and for civil society actors to advance migrant integration on the ground. This fitted both Europe's agenda to keep migrants in neighbouring countries, as well as Morocco's agenda to attract international funding for migrant integration. In parallel, Morocco actively pursued a migration diplomacy to showcase itself as a model for migration management in African and international diplomatic circles – with success.

The following sections delve into the power dynamics characterizing Moroccan immigration policymaking within and among this plethora of state, civil society and international actors. They showcase that while policy processes highlighting the role of domestic politics approaches or legal actors seem indeed subject to a 'regime effect', policy processes central to bureaucratic politics approaches or international relations theories of immigration policymaking are also at play in autocratic Morocco.

Dynamics Within the Moroccan State[1]

Until the late 2000s, the involvement of the Moroccan state on immigration was limited to the securitarian approach of the MoI, as well as negotiations between the MoFA and European or African countries regarding specific aspects of migration facilitation or migration control. Increasing domestic and international criticism exposed the dissonance between Morocco's overall restrictive immigration policy and the King's declared political vision of a 'liberal monarchy'. The previous chapter has shown how the 2013 liberal immigration reform has not only emerged out of Morocco's monarchical regime but also consolidated it. This section dissects the dynamics underpinning this illiberal paradox. On the one hand, the institutional set-up of the Moroccan state and the room for manoeuvre of specific pro-migrant CSOs were instrumentalized to foster the image of Mohammed VI as a 'liberal monarch'. On the other hand, dissenting opinions were silenced and partisan polarization circumvented by elevating immigration policy into a national undertaking. This showcases the fundamentally different role civil society and political parties play in autocracies. Yet, while the royal impetus assured the adherence of key state actors to the reform, it did not prevent inter-institutional conflicts and inconsistent implementation well known from the institutionalist immigration policy literature on democracies.

Consolidating the 'Liberal Monarchy'

For all my Moroccan respondents, the centrality of the King in initiating the 2013 reform was undeniable: 'If there had not been the royal impulse, there would not be this policy' (M16-I23). Interestingly, however, the policy duality characterizing the reform, with violence continuing alongside the regularization and integration programs, did not challenge the progressive image of the King as a 'liberal monarch'. This is because the set-up of the Moroccan state – with the King and his entourage on one side and the administration on the other – has allowed to cast progressive developments as royal initiatives and to blame the reform's shortcomings on the administration. At the same time, the room for manoeuvre and public profile of specific actors – the CNDH, close to the Royal Palace, but also CSOs such as the GADEM or the Democratic

Organization of Immigrant Labour (ODTI) – was strategically increased to ensure the legitimacy and diplomatic success of the reform.

A 'Good Cop/Bad Cop' Dynamic Between the King and the Administration. First of all, the immigration reform was characterized by a 'good cop/bad cop' dynamic, in which the King was portrayed as guardian of the reform's liberal spirit, while other state actors – political parties, the MoI, security forces, the administration – were made responsible for violent backlashes, inconsistencies and reactionary tendencies (see also Ferrié and Alioua 2018: 20–21). The outcome is a split image of the state that ultimately legitimizes the monarchical institution in Morocco. As one of my respondents summarized:

> The migration dossier has profited from the same mechanism as all reforms in Morocco: … The King is the driving force behind the migration policy – from him come the big gestures, the big promises, but the implementation is left to the MoI. And there are defensive reflexes in the administration that mitigate these big gestures and make sure that they don't become too dangerous for the state (M17-I4).

The regularization process is exemplary for this dynamic: foreigners' bureaus were created by the MoI in each of the eighty-three prefectures across the Moroccan territory to register regularization claims. Local regularization commissions, composed of Moroccan security services and police representatives, as well as two civil society representatives appointed by the CNDH, were set up to rule on applications (MoI and MCMREAM 2013). Three thousand civil servants were mobilized to carry out the regularization (Parliament 2014). Most applications were rejected at first instance because of insufficient residency or work proofs (PNPM 2014). In September 2014, Migration Minister Anis Birou blamed the administration for not having turned the regularization into a success: 'The number of regularization requests is below our expectations. This is probably due to the difficulties illegal migrants have in providing the administration, sometimes a little too fussy, the documents attesting to the length of their stay' (quoted in: Benjelloun 2018b: 46).

The good cop/bad cop dynamic also became evident during the 'Figuig refugee crisis' in April 2017, when forty-one Syrian refugees were left without food and shelter at the Moroccan–Algerian border, as both Moroccan and Algerian security forces refused to accept them on their territory.[2] On 20 June, World Refugee Day, the King intervened by granting these Syrian refugees the right to enter Morocco, an 'exceptional' decision 'dictated by humanist values', as the press release of the Royal Cabinet specifies.[3] Episodes such as these portray the King as a 'saviour' of vulnerable groups and guardian of human rights in a repressive national environment.

Such distinction between King and security actors is also visible in civil society reactions to recurrent violence against migrants: in demonstrations for more migrants' rights in Rabat, for instance, one almost always finds migrants holding up portraits of the King. And speaking about the mass displacements from northern to southern Morocco in summer 2018, one interviewed migrant from Côte d'Ivoire concluded, 'There is a big difference between official discourse and reality. We see that the King wants that we have our rights, but it is not always easy with the authorities here.'[4]

The CNDH: Monarchy's Poster Child? A second public actor that has been crucial for Morocco's consolidation as a 'liberal monarchy' is the National Council for Human Rights (CNDH). Created in 2011 as a successor to the Consultative Council on Human Rights (CCDH) that had existed since 1990, it became the institutional safeguard of the migration reform by serving as a corrective to administrative restriction when needed and acting as a mediator between the state and civil society.

Indeed, the CNDH redressed administrative developments when things did not go as announced – such as in the regularization campaign. As just mentioned, the local regularization committees chaired by the MoI and Moroccan security services first rejected a considerable number of applicants. The appeals could have taken place in front of an administrative tribunal, but in June 2014, a National Appeals Commission was created under the presidency of the CNDH. Composed of ministerial representatives, as well as ten civil society and migrant representatives (CNDH 2014), it functioned as a counterweight to the local regularization commissions dominated by security concerns. For respondents, this institutional set-up was a conscious choice:

Those who designed the policy created safeguards such as the National Appeals Commission that enabled the solving of 80% of the cases, but with the idea of finding an honourable way for all parties involved (M17-I12).

In fact, the creation of the National Appeals Commission offered room for alternative interpretations of the regularization criteria, such as deciding to regularize all women and children regardless of their length of stay and to accept alternative proof of work and length of stay, without infringing upon the power of the MoI. As one commission member said, 'The aim was to regularize as many people as possible' (M16-I26). Ultimately, the CNDH was key in regularizing the majority of applicants during the 2014 and 2017 regularization campaigns,[*] thereby turning the campaign into a successful geopolitical marketing tool.

The CNDH has also become the principal mediator between state actors and civil society, not without ambiguities, as respondents have highlighted: 'CSOs are obliged to pass through the CNDH to reach institutions with their advocacy' (M16-I3). Indeed, the CNDH functions as a 'gatekeeper' for civil society to access the Moroccan state apparatus, indirectly controlling which civil society voices are heard – and which not. As respondents have highlighted, certain CSOs such as GADEM, the OMDH or the ODTI had already close ties to members of the CNDH before the 2013 reform and could now capitalize on these relations to channel their demands to the centre of the state. Other migrant associations or human rights organizations lamented such selective partnerships and limited access to the CNDH. Ultimately, however, as highlighted by Üstübici (2016: 312), 'despite criticism that it is a state agency with closed membership and a lack of independence, CNDH has been a crucial channel for the lobbying efforts of civil society'.

Due to the high-level profile of its presidents[†] and their close relationships with the royal cabinet, the CNDH can act as an agenda-setter or influence decision-making within the Moroccan state based on select civil society input. As interviews have shown, interpersonal and informal negotiations are a crucial tool for the CNDH to achieve change, rather than direct advocacy or outspoken criticism of state actions. Nonetheless, the 'red lines' of the regime also constrain the CNDH's influence: 'There are things that cannot be done because they are not ripe enough at the institutional or societal level – things like nationality or religious issues' (M17-I17). The CNDH's capacity for influence, therefore, also depends on civil society – national and international – to continue its advocacy for migrants' rights.

Room for Manoeuvre for Civil Society. The third actor that fostered Morocco's image as a progressive, rights-respective state and hereby paradoxically strengthened its autocratic regime was indeed Morocco's flourishing domestic civil society. As respondents highlighted,

---

[*] The 2017 regularization used the same criteria as those initially devised in 2014. As a consequence, the Appeals Commission once again relaxed the criteria in March 2018, particularly for non-accompanied minors and foreigners with a secondary school education. See HuffPostMaghreb, *Le Maroc assouplit ses critères de régularisation des étrangers clandestins*, 28 March 2018.

[†] Driss el Yazami was nominated president of the CNDH in 2011, upon its creation. In December 2018, Amina Bouayach – a Moroccan civil society activist and political figure since the 1980s – succeeded him.

one key reason for the relative freedom of Morocco's pro-immigrant civil society in the 2000s was its convergence with the royal agenda. Back in 2011, one civil society respondent stressed that 'the King's will is indisputable in opening the door to people who advocate for a new Morocco .... There is an impetus from above to open up for influences from below' (M11-I4). This explains why migrant associations such as the CMSM and CSOs such as AFVIC or GADEM enjoyed relatively broad freedoms already before 2013, despite operating without legal status: 'That's not how things are normally done in Morocco – an illegal association in Morocco, they're normally imprisoned, they're stopped' (M17-I5). By granting CSOs visibility in the public sphere and showcasing the respect of political freedoms, the monarchy consolidated its domestic legitimacy. Simultaneously, however, this strengthened control over the human rights discourse and thereby reduced the risk that civil society activism could jeopardize the monarchy.

These dynamics were reinforced after 2013, as the monarchy needed civil society involvement to successfully implement the regularization and to showcase the democratic character of the migration reform internationally. In fact, many irregular migrants were at first sceptical of the regularization, fearing a trap through which Moroccan authorities would lure them into providing their identity and fingerprints just to expel them more efficiently afterwards. The success of the regularization thus depended on CSOs and migrant leaders to vouch for the sincerity of Morocco's regularization offer (Benjelloun 2018b: 46–47). As the head of the Directorate of Migration Affairs at the MCMREAM said at a conference in March 2017, 'During the first regularization, there was a certain suspicion from the migrants, it's after the intermediation by civil society that this has changed' (M17-D8). Migrant associations led awareness-raising campaigns within their respective national or local communities and encouraged migrants to legalize their status. For instance, the ODTI distributed flyers summarizing the regularization criteria and providing instructions on how to submit a regularization claim (see Figure 5.1). Had migrant associations not played this facilitator role, the regularization campaign would have been unsuccessful – both in terms of its actual impact on migrants' lives and its symbolic geopolitical power.

These dynamics showcase the extent to which the Moroccan monarchy is dependent on a critical – although not too critical – civil society to fortify its liberal image. However, this dependency between the regime and civil society is reciprocal: as shown later, CSOs also need the monarchy as protection from the security apparatus that regularly jeopardizes civil society activities.

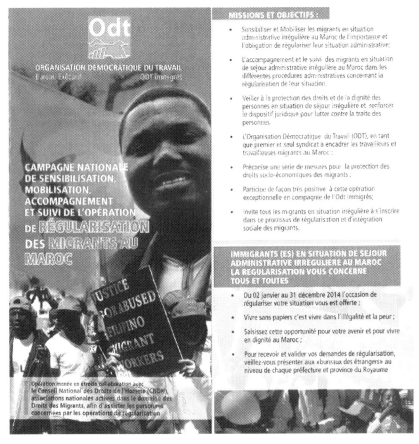

Figure 5.1 ODTI flyer from 2014 encouraging migrants to regularize.
Source: Photo made by the author

The Administration's Internal Dynamics

In parallel to dynamics strengthening the royal institution, the 2013 reform reinforced old and triggered new dynamics within the Moroccan administration that are well known from the institutionalist immigration policy literature. Although respondents regularly compared Moroccan bureaucracy to a 'machine' set in motion by the King's intervention – 'in Morocco, as soon as it's royal, it progresses, everyone runs' (M16-I16) – such a mechanical understanding of Morocco's political system, with little agency and room for manoeuvre for actors other than the King, is inaccurate. While the 'royal impulse' guaranteed a generalized dynamism on immigration within the administration, it did not prevent inter-institutional conflicts and contradictions in the way the royal vision was translated by different parts of the administration: in fact, central- and local-level institutions appropriated the reform for their own agendas, approaching immigration according to their respective institutional interests. Also in autocracies, then, immigration is just another policy area that is subject to institutional conflicts over power and resources within the state.

Turf Wars and Institutional Worldviews. First, the 2013 reform reinforced the long-standing turf wars between the MoI and the MoFA that have characterized the emigration dossier since the early 1990 and, more recently, also the immigration dossier. As El Qadim (2015: 207) writes on emigration policies,

Institutions are created, restructured, removed, recreated, giving rise to tensions, competitions and compromises in defining the competencies and budgets of each of them. If these administrations are in principle subjected to a national objective that seems largely depending on the royal will, the institutional diversity and tensions that span the state domain point at the role of administration in the definition of Moroccan migration policies.

Indeed, the Ministry for Moroccans Residing Abroad (MRE) created in 1989 was downgraded to a department in 1997 and re-created as a ministry under the umbrella of the MoFA in 2002. In 2007, it was once more detached from the MoFA, attached to the Prime Minister and granted a budget of its own (Sahraoui 2015), before being transformed into the MCMREAM in the wake of the 2013 reform. In parallel, questions of border controls, irregular immigration and emigration have been in the hands of the MoI since the creation of the Directorate of Migrations and Border Surveillance (DMST) in December 2003.

Such institutional dynamics have also affected the immigration reform, particularly the asylum law. As respondents highlight, the central negotiation point is the institutional tutelage of the future asylum office, fuelling conflict between the MoI and its historical opponent, the MoFA: while the MoFA argues that the new institution should be under its tutelage because of the historical attachment of the BRA to Foreign Affairs, the MoI refers to the situation in many European countries, where asylum agencies are generally attached to MoIs. The fact that in April 2017, the MCMREAM was downgraded to a Delegate Ministry and attached to the MoFA as 'a way to please the MoFA' (M17-D10) suggests that the MoFA is successful in expanding its powers on the migration dossier.

Alongside the deepening conflict between MoI and MoFA, the institutional set-up of the 2013 reform – with different aspects of the policy entrusted to different ministries: the regularization to the MoI, the work on refugees to the MoFA, the elaboration of the legal framework to the DIDH and the implementation of the SNIA to the MCMREAM – guaranteed that royal intentions would be appropriated by each actor within their own logic of action, based on their sectoral interests and institutional identities: 'Each institution had a different approach towards migrants and also followed a different path' (M17-I17). In particular, the security perspectives of the Ministries of Interior and Justice regularly clashes with the humanitarian perspectives of the Ministries of Health and Education. An MoJ respondent highlighted this: 'We at the Ministry of Justice have a repressive vision: security, penalties. Other departments, health, education, have a human approach, a more social vision.' Indeed, the MoH action plan targets migrants regardless of their legal status because of the imperative to secure public health, and the public service provider Entraide Nationale (EN) has opened its services to both regular and irregular migrants. This created open conflict with the MoI, as one respondent from the EN recounted:

In one of the steering committees I said that we opened our centres to all migrants whether they are regularized or not regularized, and the person of the MoI tells me: you do not have the right to welcome unregulated people. I said: ... I work with human beings; I do not care if they are regularized or not. ... The EN does humanitarian work.

These inter-institutional dynamics are not new but have been accelerated and deepened by the reform. Back in 2012, respondents already highlighted that 'institutions are in a state of conflict and each ministry establishes its own strategy' (M11-I8). As suggested by the typology advanced in this book, immigration priorities of specific ministries might be closer to each other across countries than approaches of different ministries within one country, suggesting that specific institutional dynamics are triggered by the nature of immigration policies rather than by regime specificities.

Policy Incoherence and Inter-Ministerial Coordination Problems. Alongside turf wars and diverging institutional visions, policy incoherence and a lack of coordination characterize Moroccan immigration policymaking. The most important dynamic limiting the reform process is that the discursive adherence of the entire Moroccan administration to the immigration reform has not been matched with increased institutional dynamism on the ground. In particular, while the MCMREAM has been assigned a coordinating role by the King, it faces resistance from other ministries to integrate immigrants into their sectoral policies.

To implement the SNIA, the MCMREAM is dependent on the willingness of other ministers to enact changes within their domains. Yet, without financial incentives attached, these ministers have shown little enthusiasm to implement the changes announced in the SNIA: 'The MCMREAM does not have the power to impact line ministries with big portfolios, large resources, and a lot of staff, such as the MoI, the MoL, the MoE' (M16-I16). Such disinterest is also visible in the fact that the civil servants from the MCMREAM are faced with constantly changing interlocutors in other ministries. Talking about cooperation with the MoH, one MCMREAM civil servant recounts,

> At the beginning, we worked with one department [in the MoH], and we made progress, but then, no, it's not that department anymore, we have to start over again with another department. Now it's already the third department, so that's difficult (M17-I14).

The low numbers of migrants concerned, and the fact that healthcare services for Moroccans are also insufficient, partly explains this low interest for the migration dossier: 'The priority is the Moroccan population. Take for instance health: hospitals in Morocco are still catastrophic ... So migrants' health is not a priority' (M16-I16). Next to disinterest, the MCMREAM is also facing active resistance towards some of its initiatives. This leads to situations in which efforts by the MCMREAM are cancelled out, for instance, by the MoI, as UNHCR Director Jean-Paul Cavalieri describes, for example, in the case of refugees:

> That's where we touch upon the paradox and the painful side of the situation. UNHCR, the MCMREAM, and the ANAPEC invest heavily in the employability of refugees. ... On the other hand, these employable refugees are blocked at the delivery of their residence permit.[5]

Caught in the middle between MoI, MoFA and other large ministries, the MCMREAM did not have the institutional powers to effectively coordinate the implementation of the National Strategy on Immigration and Asylum (SNIA). As a result, the governance structure set up to implement the SNIA has become dysfunctional. The downgrading of the MCMREAM into a Delegate Ministry in 2017 and its ultimate integration into the MoFA in 2019 have further reduced the institutional power of those who are in charge of Morocco's immigration strategy.

Centre-Periphery Dynamics. Lastly, the implementation of the 2013 reform is also structured by the gap between the (geographical and power) centre of the state and its periphery, which creates leverage for individual bureaucrats and local authorities. Although ministerial respondents assured me of the effective communication within their institutions – 'we give an order, and it's executed' (M16-I24) – policy interpretations diverge between high-level civil servants and street-level bureaucrats within the same ministry: 'Everyone understands the minister's circular in his own way' (M17-I1). In addition, policemen, doctors or school administrators were often unaware of decisions taken by their ministry in Rabat: 'The policemen or border customs officer in Oujda has no idea of what is going on in Rabat at the central level in his ministry' (M16-I15).

As a result, the 2013 reform is implemented inconsistently across regions: 'In Rabat, the law is not the same as in Marrakesh or Tangier' (M16-I10). Migrants were, for instance, required to hand in work or housing contracts for the renewal of their residence permit in Tangiers or Salé, but not in Rabat. As Diallo (2016) showed in his study of decision-making practices on residence permit applications in Morocco, 'each local service claims the monopoly of administrative know-how in the process of selecting those who are entitled to a residence permit'. Access to work, healthcare or education also varies across the territory: 'You find schools where they accept migrants and others where they don't accept anyone' (M17-I1). Despite the centrality of the Moroccan administration, local bureaucrats therefore do have room for manoeuvre in the governance of foreigners.

Such centre-periphery dynamics can also be consciously mobilized by regional or local authorities to advance agendas that might not be supported by the central government. While such dynamics mostly go unnoticed, the incident in 2019 involving Moroccan bus companies brought the role of regional authorities to the fore: in October, Moroccan bus companies suddenly required 'Africans' – as written on the improvised posters fixed to bus station counters, but de facto targeting Black people – to show valid residence permits to board long-distance buses. The incident triggered large-scale civil society outrage and was condemned by the CNDH, as well as Moroccan parliamentarians, particularly when internal documents revealed that bus companies were acting on the request of regional transport and security authorities that explicitly sought to limit freedom of movement of potential irregular migrants through such informal privatization of internal migration control.[6] The internal dynamics of the Moroccan administration – both within and between ministries at the central and local level – are thus crucial to understand how immigration policy is performed on the ground.

Immigration as a 'National Undertaking': The Absence of Party Politics

Alongside the monarchy and the Moroccan administration, a third state actor deserves attention – not for its actions, but for its passivity: political parties and the Parliament. In stark contrast to dynamics across democracies in Europe and North America, until now, immigration is not subject to Moroccan partisan dynamics, as the King has depolarized immigration by elevating it into the royal realm. Fieldwork insights indeed suggest that the royal intervention has transformed immigration into a 'national undertaking' (M17-I5) that stands above party politics. As a result, open discontent with the 2013 reform is frowned upon and has made immigration relatively immune to exploitation by domestic political actors. According to one Moroccan deputy,

> From the moment that the King says it's a state policy, we cannot have a discourse like the European far-right here in Morocco. The fact that the policy has been initiated by the King prevents immigration from being politicized for electoral ends.

Indeed, elected politicians or party leaders have refrained from polarizing around immigration because it falls in the realm of royal prerogatives and has one of the 'untouchable topics' (M17-I6). When a Moroccan deputy criticized the immigration policy in May 2017 by claiming that 'Moroccan cities are now polluted by sub-Saharan migrants',[7] this triggered a wave of political and media outrage. Similarly, when in May 2019, a deputy from the Islamist PJD representing the southern city of Tiznit lamented the negative social impact of 'sub-Saharan' African migrants in a written question to the MoI, the PJD leadership intercepted the written question before reaching the Minister of Interior, stating that such language drawing from far-right European parties was 'incompatible with the principles of the party'.[8]

Also, there is no electoral advantage for Moroccan political parties to politicize immigration given the limited number of immigrants: 'They don't matter, how many immigrants do we have? 80,000? So what, compared to 33 million Moroccans' (M17-I6). Migration is thus not central to public debates on the labour market or social policy – it is seen as a foreign policy issue that does not affect domestic politics. This also explains why the MCMREAM is not a sought-after ministerial position: 'This ministry is not a bonus, but a burden ... it has no political weight and cannot provide any direct services to the population' (M17-I14). The progressive integration of the MCMREAM into the MoFA since 2017 has only reinforced this.

Immigration policy continuity is thus largely guaranteed throughout elections: 'Even if the Minister of Migration changes, the content and priorities remain the same, it is a national priority' (M17-I19). This highlights the imperative nature of the King's will over potential domestic politics dynamics such as partisan instrumentalization of immigration. As shown next, however, the absence of meaningful party politics means that the politicization of immigration in Morocco has been mainly channelled through civil society activism.

Civil Society Dynamics

Despite Morocco's autocratic political context, civil society accusations of migrant rights' violations throughout the 2000s played a crucial role in preparing the ground for immigration reform. Yet, while the 2013 liberal reform fundamentally reshaped civil society activism, it has not univocally strengthened civil society's place in political processes. Instead, it has made its role more ambiguous. On the one hand, CSOs have consolidated their position in Morocco's immigration policy landscape since 2013. In the past, Morocco's pro-immigration CSOs operated without authorization and assured their political survival through support from abroad. With the regularization of CSOs and migrant associations, civil society has become an institutionalized political actor, and increased interaction with state institutions offered more scope for influencing public policies directly or indirectly. Also, the heightened international attention to migrants' rights in Morocco has created more opportunities for civil society to point at inconsistencies and denounce backlashes. On the other hand, civil society increasingly struggled to reposition itself in response to Morocco's 'liberal' agenda. The mushrooming of CSOs as a result of political and funding opportunities has triggered market dynamics, such as growing competition among CSOs and a fragmentation of the civil society agenda. At the same time, public funding and the integration of CSOs into certain decision-making processes has led to its partial cooptation and silencing. While civil society was clearly positioned against state authorities in the past, denouncing their securitarian approach and violence, after 2013, the involvement of a growing number of state actors on immigration has diffused responsibilities for continued migrant rights' violations and forced civil society to adjust its advocacy strategies.

The Civil Society 'Market'

After 2013, civil society work on immigration in Morocco mushroomed as CSOs took advantage of domestic and international funding opportunities: the Swiss Development Cooperation (SDC) that had supported Caritas and GADEM for years increased their funding, and new international development actors arrived, such as Belgian and American foundations, or the German Development Agency (GIZ): 'Migration has become a courted, sexy subject, there are plenty of funders who desperately want to work on migration' (M16-I16). In parallel, Moroccan authorities sought to diversify their civil society interlocutors beyond the 'usual suspects' (the GADEM, Caritas, a few migrant organizations, and European NGOs). To 'moroccanize' civil society around immigration, the MCMREAM started to issue yearly calls for proposals in 2014 for social and humanitarian assistance or cultural integration projects. 'We have associations working in neighbourhoods with women, children, etc., so the idea was to infuse migration into these projects. ... We wanted to work with Moroccan society – it was a choice,' one respondent within the MCMREAM said. In 2014, sixty projects were funded with a total of nearly 25 million dirhams [around 2.95 million USD]; in 2015, sixty-four projects with a total of 11.6 million dirhams [around 1.36 million USD] (MCMREAM 2016: 115–16).*

While one respondent highlighted that such national funding opportunities are 'of course a control reflex' (M17-I4), they allowed CSOs to start or expand their work with migrants: by 2016, the MCMREAM listed twenty-seven CSOs specialized in migration and sixty-four generalist CSOs who have expanded their work to migrants (MCMREAM 2016).† CSOs also increasingly joined forces within collectives: in 2016, the Civil Council for the Fight Against All Forms of Discrimination was created by fourteen CSOs; in 2018, the Platform of Sub-Saharan Associations and Communities in Morocco (ASCOMS) was launched by initially seventeen members; and in 2019, a civil society collective of six associations was created to support of victims of human trafficking.

However, increasing funding opportunities also triggered market dynamics, as civil society actors increasingly competed for funds. In the words of one of my respondents, 'The new migration policy has created a wave of project hunters' (M16-I9). This competition has materialized along four dividing lines: between Moroccan and international CSOs, as, according to civil society respondents, 'some associations think they are

---

* These are rather meagre financial investments compared to other migration policy domains. For instance, over the same period, the MoI spent more than two billion dirham 'to reinforce the integrated border management to limit irregular migration' (MCMREAM 2016b: 78).
† For an overview of CSO activities and projects on migration in Morocco between 2013 and 2018, see MCMREAM (2016: 30–77) and MDCMREAM (2018: 25–67).

superior to others because of their international reputation' (M17-I3); among Moroccan CSOs, in particular between those accepting international funding and those rejecting it, fearing their instrumentalization for Europe's migration externalization agenda; between migrant associations and Moroccan CSOs that started to work on migrant integration as a result of authorities' 'moroccanization' policy; and finally, among migrant associations themselves. As one respondent concluded, 'There is money now, so everyone tries to get his part of the cake' (M16-I23).

Besides funding, competition materialized most visibly on the legitimacy to speak for or decide on behalf of migrants. Given the high turnover of migrant organization leaders, Moroccan authorities and European funders often prefer to work with more established, international CSOs: 'They don't want to lose time investing in small structures and migrant associations that might not have the competence' (M16-I6). While CSOs still depend upon each other for effective migrant protection and successful political mobilization (Üstübici 2016), civil society increasingly fragmented after 2013. In December 2016, Hicham Rachidi, a central figure of the GADEM, describes these lines of tension:

Once partners, Moroccan and international civil society structures now differ in their readings of the national/regional context. ... Migrant and refugee associations face tensions stemming from ideological, ethnic, nationalistic and personal leadership disparities ... that put brakes on their common efforts ... to position themselves as credible interlocutors in front of public authorities and to be able to carry the voice of the voiceless at the political level.[9]

Ambiguous State–Civil Society Dynamics[10]

Despite these internal dynamics, CSOs have consolidated their presence in front of Moroccan authorities. Back in the early 2000s, interactions between civil society and state actors were minimal and CSOs under constant surveillance from Moroccan security services. Even in 2012, respondents painted the picture of an impenetrable administration: 'All doors are closed ... Our requests are not taken into account' (M12-I3). While state institutions started to engage with specific CSOs such as the GADEM, the Democratic Organization of Immigrant Labour (ODTI), or the OMDH after 2011, 'the generic mode of operation in Morocco is that civil society is not yet recognized as a valid interlocutor' (M12-I13).

Selective Openings and Partial Co-Optation. The 2013 reform opened the state's doors to civil society. Particularly the CNDH, the Ministry of Health (MoH) and the MCMREAM have

Civil Society Dynamics 125

developed informal contacts and formal cooperation with CSOs and migrant organizations.[11] Even Moroccan security services became more cooperative after 2013 in resolving critical situations of migrants blocked at the border:

There is now a certain reactivity of the General Directorate for National Security (DGSN) and national police when there is a communiqué by associations such as GADEM or the Protection Platform. ... So there is a certain change in the modus operandi (M17-I21).

However, the state opening to civil society has remained partial. Interviewees framed the political arena as a space with limited access that required an entrance 'ticket' (M17-I1, M17-I3, M17-I10). Indeed, not all CSOs have profited from improved cooperation with state institutions: 'For sub-Saharan associations relations have improved, for Moroccan associations it depends on the topic they work on and whether they do a lot of advocacy or not' (M16-I8). While CSOs such as GADEM or ODTI have profited from their close relations with the CNDH to make their voice heard, relations between the state and the Moroccan Association of Human Rights (AMDH) – the most critical human rights organization in Morocco and subject to regular crackdowns by authorities – rather worsened over the years.

Ultimately, however, most state-civil society interactions seem, first and foremost, symbolic, aiming at showcasing the participatory character and inclusiveness of the migration reform rather than seeking meaningful bottom-up input. While the MCMREAM's *Guide des associations* promised 'the involvement of civil society and its active participation in all stages of the development and implementation of the national immigration strategy and asylum, through a permanent mechanism of consultation' (MCMREAM 2016: 3), state institutions did not live up to this promise:

The Minister [of the MCMREAM] wanted to establish a new system; he wanted to talk to associations every four weeks to get to know the ground, to have regular contact. We started, but after two meetings, it stopped (M16-I10).

After an initial period of euphoria, some CSOs have therefore reduced their involvement with state actors, realizing their limited influence on public actors, as well as the continuation of violent state practices that they thought were over.

In parallel to such limited openings, state institutions have also sought to co-opt CSOs and their activities. The regularization of associations and the public funding of pro-immigrant activities allowed the state to cooperate with CSOs that used to be their opponents. The GADEM, for instance, has been a central partner of the state during the first years of implementing the SNIA – 'to the extent that some consider [the GADEM] the 4th Directorate of the Migration Ministry' (M16-I6). Also, state institutions took over successful civil society activities by rebranding them as their own. For instance, the yearly 'Migrant Week' (*Semaine des Migrants*), organized by the ODTI since December 2012, has been reframed as an initiative of the MCMREAM since 2015. Symbolically, the event was also renumbered accordingly: as the advertisement flyers collected during fieldwork show, the 2015 event was marketed by the ministry as the first edition of the migrant week, although it was in fact the fourth. Lastly, state institutions such as the CNDH or the MCMREAM have hired civil society activists known for their advocacy work on migration. This 'Makhzenization' of civil society has somewhat silenced criticism of migrants' rights abuses by the Moroccan state.

Adapting Advocacy Strategies. Ultimately, by bringing CSOs on board, Moroccan authorities have made it more difficult for civil society to criticize migrant rights' violations openly and to provide a robust counter-discourse. Interviewees noted the silence of previously vocal civil society actors on the ongoing violence of state actors towards migrants in the North or at the borders: 'some migrant associations that were always very vocal in criticizing the government, they don't talk anymore' (M16-I22). Analysing such state-civil society dynamics, Norman (2016a: 431) concludes that 'Moroccan civil society organizations thus paid a heavy price by choosing to transform "… their practices and policies from mobilization and street activities to participation in public policies and cooperation with the authorities" (Vairel 2013: 43)'.

As a result of these dynamics, Moroccan civil society faced two new challenges: on the one hand, the growing number of state actors working on immigration has diffused accountability and created ambiguity about who is accountable for misconduct or the lack of improvements. The key question now is whom CSOs should target institutionally with their criticism. On the other hand, CSOs have to strike a balance between welcoming changes and continuing their criticism of migrant rights' violations:

Before 2013, it was all securitarian at the level of government policy. So for civil society, it was easy to do advocacy, you just needed to denounce the policy and the lack of political will, so civil society was more cohesive. With 2013, it has become more difficult (M16-I22).

Civil Society Dynamics 127

In response to the progressive change and continued violence of Morocco's immigration policy, civil society adapted its advocacy strategies, oscillating between confrontation and cooperation with state actors. As GADEM acknowledged in a statement in December 2018,

> If we have oscillated in recent years between support and advocacy, it is because our country itself balances between integration, reception and border management. The complexity of GADEM's positioning is, in fact, the exact replica of the positioning of the Moroccan state.[12]

For instance, CSOs now mobilize their newly acquired personal contacts within the administration to advance specific dossiers informally, in particular with the CNDH and the MCMREAM. Also, civil society capitalizes on Morocco's self-portrayal as a leader on migrants' rights – both internationally and in Africa. As one civil society respondent explained,

> Morocco was tasked with the migratory dossier at the AU, so I think we will play on that: You cannot present and suggest things at the AU level if you yourself don't have these laws in your own country.

In 2018, for instance, the adoption of the UN Global Compact on Migration in Marrakesh allowed Moroccan civil society to capitalize on heightened international attention: together with eight other NGOs, GADEM launched the 'hits and wounds' (coups et blessures) campaign in September to monitor violence against migrants in Morocco ahead of the high-level meeting in Marrakesh in December, prompting condemnations by Amnesty International (AI) and the UN Human Rights Council (UN-HRC 2019).[13]

Moroccan civil society also increasingly uses migrants' rights as an entry to advocate for Moroccans' political and socio-economic rights more broadly. For organizations such as GADEM, OMDH, or AMDH, the denial of West and Central African migrants' rights is intrinsically related to the general human rights situation in Morocco: 'If we want to be a state of law, then procedures and rules have to be respected – for everybody' (M17-I17). Not respecting refugee residence permits is thus framed as 'a question of rule of law in Morocco' (M16-I2), and security forces' violence against migrants become instrumental in denouncing general misconduct and lacking reform in the Moroccan security system. Similarly, interviewees turned their critique of deficiencies in migrant protection into a broader critique of Morocco's poor social system: 'Migrants now are accepted in hospitals and emergency rooms under the same conditions as Moroccans – that means with material insufficiencies and doctors' unavailability, that's the same for everyone' (M17-I11). By linking migrants' rights to the broader human rights situation in Morocco, migrants become instrumental in engendering a more general anti-system critique.

The ODTI, Morocco's First Migrant Workers' Union.

The dynamics around migrant unions in Morocco exemplify the different trends sketched: the prevalence of internal conflicts within the migrant community, the ambiguous role of civil society as a bridge between state institutions and migrant communities, but also the legacy of Morocco's emigration experiences in shaping civil society developments.

Back in 2011, Khrouz (2011: 50) writes, 'Unions are absent and currently seem hesitant to defend the rights of migrant workers, even if their administrative situation is regular.' That same year, the encounter between Marcel Amiyeto, a Congolese citizen living in Morocco since 2005 and founder of the Collective of Migrant Workers in Morocco (CTMM), and Driss el Yazami, the then-president of the Council for Morocco's Community Abroad (CCME), planted the seed for the creation of the first migrant union in Morocco. The historical role played by unions in the French immigration debate provided a blueprint for the labour union engagement in Morocco. Amiyeto received initial support from the French Association of Maghrebi Workers (ATMF) to contact Morocco's established labour unions, who, however, showed no interest in incorporating migrant workers. Only the Democratic Organization of Labour (ODT), a young and relatively small union that sought to gain ground in a territory dominated by older and much larger unions, was ready to accommodate a migrant section. Marcel Amiyeto recounts,

I met them in March 2012 ... I presented them with my project, they said: In principle, we defend all workers without distinction of race or religion, whether they have papers or not. So come with your project, we will give you our weight, our syndical support. ... It was an instrumental alliance of interests, a marriage of convenience.

In July 2012, the Democratic Organization of Immigrant Labour (ODTI) was founded as Morocco's first migrant union. In December the same year, the ODTI organized its first Migrant Week (Semaine des migrants) under the overall slogan *For a policy of regularization of irregular migrants in the context of Morocco's constitutional reform*, hereby somewhat anticipating the framing and substance of the 2013 policy change. While the ODTI was at first dominated by workers from Western and Central Africa, in 2014, a sub-section was created to represent Filipino houseworkers.

In 2017, three large Moroccan unions – the Moroccan Labour Union (UMT), the General Union of Moroccan Workers (UGTM), and the Democratic Confederation of Labour (CDT) – announced the creation of migrant sections within their structures. To what extent Moroccan unions will become central actors in defending migrant workers remains unclear. On the one hand, the labour market situation in Morocco is difficult, and defending irregular migrants does not create consensus within unions. For instance, labour unions remain reluctant to support a reform of the national preference in the Labour Code (the so-called ANAPEC procedure) that would facilitate foreigners' access to the labour market: 'We have to start our fight within the unions' (M17-I3), one member said. On the other hand, unions have started to become more vocal when migrants' labour rights are violated by employers.

This ambiguity is reminiscent of the historical development of European labour unions' positions towards immigrants, first sceptical and exclusionary, then subsequently discovering migrants as potential union members (Castles, de Haas and Miller 2014; Haus 1999). An interesting Moroccan specificity is that employer and labour unions are represented in the second chamber of the Parliament: 'If migrants are part of unions, the migrant component is directly in the Parliament' (M17-I13). Thus, if the migration issue is genuinely taken up by unions, it might get politicized through unions' presence in the second chamber instead of party politics dominating the first chamber.

The Democratic Challenge. Despite the politicization of immigration by the Royal Palace and growing pro-migrant advocacy in some parts of civil society, immigration has remained a relative 'non-topic' across Moroccan society. The fact that geopolitical interests rather than public demand drove the 2013 liberal reform raises the question of public adherence. In the words of one of my respondents, 'The big challenge is that the Moroccan people accept this policy' (M16-I6). This challenge is two-fold: it requires a de facto acceptance of migrants as jobseekers, patients or schoolmates in the short term; and a *symbolic* acceptance of migrants as family members or potential nationals with different cultural or religious traditions in the longer term.

Research on Moroccans' opinions on the 2013 reform is scarce. The 2018 Afrobarometer and its special module on migration, however, gives some insights into the overall reticent yet mixed attitudes of Moroccans towards immigration. It shows that a majority of Moroccans would want no (26 per cent) or only a few (30 per cent) immigrants and refugees in Morocco, compared to 23 per cent who would allow some and 13 per cent who are in favour of allowing many to immigrate

(Appiah-Nyamekye Sanny and Abderebbi 2019). More generally, 43 per cent consider that Morocco already hosts enough immigrants, and 35 per cent state that it would be bad if more migrants would come to live in Morocco. Compared to earlier surveys, however, Moroccan respondents are slightly more positive in 2018 when it comes to having a migrant or someone from a different religion or ethnicity as a neighbour (Afrobarometer 2015a, 2018a).

These insights are confirmed by a national survey of 1,000 Moroccans conducted in early 2018, showing that opinions on whether Morocco should be a host country for migrants from Western and Central Africa are split: 36 per cent of Moroccan respondents are opposed, 38 per cent in favour, and 15 per cent are in favour under certain conditions. Interestingly, respondents from Casablanca and the southern regions are most hostile towards immigrants, while respondents from the regions that already host large parts of Morocco's Western and Central African migrant population (Rabat-Salé, Tangier-Tétouan and the Oriental region in the north-east of Morocco) are largely favourable towards immigrants.[14]

My interviews point towards two explanations for such mixed attitudes towards immigration: on the one hand, popular support for the new migration policy is lacking because opening the labour market, social assistance, or healthcare to migrants is considered problematic by Moroccans who face unemployment and lack social support themselves:

Honestly, I think that Moroccan society will react like all other societies, there will be excesses of xenophobia, social clashes, and rivalries between the poor over resources ... The key issue is: will we avoid political instrumentalization or not (M17-I16).

On the other hand, respondents have mobilized the mirror effect to justify why Moroccans will ultimately adhere to the policy liberalization: 'Every Moroccan family has a migrant abroad, so there is a psychological acceptance of the other, because we are the other there' (M17-I13). Concerning migrants' access to education, one respondent recounted:

There were Moroccans who were against it [schooling children of irregular migrants]. But I told them: You know, Moroccans left to Europe in the 1950s, 1960s, 1970s, they were not told – you are irregulars, so your children will not go to school. They were simply put into schools, it is their right. And it's the same thing here (M17-I20).

Beyond the question of access to jobs, education or healthcare, immigration to Morocco also interrogates Morocco's national identity. The fact that many migrants are Black or Christian (re)introduces issues such as mixed marriages, religious diversity and race into Moroccan societal debates. Aware of this, Driss el Yazami, director of the CNDH, has suggested the public construction of churches to respond to the spiritual needs of Christian migrants in Morocco and to avoid the mistakes of European states in the 1970s, when Muslim migrants had to exercise their religion in secrecy.[15] The long-term immigrant settlement will also trigger questions about the Muslim component of Moroccan citizenship. In the words of Mourji et al. (2016: 112–13): 'To be consistent with the liberal references of its Constitution, Morocco will have to consider opening the conditions of acquisition of its nationality. ... This coherence would have a political price since it would be a question of redefining the foundations of the nation.'

How the Moroccan population would react to such measures remains unclear. On the one hand, Moroccans have been exposed to the King's Africa policy and the plural identity framing since the late 2000s: 'You constantly hear: "the King left for Africa", "we want to foster the relations with Africa", people start to become receptive to this message' (M17-I11). On the other hand, racist attacks on Western and Central African migrants regularly make Moroccan headlines,[16] and according to a 2015 survey, most migrants rarely interact with Moroccans, a quarter of them almost never (Mourji et al. 2016: 98). Thus, despite the official recognition of an 'African belonging', the incorporation of the African dimension into Morocco's identity referential remains largely symbolic and theoretical. In the words of one migrant association representative, 'Moroccan authorities committed themselves, but the country is not ready.'

The Role of International, Economic and Legal Actors

Besides state and civil society actors, international organizations, the private sector and legal actors all participate in Morocco's immigration policy field, albeit to different degrees. As already shown, foreign policy interests are essential to understand Moroccan immigration policy. Yet, as this section demonstrates, while the 2013 reform has increased international influence on national policy processes, Moroccan authorities remain in control over the direction and extent of such external influence. In contrast to international dynamics, employers and lawyers – central to explanations of immigration policy in Western liberal democracies – are not key players in Moroccan immigration politics. I suggest that the size of Morocco's informal economy and the confluence of interests between employers and the King explain the negligible public role of employers, while the limited role of legal actors is a result of Morocco's autocratic regime.

The International Dimension

The Extent and Limits of External Influence. The 2013 reform has opened up numerous opportunities for external actors – IOs, development agencies, diplomatic representations – to work with Moroccan institutions on immigration: 'You cannot imagine, projects are launched everywhere … IOs are in a craze to work on this policy' (M17-I5), one respondent exclaimed. In particular, international actors provided increased funding to support public institutions in implementing the immigration reform: UNHCR sponsored the creation of a position within the CNDH to work specifically on asylum; the GIZ worked with local Moroccan authorities to advance the 'territorialization' of the SNIA; and IOM has stepped up its cooperation with the MoH to integrate migrants into public healthcare, as well as with the MoI to expand its voluntary return program. UNHCR, IOM, ILO and others also regularly organize workshops on migrant rights for Moroccan civil servants across ministries, parliamentary groups and professional bodies such as police, judges or labour inspectors. The 2013 reform thus clearly multiplied relations between external actors and public authorities:

There is before and after the 9 September 2013. Until then, nothing worked and it was a struggle to work in Morocco. Afterwards, it was a whole different dimension and dynamic. The work with the MoI and MoFA suddenly became much better (M16-I4).

According to respondents, the lack of expertise on immigrant integration within Moroccan institutions reinforced this willingness to cooperate. Such interactions allowed external actors to shape the agenda of public authorities and bring their visions on migration and integration to Morocco. For example, the annual immigration conference organized by the MCMREAM reflected, in 2017, the topic of the GIZ-funded RECOMIG project, namely the territorialization of migration policy at the local level. However, these new opportunities for policy influence have not automatically increased the weight of external actors on Moroccan policymaking. While IOs have gained influence in Moroccan institutions due to a lack of and need for expertise, the 2013 reform also offered Moroccan authorities an opportunity to limit or shape the extent of international influence.

On the one hand, administrative bodies actively resisted external involvement in some instances: against common practice, the GIZ was not given an office for its expert within the MCMREAM. Also, while IOs had significant leverage in shaping specific projects within the SNIA, their contribution to the legislative process has been minimal – particularly compared to Tunisia: although UNHCR was allowed to give feedback on the draft asylum law, it was not involved in its elaboration, and IOs were not given access to the draft law on immigration.

On the other hand, external funding and involvement largely mirrored the goals of Moroccan authorities to move attention away from migrant protection and towards migrant integration. In the past, international actors focused on providing basic humanitarian support to irregular migrants or on lobbying for more migrant rights. Now 'there is little funding from donors dedicated to issues of protection and humanitarian assistance, especially for irregulars, everyone is on integration issues, they follow the discourse and will of public institutions' (M17-I21). This new focus on integration also suited European funders, as it fitted within the European political climate seeking to encourage neighbouring countries to provide more attractive living conditions for migrants. It was also a less problematic topic for funders in terms of cooperation with Moroccan authorities compared to funding advocacy work or support structures for irregular migrants. As one respondent explained, 'Irregular migrants are a category that will always remain under-financed because it's the most difficult category to justify in terms of political dialogue with the government' (M17-I21).

Ultimately, the 2013 commitment to a human rights–based immigration and integration policy also bolstered Moroccan authorities' migration diplomacy towards Europe. On the one hand, it allowed Morocco to more easily reject EU cooperation proposals that neglect human rights, such as forced returns of Moroccans from Europe or the establishment of asylum-processing camps. As one high-level civil servant highlighted, 'Morocco now possesses a negotiation tool to say: No, I have a policy, I have rules to respect'. On the other hand, the 2013 reform allowed Moroccan authorities to mobilize the demonstration effect, instrumentalizing its liberal immigration policy to advance diaspora policy goals in Europe.

The Absence of African Actors. But what about African actors? Do Ivorian, Senegalese, Congolese or Malian embassies lobby for better treatment of their citizens in Morocco, or, if not, why? Asking this question to representatives of the embassies of Senegal, Mali and Ivory Coast in Rabat has been challenging, given that they were not available for interviews. According to other respondents, however, African embassies do not lobby to improve their citizens' situation in

Morocco: 'It was not them who worked for the protection of the rights of their nationals in Morocco' (M16-I26). The incident around the Senegalese embassy in 2013 is emblematic of this: in May, Senegalese citizens in Morocco held a sit-in in front of their embassy in Rabat to protest against the expulsion of sixteen Senegalese from Morocco. The sit-in ended in clashes with the Moroccan police and arrests of Senegalese citizens. But instead of defending its citizens, the Senegalese embassy lodged a complaint against them.[17]

Similar dynamics have been at play in 2018, when large-scale migrant expulsions triggered civil society outrage, including local demonstrations by migrants in Tangiers and condemnations by international human rights organizations: To forestall diplomatic problems, on 30 August 2018, Moroccan Ministries of Interior, Foreign Affairs and Migration invited the African diplomatic corps to a meeting to justify the migrant displacements and request support by origin countries to return some of the migrants concerned. According to Driss el Yazami, president of the CNDH, African ambassadors 'saw no objections' to such proceedings.[18] As highlighted by local civil society representatives, it even seems that in 2020, Senegalese and Ghanaian consulate employees were actively involved in identifying their nationals to be forcibly removed from southern Morocco.[19]

There are two main reasons why African states are not engaged in protecting the rights of their citizens in Morocco: on the one hand, advocacy for their citizens' rights abroad would render the domestic problems that make them leave the country in the first place more visible. On the other hand, states who themselves pursue a policy of migration securitization lose their legitimacy in lobbying for their migrants' rights abroad – as Morocco until the 2013 reform. In the words of one respondent, 'Origin states where citizens are subject to repression are themselves involved in the politics of control, so they cannot protest.' Despite the centrality of Morocco's Africa policy in the 2013 reform, African diplomatic actors have thus remained relatively marginal.

The Private Sector: The Ambiguous Role of Employers

While international relations dynamics around immigration policy appear to vary according to a country's position in global migration systems, the involvement of the private sector in immigration seems related to the structural characteristics of a country's economy and labour market. In Morocco, apart from the recruitment of skilled African workers as part of their expansion into African markets, business interests have been secondary to understanding immigration policy processes because of Morocco's large informal labour market and tight imbrication between economic and political elites.

Moroccan banks, construction companies, energy and telecommunication providers expanding their activities into African markets have indeed been actively recruiting foreign employees. Royal Air Maroc (RAM) started to hire stewards from Western and Central Africa to cater to their African clientele from the late 2000s onwards (Infantino 2011).[20] Under its previous president, Driss Benhima (from 2006 to 2016), the company also asked the CNDH to conduct 'diversity trainings' for their employees to raise their awareness of racial discrimination. Within the General Confederation of Enterprises in Morocco (CGEM), the appointment of Abdou Souleye Diop, a Senegalese migrant resident in Morocco since 1986, as president of the CGEM's Africa Commission reflects the growing role of African clients and partners in Moroccan economic life.[21] Since 2014, employers are also integrated into the institutional set-up of the SNIA: CGEM representatives participate in the committees on employment and professional training of regularized migrants; they cooperate with ILO on projects related to migrant labour (both of Moroccans abroad as well as foreigners in Morocco), and in May 2018, the CGEM signed a partnership with UNHCR and the MCMREAM on the employability and economic integration of refugees.[22] This institutional involvement might create incentives for employers to engage more actively in immigration in the long run.

Despite these small-scale developments, however, three structural characteristics of the Moroccan economy and labour market restrain employers from becoming more active on labour immigration: first, the structure of the Moroccan economy – with 90 per cent of firms being small or medium enterprises (SMEs) or family businesses rather than large corporations (Abdel Aziz 2013) – does not lend itself to extensive political lobbying or to the strategic hiring of migrant labour. Because the official procedure to hire foreign workers is lengthy and costly for the employer,* many family businesses do not have the knowledge to recruit foreigners.

---

* The national employment office (ANAPEC) has to attest that there is no Moroccan citizen with the required profile before giving a work authorization to a foreigner (national preference procedure; see Decree 1391-05 of 25 November 2005 of the MoL). This procedure requires the employer to publish a recruitment ad in two newspapers with a circulation of at least 10,000 and wait officially at least ten days, in practice often four to six weeks. As a result, most foreign workers, both high-skilled and low-skilled, are employed without permit. See L'Economiste, *Mobilité des cadres: Les compétences marocaines d'abord*, 9 December 2014.

Second, the extent of the informal labour market – estimated at 59 per cent of the Moroccan workforce (ILO 2018) – means that cheap and flexible labour can be found informally. According to a survey, 70 per cent of migrants work in the informal sector (Mourji et al. 2016: 66). Although respondents emphasized that employers seek to stimulate competition between workers on the national labour market, there is no need to lobby for more open immigration rules, as it would only strengthen the position of foreign workers in Morocco. Indeed, 'employers have a preference for irregular workers. They know that those who have a residence permit are protected by law' (M16-I10). Thus, from an employer perspective, the current system of informal employment works well: fines for irregular employment are minimal, labour inspectors do not systematically inspect workplaces, and an informal system of exemptions allows major international corporations and specific economic sectors to bypass the restrictive labour code (Khrouz 2016: 232). As former Labour Minister Abdeslam Seddiki said on TV in March 2015, the 'derogatory system' concerning work permits for foreign workers is 'very developed'.[23]

Lastly, there is a confluence of interests between large Moroccan firms and the royal cabinet because the King is a major economic actor and employer himself. As one respondent reflected, 'Maybe they [employers] do lobbying in a discrete way, but it's not like in Europe. The relation between the economy and political power is different' (M17-I9). Within the context of a large informal economy and the tight imbrication of economic and political power, there is thus little incentive for employers to openly mobilize for more legal employment opportunities for foreigners.

The Legal Sector: Lawyers, Judges, Courts

Prompted on the role of legal actors, most respondents highlighted the weakness of Morocco's judicial institutions, while some sketched a more optimistic picture, referring to situations in which legal actors set limits to state violence. For instance, Moroccan judges took a first step to protect refugee rights in the summer of 2009: a sit-in of refugees asking for protection and resettlement in front of the UNHCR office had turned violent. Stones were thrown, and protesters were arrested. During their trial, judges at the first instance tribunal in Rabat decided to sentence the refugees only for their violence, not for their irregular status, hereby drawing a clear line between refugees and irregular migrants (Planes-Boissac 2012a: 27):[24]

They were condemned only for violent acts, they had already been in detention and were released, and it was explicitly stated that they were refugees and they are allowed to stay on the territory of Morocco. So in the end, it became a victory (M16-I31).

After the 2011 constitutional change, judges also created an independent association – the *Club des Juges* – that publicly denounced the arbitrary detentions of irregular migrants without judicial control.[25] In the context of the MoI's large-scale security operation after the end of the first regularization campaign in February 2015, the legal intervention of a judge from Casablanca was essential in condemning the internal displacements and arrests of irregular migrants as illegal, leading to their release.[26] Ethnographic accounts of the workings of Moroccan courts (Khrouz 2016) confirm this picture of reluctant but emerging legal activism in Morocco: 'Judges become more and more visible as an actor. They are reticent, it's not easy, but we had a few good judgements' (M16-I6). These few instances remain the exception to the rule, however, as court decisions remain incoherent and arbitrary: 'Sometimes, in the same audience, with the same judges, you can get totally different decisions' (M16-I28).

Lawyers have been more active on migrants' rights than courts. Back in 2007, UNHCR started to cooperate with the OMDH and a lawyer from Rabat to offer legal assistance to asylum seekers and refugees, building up a small but steadily growing jurisprudence that forced at least minimal consistency in court rulings. In 2013, the law practice *Droit et Justice* in Casablanca launched a project to provide legal assistance to refugees and training for other lawyers, and in November 2015, the *Clinique Hijra* was created in Tangier to provide legal assistance to migrants more generally – be they regular or irregular foreigners in Morocco or Moroccans abroad. Thus, despite the fact that the power of legal actors in Morocco is not comparable with that of courts and judges in democracies because of Morocco's weak rule of law and the limited independence of the judiciary, there have been attempts by national civil society, lawyers and judges to hold public authorities accountable through legal tools.

How Authoritarian Consolidation Shapes Immigration Politics

Writing about the reform of the Moroccan family code (*mudawana*) in 2004, Cavatorta and Dalmasso (2009, 488) argue that 'the process through which the new family code was passed highlights the crucial institutional role of the monarch, whose individual decision-making power has driven the whole process. Authoritarianism finds itself strengthened in Morocco despite the liberal nature and outcome of the reform'. They conclude that 'in Morocco, the King managed to reassert his grip on power by presenting himself as the defender of women's rights' (Cavatorta and Dalmasso 2009: 489). By replacing women with migrants, this sentence also accurately circumscribes the dynamics around immigration policy in Morocco. Yet, despite the centrality of the King in the policy process, this did not absorb resistances and diverging views within the administration with regards to agenda-setting and policy implementation.

Together with the analysis of policy drivers in Chapter 4, the Moroccan case study has provided key insights into autocratic immigration policymaking and the boundaries of the 'regime effect': first, autocratic leaders can, if it suits the regime's legitimation strategies, drive immigration policy liberalization because of their relative independence from societal and legal actors, a dynamic I call the illiberal paradox. However, there seem to be three main limitations to this illiberal paradox. First, permissive immigration reforms might not always be followed through in practice, as welcoming immigration discourses might, first and foremost, fulfil a symbolic role towards a specific (often international) audience. Second, while autocracies seem less bound by legal constraints than democracies and can more rapidly open up their immigration regimes if they wish to do so, this also increases the vulnerability of liberal reforms to sudden restrictive backlashes. Third, immigration and integration do not automatically go hand in hand. As Ruhs (2013) has argued, there is a trade-off between allowing large-scale immigration and granting extensive integration rights (Breunig, Cao and Luedtke 2012; Shin 2017). As a consequence, the illiberal paradox might be particularly relevant for countries in which the volume of immigration is low or where liberal entry regimes do not spill over into a general liberalization of migrants' rights.

However, the Moroccan case study also showcased that even within autocratic systems with largely top-down decision-making, inter-institutional and bureaucratic dynamics on immigration policy are more comparable to those identified in the literature on liberal democracies than often presumed, making institutionalism key to understanding immigration policy processes across political regimes. Looking at the role of civil society activism, I find that it can play a crucial role in setting the political agenda in an authoritarian context such as the Moroccan one by providing the primary outlet for channelling citizens' interests into the political system in the absence of party politics. The weight of civil society is expected to be particularly strong at a moment of heightened international attention to the topic. However, the opening of the state towards civil society does not necessarily strengthen its weight on policy processes, as increased opportunities for civil society influence might be cancelled out by state co-optation attempts and market dynamics within civil society. Thus, political economy approaches to immigration policy-making are not neatly applicable to more autocratic contexts.

It remains unclear whether Morocco's liberal migration agenda initiated in 2013 will prevail in the long term, particularly in a scenario where the royal will to keep up this liberal agenda might wane. Thus, one of my respondents asked, 'What will happen to the migration policy now that Morocco is back in the African Union, now that the King got what he wanted?' (M17-I12). Will the dossier lose its dynamism, or are the administrative structures and civil society institutions in place strong enough to keep the system going? On the one hand, dynamics of path dependency (Pierson 2000) would suggest that as soon as the 'royal impulse' disappears, institutions fall back into their deeply rooted behaviours – for the MoI, a purely securitarian approach; for the MCMREAM, a focus on Moroccans abroad; for the MoH, MoL or MoE, a policy of laissez-faire and ignorance of the migrant population. This would lead to a return to pre-2013 politics. On the other hand, institutions or policies, once created, can take on a life of their own (see Tilly 1975: 117). Setting up institutions such as the CNDH or the MCMREAM – even if they might be façade institutions initially – can create institutional incentives and dynamics that were not originally planned. The integration of new actors in the Moroccan policy process could thus, in the long run, trigger dynamics of a self-fulfilling prophecy. Some interviewees were thus optimistic: 'Now, if we act as if Morocco followed a rights-based approach, we might end up with a rights-based approach' (M17-I6).

Keeping these complex dynamics in Morocco's authoritarian context in mind, the next two chapters now zoom into the Tunisian case, where immigration policy has remained strikingly restrictive – and unchanged – throughout the democratic transition that the country experienced in the decade after January 2011.

6 Regime Change and Immigration Policy Continuity in Tunisia

The Origins of Tunisian Immigration Policy: State Imperatives, Geopolitical Priorities and National Security

As in Morocco, immigration control was not a major preoccupation in Tunisia until the 1930s. While Tunisia's local authorities started regulating foreigners' rights to enter and work over the nineteenth century, when immigration started to grow, this was mainly through bilateral treaties that privileged certain nationals such as French, Italian and British citizens over others (Perkins 2004: 32). This system was largely maintained after France colonized Tunisia in 1881. Although a decree in April 1989 asked foreigners to declare and justify their residence in Tunisia, no measures were taken to restrict immigration. Only in 1930, just after the economic crisis hit Europe, French authorities limited work permits in Tunisia to highly qualified foreigners by introducing a work and residence permit, as well as a preference for national workers. Work regulations were further restricted in July 1953, when high administrative taxes for employers were introduced for every new or renewed work contract, as well as for the visas of workers' families.

After independence in 1956, Tunisia replaced the immigration laws inherited from the colonial period through legal reforms in 1968 and 1975. But while Tunisia got formally rid of the French colonial legacy in immigration law much earlier than Morocco, the restrictive substance of Tunisia's immigration policies, as well as the system of visas, work permits and related sanctions for foreigners, remained essentially unchanged. Over the post-independence decades, Tunisia's leaders complemented this generic legal framework by a set of scattered, small-scale policy initiatives in view of strengthening international support for their regimes: both the selective openings towards certain refugees and labour migrants under Bourguiba, as well as the combination between exemption regimes for high-skilled workers and restrictive policies towards irregular migrants under Ben Ali, were significantly shaped by geopolitical interests.

Foreign policy, in particular President Bourguiba's ideals of regional integration with the Maghreb, Western and Central Africa, dominated Tunisia's policy on student and labour migration until the 1980s: personal friendships between Bourguiba and Léopold Sédar Senghor, President of Senegal, or Félix Houphouët-Boigny, President of Côte d'Ivoire, were key in crafting bilateral agreements on development cooperation or student exchanges in medicine, agriculture or engineering. Tunisia also signed bilateral agreements with Algeria, Morocco and Libya in the 1960s to facilitate regional mobility, even if these were implemented inconsistently over the years depending on the diplomatic climate between the countries.[*]

Also Tunisia's approach to refugees was driven by strategic considerations, as authorities granted residence permits to refugees on a case-by-case basis, depending on whether the protection of that particular group would fit into the overall political narrative of the regime and would help secure its power at home or abroad. For instance, when Algerian refugees arrived in Tunisia during the Algerian War of Independence (1954–1962), Tunisia welcomed them in a spirit of brotherhood between two independence-seeking nations. Similarly, Palestinian refugees and militants were welcomed by Bourguiba in the early 1980s under the banner of pan-Arab solidarity and because their liberation struggle aligned with Tunisia's geopolitical priorities at the time. In contrast, Algerian refugees who arrived during Algeria's civil war in the 1990s were met with suspicion by Tunisian authorities, as Ben Ali's regime perceived Algerians as a security risk and feared that the Algerian conflict would spill over to Tunisia.

Apart from these geopolitically motivated refugee policies, however, Tunisia did not have a consistent approach towards granting political asylum: as in Morocco, the Geneva Convention came into force on 2 June 1955, while Tunisia was still under French colonial rule. UNHCR started operations in Tunisia in May 1957, when President Bourguiba called upon the UNHCR to assist the government in the accommodation, care and eventual repatriation of more than 150,000 Algerian refugees (UNHCR 2000: 38–42). Shortly afterwards, the Tunisian government confirmed its adherence to the Convention in a letter sent to the Secretary-General of the UN on 24 October 1957

---

[*] Although exempted from the work permit requirement, since the 1990s Moroccans and Algerians need to request a 'certificate of non-submission of a work contract' by an inter-ministerial commission. This certificate is an administrative absurdity, as it requires those who do not need to submit a work contract for approval to the MoEPF, to request a certificate by the same ministry that explicitly exempts them from such approval.

(Boubakri 2007). Yet, Tunisia never established a national refugee determination procedure. While UNHCR opened an honorary representation in Tunisia in 1963, but with only two employees and led by a Tunisian diplomat close to the regime, its presence remained largely symbolic. In 1992, the Tunisian MoFA signed an agreement with UNHCR to officially grant it the right to register asylum seekers and determine refugee status (Planes-Boissac 2012b: 26). According to respondents, however, UNHCR conformed to an informal quota set by Tunisian authorities in their refugee determination:

> People went to the Red Crescent, who transferred the dossiers to the UNHCR in Tunis, who then delivered the refugee status. But it was never more than a hundred people a year. They said that this was a verbal instruction by the Tunisian government, to not open the doors, to not create any pull factor (T17-I32).

Historical data indeed shows that between 1992 and 2002, UNHCR registered on average 261 refugees each year (CARIM 2003), but that only around 40 per cent of refugees recognized by UNHCR between 1992 and 2010 actually received a Tunisian residence permit (Laacher 2007, cited in Planes-Boissac 2012b: 26).

Over the 1990s, Ben Ali complemented Tunisia's overall strict migration policy by a wealth of exceptions in line with the regime's economic and foreign policy priorities: in 1992, the Ministry of Interior (MoI) gained discretionary powers to hand out special residence permits to investors and business people; in 1993, the Investment Code allowed fully exporting firms to recruit management personnel from abroad, and created exemptions for sectors such as mining and hydrocarbon exploitation. Also, the regime officially welcomed specific migrant groups as 'guests', such as employees of the African Development Bank (AfDB) in the early 2000s, to bolster Ben Ali's geopolitical standing.

In parallel, immigration control was progressively stepped up – through the introduction of a penalty for irregular stay and employment in 1994 and 1996, as well as readmission agreements with Italy in 1998 and 2003 – and became a central tool to bolster the international legitimacy and domestic grip of the Ben Ali regime. Ultimately, Law 2004–06 legally cemented the securitization of migration by putting sanctions for irregular migration and anyone in contact with them on par with those for terrorist activities. Migrants caught without papers were detained in so-called Welcome and Orientation Centres, such as the El Ouardiya centre outside Tunis.[*] Because Tunisia did not have a

---

[*] For personal insights into El Ouardiya, see the accounts of Jean Fontaine (2012), a Christian missionary living in Tunis who was authorized by the MoJ to visit foreign

formal return policy, irregular migrants – once detected and detained – were required to pay their flight tickets home or otherwise risked being abandoned by the Tunisian army in the Algerian desert or at the Libyan border (see also Ben Jemia 2009; Boubakri 2011; Garelli and Tazzioli 2017: 31–32).

Interviewees overwhelmingly saw the 2004 repressive law as a direct result of Tunisia's close cooperation with Italy in the early 2000s, as well as of the generalized pressure exercised by the European Union on North Africa in the context of migration control externalization (Ben Jemia and Ben Achour 2014; Boubakri 2009). Indeed, as in Morocco, the law was a relatively cheap instrument for the Tunisian autocratic regime to foster its image as a reliable cooperation partner abroad and to guarantee external support. In the words of one respondent: 'There is the economic aspect, the blackmailing logic with the EU – you protect our borders, and in return you receive economic aid – but also: we will support this regime and this dictatorship' (T17-I13).

However, the 2004 law not only allowed Ben Ali to respond to European expectations and thus consolidate the external legitimacy of his regime; it was also a tool for the authoritarian state apparatus to increase surveillance over Tunisian society (Geisser 2019: 5–6). As Ben Jemia (2006, in Boubakri 2009: 16) notes, 'the "repressive spiral" intended for clandestine migration will put us all under constant surveillance and the rule of arbitrariness'. Like in Morocco, external factors can only partly explain the law's enactment, which was also driven by domestic political goals to increase national surveillance and security.

To conceal these goals, Tunisian authorities framed the law as a necessary legal adjustment to step up Tunisia's 'war against terrorism', pursued more forcefully after the terrorist attacks in the Tunisian beach resort Djerba on 11 April 2002 and the enactment of Law 2003–99 against terrorism. Linking irregular migration to terrorism and national security justified the fact that penalties for irregular migration were on par with sanctions of terrorism and transnational crime (Ben Jemia 2009: 270–71). At the same time, Law 2004–06 was presented as a tool to fight human trafficking of foreigners and Tunisians alike, and thus as a means to protect Tunisia's youth (Meddeb 2012: 377–78). In 2004, Interior Minister Hadi Mhenni emphasized before the Tunisian Parliament: 'President Zine El Abidine Ben Ali is paying close attention to the question of clandestine immigration because this issue is mainly

prisoners in Tunisian prisons between 2004 and 2010. For a more recent insight, see the testimonies collected by Glenda Garelli, Federica Sossi and Martina Tazzioli, *Réfugiés en Tunisie: entre détention et deportation*, 18 April 2015.

concerned with Tunisian youth. Our duty is to preserve Tunisian human beings' (J.O.R.T. 2004). De facto, however, the law allowed Ben Ali's regime to tighten its grip over population movements into, across and out of the national territory and thus contributed to internal regime stability. As one of my interviewees summarized, 'the 2004 law has been enacted in a logic of internal control' (M17–I2).

Given this securitarian grip on immigration, the field of immigration politics was dominated by the President, the MoI and security actors. Civil society activism was minimal, limited to humanitarian support by a few associations, and international organizations such as IOM and UNHCR, although present in Tunisia, did not venture into advocacy for migrants' rights and operated under surveillance of the state apparatus: 'No one was allowed to move on this topic other than the state' (T17-I1). This low level of civil society mobilization on migration reflected the more general absence of freedom of association under Ben Ali's regime, which denied critical associations legal registration and made funding from abroad inaccessible or channelled it through the regime (Bellin 1995; Boubakri 2013: 20): 'everyone was under surveillance' (T16-I4). Until the turn of the twenty-first century, migrant rights' violations were therefore, if at all, criticized only by European human rights activists or Tunisians living abroad. Although the advent of the Internet and social networks in the late 2000s did offer new opportunities for voicing discontent, my respondents highlighted how immigration was subjected to the so-called omertà[*] and therefore silenced in the public sphere.

Thus, when the revolution in January 2011 put an end to Ben Ali's autocratic rule, Tunisia's immigration policy was a patchwork of laws, bilateral agreements, exemptions and informal practices adopted over decades in view of ensuring the sovereignty as well as the internal and external legitimacy of the authoritarian regime in place.

The 2011 Revolution: A Window of Opportunity for Change

From the outset, revolution and migration were intrinsically linked, and immigration gained political salience in the public sphere, not only because freedom of movement was a central claim of revolutionaries

---

[*] Omertà refers to the code of silence that the mafia in Southern Italy requires from their members as part of their code of honour. It requires silence about criminal activity and a refusal to give evidence to the police in the context of questioning by authorities or other outsiders.

who would otherwise have voted with their feet but also because the political situation in neighbouring Libya prompted the arrival of large numbers of refugees and migrants in the south of Tunisia (Natter 2015b). The societal response to these large-scale arrivals was exemplary: families and hotel owners made their rooms available for refugees, and activists from Tunis travelled to the border areas to help distribute food, blankets and medicine: 'There was a momentum of popular solidarity' (T17-I20). At the same time, UNHCR stepped up its institutional response by setting up the Choucha refugee camp in February 2011 near Ras Jadir, a few kilometres away from the Southern Tunisian border with Libya. At the peak of the crisis, it received 18,000 people a day. For respondents, 'Choucha' became a code word to capture the emergence of immigration on the public and political agenda: 'Before there was no public debate, then there was Choucha ... This has changed things completely, it has turned immigration into an issue' (T16-I8). Such dynamics challenged the securitization and silencing of immigration that had dominated until 2011 and culminated in the institutional recognition of migration as an issue through the creation of the State Secretariat for Migration and Tunisians Abroad (SEMTE) in 2012. The 2011 revolution thus provided a window of opportunity for new actors to raise their voices and new interests to emerge.

New Faces, New Priorities: The Reshuffling of Domestic Politics

First of all, the democratic transition partially renewed Tunisia's political and administrative elite: while low-level civil servants often kept their positions, many high-level civil servants, deputies and ministers were replaced. In particular, the return of leftist and Islamist politicians from exile, and their integration into Tunisian institutions at the highest level, was central in politicizing migration in the immediate post-revolutionary period. Former political exiles who joined the Tunisian administration after 2011 brought their personal migration experiences with them and integrated concerns around migrants' political participation and discrimination into their political actions. In the words of Tunisia's first State Secretary for Migration and Tunisians Abroad, Houcine Jaziri, an Ennahdha politician formerly exiled in France: 'I was exiled for twenty years, so I knew migration as a subject, I was a subject of emigration.'

As a result, returnees crucially shaped immigration politics in the immediate aftermath of the revolution: for instance, Kamel Jendoubi, a human rights activist exiled in France for decades, was appointed president of the Independent Superior Commission for Elections (ISIE) in charge of organizing the 2011 elections and was a central figure behind the decision to grant Tunisians abroad eighteen seats in the National Constituent Assembly (NCA). Also, Radhouane Nouicer, the State Secretary of Foreign Affairs in Tunisia's transitional government (January to December 2011), played a key role in accelerating the negotiations for the UNHCR headquarters agreement, signed on 18 June 2011. As the head of the UNHCR Bureau for the Middle East and North Africa until 2010, his role as broker between his previous employer, UNHCR, and the Tunisian government was central to establishing the necessary trust between both parties to finalize the negotiations.

More generally, Members of Parliament (MPs) who had previously been exiled shaped the discussions on migration and asylum during the 2011–2014 constitution-making process. Indeed, there was no substantial debate within the NCA or its committee of rights and liberties on Article 26, which enshrined the right to political asylum,[*] according to respondents for two main reasons: on the one hand, the politically salient situation within the Choucha camp made NCA members aware of the necessity to create a legal framework on asylum. On the other hand, numerous NCA members (both Islamists and human rights activists) had been former political refugees in Europe themselves: 'These people were granted asylum rights in Europe, so they were grateful and wanted refugees to be treated with dignity [in Tunisia]', one high-level civil servant concluded.

Shifting from International to Domestic Political Legitimacy

Democratization provided the new regime with domestic legitimacy and thereby reduced the need for external façade support. However, while authoritarianism allowed Ben Ali's regime to mute public or political discussions on immigration and to conduct a policy dominated by foreign policy and security interests, democratization now required politicians to legitimize their political positions in front of the Tunisian electorate. Thus, the democratic transition shifted the emphasis of policy considerations from the international to the domestic political sphere.

This shift has been prominent in how Tunisian authorities repositioned themselves on migration in front of European actors in the immediate post-revolutionary period. In particular, Tunisian politicians referred to domestic demands and civil society pressure to refuse

---

[*] The right to political asylum was not included in the first constitutional draft of 14 December 2012, but only in its second draft of 22 April 2013. In all subsequent constitution drafts, the article has not been substantially changed. All drafts of the constitution can be accessed at http://majles.marsad.tn/fr/constitution/4.

European attempts to securitize Tunisian borders further and to sign a Europe-wide readmission agreement. Indeed, CSOs such as the Tunisian Forum for Economic and Social Rights (FTDES), the Association of African Students and Trainees in Tunisia (AESAT), Caritas or Terre d'Asile Tunisie (TAT) started to advocate for the protection of migrants, both of Tunisians disappeared in the Mediterranean Sea as well as of refugees and workers from Central and Western Africa (Boubakri 2013; Natter 2015b). In 2012, Tunisian authorities thus rejected the first version of the Mobility Partnership drafted by the European Union and came up with a proposal based on Tunisian priorities instead, namely job opportunities and visa facilitation for Tunisians, as well as the promotion of migrants' rights (Fargues and Fandrich 2012: 7–8). The eagerness with which Tunisian authorities before 2011 sought to polish their image abroad through paying lip service to European migration control imperatives thus seemed to have disappeared in the immediate post-revolution period.

Interviewees also highlighted that since 2011, Tunisian citizens' adherence to policies has become vital for their success, leading post-2011 governments to frame policies as 'home-made': politicians now emphasize that policies address domestic demands and are backed by Tunisian society instead of being imposed by external actors such as the United Nations or the European Union. Talking about the asylum law, one respondent stresses, 'If people say no, then parliamentarians will have a lot of difficulties to pass the law' (T16-I20). As a consequence, CSOs and IOs who lobby for migrants' rights focus on raising awareness within the Tunisian population and among parliamentarians. This contrasts with the situation in Morocco, where lacking democratic or parliamentary adherence to the 2013 reform has been highlighted as problematic by respondents, but not as an obstacle to policymaking in the first place.

In sum, the atmosphere of political change, the need for domestic political legitimation, and the integration of migrants and former exiles into the Tunisian state apparatus resulted in the institutional recognition of immigration: the State Secretariat for Migration and Tunisians Abroad (SEMTE) was created within the MoSA in 2012, and the right to asylum was enshrined in the 2014 Constitution. Also, Tunisia's transitional government relaxed the dispositions of the 2004 law that criminalized irregular migrants in March 2011, and work on the national migration strategy, as well as asylum and trafficking laws started. As one respondent from within the newly created General Directorate for International Cooperation on Migration (DGCIM) attached to the SEMTE said, 'Everyone got started.' Such dynamism demonstrates

Tunisia's attempt to leave behind the securitized approach and reform its immigration regime in the immediate aftermath of the revolution.

Democratization: The Drivers of Immigration Policy Continuity

This initial dynamism on immigration, however, died down over the course of 2013, when economic and security issues became more pressing. Besides fears that Libya's civil war next door would spill over into Tunisia, a series of political assassinations in 2013 triggered a national security crisis. In parallel, a sharp drop in foreign investments and tourism aggravated the economic crisis. These developments triggered institutional and domestic politics dynamics that drove the continuation of Tunisia's securitarian framing of immigration and of pre-2011 detention and expulsion practices, as well as the increasing administrative hassling of migrants. For instance, policy and law-making initiatives such as the *National Migration Strategy* (SNM) or the asylum law that were launched in 2011 never saw the light of day. Also, penalties for irregular stay were doubled in 2013, and students were facing increasing difficulties in accessing visas. Only Libyan immigrants continued to be tolerated by authorities based on Tunisia's foreign policy priorities. Ultimately, as democratization required political leaders to legitimize policies in front of an electorate, strategic depoliticization and policy continuity seemed the safest option when faced with conflicting domestic demands on immigration.

Institutional Drivers: The Fizzling Out of Legal and Policy Initiatives

The absence of legal change and the fizzling out of policy initiatives launched after 2011 epitomizes the continuity of Tunisia's authoritarian immigration regime: while work on the *National Migration Strategy* (SNM) and the draft laws on asylum and trafficking started shortly after the revolution, only the law on trafficking has been enacted by the end of 2020 and thus the centrepiece of Tunisia's immigration regime, Law 2004–06, remains untouched. Ultimately, governmental volatility and institutional instability have been major drivers behind the continuity of Tunisian immigration policy.

In 2012, the SEMTE, and in particular Khalil Amiri and the advisor of State Secretary Houcine Jaziri, started to elaborate the SNM. A first draft was presented at the end of 2013 (MAS 2013) but was not approved by the Council of Ministers due to a governmental change. The strategy was taken up again in 2015 within the framework of Tunisia's work on its five-year development plan (2016–2020). Workshops were organized throughout the Tunisian territory to discuss the SNM with international stakeholders, local authorities, social partners and civil society actors. A second version was circulated in November 2015 (MAS 2015), but the governmental reshuffling of early 2016 once again prevented the political validation of the strategy. The General Directorate for International Cooperation on Migration (DGCIM) within the MoSA continued to work on the strategy, publishing a third version in July 2017 (MAS 2017) that was under consideration of an intergovernmental commission in April 2019. In September 2020, a fourth revision of the strategy was on its way. Throughout these reviews, the four main pillars of the strategy – protecting the rights of Tunisians abroad, reinforcing the contribution of migrants to Tunisia's socio-economic development, promoting Tunisians' regular migration and preventing irregular migration, and protecting the rights of immigrants in Tunisia, including asylum seekers and refugees – have remained untouched. What is striking, however, is that the level of detail has *decreased* with each draft: from a dense, thirty-seven-page document in 2013 that included a detailed action plan, the SNM was reduced to a double-spaced, twelve-page document in 2017. This showcases how with every round of consultation, the common ground in terms of substance and strategic thinking has progressively declined.

Work on the asylum law also started early on, as the refugee crisis at the Tunisian–Libyan border attracted continuous political attention, and the 'post-revolutionary passion for human rights' (T17-I26) motivated policymakers to translate Tunisia's ratification of the Geneva Refugee Convention into domestic law. In October 2011, the Centre for Legal and Judicial Studies (CEJJ) of the Ministry of Justice (MoJ) was charged with elaborating the asylum law. A first draft was finalized in the spring of 2012 but withdrawn when UNHCR joined the CEJJ in the law-making process. Between 2013 and 2016, the CEJJ and UNHCR revised the draft asylum law, but the strained political situation and the government's economic and security priorities repeatedly delayed the process. New drafts of the law were presented by the MoJ in 2016 and 2018 and then forwarded to the Prime Minister's office, waiting to be sent to the Parliament (Ben Achour 2019; FTDES and Migreurop 2020: 38).

One civil society representative brought these dynamics to the point during a conference in Tunis in November 2016: 'The law is in elaboration – so we see that there is a political will – but it is in elaboration since 2011, so we also see that there are political brakes at work' (T16-D9). According to respondents, Tunisian authorities – in particular, the

Ministry of Interior (MoI) – are reluctant to enact an asylum law because of its potential pull effect attracting more refugees to Tunisia: 'The law is never going to pass I think. When you talk to public authorities, they tell you: honestly, no' (T17-I11). Over the years, these dynamics have changed little: in December 2020, at the occasion of the *International Migrant Day*, the FTDES, ATFD, EuroMed, TAT, LTDH and IADH once more called upon Tunisia's President to move forward with the enactment of the asylum law and to legally enshrine the protection of migrant rights.[1]

The dynamics around the asylum law illustrate the overall political climate on immigration: an initial dynamism due to a post-revolutionary euphoria for human rights, followed by a political stalemate because of dominant economic and security concerns. In particular, respondents argued that, once in power, new political leaders moved away from their initial, ideological positions and, faced with the realities of economic and security dynamics, adapted their political priorities accordingly:

The bottom line is always control. … Even the former Secretary of State Jaziri did not have the same speech in 2011, when he took the Secretary of State, compared to 2013, when he said that we must control [migration]. In 2011, he had an opening speech, free movement, resist Europe and all that. In 2013, we heard the same speech that we heard before 2011 and that we still hear today. … So there is the permanent need for control that imposes itself on everyone (T17-I32).

Such deeply ingrained institutional dynamics that led to the fizzling out of legal reform plans showcase the pre-eminence of security interests in driving immigration politics. However, policy continuity was also shaped by the newly emerging domestic politics around immigration.

Domestic Politics: Tunisians First[2]

Contradictory Popular Demands. Democratization opened up political processes for civil society input and popular requests. But Tunisian policymakers were confronted with conflicting claims by the population: the unprecedented increase in civil liberties prompted civil society activism for more migrants' rights, but the liberalization of the public sphere also spurred racist backlashes against migrants. It allowed both those who felt discriminated to voice their concerns and request equality, such as Black Tunisians, students from Central and Western Africa or rejected asylum seekers stuck in the Choucha camp, as well as those who felt endangered by diversity to express their fears and aggressions. These contradictory demands explain why the democratic transition did ultimately not translate into a human rights-based immigration reform.

As developed earlier, official national identity discourses before 2011 highlighted Tunisia's homogeneity, and authoritarianism promoted a single national identity conception cast around republican ideals. After 2011, talking about 'diversity' became possible: 'With the revolution, all those who were repressed and who did not have the right to speak were given space' (T17-I14). Opinions on politics, religion and identity started to diverge (Pouessel 2012a): 'Before the revolution, we spoke of *the* Tunisian, period. ... After the revolution, everyone was talking about differences, about the Black, feminist, Muslim, atheist Tunisian and so on' (T16-I12). In December 2011, Black activist Maha Abdelhamid published an open letter that kick-started the politicization of the racial question in Tunisia.[3] Associations were founded to raise awareness about Tunisia's Black minority and deeply racialized society, such as the collective ADAM, the Tunisian Association for the Support of Minorities (ATSM) and the association M'nemty (My Dream). Many of my interviewees, for instance, talked about El Gosba, a village in the South of Tunisia that had made headlines because of its racially segregated school buses – for 'White' and 'Black' Tunisian schoolkids, respectively.[4] Also TV programs took on the issue of anti-Black racism and discrimination of ethnic minorities (Scaglioni 2017).

The newly gained freedom of expression, however, liberated not only calls for human rights and diversity but also racist and exclusionary sentiments, with Black Tunisians and migrants from Western and Central Africa alike facing growing racist aggression – verbal and physical – in the Tunisian public sphere (Scaglioni 2017: 23–27; TAT 2018). As one respondent highlighted, 'What is new is that racism has degenerated into aggressions. There is a lot of verbal aggression in Tunisia since the revolution that was not there before' (T17-I20). In part, the falling away of institutional protection of select migrant groups through Ben Ali's regime can explain this overt racism. As one respondent recalls, 'At the time you were left alone, no one disturbed you, no one insulted you on the street – no one dared to, because somehow foreigners were well protected by the police, they were the President's guests' (T16-I25). Indeed, Western and Central African migrants' presence in Tunisia was seen as intimately related to the old regime: 'Once the President was on TV and informed all Tunisians that the AfDB was there for their benefit, that they should not touch them [African employees], that they had to respect and welcome them' (T17-I21). In an oppressed political context, this created a relatively safe environment for Western and Central African students and irregular workers who, according to one respondent, 'managed to blend in with the AfDB population' (T17-I6). This does not mean that racism against Black Tunisians or immigrants was not widespread before 2011,[5] but it can explain why suddenly migrants from Western and Central Africa became an open target once Ben Ali's police state was toppled: 'When the revolution happened in 2011, all this grudge exploded' (T16-I16).

Strategic Depoliticization. In response to these contradictory popular demands, Tunisian politicians strategically depoliticized immigration and privileged policy continuity to avoid the issue altogether. Policymakers highlighted the need to unite the Tunisian population under a common identity instead of politicizing its diversity. Indeed, after the 2014 Constitution put an official end to national identity debates, political leaders sought to avoid further societal polarization and concentrated on fostering unity among Tunisians: 'We are in an atmosphere of consensus where everyone agrees that we should not be debating or should not be fractured as a population' (T17-I31). Civil society calls to recognize Tunisia's ethnic and racial diversity did not fit this agenda. Instead of seeing them as a contribution to Tunisian democratization, politicians cast CSOs working on immigration and discrimination as unpatriotic and dividing the Tunisian nation. One civil society respondent recounts:

You often hear people say: You talk about discrimination? Who paid you to talk about that? We need unity now, not the division of society ... So there is no room for difference in this vision, for them speaking of discrimination is division.

Next to this discourse of national unity, respondents across the board framed immigration as a non-priority in the face of more pressing socioeconomic and security issues. Public and political agendas put 'Tunisians first' and concentrated on issues such as terrorism or unemployment to improve citizens' living conditions. When prompted on the need for immigration reform, interviewees overwhelmingly responded, 'it's not the right moment' (T16-I12); 'they have other fish to fry at the moment ... It's a luxury to think about questions like immigration' (T17-I4). The Afrobarometer (2015b) confirms this, with unemployment (57 per cent), crime and security (43 per cent), poverty and destitution (31 per cent), the management of the economy (28 per cent) and education (17 per cent) as the top five priorities of Tunisians at that time.

This 'navel-gazing' (T17-I6) was cast by respondents as a logical consequence of the revolution, as Tunisians first and foremost had to redefine their own priorities – leaving little space to deal with 'the other': 'Of course you start first with yourself ... before you start to think about foreigners in Tunisia' (T17-I10). As a result, policymakers have consciously depoliticized immigration. For respondents, this 'non-management of migrants in Tunisian reflects a choice' (T16-I3), as politicization would require taking a position:

They are there, they live, they work, they have families, they rent apartments, but we are ignoring it, certainly for political reasons, because we would have to explain how and why we accept people coming in.

While this non-policy succeeded in avoiding partisan and popular polarization on immigration in the first decade of democratization, it remains to be seen whether depoliticization is sustainable in the long term.

Foreign Policy Drivers: The Libyan Question

While depoliticization can also partly be explained by the small scale of immigration in the case of European and Western or Central African migrants, which hover around a few ten thousand, the magnitude argument does not explain the laissez-faire policy adopted towards Libyan immigration. Although reliable statistics are lacking, one can reasonably estimate that around 500,000 Libyan citizens permanently reside in Tunisia. This corresponds to roughly 5 per cent of the Tunisian population. Libyan migrants have affected Tunisia's everyday life, in particular the rental market, private health sector or food and oil prices. Yet, their presence is not politicized, no political party has tried to scapegoat Libyan migrants, and no decisions are taken to regulate or limit their presence in Tunisia.

Tunisia's approach is one of 'laissez-faire' (T17-I7, T17-I10, T17-I13, T17-I14). According to respondents, an internal governmental note stipulates that Libyans should be tolerated regardless of their legal status. In 2014, a circular of the Ministry of Education (MoE) allowed the creation of Libyan private schools, as well as the enrolment of Libyan children in Tunisian public schools. And in November 2014, Tunisia's then Head of Government, Mehdi Jomâa, pointed at the socio-economic and security challenges raised by the presence of allegedly 1.2 million Libyans in Tunisia, concluding, however, 'Our Libyan neighbours will always remain welcome.'[6] Why has Libyan migration not been politicized in Tunisia?

Interviewees highlighted pragmatism as a driver for this laissez-faire approach: because Libyans can enter and leave Tunisia freely, the Tunisian government is not forced to act – 'Why make laws, procedures, residence permits if Libyans can circulate freely?' (T17-I32). Pragmatism also characterizes UNHCR's justification for not recognizing Libyans as refugees, given that Tunisia offers Libyans '*de facto* protection' by letting them enter and stay on its territory. Other respondents suggested that UNHCR has been instructed by the Tunisian government not to deal with Libyan applicants for political reasons. As Boubakri (2015: 18–19) notes, 'Tunisian authorities want to avoid Libyans accessing the refugee status to accelerate their return once the conflict is over.' In this vein, only about thirty Libyan citizens requested support from UNHCR in 2018–2019.[7]

Underlying this 'pragmatic neutrality' (Murphy 2014: 243) – characteristic of Tunisian foreign policy more broadly – are geopolitical considerations: Tunisian governments are acutely aware of the potential economic powerhouse that Libya represents and, with two Libyan governments next door, Tunisia's overarching foreign policy imperative is to remain neutral towards Libya's internal conflict and to secure future cooperation no matter the outcome of the civil war (Natter 2021c). Indeed, once Libya recovers from its internal crisis, Tunisia will be 'the first one to profit' (T16-I7). Libya has been an important destination for Tunisian workers since the 1970s and Tunisia's second-largest economic partner after the European Union throughout the 2000s in terms of imports and exports. Since 2003, Libyans have also become an important clientele for Tunisian private health clinics and the tourism sector (AfDB 2011). Although economic exchanges with Libya collapsed over the course of 2011, Tunisia has profited from the presence of Libyans after the revolution, who were welcome consumers in a difficult economic situation. In the words of one of my respondents, 'It [laissez-faire] is a very realistic position, especially if you look at the power balance, with small Tunisia and the very rich, huge Libya next to it' (T16-I17).

Furthermore, as both supporters and opponents of the Gaddafi regime have sought refuge in Tunisia, Tunisia seeks to avoid importing Libya's conflict at all costs. In summer 2014, the Tunisian government reiterated that Libyans are welcome provided that they do not engage in any political activities.[8] According to one interviewee, there is even an implicit agreement between the Tunisian Ministry of Interior (MoI) and the heads of Libyan communities guaranteeing that Libyans will not exercise any political activities in Tunisia: 'Libyans have really tried to use Tunisia as if it were Switzerland' (T17-I29), as a neutral, safe haven. Tunisia's deliberate laissez-faire policy reflects this strategic neutrality towards Libya: 'Libyans are left in the dark, but they are tolerated. ... It is crystal clear: They [Tunisian authorities] want to retain the current situation, the current status quo' (T17-I20).

Tunisian authorities legitimized this laissez-faire policy with an official discourse that cast Libyans as 'guests' or 'brothers'. A discourse of brotherhood, fraternity and hospitality also dominated my interviews with civil society and state respondents, who highlighted the shared cultural habits and family bonds between Libyans and Tunisians, particularly in the South. Indeed, Southern Tunisia has always seen transborder commerce and the irregular movements of goods and people between Tunisia and Libya, and Tunisia has always been a destination for Libyans to do business and receive healthcare. When prompted on the Libyan presence in Tunisia, standard answers were: 'Libya is a special case' (T16-I2); 'Libyans are not immigrants, they are our brothers, our guests' (T16-I11); 'It's as if they were at home … they are like Tunisian citizens' (T17-I28).

While this discourse suggests that Libyans are tolerated in Tunisia, the laissez-faire policy ultimately subjects Libyans to the same risks as other migrants: legal uncertainty, difficulties in accessing public healthcare and education, as well as the arbitrariness of Tunisian administration and security forces. As one civil society respondent said, 'They cannot have residence permits, they cannot work officially, we see a lot of precarity and protection issues also for Libyans' (T17-I3). In particular, while Libyans arrived in Tunisia with considerable financial reserves in the early 2010s, as time passed and the situation in Libya deteriorated, they experienced increasing financial difficulties (Mouley 2016). The framing of Libyans as guests has also sidelined them in civil society work: Tunisian CSOs mobilized on immigration mostly do not include Libyans in their work, with the exception of the TAT and the Media and Human Rights Observatory who provide Libyans with healthcare and psychological support.

Although not dominating socio-political debates, an 'anti-Libyan' discourse has also started to emerge over time on particular issues (Mouley 2016: 59). For example, the Tunisian government's decision to facilitate property purchases for Libyans in autumn 2016 – a measure intended mainly to attract investments in the housing sector – has led to a public outcry. In reaction to protests by Tunisians fearing a further rise in housing prices, the decree was amended a few months later to limit these facilitations to properties worth over 200 million dinars [around 100 million USD at the time].[9] Paradoxically, Libyans are made responsible not only for the rising house and food prices because of their wealth and purchasing power, but, at the same time, also for burdening the public healthcare and food subvention system because of their increasing poverty. Thus, although the laissez-faire policy adopted by successive Tunisian governments seems indeed a pragmatic response towards Libyan immigration as it has kept its political salience low (see also Roman and Pastore 2018), the question remains how political parties and the population at large will respond to the protracted stay and impoverishment of Libyans in the longer term.

Pressures from Within, Below and Outside: The Drivers of Heterogeneous Developments

Although immigration was largely sidelined by political actors for domestic and foreign policy reasons after 2013, this did not preclude a total absence of policy developments. Yet, the changes that have been enacted showcase a striking continuity with Tunisian authorities' historically engrained, piecemeal approach towards immigration that maximizes state power over immigration. Two drivers have been key in reinforcing the 'very ambiguous, scattered and incoherent' (T16-I25) nature of Tunisia's immigration regime: on the one hand, institutional dynamics and the priority to secure state control over population movements explain why those changes that have occurred on immigration have remained either group-specific or at the level of informal arrangements. On the other hand, international norm adherence and year-long pressures from civil society and external actors drove a discursive shift among public authorities, as well as minor legal changes on human trafficking and racism by effectively linking migrants' rights to Tunisians' rights. However, these scattered changes did not affect the core of Tunisia's immigration regime: residence permits. With the laws on immigration and asylum untouched, Tunisia's administration has so far remained immune to bottom-up and external pressures for liberal reform.

Institutional Drivers: Securing the State's Room for Manoeuvre[10]

Ambiguity and Informality as Power. The overall immigration policy continuity in Tunisia has indeed been accompanied by minor policy changes. As in Morocco, however, Tunisian policymakers have preferred informal arrangements over legal reform to secure the state's discretionary power. In the words of one Tunisian respondent:

Tunisia does not want to be held accountable by something that is written, that is palpable, like a residence card, a law, a circular. ... Whatever domain you are looking at, you will find the same logic, keeping the ambiguity, so that discretion remains the basic framework for managing migration (T17-I32).

Tunisia's approach to refugees is exemplary in this regard: in principle, refugees with a UNHCR certificate do not receive a residence permit from the Ministry of Interior (MoI), as Tunisia does not officially recognize the document. But there is some room for manoeuvre within state institutions: in January 2015, the NGO ADRA launched a project together with UNHCR on the labour market integration of refugees in Tunisia. Although not provided for in the law, the Bureau of Emigration and Foreign Labour Force within the Ministry of Employment and Professional Training (MoEPF) now hands out work permits for refugees based merely on a UNHCR certificate and a work contract. The work permit then allows refugees to apply for a residence permit at the MoI. While this has created an informal regularization mechanism for refugees via employment, refugees' access to residence permits remains highly arbitrary given the case-by-case basis of this informal procedure. As a further step, an administrative note of the MoSA from May 2019 allowed such refugees registered with UNHCR that have contracts authorized by the MoL to access Tunisian social services via the National Social Security Fund (CNSS). In June 2020, a refugee has for the first time officially joined the CNSS.[11]

Informal arrangements also prevail regarding student visas. During a meeting of the association Doctors of the World Belgium (MdM-B) and the MoI in February 2017, the Directorate of Borders and Foreigners committed to changing its practice of delivering seven-day visas to students at the airport, and instead agreed to grant them a one-month visa to prevent them from falling into irregularity after one week. However, as the representative of MdM-B said at a public event in May 2017, 'The director committed to deal with this on a case-by-case basis. ... We did not get a written commitment from the MoI, they did not want that' (T17-D6).

Similarly, IOM and TAT were capable of negotiating case-by-case exemptions from irregular stay penalties with the Ministry of Finance (MoF). According to respondents, this was an informal arrangement with one specific civil servant at the MoF, who used their discretionary power to resolve individual cases. When he/she changed position in April 2016, this informal procedure was ended: 'The new person in charge said there is no legal text that allows the penalties to be cancelled, and so they will stop doing that' (T16-I8). This ambiguity and informality grant the Tunisian administration considerable discretionary power to reverse its standpoint at any moment and thereby jeopardizes the situation of migrants on the ground.

Lastly, civil society work on irregular migrants remains fragile because the restrictive law of 2004 is still in place. Although the sanctions for assisting irregular migrants have not been implemented since 2011, 'the law is like a sword of Damocles ... it's true that the law is not enforced, but it is still there' (T17-I15). By not reforming the 2004 law, the Tunisian executive retains the power to enforce or suspend such dispositions according to its priorities. CSOs are therefore not safe from a potential backlash – as a member of TAT told me: 'When we asked the former State Secretary to give us a paper that recognizes our work in case the 2004 law would be enforced again at some point, this was not possible.' Repealing or replacing the law with a new legal framework would bind the state to guarantee migrants' rights. For some respondents, it is paradoxically the non-enforcement of the 2004 law that epitomizes the continuity of autocratic political practices: 'In a democracy, it is the law that counts, when we do not apply the law, we are not in a democracy' (T17-I29).

Group-Based Exemptions. In parallel to informal arrangements, a series of small, ad-hoc measures has facilitated entry or alleviated problems for specific migrant groups since 2011, mainly driven by economic interests: in June 2012, the Tunisian government removed all requirements for Algerian workers to comply with the 1963 Establishment Convention; they can now work in Tunisia with a simple work contract. Within Tunisia's dire economic context, this unilateral decision was taken with the expectation that Algeria would, in return, remove limitations for Tunisian workers. In April 2015, the Ministry of Foreign Affairs (MoFA) removed visa requirements for Burkina Faso, the DRC, Congo-Brazzaville, Zimbabwe, Botswana and the Central African Republic to boost tourism and encourage trade – a decision that has apparently not been implemented by the MoI.[12] And in 2016, a new investment law broadened the possibilities of companies to hire foreign workers at the managerial level or with specific skills. This option had existed for fully exporting companies in the past; it is now available to all companies operating in Tunisia.

Most importantly, however, the decree on irregular stay penalties, which had been amended back in 2013 to double the fine, was revised once more in response to relentless lobbying by international and civil society actors. While most migrants enter Tunisia regularly, more than 70 per cent of migrants – workers, students and refugees alike – fall into irregularity at some point (Nasraoui 2016; TAT 2016). In their survey of 314 migrants, Terre d'Asile Tunisie, for instance, found that 11 per cent had already been in detention (TAT 2016: 46–47). More generally, it has become difficult for migrants to regularize their stay and 'to seize the sesame, the famous residence permit' (T16-I23). Given the number of migrants affected, Tunisian and international actors – in particular, TAT, the UGTT, ILO and IOM – started exercising pressure on the Tunisian government from below and outside to advocate a reform of the decree, highlighting its negative repercussions for Tunisia's attractiveness as a destination for African students and entrepreneurs. To raise awareness, civil society respondents emphasized that penalties pushed migrants to risk their lives in the Mediterranean Sea:

If you have a migrant who stayed three years in Tunisia in an irregular situation, he has to pay 4,000 dinars *[equivalent to around 2,000 USD in 2016]*, that's more than what he would pay to go to Lampedusa, today to go to Lampedusa you pay 800 euros (T16-I16).

Respondents also pointed at the decreasing number of Western and Central African students in Tunisia to show how penalties jeopardized Tunisia's image as a student destination: according to AESAT, Tunisia's Western and Central African student population has decreased from 13,000 to 6,000 within ten years.[13] And in 2015, a survey within the African student community showed that out of 400 people, 100 per cent wanted to leave Tunisia. This is particularly dire for Tunisia's private education sector, as African students are a significant source of income (TAT 2018: 8–9).

These advocacy efforts were at least partly successful: although penalties were not cancelled, a decree from the MoF in September 2017 set an upper limit of 3,000 dinars for penalties (corresponding to roughly three years of penalties or around 1,200 USD at the time), and exempted refugees and victims of trafficking from paying the penalties altogether. In April 2018, students and trainees were also exempted (TAT 2018: 29). Although a victory for part of Tunisia's migrant community, the high upper limit and the small number of people effectively exempted by the revision confirm the symbolic nature of change. Even the legal reforms on human trafficking and racial discrimination discussed next, which resulted from external and domestic pressures, respectively, do not challenge the overall policy continuity in Tunisia's immigration regime.

External and Internal Pressures for International Norm Adherence

External Agenda Setting: The Law Against Human Trafficking. As in Morocco, international norms and actors were key in triggering the only legal policy change on immigration in Tunisia since 2011: the law against human trafficking. Back in 2009, under the regime of Ben Ali, an ad-hoc inter-ministerial group led by the MoJ had already initiated work on a draft law on trafficking (IOM 2013: 49). In 2012, the American State Department upgraded Tunisia in its yearly Trafficking in Persons Report and financed the first countrywide study on trafficking (IOM 2013) – only to downgrade Tunisia again to the 'Tier 2 Watch

List' in 2013 (J/TIP 2017). According to respondents, these developments prompted Tunisia's work on human trafficking legislation.

As a result of this 'external agenda setting' by foreign governments and IOs, human trafficking has been turned from a political taboo into a 'fashionable subject. ... Now everyone is convinced that there is trafficking, everyone is talking about it' (T17-I23). *Law 2016–61 relative to the prevention and the fight against human trafficking* was elaborated by the MoJ in close collaboration with IOM and passed on 3 August 2016. Although the effectiveness of protection mechanisms provided by the law remains unclear – trafficking victims only receive a residence permit in Tunisia for the duration of the legal procedure, even if they denounce the organizers of trafficking – the law was successful in that it removed Tunisia again from the American State Department's watch list in 2017 (J/TIP 2017).

Two other elements explain the smooth enactment of the anti-trafficking law in contrast to the political stalemate on asylum – and they mirror those in Morocco: first, the law not only protects foreigners trafficked into or through Tunisia, such as Ivorian housemaids, but also Tunisian victims of trafficking – in particular, those working in the Gulf. Framing trafficking as a problem affecting Tunisians increased the societal relevance of the law and the engagement of national policymakers: 'It was much easier to gather people around this issue' (T17-I15). Second, it was a 'low cost–high gains' law, with high geopolitical image gain, little impact on public life, as well as few efforts required for its implementation. Adopting a law against trafficking provided Tunisia with an opportunity to internationally showcase Tunisia's adherence to a community of modern, liberal states. In the words of Lorena Lando, head of IOM in Tunisia, at a public event in May 2017: 'We see that Tunisia has the willingness to act on trafficking, and to be part of the countries that attack this problem.'

Bottom-Up Pressures: The Law Against Racism. Norm adherence also drove Tunisia's law against racial discrimination, but instead of being incited from outside, it was prompted by civil society activism. Back in 2011, civil society had called upon the National Constituent Assembly (NCA) to integrate the prohibition of racial discrimination into the new constitution – without success: 'Even though some deputies at the time were supporting the initiative ..., the majority said, no, there is no discrimination problem in Tunisia' (T16-I12). With Black Tunisians and migrants from Western and Central Africa facing increasing racist aggression, migrant associations and CSOs became more vocal on the topic. On 21 March 2016, three Tunisian CSOs – the Tunisian Forum for Economic and Social Rights (FTDES), Euromed Rights, and the Committee for the Respect of Liberties and Human Rights (CRDHT) – presented a draft law against racial discrimination.[14] In June, eighteen Members of Parliament (MPs) submitted it to Parliament for consideration. Despite receiving cross-partisan support at the time, the draft law was not discussed in Parliament for over two years.

Repeated, racially motivated attacks in the public sphere, however, increased civil society pressure. In October 2016, a young Black Tunisian, Sabrine Ngoy, denounced the indifference of police and politicians towards racial aggressions: 'I am asking myself: Do I not have the right to walk through the streets of my country without hearing insults because of my skin colour?'[15] This prompted an official excuse by Mehdi Ben Gharbia, minister for relations with constitutional bodies, civil society, and human rights, a few days later. Only two months later, however, in December 2016, three Congolese students were attacked with knives in the centre of Tunis, triggering protests and a social media campaign by AESAT and TAT around the slogan: 'I don't want to die in Tunisia because I'm Black.'[16] Media coverage of these events forced institutional actors to react: On 26 December, the *National Day Against Racial Discrimination*, Prime Minister Chahed called for accelerating the work around the draft law against racism.[17]

In early 2017, the government took over the revision of the draft law – reducing the initial thirty-six articles to eleven articles. The final draft was discussed in consultation with civil society and UN bodies on 20 November 2017, and *Law 2018–50 for the Elimination of all Forms of Racial Discrimination* was adopted on 9 October 2018. It punishes racist statements and acts by a prison sentence of one month to one year and a fine of up to 1,000 dinars [around 370 USD at the time] and creates a *National Commission to Fight Discrimination,* ultimately launched in July 2020. The law was welcomed by political leaders, civil society and the international community: Messaoud Romdhani, president of the FTDES, called it 'a turning point in the history of Tunisia, equal to the abolition of slavery',[18] and the independent deputy Raouf El May said, 'We took time to do it, but now it's there, and we can be proud to be the first in the Arab world.'[19]

Despite their involvement in the law-making process, however, CSOs have been the first to criticize the law's limitations.[20] According to them, the law is first and foremost symbolic, as Black communities need to gain confidence in Tunisia's police and legal system before the law can show its effects on the ground. For activist Khawla Ksiksi, [the law] remains on paper; the reality on the ground is very different. Victims do not have the financial means to start costly legal proceedings, they cannot wait years to win a case, and in some instances, it is not socially realistic or acceptable to file complaints against neighbours or family members.[21]

In 2019, CSOs set up a network of nine Anti-Discrimination Points (PAD) across the territory to monitor discriminations on the ground, and in June 2020, in the context of the Black Lives Matter protests in the United States, protests erupted again: on 6 June, thirty-one Tunisian associations organized a large-scale anti-racism protest in the centre of Tunis.[22] Saadia Mosbah, heading the association M'nemty that led the protest, denounced:

We do not change society by decree. You need genuine political will to launch educational programs and to raise awareness amongst citizens. But the government is not completely here because black lives are not a priority.[23]

Little has thus changed in practice, both for victims of racial discrimination as well as migrants more generally. The progressive changes that have been enacted within Tunisia's broader immigration regime have been either largely symbolic or limited to particular migrant groups that benefit from combined international and civil society support. These policy dynamics and the scattered, ambiguous immigration regime that results from it showcase the striking continuity of restrictive immigration policy substance, as well as of Tunisian authorities' historically engrained, piecemeal approach towards immigration that privileges internal and external regime stability over legal reform and human rights.

Shifting Configurations of Immigration Policy Drivers in Tunisia

This chapter has analysed the drivers of Tunisian immigration policy before, during and after the 2011 regime change, showcasing that the main consequence of democratization has been the increased centrality of domestic politics. While in the past, immigration policy was almost exclusively a tool to consolidate state sovereignty and the international legitimation of Tunisia's authoritarian regimes, democratization has shifted the emphasis of immigration policy drivers from foreign policy towards the domestic realm, showcasing the centrality of political economy explanations of immigration policy in democratic contexts. At the same time, the role of deeply engrained national identity narratives and the imperative to secure state power over immigration remained relatively unaffected by regime change.

Migration was set on the agenda in 2011 because the post-revolution euphoria for human rights and the will to create a transparent, inclusive Tunisia spilt over into migration issues. Also, previously exiled politicians who were integrated into Tunisian institutions after 2011 brought with them their experiences as migrants and refugees. Yet, the democratic transition and the increase in freedom of expression affected the politicization of immigration in two opposite ways: it created more space for civil society activism on migration, but it also freed up previously repressed racist sentiments, leading to increasing stigmatization of Black Tunisians as well as Western and Central African immigrants in the public sphere. As a result of these conflicting claims and the more pressing economic and security issues in transitional Tunisia, the initial dynamism on immigration reform waned after 2013, and migration largely disappeared from public and political debates.

To ensure democratic accountability, political legitimacy and social stability, domestic policymakers put 'Tunisians first' and reverted to predominant security imperatives. This explains why policymakers have strategically depoliticized immigration and been reluctant to engage in more liberal stances towards foreigners (European, Western and Central African, and Libyan alike). Such insight also resonates with broader research conducted on racial immigration policies in the Americas (FitzGerald and Cook-Martín 2014) or asylum politics in Africa (Milner 2006), suggesting that, paradoxically, democratization and immigration restrictions can go hand in hand.

Only through lobbying from below and outside have the fringes of Tunisia's immigration regime – racial discrimination, human trafficking and irregular stay penalties – been reformed or adapted through informal, case-by-case arrangements. While the laws on human trafficking and racial discrimination suggest some movement in the overall policy continuity, these changes are primarily symbolic, seeking to showcase Tunisia's adherence to international human rights, but with limited effects in terms of the number of people concerned and the rights granted to them. As the asylum law and a reform of the 2004 law are out of sight, the core of Tunisia's immigration regime – entry and stay rights – has remained untouched. This demonstrates the resilience of the pre-revolutionary, restrictive approach to immigration and the importance of deeply engrained, national path dependency dynamics in understanding not only immigration policy change but also continuity.

One issue that is becoming central to civil society advocacy, but has been ignored by Tunisian policymakers so far, is the regularization of irregular migrants. Inspired by Moroccan policy developments, CSOs are increasingly requesting a regularization campaign in Tunisia, most recently in 2020, as a possible solution to protect migrants in the context of the COVID-19 pandemic. Tunisian authorities' reaction to such demands will set the direction for future developments: on the one hand, regularization is a one-off policy measure and as such does not engage the Tunisian state in the long term. It could thus be one more layer in Tunisia's ambiguous, provisional approach. On the other hand, a regularization would make Tunisian authorities enter policy territory that they have avoided until now: the question of residence permits. In the medium-term, this could increase pressures on the state to reform the 2004 law and enact an asylum law. The immigration history of Western Europe and the current developments in East Asian countries such as Japan, South Korea or Malaysia suggest that Tunisia's policy of ignoring immigration is unlikely to be sustainable in the long run: at some point, governments end up acknowledging the reality of immigration and, willingly or grudgingly, accommodate it (Castles, de Haas and Miller 2014).

The state-civil society dynamics that characterize such immigration policymaking stand at the centre of Chapter 7. In particular, it dissects the inter-actor power plays that underpin the ambiguous effects of democratization in Tunisia, whereby the greater inclusion of political and societal actors in policymaking has not led to progress in terms of human rights but to policy stalemate and the re-emergence of security imperatives.

7 The Ambiguous Effects of Democratization

A Changing Cartography of Actors in Tunisia's Immigration Policy Field

Over the years, Tunisia's decision-making landscape on immigration and power relations between state, civil society and international actors became increasingly complex. Before 2011, immigration policymaking was highly secretive, controlled by the MoI and the President and dominated by a security approach. While other ministries (Employment, Social Affairs, Finance) were in charge of certain aspects of immigration control, the lack of inter-ministerial coordination ensured everyone was working in silos, following presidential instructions. Civil society activism was minimal, limited to humanitarian support by a few associations such as Caritas or the FTDES. IOM and UNHCR, although present in Tunisia, did not venture into advocacy for migrants' rights and operated under surveillance of the state apparatus. External influence on immigration policy was strictly limited to diplomatic channels, mainly with Italy or France, or select international actors such as the African Development Bank hosted in Tunis since 2004.

In this context, '2011 was a game-changer' (T17-I32). The political landscape opened up to accommodate numerous actors from within the Tunisian state, civil society and the international sphere. Compared to the autocratic power monopoly of the MoI before 2011, the immigration dossier now lies at the intersection of different ministerial portfolios: the newly created SEMTE is in charge of drafting the National Migration Strategy, the CEJJ within the MoJ is responsible for elaborating laws on asylum and racial discrimination, Ministries of Health, Employment and Higher Education of providing their services to migrants. Yet, inter-ministerial cooperation, although attempted anew, has been largely unsuccessful, with diverging visions impeding policy processes and turf wars creating policy inconsistencies. Generalized political volatility at the governmental level has only aggravated this.

The fact that Tunisian Parliament, civil society and social partners now participate in policymaking further complicates the picture. In particular, civil society activism has been mushrooming since 2011: migrant organizations were created, the work by Tunisian human rights NGOs amplified, and local branches of international NGOs were set up. Funded mainly by international and European actors, this burgeoning civil society has markedly increased pressure on Tunisian state institutions to secure immigrants' rights, but it has also faced challenges of internal competition and overlapping projects that has diminished its striking force. In contrast, political parties and Members of Parliament (MPs), although key actors in Tunisian politics over the past decade, have not been central in initiating immigration policy debates on immigration so far, in line with the strategic depoliticization of immigration.

Lastly, European diplomatic actors and international organizations have been keen on supporting Tunisian civil society and administration in advancing justice reform, security reform or economic development in the context of Tunisia's democratization – tying in the migration issue wherever possible. In early 2011, IOs specialized in migration (UNHCR, ILO, ICMPD) arrived in Tunisia to respond to the large-scale arrivals from Libya and have since consolidated their position as key actors in Tunisia's immigration policy field. While European pressure on Tunisia to control irregular migration has not subsided over the past decade, Tunisian governments are increasingly aware of Tunisia's interests in the African neighbourhood and continue to resist European externalization attempts, invoking the interests of the Tunisian democratic electorate that largely sees migration as a right. As in Morocco, Tunisian immigration politics thus increasingly takes place within a three-level game.

The following sections delve into the power dynamics characterizing Tunisian immigration policymaking within and among this plethora of state, civil society and international actors. They showcase that the 'regime effect' – that is, the fact that specific immigration policy dynamics are inherent to liberal democracy – primarily concerns policy processes that are central to political economy approaches and specific aspects of institutionalism.

Dynamics Within the Tunisian State

The democratic transition has affected the Tunisian state at its core. Despite continuities within lower-level administration, Tunisia's political institutions – government, Parliament and high-level ministerial positions – have undergone significant changes. Democratization also fundamentally reshaped regime strategies for political legitimation, as political leaders now had to legitimize (immigration) policies in front of Tunisia's electorate. How have these changes brought about by democratization affected immigration policymaking dynamics within the Tunisian state? The end of authoritarianism meant that high-level civil servants reclaimed political initiative and that inter-institutional dialogue was attempted anew – also on immigration. While the involvement of state institutions on immigration was limited to the MoI's security approach before 2011, the revolution set immigration on the agenda of a plethora of state actors. However, while democratization has empowered institutional actors, it has also propelled diverging institutional identities – and hence conflicting visions on immigration – to the fore, triggering policy stalemate instead of dynamism. Rather than pushing the reset button, democratization has highlighted the inherently complex administrative architecture of the modern state. In addition, the volatility of Tunisian governments in the first decade of democratization obstructed attempts to move beyond economic and security priorities. This explains why previously exiled politicians did ultimately not act upon the mirror effect by translating their migratory experiences into liberal immigration policy changes. In this context, policy continuity – which did not require taking a position – seemed the safest option. Such insights highlight the importance of institutionalist approaches in making sense of immigration politics not only in consolidated liberal democracies but also in times of regime change.

An Autocratic Monopoly on Information and Decision-Making Until 2011

Under Ben Ali's authoritarian regime, only the President, the Tunisian security apparatus, and the Ministry of Interior (MoI) – called 'a state within the state' (T16-I23, T16-I16) – were involved in immigration policymaking (Boubakri 2009): 'Immigration was nearly a state secret' (T17-D1). In the late 1990s, Ben Ali adopted a divide-and-rule strategy that sought to isolate departments from each other to retain control over the administration. Decision-making responsibility was taken away from high-level civil servants – 'everyone, even General Directors, were transformed into implementers!' (T16-I23). The resulting compartmentalization of the state administration reinforced the power of the MoI and its Directorate of Borders and Foreigners. Although units within the MoFA, the MoHE or MoEPF were in charge of specific aspects of Tunisia's immigration policy, they were not communicating with each other and not involved in central decision-making: 'Other departments had no say at all ... it was the MoI who managed foreigners' (T16-I16).

168   The Ambiguous Effects of Democratization

These bureaucratic dynamics explain Tunisia's opaque and arbitrary approach towards immigration over the 1990s and 2000s: regulations on foreigners were generally confidential, no effective legal tools were available to foreigners to appeal against denied residency permits, and systematic references to notions of public order provided a convenient justification for discretionary powers of police and MoI (see Ben Jemia 2006; Planes-Boissac 2012b). As one respondent highlighted with regards to granting stay permits to refugees:

> Some [refugees recognized by UNHCR] had documents in due form, a stay permit and travel documents, others had an entirely irregular status ... We know that the Ministry of Interior delivers these permits, but then does the person need to have lived here regularly for certain years? Does the person need to fulfil specific conditions? This is all very vague (T17-I26).

The absence of counterpowers within the state further strengthened the MoI's monopoly on immigration: Tunisia's Parliament did not play a key role in policymaking, as 'every law that arrived at the national assembly was voted immediately, without discussion' (T16-I16). The parliamentary proceedings around Law 2004-06 on irregular migration, for instance, show that the law was recommended without comments by the Committee on Political Affairs and External Relations and the Committee on Public Legislation and Public Administration, who were in charge of examining the law. And while some MPs did criticize aspects of the law during the parliamentary debate held on 27 January 2004 (J.O.R.T. 2004) – particularly Tunisia's role as Europe's border guard and the ineffectiveness of a security approach to address the fundamental socio-economic drivers of (irregular) migration –[*] the law was ultimately adopted unanimously: 'There was no discussion on the law, it was simply imposed' (T16-I23).

Democratic Institutions After 2011: Drivers and Obstacles for Immigration Reform

The democratic transition bolstered the weight of the Parliament and political parties in policymaking: 'Before everyone played a theatre

---

[*] For instance, Deputy Jalal Al-Akhdar exclaimed, 'Is it our fate to do the policing job to guard the castles of rich countries?' and Deputy Mohamed Mokhtar Al-Jalali criticized the underlying motives of the law, asking, 'Does the desire to please Europe and to defend its borders from the migration coming from the south explain this exaggerated intensity [of irregular migration sanctions]?' Criticism also came from Deputy Mohamed Thamir Idris, who argued that 'addressing irregular immigration is only possible by providing the conditions for people to develop their personality in their homeland. ... I believe that this law is a declaration of failure [to keep our youth at home]' (J.O.R.T. 2004).

piece, ... Now it's very different. The Parliament is the centre of power now' (T17-I20). Fieldwork insights, however, show that while democratization empowered Members of Parliament (MPs) to initiate legal change, it also subjected them to domestic politics dynamics that eventually obstructed progressive immigration reform.

A Blurred Mirror: The Ambiguity of Political Remittances. In 2011, the attribution of 18 parliamentary seats (out of 217) for representatives of Tunisians residing abroad (TRE) laid the ground for an institutional integration of migration in Tunisian politics. Many of those who were elected into Tunisia's first democratic Parliament as TRE deputies had been politically active on human rights or migrant integration in Europe before 2011, and some used their mandate to raise issues of racism and discrimination in Tunisia (Pouessel 2016: 178–79). By feeding their experiences of being stigmatized as 'Muslim' or 'Arab' migrants in Europe back into Tunisian political life, they generated so-called political remittances (Jaulin and Nilsson 2015; Levitt 1998).

Two MPs from the Islamist Ennahdha party have become particularly vocal on immigration and racism. Houcine Jaziri, State Secretary for Migration until 2014 and MP for Tunisians residing in France afterwards, explained his engagement for migrants' rights in Tunisia through what I call the 'mirror effect', namely the translation of Tunisia's history of emigration and concern for its migrants in Europe into calls for immigrants' rights in Tunisia: 'I cannot ask for my rights abroad if a foreigner here does not find these rights ... What I do not want for a Tunisian, I do not want for an African.' Also, Jamila Debbech Ksiksi, Tunisia's first female Black deputy, has repeatedly condemned racism and xenophobia in Tunisian society: in February 2015, for instance, she denounced the racist attacks that had occurred after Tunisia's national football team lost against Equatorial Guinea in front of the Parliament; and in December 2016, after the racist aggression against three Congolese students, she organized a meeting between the AESAT and the President of the Parliament to discuss the draft law on racism.[1]

Yet, this integration of emigration experiences in Tunisian politics has ultimately not spilt over into a reform of Tunisia's immigration regime. The need for democratic legitimation has prevented formerly exiled politicians from acting upon the mirror effect, which remained primarily discursive: 'Even after 2011, the reflex of politicians who were immigrants themselves was not to set up an immigration policy. They were asking for protection of Tunisians abroad, not of immigrant workers' (T16-I23). Indeed, due to the nature of democratic politics and focus on re-election, MPs privileged their electorate (Tunisians, including TRE) and disregarded immigrants in Tunisia. In addition, politicians who returned from exile faced hostility from part of Tunisia's political establishment who pointed at their long absence from Tunisia, their imperfect Arabic, and their lacking knowledge of Tunisian economy and politics (Pouessel 2016). As one respondent highlighted, 'There was at the beginning a true rejection on the part of Tunisians – you did not live what we lived, you were in exile, so you do not understand anything' (T17-I6). As a result, some MPs have tried to become 'more royalist than the King' (T17-I6), showcasing their *tunisianité* and abandoning issues of racial discrimination or immigration along the way. While there was an initial attempt to integrate migratory experiences into the Tunisian political landscape in the immediate aftermath of the revolution, over the years, previously exiled politicians increasingly focused on domestic issues.

Elite Consensus: The Absence of Partisan Cleavages.
More generally, fieldwork insights suggest that there are no fundamental cleavages on immigration across Tunisia's political party landscape. This does not necessarily imply ideological agreement on immigration. Rather, each party had different reasons to adopt a relatively benevolent position on immigration after the revolution: Ennahdha mobilized on migration issues because many of its members had just returned from exile abroad; liberal parties approached immigration through the lens of Tunisia's commitments to human rights and democratic reform; and left parties saw immigration as part of international solidarity and the anti-racist cause (see also Pouessel 2016). Indeed, ahead of the 2011 elections, all political parties refused a securitized approach to migration and favoured a human rights–based approach towards refugees in their party programs (Boubakri 2013: 19–20).

Over the years, this initial pro-immigration stance has waned, but parties have refrained from polarizing around immigration, in line with the more general depoliticization of immigration by political elites discussed earlier. This consensual political climate shines through in the cross-partisan votes on immigration issues: in 2014, Article 26 of the constitution that enshrined the right to asylum was voted in unanimously; in 2016, the law against human trafficking was voted in unanimously; and in 2018, the law against racial discrimination was voted in by 125 votes for, one against and five abstentions. Interestingly, the one vote against the law was by Yassine Ayari, an independent MP representing Tunisians in Germany since February 2018. The abstentions were largely driven by MPs from the left-wing Democratic Bloc, two of which represent Medenine in the south-east of Tunisia, a centre for migrant arrivals since 2011.[2] This focus on national unity reflects broader dynamics within the Tunisian party landscape in the 2010s, which has been dominated by a climate of partisan consensus on the fundaments of the democratic transition (see also Marzouki 2016; Murphy 2013; Yardımcı-Geyikçi and Tür 2018).

A second reason why Tunisian political parties do not exploit the topic of immigration for political gains is that there is no popular polarization around the issue (see also Roman and Pastore 2018: 9). Even more so than in Morocco, surveys on Tunisians' attitudes towards immigration are scarce. Only the *Afrobarometer* offers minimal insights, revealing that immigration is not a strongly polarized issue: in 2018, 74 per cent of respondents would not care about having an immigrant as a neighbour, 16 per cent per cent would strongly or somewhat dislike it, and 8 per cent would somewhat or strongly like it. Similar response patterns appear regarding having a person of a different religion (68, 25 and 6.5 per cent, respectively) or ethnicity (73.5, 18 and 6 per cent, respectively) as a neighbour (Afrobarometer 2018b). This limited salience differs strongly from the central role immigration plays in European or American public debates and party politics.

Yet, this is not set in stone: polarization might simply be a question of time. In fact, the ongoing reconfiguration of the Tunisian party system, with the numerous creations, mergers or splits of parties since 2011, has hindered the emergence of stable party identities (Allal and Geisser 2011; Schäfer 2017). As Yardımcı-Geyikçi and Tür (2018: 791) write, 'in the case of Tunisia, it is difficult to measure the parties' positions on the ideological spectrum as they are still unpredictable'. This is likely to change with the continued maturing of the Tunisian party system. According to respondents, links between immigration and questions of security and terrorism could ultimately prompt anti-immigration voices or parties to emerge also in Tunisia.

The Challenge of Governmental Volatility. Alongside the Parliament and political parties, the second political actor that depends on democratic legitimation in post-2011 Tunisia is the government. With nine governments in the first ten years after the revolution and many more cabinet reshufflings, the executive's volatility has jeopardized its capacity for action. In particular, governmental volatility has triggered repeated delays and priority shifts, requiring civil servants, CSOs and IOs to restart work from scratch with each new minister and state secretary: 'Each time there is a government change, there is a change of perspective, a change in direction' (T16-I7).

The State Secretariat for Migration and Tunisians Abroad (SEMTE) has particularly suffered from governmental volatility.* It was first created in January 2012 as a secretariat with responsibility for three new directorates within the Ministry of Social Affairs (MoSA): the General Directorate for International Cooperation on Migration (DGCIM), the General Directorate for Planning and Follow-up (DGPS), and a National Migration Observatory (ONM), which has only been functional since June 2015. As part of the governmental change in January 2014, the state secretary post was removed. The next governmental change in February 2015 recreated it *without* responsibility for the three directorates that had continued to function within the MoSA in the meantime. In February 2016, the state secretary post was abolished again. The governmental reshuffling of August 2016 recreated the secretariat, but this time under the umbrella of the Ministry of Foreign Affairs (MoFA). This decision triggered a turf war between the MoSA and MoFA that was politically resolved by moving the SEMTE back to the MoSA in September 2017. In November 2018, the migration dossier was upgraded to a ministry attached to the head of government, but disappeared again in the new government of February 2020, only to be recreated at the next government formation in September 2020, this time however once more attached to the MoFA. In sum: 'The SEMTE is created one day, removed the other day, put back the next, thrown from one ministry to the other' (T16-I16).

The repeated creating and dismantling of the SEMTE has rendered it powerless and incapable of living up to its mission of steering Tunisia's migration policy, as governmental volatility has slowed down and blocked strategic decision-making: several Council of Ministers dedicated to migration were cancelled over the years, delaying the adoption of the *National Migration Strategy* (SNM). Governmental changes also led to frequent shifts in political priorities, requiring civil servants and their partners to restart work from scratch. This has demoralized actors: 'The Minister arrives, he has six months to look at the file, then he leaves.

---

* List of State Secretaries related to migration, 2012–2020: (1) Houcine Jaziri (Ennahdha), State Secretary on Migration, MoSA, January 2012–January 2014, (2) Belgacem Sabri (Independent), State Secretary on Migration and Social Integration, MoSA, February 2015–February 2016, (3) Radhouane Ayara (Nidaa Tounes), State Secretary on Migration, MoFA, August 2016–August 2017, (4) Adel Jarboui (Nidaa Tounes), State Secretary on Migration, MoSA, September 2017–November 2018, (5) Radhouane Ayara (Nidaa Tounes), Minister in Charge of Emigration and Tunisians Abroad, Head of Government, November 2018–February 2020, (6) Mohamed Ali Nafti (Independent), State Secretary in Charge of Immigration and Tunisians Abroad, MoFA, since September 2020.

This volatility blocks any strategic vision of foreign policy, development policy or migration policy!' (T17-I14).

Tunisia's policy response to a potential second large-scale arrival of migrants from Libya is exemplary in this regard: in 2014, Tunisian authorities elaborated a contingency plan with IOs, setting out the responsibilities of the Red Crescent, the IOM, UNHCR and other UN organizations, as well as the different Tunisian ministries and local authorities in the event of large-scale migrant arrivals. The document is not publicly available, but respondents involved in its elaboration highlighted that Tunisian authorities have repeatedly switched their approach: in 2014, authorities advocated to host refugees in urban areas due to the 'bad experience with the Choucha camp' (T16-I20). Indeed, UNHCR and Tunisian institutions are not keen to look back on the Choucha camp episode: 'UNHCR does not want to talk about 2011, they had a bad experience with Choucha, they had lots of problems, so they want to move beyond it' (T16-I20), one respondent said. The internal evaluation report of UNHCR's mission in Tunisia confirms this assessment (UNHCR 2013). In contrast, in 2016, the government returned to a camp approach due to Tunisia's increasing fears of terrorist infiltration from Libya. In spring 2019, the contingency plan was updated once more in response to growing arrivals from Libya, and in January 2020, a site was identified in Bir El Fatnassiya where a camp could be set up from one day to the next in case arrivals would cross the threshold of 300 a day (FTDES and Migreurop 2020).[3]

The Administration's Internal Dynamics[4]

While the democratic transition visibly reshuffled the powers and priorities of democratic institutions to accommodate new interests and electorate groups, the impact of democratization on Tunisia's administration – 'the backbone of the Tunisian state' (M17–I2) – has been more subtle. On the one hand, the authoritarian politics of compartmentalization and isolation started to break down, and many civil servants regained confidence in their responsibilities. On the other hand, the day-to-day workings of the administration have not changed fundamentally, as the authoritarian heritage of distrust and top-down command structures still weighs on policy practices. It is this clash between a decades-long legacy of policy practices and a fundamentally new political environment that can account for many of the dynamics observed within the Tunisian administration, such as turf wars and diverging visions on immigration, that remind strongly of those described in the Moroccan case.

Securing Institutional Territory Through the Democratic Transition. With the restructuring of institutional powers after the revolution, institutions have focused on securing their turf throughout the democratic transition: 'The administrative organization is scattered, it's disastrous. ... Each ministry wants to secure part of the migration issue,' one high-level respondent within the Tunisian administration exclaimed. Indeed, in contrast to the pre-2011 period, the migration dossier is now split up among different ministries: while the MoI continues to be in charge of visas and residence permits, as well as detention centres, the MoF is responsible for the penalties for irregular stay, the MoJ for migrant expulsions from the territory, the MoEPF for the authorizations for foreign workers, the MoHE for international students, and the SEMTE is supposed to coordinate Tunisian institutions and their relations with international partners and civil society.

This multiplication of voices within the Tunisian state apparatus has made policymaking more incoherent and fostered a stalemate on immigration. In particular, the democratic transition empowered civil servants to take responsibility and to participate in political debates: 'They [civil servants] feel that now they have a responsibility towards society. ... Now they feel like actors' (T17-I23). This triggered an 'overshooting of democratic responsibility', as civil servants who felt empowered to raise their voice ultimately blocked the policy process: 'There are individuals who can block everything because they disagree. ... I would say they are discovering the power of saying no' (T17-I20). A former State Secretary of Migration I interviewed criticized the endless discussions and lack of decision-making: 'In Tunisia now discussions are fashionable [*laughs*]. There is always someone who does not agree.' The resulting inter-institutional conflict on immigration in post-2011 Tunisia is structured by two main dividing lines: between the Ministry of Interior (MoI) and most other ministries, as well as between the Ministries of Social and Foreign Affairs.

First, the growing sense of responsibility among administrative actors after 2011 has created friction between the MoI and a range of other ministries. While the MoI remains the central actor on immigration in Tunisia, it now has to actively defend its institutional territory. For instance, when the Choucha camp closed in July 2013, around 200 asylum seekers were still living there – refusing to return to their countries of origin but also lacking refugee status or a Tunisian residence permit. The Minister of Social Affairs at the time, Khalil Zaouia, offered the remaining asylum seekers a residence permit if they registered their fingerprints at the local police station in Ben Guerdane (see also Garelli and Tazzioli 2017: 23). However, none of the asylum seekers who took up this opportunity ever received a residence permit. According to respondents, the MoI blocked the initiative of the MoSA. Similarly, the removal of visa requirements for six African countries announced by the MoFA in April 2015 to boost tourism and encourage trade has never been enforced by the border police – which is under MoI tutelage and continues to require visas for citizens of these countries. These two examples reveal how 'the MoI used its veto right' (T17-I15). As one respondent concludes, 'In Tunisia, what counts in the end, on all topics, is the position of the MoI' (T16-I2).

The second line of division on immigration within the Tunisian administration runs between the MoSA and the MoFA and focuses on the tutelage of the State Secretariat for Migration and Tunisians Abroad (SEMTE). In August 2016, the SEMTE was transferred from the MoSA to the MoFA to accommodate deputies representing Tunisians abroad and who lobbied for a 'more prestigious' (T16-I8), high-level treatment of the migration issue. This shift in tutelage triggered open discontent from the MoSA: the directorates formerly attached to the SEMTE – such as the National Migration Observatory (ONM) or the Office for Tunisians Abroad (OTE) – refused to work with the new State Secretary at the MoFA, and their offices remained in the buildings of the MoSA. This conflict between the MoSA and the MoFA deepened the impasse around immigration, as it jeopardized cooperation with other ministries, civil society or international actors, and created institutional uncertainty about who the right interlocutor was in the first place: 'Cooperation partners don't even know how to reach us, or whether they should send invitations to the MoFA or the MoSA' (T17-I30). This lack of institutional clarity has made policy processes inefficient and long-term strategic planning almost impossible for over a year. Most strikingly, both the MoSA and the MoFA worked separately on a revision of the SNM throughout 2016 and 2017, duplicating efforts. The inter-institutional conflict has been ongoing since then: while the September 2017 governmental change moved the SEMTE back to the MoSA, in September 2020, the new government once more attached it to the MoFA.

Lacking Inter-Institution Coordination and Diverging Visions on Immigration. In addition to such turf wars, inter-ministerial cooperation has remained difficult since 2011, as the compartmentalization and disempowering of the Ben Ali administration has left severe marks on inter-institutional trust until today, and changes in administrative practice are slow and sticky: 'You don't change a system that is inaccessible for decades within five years' (T16-I18). In particular, and despite its central role, the Ministry of Interior (MoI) has remained isolated from inter-ministerial discussions. Respondents described it as 'hermetic' (T16-I23) and as 'dialogu[ing] with no one in the government except itself' (T16-I16). Such path-dependent institutional behaviour showcases the importance of considering not only policy change but also policy continuity and for understanding the continued importance of historical legacies in shaping contemporary political dynamics. For Boubakri (2013: 29), 'the Ministry of Interior maintains its tradition of silence from the former regime and refuses any public position, any statement, and even any participation in meetings or conferences on migration'.

To exemplify such lack of inter-ministerial coordination after the revolution, interviewees pointed at the contradictory regulations migrants are subjected to, making the application for a Tunisian residence permit akin to 'fishing in the dark' (T16-I18). The procedures for international students are particularly telling in this regard: the MoI requires a certificate of presence from universities to process a student's residence permit application, universities deliver these certificates only after one month of class attendance, but often students receive only a seven-day or one-month visa at arrival (see also TAT 2018: 28–29). This makes it impossible for them to regularize their situation in time and avoid the penalties for irregular stay enforced by the Ministry of Finance (MoF): 'You get the impression that the Ministries of Interior, Finance and Higher Education don't know each other at all' (T16-I25).

The lack of inter-institutional coordination and the overall powerlessness of the SEMTE allowed institutions to pursue their own interests on immigration, depending on their sector-specific visions and institutional worldviews. As in Morocco, the Ministries of Education and Health adopted a more open, humanitarian approach towards migrants, while the Ministries of Interior and Employment took on a restrictive, security-driven stance. As one respondent said, 'Each party plays its role' (T16-I10). Indeed, respondents unanimously pointed out that the MoI's security approach to immigration was inherent to its place in the institutional landscape. 'They are in charge of the security of the country; it is their role' (T16-I18), one respondent said. 'It's somewhat the case everywhere in the world, the MoI has always a security approach to migration' (T16-I7), another one added. In contrast, the institutional priorities of the Ministry of Health explain its more open approach towards immigration:

The MoH is one of the few ministries open to migration. ... They are the first to say that health is universal, that health is for all without discrimination, including migrants, including people in an irregular situation (T17-I23).

Such positioning of the MoH since 2011 might have contributed to the more inclusive approach adopted by the Tunisian government in the context of COVID-19, with migrants being granted access to state support programs (MoI 2020).

Also the Ministry of Higher Education (MoHE), which actively frames Tunisia as a regional scientific hub and a higher education destination for African students in its 2017 strategy, promoted opening Tunisia towards immigration.[5] This goal clashes with the practices of the MoI and MoF, who obstruct the entry and stay of those students. In this context, the May 2018 exemption of students from the irregular stay penalty is likely not only the outcome of bottom-up migrant mobilization, as discussed in Chapter 6, but also of inter-ministerial negotiation and compromise between the MoI, MoF and MoHE. Indeed, exempting students from penalties seems a pragmatic approach to resolve this inter-ministerial contradiction without touching the foundations of Tunisia's immigration regime.

Tunisia's democratic transition and political volatility have certainly aggravated these internal incoherencies and conflicts by bringing them out into the open. However, the comparison with Morocco suggests that ministerial approaches towards immigration are more influenced by institutional identities than by the type of political regime in which they operate. Migration policymaking always has to accommodate diverging institutional visions, creating migration regulations that are incoherent 'by design' (Czaika and de Haas 2013) across the globe.

Civil Society Dynamics

Next to reshuffling some of the institutional power dynamics within the state, the 2011 revolution triggered an unseen level of civil society activism, including on immigration. How have developments since 2011 reshaped the role and influence of Tunisian civil society on immigration? First of all, civil society gained an independent voice in the national political sphere. Within the context of democratization, all eyes were on bottom-up political dynamics: ignoring civil society was no longer an option for Tunisian policymakers after 2011, and relations between state institutions and CSOs burgeoned. However, access to power structures did not go hand in hand with actual influence on policy outcomes because democratization required CSOs to reposition themselves in front of authorities and to develop new lobbying strategies in response to the institutional fragmentation of the immigration dossier. As a result, Tunisian civil society sought to increase its voice by entering into 'strange bedfellow' coalitions with either the Tunisian government or external actors, depending on the issue at stake. In parallel, the mushrooming of CSOs has created new dynamics within civil society, as not only joint advocacy efforts increased but also views on immigration within and between CSOs diverged.

The Relative Absence of Counterpowers Under Ben Ali: State-Controlled and Weak CSOs

Given the securitarian grip on immigration in Ben Ali's Tunisia, CSOs played a minimal role: the only Tunisian organization that directly interacted with migrants was the Red Crescent. As a humanitarian 'auxiliary of the state' (T16-I22), it provided emergency support to refugees and irregular migrants that arrived at Tunisia's southern borders with Libya or were stranded at the Mediterranean coast. It was also the official intermediary between asylum seekers and UNHCR from the 1990s until mid-2019, when the registration of asylum seekers and management of reception centres was taken over by the Tunisian Council for Refugees (CTR). Through its work, the Red Crescent indirectly contributed to keeping immigration off the wider socio-political agenda. The only migrant association that existed at the time – the Association of African Students and Trainees in Tunisia (AESAT) – was created in 1993 with the backing of the Ministry of Higher Education (MoHE) to promote cultural exchanges among African students and Tunisians. According to respondents, it de facto served the Tunisian state as a control organ to oversee the activities of the African student community. Most strikingly, the headquarters given by the state to the AESAT were located just next to a police station in the old city (medina), and AESAT members were prohibited from collaborating with Tunisian associations other than the youth movement of Ben Ali's party, the Constitutional Democratic Youth (JCD).

In the early 2000s, given the growing politicization of irregular migration in Euro–African relations, Tunisian organizations started to tacitly mobilize, first on the drowning of Tunisian youth in the Mediterranean and progressively also on the dire situation of immigrants in Tunisia (Bel Hadj Zekri 2009; Boubakri 2004, 2013; Boubakri and Mazzella 2005). Humanitarian actors such as Caritas started to offer psychological support and to distribute clothes and medicine to migrants. In comparison to Morocco, where Caritas played a significant role in politicizing immigrant rights, its activities in Ben Ali's Tunisia remained, however, very discreet.[*] Human rights actors, such as the Tunisian Association of

---

[*] Caritas had no legal status in Tunisia before 2011, but was tolerated by authorities (Planes-Boissac 2012b: 54). Its engagement was primarily humanitarian. The only

Democratic Women (ATFD), the Tunisian League for Human Rights (LTDH) and the Tunisian Forum for Economic and Social Rights (FTDES), started incorporating migrants into their work. And in 2007, Tunisia's biggest labour union, UGTT, included the issue of irregular migrants' rights in their annual conference on migrant workers, at which labour unions from France, Italy and Spain as well as Chad, Mali and Niger participated. This incipient civil society dynamism, however, differs strikingly from the consolidation of transnational civil society work on migration in Morocco over the 1990s and 2000s.

Civil society activism also remained limited because, in contrast to Morocco, the state adopted a 'policy of containment' (Redissi 2007: 112) that put civil society under constant surveillance. When the LTDH organized its first seminar on irregular migration in Tunisia together with the International Federation of Human Rights (FIDH) in June 2003, 'the police was everywhere' (T17-I32). According to respondents, CSOs benefiting from an international standing – such as the UGTT, the Arab Institute for Human Rights (IADH) or Amnesty International – had more room for manoeuvre, as their transnational connections provided them with 'a protection belt' (T17-I13) from political repression – if only to keep the regime's image abroad clean. However, immigration and discrimination really only became widely politicized in Tunisia after the revolution.

Democratization and Civil Society Activism

Statements that highlight the absence of civil society under Ben Ali – such as 'Civil society was born in 2011' (T16-D12) – do not do justice to the civil society efforts just outlined. However, the increase in civil liberties after 2011 really did prompt civil activism on an unprecedented scale, accelerating its integration into transnational networks and changing its role on the Tunisian political scene (see also Bartels 2015; Deane 2013).

The CSO Boom and its Transnational Dimension. Law 2011–88 on associations, enacted in September 2011, facilitated the creation of Tunisian CSOs and offsprings of international CSOs: before 2011, an authorization by the MoI was required to register a CSO; now CSOs simply need to inform the Secretary-General of the government of their creation. As a result, thousands of new CSOs were established in

activity with a political component were regular visits to Tunisian prisons, where they offered counsel to Christian foreigners from Africa, Europe or elsewhere.

Tunisia to advocate for more dignity, freedom, and human rights, including for migrants. The Tunisian Association for the Support of Minorities (ATSM), the Association for the Defence of Black Tunisians' Rights (ADAM), and M'nemty were created to denounce racism within Tunisian society, and Tunisian CSOs working on human or socio-economic rights stepped up their advocacy on migration: the FTDES focused on Tunisians disappeared in the Mediterranean Sea, as well as on refugees in the Choucha camp, the UGTT on migrant labour rights, Caritas became more vocal (Boubakri 2013; Natter 2015b). As in Morocco, diaspora organizations such as the French Federation of Tunisians for a Citizenship of Both Shores (FTCR), created back in 1974, got involved in immigrants' rights.

Also, migrants themselves mobilized. The first ones to make their voice heard were the rejected refugees stuck in the Choucha camp (Bartels 2015: 73–75; Boubakri and Potot 2012; Garelli and Tazzioli 2017: 36–41). Starting in 2012, camp residents began protesting against the slowness and high rejection rates of UNHCR. They organized marches to Tunis and sit-ins in front of the UNHCR head office, European embassies, and the Tunisian government to claim their right to resettlement or to a Tunisian residence permit, and were successful in gathering support from transnational solidarity groups.[*] As one respondent recalls, 'These people put a lot of pressure on the Tunisian government. ... The topic became very politicized' (T17-I23). The rejected refugees of the Choucha camp remain a policy issue until now: while the camp was officially closed in 2013, several dozen asylum seekers remained there until they were forcefully evicted by the Ministry of Defence in June 2017. Transferred to a Sport and Youth Centre close to Tunis, where twenty-eight of them still lived in 2020, they continue to (unsuccessfully) claim their recognition as refugees and resettlement outside of Tunisia.[6] Next to rejected asylum seekers, African students mobilized early on, as the student association AESAT shifted its focus away from cultural activities and started advocacy work to support students whose residence permits were delayed or who faced high penalties for irregular stay. Other student associations were created, such as Afrique Intelligence in 2012 or the Union of African Leaders (ULA) in 2016. Lastly, inspired by the unionization of migrant workers in Morocco, irregular migrant workers founded the (not officially recognized) Association of Sub-Saharan Workers in Tunisia (ASTT) in 2016.

---

[*] See, for instance, the blog of European supporters set up to coordinate a transnational solidarity campaign for refugee protests in Choucha: https://chouchaprotest.noblogs.org/about/

Compared to Morocco, however, migrant mobilization remains relatively low.

In addition to such domestic civil society activism, numerous international CSOs and IOs moved into Tunisia after 2011: Euromed Rights to facilitate networking between CSOs engaged in migration; Terre d'Asile Tunisie (TAT) and Doctors of the World Belgium (MdM-B) to offer on-the-ground support for (irregular) migrants, such as legal representation or medical care, but also to step up policy advocacy; ILO to engage the UGTT on immigrant workers; and UNHCR to advance the legal protection of refugees and their labour market integration. In the words of one of my respondents, 'There are many, maybe too many international structures and NGOs who arrived here to do their projects' (T17-I26). While the international interest and associated funding boom have created opportunities for civil society activism, it also increased civil society's dependence on foreign funding: 'We do not have any means if there are no international organizations or foreign states that finance our activities' (T16-I22), one respondent said. This is problematic in terms of the long-term sustainability of civil society activities, but also in terms of their freedom in setting their own agenda (see also Deane 2013).

In contrast to Morocco, where transnational civil society linkages on immigration have been fostered since the late 1990s, Tunisian CSOs were thus only fully integrated into the transnational community of migration activists after 2011. Today, Tunisian activists are part of an epistemic community of migration CSOs, where Maghreb migrant organizations in Europe, European human rights advocacy groups, and Maghreb migration CSOs regularly meet and share information and advocacy strategies. In this space, not only Europe but also Morocco has become a reference for activist strategies concerning, for instance, the regularization or the unionization of irregular migrants.

Cooperation Versus Fragmentation of Civil Society Agendas. Within this burgeoning, transnational civil society, however, not all activism lasted: many of the organizations created in the post-revolutionary euphoria dissolved after a while, such as the Tunisian Council for Refugees and Migrants (an association of Tunisian lawyers) or ADAM. In addition, civil society started to face two contrasting dynamics: on the one hand, a fragmentation of agendas; on the other hand, increasing cooperation.

Disagreements among CSOs emerged quickly after 2011, for instance, on the asylum law: while some criticized the involvement of UNHCR in the law-making process and the danger of injecting external interests into the national law, others upheld the need to enshrine international human rights standards and thus refugee rights. Also, on the issue of racism, disagreements prevailed, as CSOs working on the discrimination of Black Tunisians and those working with Western and Central African immigrants diverged in their priorities: 'You would think that anti-racist movements might ally with sub-Saharan students, but no ... Only because you are a minority does not mean that you show solidarity with other minorities' (T16-D12). Ultimately, such a lack of coordination and trust among civil society actors has weakened their efforts. Also, the competition for international funds has jeopardized civil society's striking force, most recently between the Red Crescent, historical partner of UNHCR and IOM, and the Tunisian Council for Refugees (CTR) created in 2016: because of alleged lack of transparency in financial management, UNHCR has decided in mid-2019 to end its contracts with the Red Crescent and to entrust the CTR with the registration of asylum seekers and management of reception centres (FTDES and Migreurop 2020: 92–93). This has had severe consequences on the migrant protection and support activities that the Red Crescent had been conducting for decades on the ground.

Despite such conflicts and disagreements, there have been increasing attempts at joining forces around specific advocacy campaigns over the years, such as on the issue of disappeared Tunisian youth in the Mediterranean in 2011 or the risks entailed in the Mobility Partnership signed by the European Union and Tunisia in 2014. Efforts to coordinate advocacy on immigration have been more recent: in 2017, Euromed Rights, TAT, and AESAT developed a joint civil society agenda to bundle advocacy efforts. During a one-day workshop, CSOs came up with a ten-point priority advocacy list, among which were the adoption of the law against racial discrimination, the abrogation of Law 2004–06 on irregular migration, and an amnesty for irregular stay penalties supplemented by exemptions for specific migrant categories. However, divisions within Tunisian civil society remain – as one civil society respondent not participating in this initiative concluded: 'We don't have the same agenda, the same vision.'

The UGTT: Caught Between International Solidarity and National Preference. The dynamics around immigration within Tunisia's largest labour union, the UGTT, illustrate the difficulties Tunisian civil society actors face. Throughout the twentieth century, the UGTT has been a central actor in Tunisian politics, reinforced through its role in the *National Dialogue Quartet* that resolved the national political crisis in 2013. Today, the UGTT is a major interlocutor for the

Civil Society Dynamics 183

government: 'Sometimes I think they are more powerful than the government' (T16-I11), one respondent stressed. As a result, respondents highlighted that without UGTT support, there would be no immigration reform in Tunisia.

The UGTT's Department of International Relations, Migration and Arab Relations set migrants' rights on its agenda in the context of Tunisian emigration and its collaboration with European labour unions. In 2007, the UGTT launched the idea of a transnational union network to defend labour migrants' rights (Ben Ahmed 2011), which was effectively created in 2009 as the Network of Unions on Mediterranean and Sub-Saharan Migration (RSMMS), with over twenty member organizations from Europe and Northern, Western and Central Africa. While this policy initiative was initially focused on Tunisian emigrants, after the revolution, international and civil society actors set the issue of immigration on the UGTT's agenda: the ILO-led IRAM project (2014–2017) effectively linked the question of Tunisian labour emigration with that of immigration to Tunisia, and TAT organized encounters between UGTT members and irregular migrant workers in 2016 that opened up discussions on the potential unionization of migrants within the UGTT. One outcome of these encounters was the creation of the first Association of Sub-Saharan Workers in Tunisia (ASTT) at the end of 2016.

Such developments progressively led to a shift in UGTT's discourse on immigration, away from competition between national and migrant workers, and towards the universality of labour rights. One respondent observed:

In the beginning, the UGTT line was: No social dumping, we must protect our labour market. ... But then they met migrants who were in a state of slavery, and I think that has changed the vision completely (T17-I20).

Beyond discourse, however, the UGTT's engagement on immigrant workers' rights has remained reticent. Given Tunisia's dire economic situation, mobilizing for foreign workers and supporting liberalization of labour market regulations is highly unpopular, and therefore, the UGTT continues to oscillate between upholding the universality of worker rights and defending Tunisian workers' interests. Also, there are internally divergent opinions on immigration within the UGTT: while the International Relations Department advocated for a more inclusive approach towards immigration, this vision is not shared by all union members, creating a 'need for internal advocacy' (T16-I7). Ultimately, this internal debate has been resolved in favour of migrant workers: in February 2019, the UGTT publicly demanded a regularization campaign and created official contact points for migrant workers in Tunis,

Sfax, Sousse and Medenine offering legal aid.[7] And on 2 December 2020, UGTT Secretary-General Noureddine Taboubi handed out the first membership cards to migrant workers from Western and Central Africa after the UGTT decided to accept foreigners as members to 'defend human and workers' rights irrespective of their nationality, type, skin colour or religion'.[8]

State-Civil Society Dynamics

Next to the burgeoning civil society activism and its complex internal dynamics, what has changed since 2011 is civil society's access to power structures: 'If you look at civil society, there has been a real revolution. They have become a real interlocutor for the authorities' (T16-I25). Yet, the influence of CSOs on political discourse or agenda-setting has not necessarily translated into policy outcomes, partly because of the fragmentation of civil society interests just discussed, partly because of the inherited authoritarian bureaucratic practices and the reluctance of state actors to open up (Youssef 2018). To increase their weight in decision-making, civil society has therefore adopted new advocacy strategies.

Accessing Power Structures Versus Influencing Decision-Making. Respondents across the board have highlighted the increased interactions between state institutions and civil society after 2011. First of all, people who had previously been labour union leaders or human rights' activists within or outside Tunisia now work within state institutions, bringing civil society perspectives with them. Most prominently, Moncef Marzouki, Tunisia's President between 2011 and 2014, was president of the LTDH (1989–1994) before going into exile to France; and Kamel Jendoubi, Human Rights Minister from 2015–2016, had been president of Euromed Rights since 2003.

In addition, civil society relations with state institutions are now more institutionalized: AESAT, TAT and MdM-B are regularly invited to meetings and conferences organized by the SEMTE, and together with the UGTT and the UTICA, they took part in the revision of the *National Migration Strategy* (SNM) in 2015. Tunisian CSOs have also established links with ministries and other state institutions: TAT negotiated exonerations from irregular stay penalties directly with the MoF and entered into a partnership with the National Migration Observatory (ONM), MdM-B offered training sessions for civil servants from the MoH to raise awareness about the universal access to healthcare and engaged the MoHE on student rights, and AESAT representatives were officially received by President Marzouki in 2014 and Prime Minister Chahed in 2016 to discuss racial discrimination in Tunisia.

Relations with the MoI have remained more limited: TAT and the Red Crescent sometimes engage with police and border guards regarding detentions and expulsions, and in 2017, MdM-B met representatives of the MoI's Directorate for Borders and Foreigners. Apart from these instances, however, 'the MoI remains closed for consultations .... This closure is just the same as it was before 2011' (T17-D6). CSOs have also expanded their contact points within the state beyond ministries by working more systematically with MPs as a means to channel their demands into the political system: for instance, Euromed Rights mobilized MPs in 2016 to submit a draft law against racism in Parliament, IADH is working together with the Rights and Liberties Commission of the Parliament on the refugee question, and MdM-B works together with the Health and Social Affairs Commission on students from Western and Central Africa.

However, CSOs' access to authorities has not necessarily increased their capacity to influence decision-making. While CSOs were successful in changing authorities' discourses and informal policy practices to a certain extent, as outlined earlier, their lobbying has not succeeded in reforming the core of Tunisia's immigration regime: stay permits and asylum. Legal change was only possible on issues that aligned with the priority of domestic political actors to put 'Tunisians first' and to symbolically display the progressiveness of Tunisian democracy, such as racism and human trafficking. Civil society respondents have expressed their frustration about this limited influence on policymaking:

There are consultations, a dialogue; there is an awareness. ... But there is not much improvement in terms of results. ... Each time you create pressure from the streets, there is some change, you win some point, but afterwards, there is no follow-up (T17-I12).

Ultimately, when reflecting on their newly gained margin of manoeuvre in Tunisian political life, civil society respondents concluded that 'the greatest achievement of the revolution is the freedom of expression' (T17-I5): 'On substance, there has been no change ..., but we can talk, we can complain, we can highlight the question of migrants' rights' (T17-I32).

Diversifying Lobbying Strategies. Despite limited influence on decision-making, the dynamism and institutionalization of civil society as a political actor nurtured hopes among respondents that civil society would eventually succeed in driving policy change: 'The change will not come from the political elite, also not from the Parliament. ...

The most vibrant political interlocutor remains civil society today' (T16-I17). At the same time, Tunisian activists recognized that as part of the broader democratization process, civil society still needed to acquire professional lobbying skills to fully exploit their room for manoeuvre within Tunisian policy processes (Cassarini 2020; Deane 2013):

> Very few NGOs actually know that they can request a hearing, that they can enter the Parliament. ... This is a mutual effort where MPs need to become more open, but also civil society needs to learn how to lobby (T17-I31).

As part of this learning process, CSOs have developed new lobbying strategies over recent years to make their voice heard by authorities. Like Moroccan civil society in the 2000s, Tunisian activists increasingly mobilize the mirror effect by leveraging authorities' interests for Tunisians abroad in their advocacy for immigrants' rights within Tunisia:

> The strong argument is that we defend the rights of TRE with a lot of vehemence. And for the sake of consistency, we must also be concerned about the issue of migrant workers in Tunisia. This is an argument that works pretty well (T16-I7).

CSOs have also strategically started to first engage authorities on 'easy' topics, such as student migration, economic cooperation with Africa, or public health, before putting thornier issues such as irregular stay penalties or access to work and residence permits on the table. As one representative from Doctors of the World Belgium (MdM-B) put it in a public debate: 'They want to talk about students, we talk about students. Then the message passes. But inevitably, by talking about students, one day we will start talking about workers.'

Another strategy devised by Tunisian actors has been to mobilize international norm adherence, key in the context of Tunisia's human rights agenda, as an 'entry door' (T17-I14) to advocate for change on migrants' rights. This has been effective in pushing for a law against racial discrimination, as discussed previously, but it has also succeeded in opening the education system to undocumented children. Speaking about the rights of refugee children to attend school, one respondent recalled, 'At the beginning, the MoE and MoSA refused to deal with this issue, but then they understood that Tunisia adhered to the International Child Protection Convention and that we are obliged to accept this' (T17-I27). In a similar vein, Education Minister Fethi Jarray in August 2014 justified the decision to enrol Libyan children in public schools through Tunisia's commitment to international norms:

> In addition to the duty of fraternity and neighbourhood, we are required to ensure the schooling of these children as the first Arab signatory of the International Convention on the Rights of the Child.[9]

As in Morocco, Tunisian CSOs have also started to integrate migrants' rights into the broader democratization debate to make their voice heard: 'You cannot claim to be modern, be considered to defend universal values, and not respect migrants' rights' (T17-I7), one respondent concluded. While the impact of civil society on decision-making in the realm of migration has remained relatively limited so far, the diversification and professionalization of advocacy strategies might, in the mid-term, raise the structural weight and impact of civil society on policy processes.

'Strange Bedfellows': Shifting Alliances Between Civil Society, State Institutions and IOs. [10] A last strategy devised by civil society to make its voice heard has been to mobilize alliances with either state institutions or international actors strategically, depending on the issue at stake: while CSOs team up with IOs against state authorities to lobby for migrants' rights, CSOs team up with state authorities against IOs to defend Tunisian politics from external interference. As one civil society respondent said, 'we are in a relationship of both criticism and collaboration with the authorities' (T17-I14).

On the one hand, civil society fulfils the traditional role of counterpower to government and administration, monitoring state action and uncovering abuses of migrants' rights. Acting in this role, Tunisian CSOs mobilize their international networks to exercise pressure on national political actors from below and outside, akin to the 'boomerang effect' theorized by Keck and Sikkink (1998). Also, because Tunisian governments now need to legitimize their policies democratically, the absence of civil society in policy processes symbolizes a lack of democratic adherence that CSOs can use as leverage to pressure authorities to take on board their positions. In return, IOs try to get civil society on board to back up their demands with domestic legitimacy. However, CSOs and IOs form a coalition of 'strange bedfellows' (Zolberg 2006): although their goals overlap, the interests underlying their respective positions are often antagonistic. The asylum law is a good case in point: while EU actors are guided by the European agenda to transform Tunisia into a safe refugee destination that would reduce the pressure on Europe's southern borders, Tunisian civil society pushes for refugee rights in the context of Tunisia's democratization and the consolidation of the rule of law.

On the other hand, however, civil society partners up with state institutions in order to increase their joint leverage against external actors' demands (see also Roman and Pastore 2018). For example, the Tunisian MoFA has used civil society criticism of EU migration policies as a tool in their refusal of EU migration control demands on readmission. As one civil society respondent said,

We have our red lines, and apparently, they converge with those of the MoFA and the SEMTE. ... The sign we received from the MoFA is: Go for it! Like that the MoFA can tell Europeans that civil society is opposing these agreements and thus they cannot sign them. In a sense, our work gives them more strike force.

The democratic character of post-2011 Tunisia has thus allowed the government to better face European pressures by pointing at the need to respond to domestic demands and actors.

In these complex state-civil society dynamics, a third dynamic is at play: paradoxically, civil society projects that provide temporary relief to migrants' difficulties can have the counterproductive effect of lowering pressures on the state to act. For instance, legal or healthcare support for irregular migrants relieves the state of its responsibility to provide such services in the first place. Also, IOM's so-called voluntary return program that offers an alternative to expulsion or self-paid return indirectly thwarts civil society advocacy: 'IOM is the comfort solution for Tunisia now because some of these people put a lot of pressure on the Tunisian government ... Entrusting those cases to IOM suits Tunisia, as it allows them to avoid a real reflection on a policy of return' (T17-I20). Such dynamics are reminiscent of the balancing act that Moroccan CSOs face, between supporting migrant integration programs launched by the state and keeping the pressure on authorities to live up to its legal reform promises.

The Role of International, Economic and Legal Actors

Besides state and civil society actors, international organizations, the private sector and legal actors participate in Tunisia's immigration policy, albeit to different degrees. With migration being an intrinsically international policy issue, the role of IOs as well as diplomatic interests towards the European Union and increasingly also Africa are key. In contrast to Morocco, however, where the monarchy strategically instrumentalized immigration in a three-level game, the deliberate depoliticization of immigration in Tunisia has opened opportunities for international cooperation at the level of technocratic capacity building. Employers and lawyers have not played a central role in Tunisian immigration politics in the first decade after the revolution despite their centrality in theorizing immigration politics in democracies. With democratization advancing, there are signs that this will change in the case of legal actors, as they are increasingly solicited by CSOs to challenge the legality of arbitrary administrative decisions. The role of employers, however, is unlikely to change given the continuities in Tunisia's economic structure and high levels of informality in the labour market.

The International Dimension

Democratization has opened up space for external actors to intensify cooperation with Tunisian state institutions and CSOs. Yet, this has not automatically increased external influence on Tunisian policymaking: although external agenda-setting has been successful in some instances, such as the law against human trafficking, the discursive acknowledgement of immigration or more technocratic cooperation projects that aimed at strengthening the institutional capacity of the Tunisian state, Tunisian authorities largely resisted external political pressures, in particular by referring to their democratic legitimacy.

From a Controlled Partner to a Complex Web of Interactions. Under Ben Ali, IOs were under tight state surveillance, and interactions between external actors and Tunisian institutions were centralized within specific Directorates of the MoFA or the MoI. Prior to 2011, the state's grip on IOs made them reluctant to engage in advocacy work. As already mentioned, UNHCR opened an honorary representation in Tunis in 1963 and since 1992 registered asylum seekers within the informal quota set by the Tunisian state. The IOM opened a small office in Tunisia in 2001 but limited its activities to the return of Tunisians. According to a respondent, when prompted on the human rights violations contained in the 2004 law, 'they [IOs] totally refused any act of denunciation of this policy. ... They said no, we fear the regime, please leave us aside' (T17-I7).

The revolution opened up the Tunisian state apparatus to outside actors – European diplomatic actors, funding agencies and IOs (Cassarini 2020; FTDES and Migreurop 2020). The situation at the Libyan–Tunisian border in early 2011 prompted UNHCR and IOM to step up their operations in Tunisia. Over time, their activities moved from emergency support to more structural work, such as migrant integration projects and policy advocacy. Numerous other international actors started working on migration in Tunisia after 2011, partly for institutional funding logics I have already outlined for Morocco:

It's the same everywhere when there are fashionable topics. ... We all run after budgets, and people start working on subjects on which they do not necessarily have expertise just because there is a funding opportunity (T17-I23).

Not only international actors have mushroomed, but also their interactions with Tunisian institutions have proliferated: IOM and UNDP now cooperate with the Ministry of Health (MoH) to integrate immigrants into Tunisia's public health strategy; the French Development Cooperation (AFD) works closely with the SEMTE and the national employment agency ANETI; the ILO links up the MoSA with Tunisia's social partners (UGTT and UTICA) on labour migration; ICMPD has launched multiple projects with the SEMTE to support it in finalizing its migration strategy and with municipal authorities to foster local migrant integration; and UNHCR deepened cooperation with the MoJ, the MoH and the border police to improve the situation of Tunisia's refugees. Compared to the minimal, centralized relations between Tunisian institutions and external actors in the pre-2011 era, the current situation is a complex web of interactions.

Yet, as in Morocco, diplomatic engagement on immigration has been mainly dominated by European actors. African embassies have been reluctant to take an active position on Tunisia's mistreatment of immigrants according to respondents: 'Sub-Saharan embassies don't defend the sub-Saharans when they are victims of violence or administrative abuses from the police; they always try to keep their distance from the Tunisian government' (T17-I5). Even when the second advisor of the Senegalese embassy became the victim of aggression at the Tunis airport because he was thought to be an irregular migrant, the Senegalese MoFA summoned the Tunisian ambassador to Senegal but never politically or legally followed up on the incident.[11] Despite this limited engagement of African diplomatic actors on immigration in Tunisia so far, Tunisian authorities and business elites have become increasingly aware of the economic potential of Western and Central African markets, as outlined later. This introduces a new variable into Tunisian immigration politics that might change the balance in Tunisia's three-level game in the future.

Foreign Expertise as a Double-Edged Sword: External Agenda-Setting and Tunisian Resistances. With interactions between state authorities and external actors multiplying, opportunities for 'external agenda-setting' increased. Indeed, IOs did not only bring their funds to Tunisia but also their interests and discursive frameworks. Most importantly, external actors have wanted to set immigration on Tunisia's governmental agenda and, despite initial reticence from Tunisian authorities, succeeded. As respondents recount, IOs have nudged Tunisian state actors time and again to include pilot activities on immigration into their broader migration cooperation: in a cooperation project on the return of Tunisians from Europe, for instance, European partners added a sub-project on the return of Western and Central African migrants from Tunisia, whereby the administrative service set up to deal with the reception and reinsertion of Tunisian returnees should ultimately also be able to manage the return of irregular migrants from Tunisia. Also, international lobbying throughout

2011 and 2012 has pushed state authorities to include immigration in the draft *National Strategy on Migration* (SNM). According to a respondent, 'the first reflex was a total denial and a refusal to address the issue [immigration]. ... The evolution comes following the pressure of the international community ... until they realized that they could not ignore immigration anymore' (T16-I23). Confirming this external agenda-setting dynamic, one representative of the Ministry of Foreign Affairs said at a public event in May 2017, 'The fifth axis of the migration strategy [on immigration] takes up the priorities of the international community.'

To further increase their leverage on national actors, the Swiss Development Cooperation Agency (SDC) and the EU Delegation in Tunis established a migration working group bringing together all major IOs, funders and European NGOs working on migration. Over the years, they have developed a joint advocacy agenda with six priorities, among which are the reform of the irregular stay penalties, the enactment of the asylum law, or the improvement of Tunisian inter-institutional coordination. Such coordination might explain the relative success of external agenda-setting in Tunisia compared to Morocco, where international actors work mainly bilaterally with the government and where there is little international coordination to avoid overlapping or conflicting lobbying efforts. Such a comparatively high level of international coordination in Tunisia might also be partly because the 2011 revolution created an 'artificial' common starting point, as opposed to the more gradual arrival of IOs working on migration in Morocco since the late 1990s.

In parallel to such external agenda-setting dynamics, external advice and technocratic input have also been explicitly sought by Tunisian state actors with limited expertise on immigration (Cassarini 2020). For instance, the DGCIM has requested external technical assistance for the operationalization of the migration strategy, and the CEJJ, in charge of drafting the asylum law within the MoJ, has engaged UNHCR to advise it on the process. Ultimately, however, external influence on decision-making only succeeds when it aligns with the state's internal interests, also in Tunisia. Regarding the law on human trafficking, for instance, external agenda-setting succeeded not only because international pressure aligned with Tunisia's interest to improve the U.S. Department of State rating but also because the law entailed limited political costs for Tunisian policymakers and only minimally affected Tunisia's immigration regime.

On politically more thorny issues, however, Tunisian state institutions have responded to external actors' pressure with open or subtle resistance: 'They know how to defend themselves', a European funder highlighted. And another IO respondent told me, 'When we want to go too far on some issues, we push, we push – boom! – at some point, the doors will be closed, and it will be for a good time.' This might have been the fate of the *National Migration Strategy*: external actors have pushed for its adoption up to the point that 'authorities may have decided to back off and say, ultimately it might not be the moment yet for this strategy' (T17-I23). Next to open resistance at the level of agenda-setting, Tunisian institutions also mobilize 'silent disobedience' at the level of policy implementation and practices, as Garelli and Tazzioli (2017: 90) highlight. Lastly, as shown earlier, democratization allowed the Tunisian government to better face European pressures by referring to the need of taking into account civil society actors and public opinion. Although cooperation with the European Union is still economically important for Tunisia, it is no longer critical for the government's political legitimation.

The Private Sector: The Ambiguous Role of Tunisian Employers

As in Morocco, the limited involvement of the private sector in immigration seems rather related to the structural characteristics of Tunisia's economy and labour market than to political regime dynamics in the wake of democratization. Indeed, Tunisia's private sector has so far remained publicly silent on immigration, suggesting that employers favour hiring migrant workers informally instead of engaging in the politically sensitive topic of foreign labour recruitment. The elaborate system of Labour Code exemptions that allow employers in specific sectors to freely recruit foreigners under certain conditions indicates that, for decades, the interests of big businesses were directly integrated into immigration politics through the tight imbrication of political and economic power. Despite the democratic transition in 2011, the foundations of Tunisia's economy have not been altered, and employers have not fundamentally shifted their position on immigration: while they need immigrant labour in the agriculture, construction or service sectors and are aware of the need to open labour markets to foster increased integration with African economies, they acknowledge the political sensitivity of opening the labour market to foreigners in the context of high national unemployment and economic stagnation.

Respondents across the board highlighted the apparent contradiction between high unemployment rates among Tunisians and employers looking for migrant workers in specific sectors: 'We are in a paradoxical situation. We have 14 per cent unemployment, but businesses have 120,000 open job positions', a respondent at the Union of Industry,

Trade and Crafts (UTICA) said, referring to a 2016 study by the Arab Institute of CEOs (IACE 2016: 15). Prompted on labour immigration facilitations, however, another respondent of Tunisia's largest employer union remains reticent:

I don't think that we should allow foreign workers to work in Tunisia. ... There are some businessmen who have asked for permission to hire foreign workers. ... But reforming the labour code, with what is happening currently, I do not think it's on the agenda.

As in Morocco, the size of Tunisia's informal economy – estimated at 53 per cent of employment (ILO 2018) – decreases employers' traditional lobbying incentives, given that they can cover their labour needs through informal (migrant) labour, which is cheaper and avoids claims around workers' rights (see also Ben Sedrine 2018; Labidi, Bennour and Jaidi 2017): 'The reality is that, yes, firms need this workforce, but no, they don't want to declare it' (T17-I20). Scarce workplace controls and low enforcement of employer penalties allow employers to bypass the restrictive labour code, to the detriment of foreign workers. Indeed, a 2017 study highlighted the dire working conditions of migrants, in terms of payment, working hours, health and exploitation (Labidi, Bennour and Jaidi 2017).

However, with Tunisian businesses seeking to expand on the African continent, particularly to Senegal, Côte d'Ivoire, and Mauritania, interviewed authorities and employer representatives were aware that – in the words of a respondent from the Ministry of Employment and Professional Training (MoEPF) – 'to open new markets in Africa, we need to open up to foreign workers as well'. While employers do not publicly defend such a position, some initiatives have been launched with regards to mobilizing the potential of African students and entrepreneurs: UTICA has signed a partnership agreement with the AESAT for the creation of a business incubator for young African entrepreneurs and is in close contact with the MoHE to promote Tunisia's higher education sector abroad. In the medium- to long-term, such initiatives and the increasing need for specialized, high-skilled immigration could increase the role of business interests in immigration policy, regardless of Tunisia's political regime dynamics.

The Legal Sector: Lawyers, Judges and the Rule of Law

Democratization, however, is likely to reshape the role of legal actors in Tunisian immigration politics. Although courts and judges are not (yet) central actors on immigration, Tunisian civil society actors and lawyers are beginning to use legal action as a tool to enforce migrants' rights.

Under the authoritarian regime of Ben Ali, judges were largely dependent on the executive, and foreigners' rights to appeal administrative decisions on residence permits or expulsions were either non-existent on paper or ineffective in practice (Ben Jemia 2009; Planes-Boissac 2012b: 33). Also, the limited jurisprudence on immigration that existed often showed inconsistencies and generally adopted a restrictive interpretation of migrants' rights, notably regarding the implementation of the 2004 law and of foreigners' labour rights (Ben Jemia and Ben Achour 2014: 15–16, 30–32). Since 2011, the judiciary has gained institutional autonomy: the Association of Tunisian Magistrates (AMT) has at times criticized the treatment of migrants by the Tunisian state, and judges are increasingly involved in international networks such as the International Association of Refugee Law Judges (IARLJ), whose annual conference was held in Tunis in 2014.

Although the jurisprudence on immigration since 2011 has remained relatively limited, mainly because practices towards immigrants are often not codified in law and can therefore not be challenged in court, this is subject to change. Human trafficking is a particularly promising issue area in this regard: the creation of the *Authority to fight against human trafficking* in February 2017, headed by a judge, substantially increased the legal opportunities to protect trafficking victims from expulsion or to enforce their social and labour rights.[12] Also, legal activism is increasing: while civil society focused on emergency support for refugees and migrants in the immediate post-revolutionary period, since 2016, CSOs have launched legal aid initiatives for migrants and refugees – Lawyers Without Borders (ASF) started working with victims of human trafficking, IADH initiated a cooperation with UNHCR to legally represent recognized refugees, and TAT launched a legal clinic for vulnerable migrants in 2017.

There is thus a growing awareness within civil society that legal action and court judgments have the potential to enshrine migrants' rights in Tunisia. For instance, since 2017, CSOs have discussed the possibility of challenging the legality of the Ouardiya detention centre – officially a 'Welcome and Orientation Centre' and therefore not, like prisons, under the authority of the MoJ – in front of an administrative tribunal. The following discussion among civil society representatives in May 2017 provides insights into such incipient dynamics:

> Participant 1: I want to suggest legal action against the existence of Ouardiya; this has been proposed to us by the Union of Judges, but we never did anything.
> Participant 2: Let's do it!

Participant 3: So we just need to have the case of one migrant and go to court?
Participant 1: Yes, and this will not be a problem. There are enough migrants there at the moment, so this will be easy! They took Migrant X last week.
Participant 2: So then we just have to go to court with Migrant X! (T17-D6).

Yet, it took some time for civil society to act upon its plans. Ultimately, the dire situation of irregular migrants held in Ouardiya during the first COVID-19 lockdown in March/April 2020 was decisive in triggering legal action. Between 6 and 16 April, migrants detained in Ouardiya entered into a hunger strike to protest the unsafe conditions in which they were forced to remain, without access to face masks and disinfectants. The hunger strike ended after a meeting between several CSOs (UGTT, FTDES, LTDH and ATFD) and the Minister of Human Rights on 16 April, in which Tunisian authorities agreed to meet detainees' demands of minimal sanitary needs and promised to eventually free detainees.[13] However, on 5 June 2020, a coalition of CSOs, among which the FTDES, Lawyers without Borders, TAT, and the World Organization Against Torture (OMCT), brought a case to the Tunis administrative tribunal to contest the legality of Ouardiya. And on 9 July 2020, in an unprecedented decision, the tribunal requested the liberation of twenty two migrants unlawfully detained in the Ouardiya centre.[14]

These initiatives showcase the extent to which mobilizing courts and the rule of law for migrant protection is specific to democracies. As one respondent summarized when talking about unlawful expulsions of migrants, 'Before 2011, there was a dictatorship, so when they caught people, they sent them back directly. ... It's not like now, with the court, where you have to respect the law' (T16-I22). Such insights suggest that legal actors will become more central to Tunisian immigration politics in the future, particularly once the Tunisian Constitutional Court is operational.[*] At the same time, the currently largely informal character of Tunisia's immigration regulations will continue to obstruct civil society efforts to unleash the potential of court-based expansion of migrant rights: 'The problem in Tunisia is that there are very few laws [on immigration], so there are very few legal disputes that can be made' (T16–I8).

---

[*] It was created by the 2014 Constitution, but was not operational until the end of 2020. Jeune Afrique, *Blocage de la Cour constitutionnelle en Tunisie: « les modernistes sont perdants »*, 12 October 2018; AA, *Tunisie : Report de l'examen de la modification de la loi relative à la Cour constitutionnelle*, 8 October 2020.

How Democratization Shapes Immigration Politics

Together with the analysis of policy drivers in Chapter 6, the Tunisian case study has provided key insights into how democratization shapes immigration politics and thus into the boundaries of the 'regime effect'. First of all, there appears to be a clear 'regime effect' regarding domestic political processes on immigration: prior to 2011, only the inner circle around Ben Ali and the MoI was involved in policymaking. The democratic transition after 2011 shifted the foundations of Tunisian political life by putting domestic political legitimation centre stage and reshuffling dynamics among state and societal actors. Since the revolution, Tunisian policymakers need to ensure popular adherence to policy changes to secure their legitimacy and parliamentarians are perceived as central policymaking actors. While so far there is a cross-partisan elite consensus to depoliticize immigration, once the Tunisian party system stabilizes, MPs could drive both progressive and restrictive immigration reform, either by translating their concerns for Tunisians abroad onto immigrants in Tunisia or by politicizing immigration from a nationalist perspective.

A 'regime effect' is also visible with regards to civil society, as democratization fundamentally reshaped civil society activism and its relationship with state institutions. Indeed, although policymaking is far from being fully transparent and inclusive, there is much more civil society consultation and external oversight. However, while civil society has been successful in reshaping Tunisian authorities' discourse on immigration, in setting issues on the agenda, and in negotiating exemptions and improvements for specific migrant categories, their influence on actual decision-making has remained limited. This is partly due to the limited maturing of Tunisia's pro-immigration civil society, as well as to its internal divisions. Such 'civil society gridlock' (Blair 1997; Lewis 2002) is not uncommon in democratizing contexts, with conflicting civil society claims ultimately paralysing political and social processes of change. Time is an essential factor in this regard: research on pro-migrant activism in South Korea or Latin America, for instance, indicates that it took nearly two decades for democratization to spill over into a broadening of immigrants' rights (Acosta Arcarazo and Freier 2015; Chung 2010). Yet, there are also numerous other cases where the democratization-migrant rights' nexus never materialized (Brobbey 2018; Milner 2009; Whitaker 2005), particularly when newly empowered voters showcase clear anti-migration preferences. Only the future will show which dynamic will emerge in Tunisia.

Alongside these apparent 'regime effects' on domestic politics and the role of civil society, however, democratization has had ambiguous effects on institutionalist dynamics within the Tunisian state and on the role of external actors. From an institutionalist perspective, the 'regime effect' seems limited to the role of legal actors: while lawyers and judges are not yet key players in Tunisian immigration politics, civil society increasingly mobilizes human rights standards and the rule of law to protect migrants' rights. The role of legal actors will thus consolidate as the political transition matures. Otherwise, however, bureaucratic dynamics on immigration showcase a striking continuity throughout the regime change: the MoI has remained the key actor on immigration in terms of veto power, and the different visions on immigration across ministries have remained largely unaffected by the regime change, rather reflecting how immigration is understood from their specific institutional worldviews. Also, while the revolution has empowered Tunisian civil servants to take a position, the post-2011 plurality of voices has multiplied inter-institutional dynamics and conflict, ultimately leading to policy incoherence or even reform stalemate. This dovetails with the broader insight from the literature that immigration regulations tend to be incoherent by design because they have to accommodate various bureaucratic and political interests, regardless of the political regime in place (Boswell 2007b; Castles 2004; Czaika and de Haas 2013).

On the other hand, while the revolution has opened up the Tunisian state and society to increasing international cooperation, external leverage on national political processes continues to be limited by Tunisian state interests. With significant increases in international funding after 2011, European governments and development agencies have partly succeeded in influencing how Tunisian authorities frame immigration and what priorities are set on the agenda. But the Tunisian administration has also actively shaped the substance of this influence, seeking out foreign support for certain activities while resisting external interferences when they cross red lines. Thus, while the room for external influence has increased, the need for external regime legitimation has shrunk because of increased domestic legitimacy, which in turn facilitates Tunisian authorities' rejection of external demands. Chapter 8 will take up these insights from the Tunisian case study and compare them with those gained in Morocco to systematically assess the role of political regimes and state transformation in immigration politics.

8 Immigration Politics and State Transformation

Immigration and the State's Imperatives of Sovereignty and Legitimation

Migrants, by definition, challenge the human and territorial boundaries of nation-states and defy the efforts of states to secure their sovereignty and legitimacy through their presence. Regardless of the political regime in place, asserting sovereignty over people and territory, as well as ensuring the legitimacy of political institutions and decisions, is crucial for states, even if the sources of legitimacy and means of preserving sovereignty might differ. Sovereignty concerns and legitimation strategies are thus central drivers of immigration politics worldwide and can account for some of the striking similarities in Moroccan and Tunisian immigration policymaking. In particular, these state imperatives can explain the disconnect between immigration politicization and the actual scope of immigration; the differences in policy approaches across migrant categories; the symbolic nature of immigration policy and resulting gaps between discourse, policies-on-paper, and implementation; as well as the tendency to safeguard the state's power by creating exemption regimes or enacting changes informally. Ultimately, the dynamics emerging from states' fundamental imperatives to secure their existence explain why security interests tend to dominate immigration politics in both autocracies and democracies.

Bending Reality: Magnitude Versus Politicization of Immigration

First of all, the imperatives of regime legitimation and state sovereignty explain why the politicization of immigration in Morocco and Tunisia is largely detached from its actual scope on the ground: while the Moroccan state intentionally inflated the scale of Western and Central African immigration for its African and European diplomacy and emphasized the extent of the 2013 liberal reform to placate its progressive civil society in the context of a three-level game, the Tunisian state has deliberately downplayed (Libyan) immigration to avoid its politicization in domestic and regional politics.

Indeed, immigration from Western and Central Africa has become a number one state priority in Morocco as part of the monarchy's authoritarian consolidation agenda, despite only gradual increases in numbers and the presence of a wide range of other migrant groups. As I have shown, Morocco instrumentalized immigration for its diplomatic agenda – to gain concessions from the European Union in terms of economic cooperation and the rights of Morocco's diaspora; as well as to garner support for the Western Sahara question within the African Union and to deepen political and economic cooperation with Western and Central African countries. In addition, the immigration reform bolstered the regime's legitimacy domestically in front of liberal, progressive parts of Moroccan society who saw migrants' rights as intrinsic to Morocco's democratization agenda.

Regardless of the reality on the ground, immigration has been inflated in political discourses to fortify Morocco's image as a modern, liberal monarchy at home and abroad: 'what happens in Morocco is not because of 80,000 immigrants' (M17-I6). In fact, it is precisely the numerical insignificance of immigration to Morocco that has allowed it to be so successfully instrumentalized, as the diplomatic returns on the 2013 reform were substantive compared to its limited domestic political costs. In the words of one of my respondents, 'It was a big publicity stunt that did not cost Moroccan society much' (M16-I2). Immigration was thus turned into geopolitical capital, but given that the liberal reform only affected a small migrant population, it did not entail significant societal changes on the ground that would have triggered domestic resistance or polarization. The policy could be kept within the symbolic realm.

In Tunisia, authorities downplayed large-scale Libyan immigration to avoid their involvement in Libyan domestic politics and hereby secure future political and economic cooperation with Libya, as well as to prevent the polarization of the Tunisian electorate and hereby safeguard national unity. This non-policy was reinforced by the fact that Tunisian authorities did not know – and were not keen to know – how many Libyans effectively reside in Tunisia:

> The census says the number of Libyans who live in Tunisia is 8,000 ... If you are asking the MoI, it will tell you there are one million. It's not one million, it's not 8,000, nobody knows exactly (T16-I11).

This conscious laissez-faire approach has been legitimized by a discourse that casts Libyans as 'brothers' or 'guests', highlights the transitory nature of their stay in Tunisia, and distracts from exclusion and migrant rights abuses on the ground. Such vocabulary of hospitality and fraternity, however, is not unique in the Arab world, as it has also been commonly used for Syrians in Turkey (Toğral Koca 2016), Palestinians in Lebanon (Ramadan 2008) or Iraqis in Jordan (Seeley 2010). How a state talks about and counts (or does not talk about and does not count) immigration thus reveals broader regime strategies to ensure the legitimacy of policy decisions.

Migrant Categorization and Racialized Politicization

The imperatives of regime legitimation and state sovereignty also explain the highly differentiated nature of immigration policies. In the words of a Tunisian respondent, 'There are foreigners and foreigners' (T17-I4). Indeed, a country's immigration regime is never only open or closed but a mixed bag of measures that target different migrant groups in different ways, depending on how they strengthen or challenge the regime in place.

For each migrant category, different norms are mobilized, different actors are responsible, and different policies are deployed: in Morocco and Tunisia, irregular migrants are framed through a national security lens, and under the responsibility of the MoI, students are framed through an economic development lens, and under the responsibility of the MoFA and the MoHE, victims of human trafficking are framed through a humanitarian protection lens, and under the responsibility of a specific authority created for their protection, and European migrants are framed through a foreign policy lens and generally overlooked by law enforcement agents. In addition, Libyan citizens in Tunisia have not been framed as refugees or migrants, but as 'brothers' or 'guests' since 2011, and in Morocco, the 2013 reform has created a new migrant category – the regularized migrant – which has received preferential treatment by the MCMREAM and the integration measures it devised. In sum, 'the quality of hospitality remains in variable geometry' (T16-I18).

Furthermore, in both countries, the way in which authorities treat specific migrant groups is highly racialized. This reflects not only Morocco's and Tunisia's unease to situate themselves on the global colour line (El Hamel 2012; Gazzotti 2021b; Hannoum 2020; Mrad Dali 2015; Pouessel 2012b; Scaglioni 2017), but also migrants' capacity (or that of their civil society support networks and origin states) to either challenge or reinforce regime legitimation. This explains why practices towards Western and Central African migrants differ markedly from those towards European migrants and are structured according to foreign policy priorities and the legacy of historical power structures and racial hierarchies. While Western and Central African migrants are the target of security services, police controls, expulsions and discrimination, Europeans can usually exit and re-enter Morocco and Tunisia every three months to renew their tourist visas. This permanent tourist status is illegal in theory but largely tolerated: 'Europeans can remain irregular without being harassed, while Black people in the same situation are arrested and imprisoned in a detention centre' (T17-D6), one respondent summarized. Also, policies that appear neutral on paper – such as penalties for irregular stay – are de facto only applied to 'sub-Saharan' migrants. Such practices of 'unequal illegality' (Garelli and Tazzioli 2017: 49) show how policies are not only a result of institutionalized racism but also of the different power balances with these migrants' origin states and the vested interests that Morocco and Tunisia have in them (see also Gazzotti 2021b).

Migrant categorization dynamics thus provide crucial insights into state priorities, being mobilized not only for exclusion and discrimination – such as in the case of the 'irregular migrant' or 'sub-Saharan African' categories – but also for inclusion and enhanced protection, such as in the case of the 'European expats' or 'regularized migrants' categories. To get a complete picture of the transformations of a country's immigration regime, disaggregating immigration policy into its different components and layers is therefore critical.

Symbolic Politics: Mind the Gaps!

The intrinsic link between immigration, state sovereignty and regime legitimation also explains why immigration is an area of symbolic politics par excellence – in both democracies and autocracies. In both Morocco and Tunisia, discourses on immigration seem to count more than actions, and political leaders often reap the fruits of policy measures through their mere announcement, regardless of whether they are ultimately enacted. This explains the wide gaps in Morocco and Tunisia between political discourses, policies-on-paper and implemented measures.

In Morocco, many of the integration measures announced in 2013 have not been effectively enacted. For instance, Moroccan politicians continue to successfully capitalize on their promise that regularized migrants would receive access to public healthcare, although the measure has not been implemented several years down the line. Also, speaking of the announcement in early 2017 that regularized migrants would receive a three-year permit instead of a one-year permit, one respondent said, 'We will see to what extent this will be implemented, but the announcement itself already has an effect' (M17-I4). Also, the fact that the institutions set up to deal with immigration – the SEMTE in Tunisia and the MCMREAM in Morocco – lack human and financial resources to fulfil their mandates exposes the extent to which Moroccan and Tunisian immigration policies are 'for show'. While the SEMTE and the MCMREAM are the main interlocutors for civil society and international actors, they have little room for manoeuvre to impose their priorities within Morocco's and Tunisia's larger administrative apparatuses.

The symbolic weight of immigration policies is also evident in the fact that decisions are made not when they are most appropriate but when they are most effective in generating media attention. For instance, although Moroccan authorities persistently highlighted the 'exceptional character' of the 2014 regularization – including in my interviews in October 2016 – a second regularization was announced in December 2016, shortly before Morocco's accession to the African Union and only a few days after Algeria – the regional rival – made negative headlines because of the expulsion of a Malian migrant.[1] Similarly, when the Moroccan King intervened to grant refugee protection to a group of Syrian families stuck at the Moroccan–Algerian border in 2017, he did so on 20 June, the *World Refugee Day*, securing himself and Morocco international press coverage. Such dynamics are aimed first and foremost at showcasing Morocco's place among the group of progressive, modern states – a dynamic I have called 'geopolitical rebordering'. These insights show the importance of looking not only at what is announced when it comes to immigration but also at what is enacted and at how these written words are translated into policy practice.

Safeguarding State Power: Exemption Regimes and Informality

Ultimately, to safeguard the state's monopoly of power over immigration, both Morocco and Tunisia have responded to claims for more immigrants' rights with a 'policy of ambivalence' (Norman 2016b) or with 'politics of uncertainty' (Nassar and Stel 2019; Stel 2020): liberal changes targeting immigrants were either enacted through ministerial decrees that introduced exemptions for particular migrant groups without touching the overarching legal framework or were kept at the level of informal promises by individual policymakers. This allowed both the Moroccan monarchy and the Tunisian democratically elected government to conduct a 'pragmatic' and 'flexible' policy that responded to civil society and international demands but at the same time ensured their ability to repeal these measures in the future.

In Tunisia, for instance, authorities' tolerance towards Libyan migrants is based on an 'administrative note that says – tolerate them, and we will not be bothered to create rules' (T16-I8). Compared to granting Libyans regular residence permits, such an approach creates room to backtrack on the policy later on. In addition, while Tunisian authorities have tolerated civil society support of irregular migrants since 2011, they have not repealed the 2004 law that officially prohibits such assistance. Also in Morocco, liberal development targeting civil society, such as the regularization of migrant associations in 2014, has not been enshrined in law. According to a high-level civil servant, 'we have acted outside of the law and had a pragmatic approach to give these associations a status' (M17-D8). This, however, jeopardizes the legal security of such associations in the longer term. Similarly, progressive changes such as the exemptions for regularized migrants from the labour market test in Morocco or for specific migrant categories from the irregular stay penalty in Tunisia have not been enacted through laws but through ministerial decrees. They can thus be gone as quickly as they came.

As a consequence, legal change in Morocco and Tunisia has only affected the fringes of the immigration regime, such as issues of racial discrimination or human trafficking that have a limited impact on the magnitude of immigration and enforceable residence rights at large. The absence of reform at the core of the immigration regime – entry and residence permits, asylum and immigration laws – shows the reluctance of powerholders to set things in stone, and the primacy of guaranteeing state power and flexibility for further backtracking, a dynamic I have developed elsewhere under the of term 'ad-hocratic immigration governance' (Natter 2021a). Such dynamics are not unique to immigration policy. As Hibou (2005: 81) argues in the context of Moroccan and Tunisian economic privatization policies, 'arbitrariness and fluidity between distinctions – such as tolerated and accepted, legal and illegal, public and private – constitute modes of government unto themselves'.

The Legacies of State Formation

Investigating the role of the polity in immigration politics requires looking beyond the strategies deployed to ensure regime legitimation and state sovereignty. The ways in which Moroccan and Tunisian actors have approached immigration are also influenced by the legacies of state formation, in particular through Morocco's and Tunisia's histories of slave trade and colonization, their different imaginations and accounts of national identity, the repertoires of action that authorities have historically mobilized to respond to political opposition and claims for internal diversity, and these countries' shared experience of large-scale emigration. These insights highlight the relevance of historical-culturalist approaches to immigration policymaking across political regimes and political geographies. They also showcase that the study of immigration policy – how a state deals with 'the other' – is inevitably a study of the essence and transformation of the state. And as state formation is an ongoing process, immigration policy analysis offers a powerful lens through which to study the permanent 'reinvention of the state'.

The Heritage of Slavery and Colonization

First of all, Moroccan and Tunisian approaches to immigration were significantly shaped by the legacies of their histories of slavery and colonization. In both countries, the trans-Saharan slave trade between the sixteenth and twentieth centuries still informs the institutional marginalization and everyday racism towards Black Moroccans and Tunisians (Badoual 2003; El Hamel 2012; Mrad Dali 2009; Pouessel 2012b). Such racial discrimination of national minorities has, more recently, become entangled with perceptions of and behaviour towards migrants from Western and Central Africa, who are often called *'abid* (slave) on the streets (Menin 2016; Scaglioni 2017). While immigrants hence suffer from this historically engrained racism, growing immigration also provides an opportunity to re-evaluate the history of slavery in both countries and to bring racism towards citizens and foreigners alike back into socio-political debates. For example, the historical legacy of slavery has importantly informed discussions preceding the 2018 law against racial discrimination in Tunisia.

Similarly, colonization still weighs heavily on Morocco's and Tunisia's immigration governance. In pre-colonial times, immigration was either not regulated or loosely organized through bilateral agreements with origin countries. Immigration regulations were first introduced by colonial administrators in the early twentieth century with a focus on controlling population movement. Upon independence, Moroccan and Tunisian authorities inherited a centralized and consolidated bureaucratic apparatus and a legal system modelled on the French administration. Regulations on immigration and access to residence and work permits were largely taken over – either through path dependency in bureaucratic practices or more active institutional borrowing of migration control tools – and continue to shape contemporary legal categories and immigration procedures. At the same time, however, the history of colonial occupation and settlement has fostered mistrust towards foreigners – in particular, in relation to their access to land ownership and involvement in politics. This sentiment re-emerged in Tunisia in 2016 during debates about facilitating foreigners' access to buying property, showing the potential of mobilizing the memory of colonization in an anti-immigration discourse. As long as there is no political or popular polarization on immigration, this dynamic is dormant. Yet, it raises the question of whether and how the colonial past might be instrumentalized in a context of growing polarization on immigration.

National Identity Conceptions

Moroccan and Tunisian contemporary debates on immigration and (racial and religious) diversity are also crucially informed by official conceptions of national identity. In both countries, political leaders in the immediate post-independence period emphasized the homogeneity of the Moroccan and Tunisian nations and the role of pan-Arabism and Islam as identity pillars (Wyrtzen 2014). In addition, the departure of (primarily Christian) colonizers and Moroccan and Tunisian Jews (mainly to Israel) after independence resulted in the religious homogenization of Moroccan and Tunisian populations and fostered the Islamic focus of national identity. Since the 1980s, national identity conceptions have diverged and reconnected with pre-colonial accounts in which *marocanité* is defined through pluralism and *tunisianité* through unicity. These conceptions have affected debates around immigration: while in Morocco, African immigration is cast as a return to Morocco's African roots; in Tunisia, discussions about racial diversity were actively sidelined in the name of national unity.

Although official Tunisian history highlights its multicultural origins at the crossroads of civilizations, the modernization agenda pursued by the leaders of pre-colonial Tunisia since the mid-nineteenth century entailed the homogenization of Tunisian national identity. After independence in 1956, Bourguiba and later Ben Ali continued this modernization agenda that fostered a 'republican nationalism built around the single party, the single syndicate, the single nation' (T16-I6). Such national identity narratives left little space for alterity. As sketched earlier, this national identity conception has survived the intense identity debates between secularists and Islamists following the 2011 revolution. The silencing of discussions on internal diversity and issues of racism and immigration in the post-2011 period can thus be partly explained through this historical legacy highlighting the homogeneity of the Tunisian nation.

In contrast, Morocco's idea of the imperial state allows more flexibility towards internal pluralism and immigration. Until the late nineteenth century, the territorial spheres of influence of the Moroccan state constantly shifted (Hibou and Tozy 2015). Although colonization accelerated the consolidation of the central state power across Morocco's current territory and Muslim identity dominated the post-independence period, since the 1980s, official discourses around Moroccan national identity have shifted towards a more 'cosmopolitan' (Mourji et al. 2016: 11) identity crafted around African, Jewish, Amazigh and Arab components. This pluralism has been more forcefully pursued with the King's Africa policy since the early 2000s and consecrated in the new preamble of the 2011 Constitution, providing a window of opportunity for a more open approach towards immigration. It is in this context that we have to understand the following statement of a Moroccan deputy: 'There are no discussions on Moroccan national identity, we are not afraid of losing our national identity through this immigration.'

Repertoires of Action Towards Pluralism Claims

A third way in which state formation continues to shape immigration governance is how Moroccan and Tunisian authorities have historically dealt with claims for pluralism from their citizens. While there are many historical parallels in the way authoritarianism has maintained itself in Morocco and Tunisia, such as through economic patronage networks, repression, or divide-and-rule tactics, the two regimes have differed in their approaches to domestic claims for political or identity pluralism.

In Morocco, the monarchy historically dealt with regime criticism from left, Islamist or Amazigh groups by first repressing them and, once repression became unsustainable, proactively integrating them into the state apparatus. In the case of leftist political parties, the 1998 'alternation government' put an end to their repression during the previous decades by integrating them into the government. To counter Islamist critiques, the Moroccan King has revitalized his role as Commander of the Faithful and regional leader of a moderate Islam (Regragui 2013) and opened the way for the Islamist party (PJD) to compete in elections and to participate in government. And in response to Amazigh activism, Moroccan authorities have created a plethora of institutions to safeguard Amazigh culture and ultimately consecrated their contribution to Moroccan national identity in the 2011 Constitution. In all three cases, authorities have limited the challenge these groups posed to the regime by internalizing their criticism (and partially their activists) and developing an active state policy on the issue. The state hereby gave voice to these groups and at the same time controlled their discourse. A similar repertoire of action shaped Moroccan authorities' response towards migrant activists: realizing that the repression of immigrants and their domestic civil society supporters would be politically too costly given the international attention to the topic, Moroccan authorities shifted towards a strategy of co-optation that would allow them to control and steer the immigration debate.

In contrast, pro-migrant activism has been actively sidelined by Tunisian policymakers under the banner of achieving a common national goal, namely democratization. This reaction is in line with how the state has historically faced demands for political and religious diversity. In fact, throughout Tunisia's post-independence period, the regimes of Bourguiba and Ben Ali silenced opposition within the ruling party, by the trade union movement or by human rights activists by referring to the need to preserve national unity in order to achieve the overarching goals of progress and development. As Bellin (1995: 127) writes, 'Bourguiba dismissed the liberal ideal of political competition as partisan and divisive, unconscionably wasteful at a time when citizens should be united in a consolidated effort for national development.' Despite the democratic transition and the partial replacement of the political elite, these discourses have remained: as shown earlier, claims for acknowledging Tunisia's racial diversity (its Black minority and the presence of immigrants) have been met with reticence by the political establishment. Successive governments engaged in strategic immigration depoliticization justified by the need to preserve national unity at a crucial moment in time. This reflects broader dynamics within the Tunisian partisan landscape after 2011, which have privileged consensus over conflict to safeguard the democratic transition. Tunisian authorities' conscious depoliticization of immigration, as well as the proactive politicization of immigration by the Moroccan monarchy, can thus be seen as a continuation of the regimes' trusted repertoires of action.

The Experience of Emigration: Mirror and Demonstration Effects

A last aspect of state formation that has provided a mould for debates on immigration is Morocco's and Tunisia's large-scale emigration history since the mid-twentieth century. In particular, the experience of Maghreb migrant mobilization in Europe strongly inspired migrant activism and civil society dynamics in Morocco and Tunisia (see also Üstübici 2015). On the one hand, diaspora groups, returnees and civil society associations have mobilized the mirror effect as a tool in their advocacy for more immigrants' rights: in both countries, CSOs have exploited the dissonance between authorities' goal to advance the rights of Moroccan and Tunisian emigrants in Europe and their denial of immigrant rights. Also, political figures who were exiled in the past and returned to Morocco or Tunisia fed their personal emigration experiences as 'political remittances' into national institutions' vision on immigration. In Morocco, Driss el Yazami was a key personality who advocated for the UNHCR's 2007 cooperation agreement, as well as for legitimizing and substantiating the 2013 reform. And in Tunisia, the integration of previously exiled leftist and Islamist politicians, as well as human rights activists into the post-2011 political system has shaped discussions over the right of asylum and accelerated the conclusion of the UNHCR headquarters agreement. Ultimately, however, the mirror effect has been cut short in Tunisia because returned politicians had to prove their *tunisianité* in front of the domestic electorate.

While Morocco's and Tunisia's history of emigration has been mobilized for immigration advocacy through the mirror effect, in Morocco, progressive immigration policies were also instrumentalized for advancing emigration and diaspora policy goals through the 'demonstration effect' (Arrighi and Bauböck 2017). Particularly, the regularization campaigns for irregular migrants have fulfilled this function, showcasing to Europe that a different, more benevolent and inclusive approach to irregular migration is possible. Yet, given the limited number of immigrants it concerned and the impact it had on Morocco's geopolitical standing, the regularization was a 'low cost–high gains' measure. In Tunisia, the demonstration effect is not really at play, mainly because the magnitude of (particularly Libyan) immigration would make demonstration motives very costly on the domestic scene. Nonetheless, state actors are aware that a more open immigration or asylum policy could be an asset for Tunisia's diaspora policy. In the words of a high-level Tunisian civil servant, 'Everything we do for the recognition of foreigners, their rights, it will help us to negotiate with Europe.' Such mirror or demonstration effects are particularly relevant in countries that transition from emigration to immigration countries – such as Turkey and Mexico right now or Italy and Spain in the past – where both emigration and immigration are politicized domestically.

The systematic contrasting and comparing of Moroccan and Tunisian immigration policymaking in this chapter not only allows to identify immigration policymaking dynamics that reflect state formation legacies or state imperatives of legitimation and sovereignty. It also provides first insights into the boundaries of the 'regime effect' – that is, the extent to which political regimes shape the role, weight and interactions of the state apparatus, civil society and external actors.

Looking Inside the State

First of all, many inter-institutional dynamics – the need to negotiate diverging interests, the role of institutional cultures, or the leverage of individual bureaucrats – are strikingly similar across political regimes. In both Morocco and Tunisia, bureaucratic politics tends to produce conflicting interests on immigration within the state and thus implementation inconsistencies or reform stalemate. However, the two countries differ in terms of the role played by legal actors and the power held by the executive, which is crucial in determining the extent of top-down decision-making autonomy and the room for divergent, bottom-up interests to unfold. This, in turn, affects immigration policy dynamics and outcomes: in Morocco and pre-2011 Tunisia, bureaucratic inertia was counteracted by a strong autocratic executive; while in democratic Tunisia, the bureaucratic stalemate on immigration was reinforced by governmental volatility and a fragmentation of political and institutional voices.

The Centrality of Executive Power

In Morocco and pre-2011 Tunisia, power is indeed concentrated in the hands of the King and President, respectively, and their leverage to take strategic decisions that break with path dependency dynamics is high. The King's decision to engage in immigration reform in 2013 after a decade of restrictiveness – and to frame immigration liberalization as necessary to achieve African regional integration and to consolidate Moroccan 'modernity' – explains the extraordinary dynamism on immigration and the (at least discursive) adherence of state institutions to the new policy. By casting immigration policy as a 'national endeavour', the King lifted immigration above the political and partisan sphere. Any deficiencies in the execution of the reform were blamed on the administration in a good cop/bad cop logic that fostered the King's image as the guardian of minorities and human rights.

This contrasts with the situation in post-2011 Tunisia, where power is by definition diffused across various democratic institutions and where the institutionalized plurality of positions slowed down decision-making and made politics prone to stalemate. The continuity of Tunisia's securitized immigration policy after 2011 and the fizzling out of immigration reforms over the years thus resulted from the conflicting societal interests that political leaders had to reconcile. According to Tunisian respondents, a central decision-maker that could have initiated fundamental changes on immigration was lacking: 'There is no King in Tunisia who could carry this project' (T17-I20).

Thus, while the 'royal will' has fostered administrative actors around a common agenda in Morocco, democratization in Tunisia has exacerbated the fragmentation of voices. The process leading up to Morocco's and Tunisia's migration strategy is exemplary for this 'regime effect': in Morocco, a detailed strategy was elaborated by a small group of civil servants and politically validated within less than a year. In Tunisia, the consultative process of elaborating the strategy has not been completed ten years down the line, and the strategy's substance has progressively shrunk with each new draft. This suggests that the more actors are integrated into the process, the smaller the common ground gets. Autocracies thus seem to provide for a centripetal force of centralization and coherence, while democracies bring with them a centrifugal force of diversity and fragmentation of interests and actors.

The Rule of Law

A second set of actors that seemed crucially affected by political regime dynamics were courts and judges. In Morocco, CSOs have prompted legal interventions by judges to uphold migrants' rights, such as in the case of internal relocations and arbitrary detentions. Also, lawyers have started challenging inconsistent and arbitrary court decisions, creating a small jurisprudence on immigration that could set precedents. However, legal actors suffer from their limited independence from the executive and are unlikely to become the guardians of migrants' rights, as has been the case in the European context (Joppke 1998).

In Tunisia, civil society has started to use legal means to safeguard migrants' rights, even if only tacitly, with a first victory in July 2020, when civil society groups successfully challenged arbitrary decisions on detention and expulsion in front of the Tunis administrative court. It thus seems only a question of time, financial support and professionalization of the Tunisian legal sector and civil society until the democratic transition establishes courts as independent actors in immigration politics. In both Morocco and Tunisia, however, the reach of legal actors is limited by the fact that many migration control practices are informal and not codified in immigration law, and thus not open to legal challenge.

Bureaucratic Politics

Despite such effects on the leverage of central executive actors and courts, authoritarianism seems not to fundamentally reshape issue-specific inter-institutional dynamics on immigration known from the literature on democracies. Rather than being a specificity of democracy, the bureaucratic politics dynamics sketched in this book seem intrinsically linked to the questions raised by the topic of immigration in terms of institutional interest alignment. Democratization, then, only brings those dynamics out into the open.

Indeed, decision-makers are always faced with a variety of interests that need to be reconciled to enact a particular policy measure. In authoritarian Tunisia, decision-makers had to weigh international prestige and economic benefits against security interests to decide whether or not to host the AfDB and to grant its support staff exemptions in terms of labour market regulations (for instance, by allowing the opening of African restaurants, hairdressers, and clubs). In Morocco, the stalemate on the asylum law since 2014 suggests that different interests collide – between actors emphasizing the law's added value in fostering Morocco's position as a regional leader on migrants' rights, and those who warn of a pull effect if Morocco is to become the only North African country with a functioning asylum system. Also, while the royal will has prevented open disagreement with the 2013 reform, it did not preclude power politics and institutional turf wars that crucially affected how royal orders were translated on the ground.

In addition, institutional identities and the overarching goal of state institutions to secure their power position within a larger administrative state apparatus have shaped their policies towards immigration. In Morocco, each institution has appropriated the royal intentions through their own sectoral visions – pitting a 'social, humanitarian vision' against a 'legalistic, security vision': while Ministries of Higher Education and Foreign Affairs generally saw immigration as a means to promote the attractiveness of the country, Ministries of Health put public safety in the foreground, and Ministries of Interior viewed immigration through the lens of national security and territorial protection. These different visions were translated into conflicting positions on immigration and can account for the often contradictory regulations migrants are subjected to.

Similarly, the personal motivation of individual Moroccan and Tunisian civil servants was central to explaining progress or stalemate on particular issues, as well as divergent policy interpretations within ministerial departments and across the national territory: 'You get results based on the will of individuals, and not based on an institutional will' (T16-I16), one respondent highlighted. As evidenced in the literature on street-level bureaucrats, also in Morocco and Tunisia, local actors often resisted decisions taken at the ministerial level, and implementing bureaucrats re-adapted measures to fit their interests. In Morocco, educational authorities acted outside the law by enrolling irregular migrant children in public schools before the 2013 policy reform; and after 2013, migrants' access to social services or residence permits varies strikingly across the national territory. In Tunisia, individual exemptions from irregular stay penalties could be negotiated informally with the Ministry of Finance. While such individual leverage creates opportunities for policy openings, it also shows how fragile advances are, especially in the context of high political volatility: 'The problem is that as long as it remains a single person who is very motivated within an institution, well the day that this person moves to another service, you have to start all over again' (T17-I15).

The Clients of Immigration Politics

Looking inside the state is thus critical to understanding immigration politics across the entire democracy–autocracy spectrum. At the same time, no regime can be sustained without at least some support from parts of the population or the international state system. As Bueno de Mesquita et al. (2003) argue, all regimes need to secure their legitimacy through support by a 'selectorate'. While both democracies and autocracies depend on a combination of domestic and international support, the centrality of popular legitimation in democracies suggests that domestic clients – the electorate, political parties or CSOs – play a more central role than in autocracies. Indeed, Tunisia's democratic transition redirected policymakers' attention to the electorate and domestic socio-economic challenges. In contrast, international clients have been central to immigration policymaking in both autocratic Morocco and Tunisia throughout its democratic transition because of the inherently transnational nature of immigration as a policy issue and the fact that both countries are navigating a three-level game between European, African and domestic interests. While autocracies seem to have more flexibility to choose which clients they want to cater to through their immigration policies – diplomatic partners, patronage networks, the country's economic elite or specific sections of the general public – the central question guiding investigations of immigration politics studies should always be: who is the 'selectorate'? Who are the clients of a country's immigration policy?

Domestic Politics

This book suggests that domestic politics dynamics are to varying degrees subject to a 'regime effect': while the role played by the electorate and political parties is clearly different across political regimes, the internal dynamics, leverage, and advocacy strategies of civil society are only partly affected by the regime in place, and economic actors' role seems detached from political regime dynamics, rather reflecting Moroccan and Tunisian economic structures.

First of all, the Tunisian case exemplifies that democratization brings domestic drivers to the foreground and puts the electorate and political parties centre stage. Under Ben Ali, immigration was silenced, there was no opposition in the Parliament, and citizens could neither mobilize for nor against immigration. In post-2011 Tunisia, political leaders need to legitimize and assure public adherence to their decisions, and political parties and MPs have become a target for civil society activism. Democratic decision-makers are, however, confronted with conflicting popular demands. Post-2011 freedom of expression enabled both those who were marginalized – such as rejected asylum seekers in the Choucha camp or victims of racist attacks – to mobilize for their rights and those who felt threatened by diversity to voice their fears. The pragmatic response of Tunisian governments and political parties has been to avoid immigration politicization and to maintain the status quo. Focusing on more pressing economic and security issues, Tunisian politicians have concentrated on their electorate and privileged policy continuity towards immigration to prevent the emergence of partisan and popular cleavages on immigration. However, polarization on immigration might simply be a question of time, depending on the maturation of the party system and the consolidation of democracy.

In Morocco, the lack of popular support for the 2013 reform might challenge the sustainability of immigration liberalization in the longer term, but it has not been an obstacle for enacting the policy in the first place. Also, political parties have been relatively absent from the migration debate despite the political salience of the topic. As a result, the Moroccan executive is relatively independent of public opinion compared to its democratic counterparts and has wider leverage to enact top-down policies shaping the place of foreigners in society. As Ferrié and Alioua (2018: 24) write, 'it is obvious that the position of Moroccan rulers makes it easier to implement an open migration policy'. So far, the exploitation of xenophobic sentiment in domestic politics has remained limited because of the low magnitude of immigration and because the political establishment has emphasized its adherence to the liberal 'state policy'. In the mid-term, however, partisan or popular polarization around immigration might become an issue both for Morocco's top-down state policy and for Tunisia's strategic non-policy.

The paired comparison of Morocco and Tunisia has also shown that political regime dynamics shape civil society's role and leverage on policy processes. In Tunisia, only CSOs protected through their international standing were allowed to engage on the topic of immigration before 2011, and their room for manoeuvre was minimal, as the Ben Ali regime responded to incipient civil society activism through a policy of containment and repression. With democratization, civil society transformed from a small group of threatened activists into a dynamic and independent voice on the political scene. At the same time, the limited maturing of the field and the emergence of civil society conflicts has in part led to a 'civil society gridlock' (Blair 1997; Lewis 2002). Given that the democratic transition is still ongoing, Tunisian civil society might not yet have reached its full potential.

In Morocco, domestic civil society has in fact also played a key role in immigration politics. However, the mechanisms through which CSOs succeeded in turning migrant rights violations into a policy issue showcase the limits of societal input in autocratic contexts: on the one hand, CSOs strategically mobilized their transnational support networks – diaspora organizations and European human rights activists – to increase their political clout on the national scene, and their privileged relations with individual powerholders within the state apparatus to channel their voice into political circles to increase pressure on the Moroccan state from within and abroad (see also Üstübici 2016). On the other hand, in the absence of meaningful party politics, CSOs have partly replaced political parties as societal interlocutors for state actors on immigration. In fact, since the late 1990s, the Moroccan monarchy has allowed migrant associations and support organizations to develop their activities, partly to prove the regime's openness, partly to control the immigration domain. Thus, while civil society needs the state's tolerance to exist, the state also needs civil society to resolve issues on the ground and sustain its liberal façade – such as in the case of Morocco's regularizations, where civil society actors were pivotal in reaching out to migrants and eventually turn the policy into an international success. CSOs' room for manoeuvre, then, depends on the extent to which they challenge (or sustain) the autocratic regime.

Despite their varying leeway and roles within democratic and autocratic contexts, Moroccan and Tunisian civil society associations face similar challenges when seeking to influence policymaking. In both countries, civil society is confronted with the balancing act of exercising pressure on the state while simultaneously supporting migrants. When creating healthcare, education, or legal counselling structures for migrants, CSOs risk replacing public functions and hereby reducing the pressure on the state to act. Also, internal civil society dynamics – such as overlapping projects, competition for funds or the risk of co-optation by state actors – are strikingly similar across both countries. Ultimately, while civil society was successful in putting certain issues in the spotlight – such as racist discrimination in Tunisia or migrants' rights violations in Morocco – their advocacy alone has generally been insufficient to trigger policy change. For policy change to occur, CSO demands need to tally with the state's interest, not only in autocratic Morocco. Also in democratic Tunisia, migrant mobilization needs at least a partial alignment with state interests to succeed. Across political systems, civil society thus seems most likely to succeed in influencing policy outcomes when its claims overlap with those of state institutions or when pressure for reform jeopardizes the regime in place.

In contrast to party politics or civil society leverage that seems critically shaped by political regimes dynamics, the role of economic actors seemed, instead, to relate to the structure of Moroccan and Tunisian economies. In both countries, businesses have not openly mobilized for or against immigration for two main reasons: large employers' interests are directly integrated into the state through patronage networks and are accommodated through a set of in/formal exemptions from labour market rules, lowering the need for active lobbying. On the other hand, the importance of the informal sector reduced incentives for employers to mobilize for more legal immigration in both Morocco and Tunisia, given that they can tap into the informal labour market and recruit locals and migrants to meet their labour needs. Indeed, in an economy where every second worker is employed informally, lobbying for migrants' rights would only weaken the power position of employers.

International Politics

While the weight and dynamics of domestic actors seem to a large extent subject to a 'regime effect', even if to varying degrees, international politics dynamics – using migration as a diplomatic rent, resisting external agenda-setting, and mobilizing international norm adherence – seem not fundamentally structured by the political regime in place. In both democracies and autocracies, foreign policy interests can drive either liberal or restrictive immigration policies, depending on which position can be better turned into a geopolitical 'rent' (Bensaâd 2005; Tsourapas 2019b).

Throughout the twentieth century, autocrats in Morocco and Tunisia used selective openings for migrants as an instrument of foreign policy cooperation: through bilateral agreements, exemptions for students from specific Western and Central African countries or workers from European countries were introduced in the generally restrictive immigration legislation. Foreign policy also informed which nationalities were granted refugee status in the absence of a formalized refugee determination procedure – such as Palestinians in Tunisia in the 1980s or Congolese in Morocco in the 1990s. In the words of one respondent, the willingness to host a specific migrant group 'depends on the relationship we have with the country in question' (T17-I14). Morocco and Tunisia also used restrictive policies on irregular 'transit' migrants as a 'bargaining chip' (M16-I22) in their relations with the European Union. For this 'migratory weapon' (Greenhill 2010; Perrin 2009) to work, migration needs to remain a top priority in diplomatic relations. Talking about the continued difficulties migrants in Morocco's northern border area experience, one respondent said, '[Moroccan authorities] know very well that the problems [in Tangiers] can be solved, but they do not want to solve them, they want to leave a difficult area – that's it' (M17-I10). The conscious politicization of immigration in Morocco can thus be seen as part and parcel of its strategic migration diplomacy to increase its negotiation potential with Europe. At the same time, immigration has become a central tool for Morocco's Africa policy. It seems, thus, that instead of being tied to the political regime in place, the role of foreign policy in immigration politics varies depending on a country's position in global migration systems. For Morocco and Tunisia, their position in between two continents and several migration systems entails that immigration policies are made within a three-level game, between the domestic political sphere, Africa and Europe.

While the importance of foreign policy in immigration policy opens up room for international policy interference, external agenda-setting seems only successful when it aligns with the goals of key domestic actors. In both autocratic Morocco and democratizing Tunisia, the involvement of IOs has been welcomed as long as it served state interests, for instance, by bringing in funding and expertise to conduct capacity building projects or to increase national security and population control. However, whenever external demands went too far or conflicted with domestic priorities – such as on readmission agreements or the elaboration of an asylum law – external actors faced clear political and administrative resistance. Such resistance happened not only at the agenda-setting and discursive level but also at the level of policy implementation: although Moroccan and Tunisian authorities have regularly paid lip service to European discourses on migration control, the enforcement of restrictive measures has remained inconsistent.

The question of whether democratization ultimately strengthens or weakens external actors' interference in immigration policy requires more research. The Tunisian case points in two different directions. On the one hand, democratization opened up state and society for international cooperation, compared to before 2011 when IOs were under the grip of the Ben Ali regime and had limited room for advocacy. Yet, the increased presence of IOs has not translated into more external influence, given the need to take into account the diversity of actors and interests across Tunisia's political landscape. Interestingly, the democratic accountability of political leaders and increased civil society activism on migration have become additional resistance tools for the Tunisian state, bolstering their refusal to accommodate external demands for more migration control: on issues such as readmission agreements or border controls, for instance, state and civil society rally against international actors to democratically legitimize the government's resistance of migration policy externalization. Although democratization has created space for external agenda-setting, it has also increased resistance to it.

Next to such international dynamics of migration diplomacy and external policy interference, the Moroccan and Tunisian cases have shown that (discursive) adherence to international norms – and international shaming when there is a deviation from these norms – is key in both democratic and autocratic contexts because of its signalling effect of being part of the 'modern, liberal' world. The 2016 laws against human trafficking in Morocco and Tunisia, for instance, have been mainly enacted because they signalled the symbolic adherence to a global epistemic community and system of norms. However, international norms and standards need to be brought in by local actors to play out, and democracy can broaden the ways in which international norms affect national policymaking. In Tunisia, civil society can now mobilize legal tools such as court rulings to enforce international standards on human trafficking, access to healthcare or labour regulations, in addition to playing on Tunisia's international image by linking migrants' rights to successful democratization. Thus, while international norms matter everywhere, the ways in which they play out might be affected by political regime dynamics, with autocracies mainly affected through reputation damage, while democracies are also vulnerable to legal activism.

The specific characteristics of the Moroccan and Tunisian cases might have in part affected insights into the role of international norms in autocracies. Indeed, the Moroccan monarchy and Tunisian presidential one-party regime were precisely vulnerable to international norm adherence because they sought to broadcast their openness and progressiveness internationally. A regime that does not care about its international image will be less reluctant to simply ignore international norms. Nonetheless, these insights will hopefully provide food for thought for further systematizing insights into the role of political regimes in immigration politics.

The Polity-Politics-Policy Nexus on Immigration

This chapter compared and contrasted power dynamics and policy processes in Morocco and Tunisia to explore to what extent political regime dynamics shape immigration policymaking. To sum up the comparative insights, the simple model of the policy cycle (Jones 1970) provides a valuable framework, as it allows assessing the 'regime effect' at three levels: agenda-setting, decision-making and implementation. The Moroccan and Tunisian cases suggest that the 'regime effect' is most clearly at work at the decision-making stage, as the centralization of power in the hands of the executive increases decision-making capabilities in autocratic systems and the range of policy options available. Thus, in Morocco, the King's will is a necessary and sufficient condition for policy change to be enacted. While this does not mean that there are no competing interests to weigh against each other and no power dynamics involved in securing support for a specific decision, the need for compromise is higher in democracies, as power is by definition dispersed among institutions and decision-making more complicated. Democratic contexts might also increase the weight of path dependency – as ultimately, it might be easier to find a majority to support the status quo as opposed to a policy change.

When it comes to agenda-setting, the picture is slightly different, as numerous actors within and outside the state contribute to setting the agenda in both Morocco and Tunisia – albeit to varying degrees, depending on the sources of legitimacy and clients of the regime in place: in democracies, political parties, civil society and the electorate are likely to play a more prominent role; while political elites and their strategic foreign and economic policy interests are likely to dominate in autocracies. Indeed, Moroccan immigration reform was initiated inside the executive and subsequently expanded to the public agenda by the state's active framing of the issue, while in post-2011 Tunisia, immigration has been set on the political agenda by CSOs but consciously depoliticized by the political elite. Lastly, in both Morocco and Tunisia, implementation powers are diffused among a range of institutional actors across and within ministries, as well as across the national territory that each appropriates the policy for their own agendas. While the Moroccan King's decision was a necessary condition for the 2013 reform, it was not sufficient for its unequivocal implementation, which required the readiness of a variety of institutions to translate the policy on the ground. Inconsistencies and contradictions in how regulations are implemented thus seem to characterize immigration policies in both democratic and autocratic contexts.

Although policymaking reality is often more complex and 'messy' than these three neatly distinguishable stages of agenda-setting, decision-making and implementation suggest (Cohen, March and Olsen 1972; Kingdon 2003), such insights are critical to start delineating the boundaries of the 'regime effect' and will hopefully serve as a springboard for more refined theory-building on immigration politics across political regimes in the future. On the one hand, the paired comparison of Morocco and Tunisia highlighted the need to analyse a country's immigration regime as a mixed bag of measures and to recognize that the drivers of particular policies might substantially differ across migrant groups (see also Abdelaaty 2021; de Haas, Natter and Vezzoli 2018). Thus, looking at both continuities and changes across different immigration policy fields, as well as disaggregating immigration policy and power dynamics along migrant groups or policy issues, should lead to more differentiated analyses of the role of state, civil society and external actors on immigration.

On the other hand, this book has shown that we need to be careful about simplistic attributions of policy dynamics to democracy or autocracy alone, as state imperatives and state formation histories provide the foundation for immigration policymaking across political regimes. Indeed, legacies of slavery and colonial population control still shape how Moroccan and Tunisian authorities govern immigration – both in terms of bureaucratic practices as well as cooperation dynamics with European and African actors. Also, the ways in which Moroccan and Tunisian regimes have historically dealt with claims for political pluralism from their citizens can explain why immigration has been forcefully politicized in Morocco and consciously depoliticized in Tunisia. And regime strategies to ensure political legitimacy and sovereignty over territory and population are the key driver behind the primacy of security interests in migration control – in both autocratizing Morocco and democratizing Tunisia.

9 Conclusion

> Thinking about immigration basically comes down to questioning the state, questioning its foundations, questioning its internal mechanisms, structures and functioning.
>
> —Sayad (1999: 6)

Resolving the Empirical Puzzle

The central ambition of this book was to leverage the contrasting cases of Morocco and Tunisia to pave the way for more systematic theory-building on the role of political regimes in immigration politics. Drawing on extensive fieldwork, the book examined the complex interplay between autocratization, democratization and immigration policy-making in Morocco and Tunisia. It explored why the Moroccan monarchy enacted a liberal reform after a decade of policy restrictiveness and what obstructed immigration policy liberalization in Tunisia after the democratic transition. The analysis showed that 'state thinking' (Sayad 1999) provided the foundation for immigration governance, as immigration policy choices were geared towards ensuring the sovereignty and legitimacy of both Morocco's autocracy and Tunisia's democracy.

In Morocco, the top-down politicization of moderate immigration and the liberal immigration reform were part and parcel of the monarchy's strategy to consolidate its power in a three-level game: internationally, the reform turned immigration into political capital for Morocco's diplomatic relations with both Africa and Europe, and domestically, it bolstered the regime's legitimacy in front of liberal, progressive parts of Moroccan society. Regardless of the reality on the ground, immigration has been inflated in political discourses and became central to fortifying the image of Morocco as a modern, 'liberal monarchy'.

The analysis of interests, ideas and institutions that drove Moroccan immigration policy since the mid-twentieth century (*Chapter 4*) showed that Morocco's immigration policy has indeed been primarily driven by foreign policy interests and domestic regime legitimation goals. Although

Moroccan immigration policy in the post-independence period was heavily shaped by laws and practices inherited from the French colonial period, the monarchy strategically enacted selective immigration facilitations to strengthen diplomatic ties with European and African countries. At the turn of the twenty-first century, in a context of growing salience of African migration to Europe, the restrictive Law 02–03 was enacted to deliberately politicize so-called 'Sub-Saharan irregular transit migrants' in diplomatic relations with the European Union, to gain concessions in terms of economic cooperation and to shift attention away from the continued (irregular) emigration of Moroccans. And in 2013, it was again the royal agenda that explained the depth and speed of Morocco's – this time liberal – immigration reform. Although transnational civil society lobbying provided the foundation for the liberal reform, and dynamics of international norm adherence created the window of opportunity, it was the alignment with the monarchy's goals to promote Morocco as a 'liberal monarchy' and to deepen cooperation with Western and Central Africa that was ultimately critical for liberal reform to occur.

However, immigration policy liberalization not only emerged out of Morocco's autocratic political structures – a dynamic I call the 'illiberal paradox'. As the analysis of inter-actor dynamics on immigration (*Chapter 5*) showed, it also consolidated them. In particular, the monarchy instrumentalized relations with the administration and with Morocco's pro-migrant civil society to broadcast its modernity and liberal nature. At the same time, the royal framing of immigration policy as a 'national endeavour' meant that elected politicians, legal actors and employers have only played a subordinate role in the reform process. Yet, the top-down, centralizing dynamic initiated by the King did not absorb resistances and diverging views within the Moroccan polity, as administrative and civil society actors kept room for manoeuvre regarding agenda-setting and policy implementation. This demonstrates that while some drivers and dynamics of immigration policymaking are closely intertwined with political regime dynamics, such as the decision-making centrality of the executive and the weight of domestic politics, the internal workings of the bureaucracy or the influence of international norms in restraining national policymaking remain largely unaffected by political regime dynamics.

Examining Tunisia, this book showed that Tunisian policymakers forcefully depoliticized large-scale immigration and opted for restrictive policy continuity to safeguard democratization. While immigration was set on the agenda in 2011 because large numbers of refugees and migrants arrived from neighbouring Libya and the revolution freed up civil society activism, immigration was ultimately sidelined politically for the sake of national cohesion and future economic cooperation with Libya. Democratic politics, in fact, spurred restrictive policy demands from parts of the public as well as incoherencies in the institutional policymaking landscape that ultimately resulted in restrictive policy continuity.

The analysis of interests, ideas and institutions underpinning Tunisian immigration policy since the mid-twentieth century (*Chapter 6*) showcased the drivers of these policy developments. Under Bourguiba and Ben Ali, foreign policy priorities and the regime's political legitimation strategies drove Tunisia's dual policy of restricting refugee, labour and irregular migration while welcoming select migrant groups. The democratic transition transferred political legitimacy to the electorate and thereby increased the weight of domestic factors such as public opinion and civil society activism in policymaking. However, the democratization of political processes did ultimately not spill over into more open policies towards foreigners. Security concerns continued to dominate Tunisia's immigration policies, changes remained informal or limited to specific migrant groups, and efforts by CSOs and IOs to initiate immigration reform were mostly unsuccessful. In fact, conflicting domestic demands – for and against immigration liberalization – cancelled each other out and were overshadowed by more pressing economic and security issues. At the same time, the proliferation of actors involved in Tunisian immigration policymaking has propelled institution-specific interests to the foreground. This has compelled policymakers to put 'Tunisians first' and ignore immigration altogether because of its potential to polarize Tunisian society.

By dissecting dynamics among and within state, societal and international actors involved in Tunisian immigration politics since 2011 (*Chapter 7*), the analysis showcased the ambiguous effects of democratization on immigration policymaking. On the one hand, despite its limited impact on Tunisian immigration policy outcomes so far, democratization has fundamentally affected specific policymaking processes: under Ben Ali's authoritarian regime, the administration was compartmentalized, and inter-institutional cooperation was practically absent. The lack of real counterpowers – be it the Parliament, civil society or IOs – reinforced the purely security-driven immigration policy of the Ministry of Interior. After 2011, policy processes became more inclusive and strengthened the role of Tunisia's Parliament and the independent voice of civil society. However, democratization has also jeopardized policy consistency and inter-institutional cooperation, as it raised actors' awareness of their 'power to say no'. Thus, growing political engagement and participation rendered politics slower, more complex, and prone to internal contradictions. Ultimately, while the weight of domestic politics and civil society actors was significantly affected by democratization, drivers and dynamics related to the inner workings of the bureaucracy or the influence of foreign policy interests in national policymaking remained largely unaffected by political regime dynamics.

The systematic comparison of immigration policymaking in Morocco and Tunisia (*Chapter 8*) offered critical insights into the complex interplay between polity, politics and policy on immigration – that is, between the institutions structuring political life, the power dynamics among actors involved in policymaking and the ultimate substance of political action. While developments in Morocco and Tunisia confirm previous research pointing out that there seems to be no direct link between *polity* and *policy*, as democracy does not necessarily bring about more liberal immigration policies (see, for instance, Adamson, Triadafilopoulos and Zolberg 2011; Guild, Groenendijk and Carrera 2009; Miller 2016; Song 2019), my analysis sheds new light on the imbrication between *polity* and *politics* on immigration. It demonstrates that while liberal immigration reform and the politicization of moderate immigration have been instrumental for authoritarian consolidation in Morocco, restrictive policy continuity and the depoliticization of large-scale immigration were key to safeguard democratization in Tunisia.

The question is whether the disconnect between immigration levels and politicization in Morocco and Tunisia can be maintained in the long term or whether there is a threshold – in terms of magnitude, permanency or velocity of immigration – at which societal politicization and polarization become unavoidable. The history of immigration in Europe and current developments in the Gulf States suggest that, in the long run, keeping immigration outside of societal debates is difficult – even in illiberal political contexts. Migration inevitably generates social change, which in turn raises new societal questions (Castles, de Haas and Miller 2014). In both Morocco and Tunisia, the settlement of Christian migrants – from Western and Central Africa but also Spain, Italy and the Philippines – starts to raise questions about religious and ethnic pluralism. With continuing immigration and settlement, issues related to political participation, religious freedom and citizenship will thus likely emerge and potentially pose challenges to the foundational myths and national identities of the polity. Any future study of immigration politics in Morocco and Tunisia will thus inevitably have to investigate the long-term effect of migrant settlement in reshaping the Moroccan and Tunisian polity.

The insights gained in this book also demonstrate the theoretical centrality of immigration to the study of modern statehood and the potential of immigration policy research to explore political regime dynamics and socio-political transformations. Viewing immigration politics in Morocco and Tunisia through such a lens offers a novel take on the complex power dynamics around immigration in North Africa, with implications for policy discussions on migration cooperation across the Mediterranean. In particular, effective cooperation between European and Maghreb countries is only possible if both sides are aware of each other's interests concerning migration – and take them into account. The empirical material in this book suggests that while development and economic cooperation with the European Union or the creation of legal emigration opportunities for their citizens remain crucial policy issues for Morocco and Tunisia, European policy actors will need to pay more attention to other drivers of North African immigration policies, such as the geopolitical and economic interests of Morocco in West Africa and Tunisia in Libya, or the role of civil society activism and the need to legitimize policies domestically – even in autocracies.

Theorizing Immigration Politics – *Quo Vadis*?

Based on the in-depth comparison of immigration policymaking in twenty-first-century Morocco and Tunisia, this book explored two core questions that are of wider relevance for migration studies, as well as political sociology and comparative politics research on modern statehood: to what extent do political regimes shape immigration politics? And what does immigration policymaking reveal about the inner workings of democratic and autocratic systems? To pave the way for more systematic theory-building, the book advanced a three-fold typology of immigration policy processes that offers a set of theoretical propositions on the boundaries of the 'regime effect' and the commonalities in immigration policymaking across political regimes.

To begin with, the typology identified three *generic policy processes* that emerge out of the very essence of policymaking in modern states and are at play regardless of the political regime in place or the policy issue at stake: first, policymaking seems intrinsically characterized by discrepancies between policy discourses, policies-on-paper and policy implementation, because states are rarely this unitary actor working towards a single interest they like to portray themselves as. Second, institutions are always made up of humans – politicians, bureaucrats or activists – whose individual ideas and personal motivations are crucial in shaping policy agendas beyond institutional identities. And third, while 'politics-as-usual' might substantially differ across countries, moments of crisis generally seem to provide a window of opportunity for new actors, interactions or policy ideas to emerge.

The typology also identified five *issue-specific policy processes* that seem intrinsic to what immigration does to state sovereignty and interest alignment – and are therefore at play across the democracy–autocracy spectrum: first, state formation trajectories and national identity conceptions seem to provide the foundations of all countries' immigration regimes because immigration policy is inherently tied to the sovereignty of modern nation-states. Second, state imperatives and bureaucratic politics seem crucial to understanding similarities in inter-institutional dynamics on immigration across political regimes. This concerns, for instance, turf wars among and within certain ministries or authorities' strategies to secure power over population movement through informal and ambiguous policies. Third, with immigration being central to a globalized world, all countries seem subject to liberal norm constraints, but the way they affect national policy processes (directly through legal instruments or indirectly through reputational damage) appears to vary depending on the strength of judicial actors and the vulnerability of the regime to international shaming. Fourth, foreign policy considerations appear to be crucial drivers of immigration politics in both autocracies and democracies, but they seem to vary according to a country's position in global migration systems. In particular, I suggest that they are reinforced in the context of a three-level game, when governments need to reconcile domestic demands with vested interests in both origin and destination countries. Lastly, the weight of business interests seems not fundamentally tied to the regime in place but rather to depend on the size of the informal labour market and the imbrication of political and economic elites.

In contrast to policy processes that are at play across political regimes – either because they are tied to the nature of modern nation-states or because they are intrinsic to immigration as a policy field – the typology also identified three *regime-specific policy processes* that are crucially shaped by a country's position on the democracy–autocracy spectrum. First, the centrality of the executive, which determines the extent of top-down decision-making autonomy and the room for divergent bottom-up interests to unfold, seems fundamentally shaped by the political system in place, with the leverage to take strategic decisions that break with path dependency substantially higher in autocratic contexts. Second, the role of independent lawyers and courts as a counterweight to executive or legislative policymaking seems structurally limited in political systems with a weak rule of law. And third, domestic socio-political actors such as political parties or civil society seem to weigh by definition less in autocratic or illiberal political contexts. This does not imply that autocratic leaders are entirely independent of civil society pressure, but that the channels used by CSOs to influence state actors differ – for instance, because they more forcefully rely on international advocacy loops.

Ultimately, autocracies appear to have greater freedom to 'choose' which 'clients' they want to cater to through their immigration policies because they are less bound by institutional path dependency and societal demands for restrictions. As a consequence, executive actors in autocracies seem to paradoxically have more leeway to enact liberal immigration reforms compared to their counterparts in democracies. While the Moroccan case provided the foundation for developing this illiberal paradox hypothesis, scholarship on autocracies such as Guinea (Milner 2006), Uganda (Betts 2021; Blair, Grossman and Weinstein 2020), Libya (Paoletti 2011; Tsourapas 2017) or Turkey (Norman 2020a) offer more general evidence for the strategic use of liberal immigration reform in autocratic contexts.

The three-fold typology of immigration policy processes I developed implies that we need to narrow down the 'regime effect' – that is, the claim that immigration policy dynamics are inherent to the political regime in place – to a specific set of immigration policy processes. In particular, the insights gained from contrasting Morocco and Tunisia with the broader literature on immigration politics across the Global North and Global South (*Chapter 2*) suggest that the 'regime effect' kicks in primarily for theories that locate the origin of immigration policy within society. This is the case for classical political economy approaches such as domestic politics that analyse the interests of societal actors such as political parties and civil society on immigration to determine which problems are set on the agenda and what decisions are taken. Also, theories emphasizing the role of domestic legal actors as safeguards of migrants' rights seem more relevant in democratic contexts with systematic respect for the rule of law. This does not mean that political parties, civil society or courts have no role to play in more autocratic contexts, but that their function in policy processes seems to fundamentally differ from that in democracies.

In contrast, theories explaining immigration policymaking through the interaction between international and domestic political spheres have potential relevance across regime types. Globalization theories that highlight how international norms and institutions constrain national immigration policymaking appear equally relevant for democratic and autocratic states, although the way in which these dynamics work out on the ground might differ. Also, world systems or dependency theories, which suggest that immigration policies reflect the interests of geopolitically dominant states, offer valuable tools to understand immigration politics worldwide. In fact, they have (often implicitly) dominated explanations of migration policymaking in countries such as Morocco and Tunisia because of the assumption that policy is mainly initiated from the outside.

Lastly, the typology suggests that theories focusing on dynamics within the state provide a relevant analytical lens to understand immigration policymaking across the political regime spectrum. In particular, the national identity approach, with its emphasis on how immigration policies tie into a country's specific national history, seems pertinent for any country in the world, independent of its political regime or geographical location. This is also the case for state interest approaches, which look at how states pursue broader goals such as regime legitimation, economic development or the maintenance of social peace through immigration policy. Indeed, immigration policy decisions tend to be made with regard to securing state sovereignty and the internal and external legitimation of a regime – be it democratic or autocratic. Likewise, bureaucratic politics approaches that put institutional actors, their interests and conflicts, centre stage do also not seem subject to a 'regime effect'. Although inter-institutional dynamics are less in the spotlight in autocracies, the analysis in this book suggests that they are as important for understanding immigration policymaking as in democracies.

While this book offers only a first attempt at delineating the boundaries of the 'regime effect' and the theoretical propositions on the role of political regimes in immigration politics are necessarily preliminary, they seem to indicate that the theoretical toolbox for analysing immigration politics might not differ as fundamentally across political regimes and political geographies as is often assumed. Overall, analysing immigration politics is about finding out who the 'clients' of a specific immigration policy are – sections of the electorate, socio-economic interest groups, diplomatic partners or specific state institutions – and how they contribute to the regime's domestic and international legitimacy. This suggests that the legitimation strategies of political elites, a country's political-economic structure or a state's geopolitical embedding might have more explanatory power to understand specific immigration policy dynamics than a country's categorization as democracy or autocracy.

Looking ahead, this book hopes to serve as a starting point for consolidating theory-building on immigration policymaking across the Global North/South divide. Conducting medium-N, cross-regional comparisons that focus on particular aspects of my typology would be critical to refine insights and amend theoretical propositions. In particular, it would be fascinating to zoom into the relatively underexplored role of employers across political regimes and political economies, or to compare discourses on immigration of specific ministries across countries to specify the extent to which institutional identities shape immigration policy regardless of the political regime in place. It would also be essential to systematize insights into the consequences of the three-level game for countries' immigration policies or into the mechanisms through which liberal norm constraints work out in practice.

Ultimately, the central goal of this book was to systematically explore immigration policymaking across political regimes and to mobilize immigration policy as a lens to research political change and the inner workings of modern states. As immigration lies at the heart of public and scholarly debates on national identity and political change across the globe, recognizing the shared features of modern statehood is not only crucial to better understand how states govern immigration but also to advance broader comparative politics, international relations and political sociology reflections on power and politics worldwide. In particular, the book sought to inspire readers to question the analytical power of binary categories such as democracy or autocracy for theorizing political processes, and instead to focus on categories of analysis that are grounded in the (dis)similarities of patterned social relations around the globe. Such scholarly efforts to rethink how we categorize and order the world are much needed. Although social theory often tends to reflect global power structures, it ultimately also has the power to reshape how we talk about and make sense of the world we live in.

Appendices

Appendix 1 Interviewed Actors

The following table provides an insight into the range of actors interviewed in Morocco and Tunisia. For reasons of anonymity, I do not specify the number or positions of respondents interviewed within each institution or organization.

Table A.1. *List of interviewed actors*

	Morocco	**Tunisia**
State institutions	Ministry of Foreign Affairs (MoFA)	Ministry of Foreign Affairs (MoFA)
	Ministry of Interior (MoI)	Ministry of Social Affairs (MoSA)
	Ministry of Justice (MoJ)	Ministry of Justice (MoJ)
	Ministry for the Moroccan Community Abroad and Migration Affairs (MCMREAM)	State Secretariat for Migration and Tunisians Abroad (SEMTE)
	Ministry of Labour (MoL)	Ministry of Employment and Professional Formation (MoEPF)
	Ministry of Education (MoE)	Ministry of Culture
	Ministry of Industry	Parliament
	Ministry of Health (MoH)	Centre for Legal and Judicial Studies (CEJJ)
	Bureau of Refugees and Stateless People (BRA)	Tunis Municipality
	Parliament	National Migration Observatory (ONM)
	National Council on Human Rights (CNDH)	Office for Tunisians Abroad (OTE)
	Interministerial Delegation on Human Rights (DIDH)	Regional Directorate of Child Protection
	Fondation Hassan II for Moroccans Residing Abroad	National Statistical Institute (INS)
	Consultative Council on Moroccans Abroad (CCME)	
	High Planning Commissariat (HCP)	
	Entraide Nationale (EN)	

Table A.1. (cont.)

	Morocco	Tunisia
CSOs and migrant organizations	Caritas Morocco Moroccan Organization of Human Rights (OMDH) Moroccan Association of Human Rights (AMDH) Moroccan Association for the Support and Promotion of Small Enterprises (AMAPPE) Association Droits et Justice Democratic Organization of Labour (ODT) Democratic Organization of Immigrant Labour (ODTI) La Cimade Fondation Orient Occident (FOO) Moroccan Association for Studies and Research on Migrations (AMERM) Friends and Families of Victims of Clandestine Migration (AFVIC) Anti-Racist Defence and Support Group of Foreigners and Migrants (GADEM) African Cultural Centre of Morocco (CCAM) Council of Sub-Saharan Migrants in Morocco (CMSM) Association for the Development and Sensitization of Guineans in Morocco (ADESGUIM) Association Light on Irregular Emigration in the Maghreb (ALECMA) Clinique Hijra Evangelical Church Rabat International Mutual Aid Committee (CEI)	Caritas Tunisia Tunisian Red Crescent Arab Institute for Human Rights (IADH) Tunisian Association of Democratic Women (ATFD) Tunisian Forum for Economic and Social Rights (FTDES) Al Bawsala General Union of Tunisian Workers (UGTT) Tunisian Union of Industry, Trade and Crafts (UTICA) General Confederation of Tunisian Workers (CGTT) Doctors of the World Belgium (MdM-B) Euromed Rights Mercycorps Media and Human Rights Observatory Adventist Development and Relief Agency (ADRA) Terre d'Asile Tunisie (TAT) Maison des Droits et des Migrations Association Adam Association of African Students and Trainees in Tunisia (AESAT) Union of African Leaders (ULA) Association of Sub-Saharan Workers in Tunisia (ASTT)

Table A.1. (*cont.*)

	Morocco	Tunisia
International organizations and diplomatic actors	EU Delegation in Morocco United Nations High Commissariat for Refugees (UNHCR) Morocco International Organization for Migration (IOM) Morocco International Labour Organization (ILO) Morocco German Development Agency (GIZ) Morocco Swiss Development Cooperation Agency (SDC) Morocco Friedrich Ebert Foundation Morocco Austrian Embassy Morocco European External Action Service, Brussels DG Home, Brussels	EU Delegation in Tunisia United Nations High Commissariat for Refugees (UNHCR) Tunisia International Organization for Migration (IOM) Tunisia International Labour Organization (ILO) Tunisia German Development Agency (GIZ) Tunisia Swiss Development Cooperation Agency (SDC) Tunisia Expertise France Tunisia French Office for Immigration and Integration (OFII) Tunisia International Centre for Migration Policy Development (ICMPD) Tunisia

Appendix 2 Political and Economic Indicators for Morocco and Tunisia

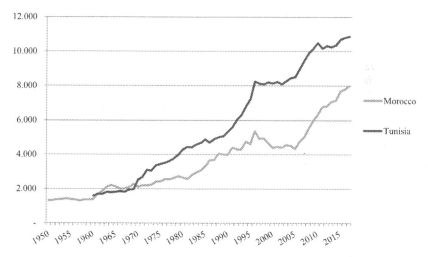

Figure A.1 Evolution of real GDP per capita, 1950–2017[*].
Source: *Penn World Tables 9.0 and 9.1 (Feenstra, Inklaar and Timmer 2015)*

---

[*] The variable measures expenditure-side real GDP at chained PPPs (in mil. 2005 USD), which allows the comparison of relative living standards across countries and over time.

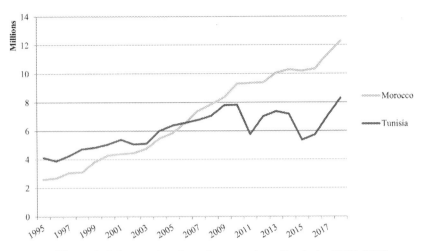

Figure A.2 International tourism, number of arrivals, 1995–2018.
Source: World Bank (2020)

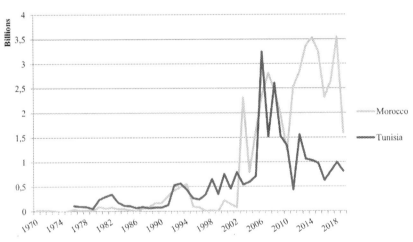

Figure A.3 Foreign direct investment (net inflows, current USD), 1970–2019.
Source: World Bank (2020)

Appendices

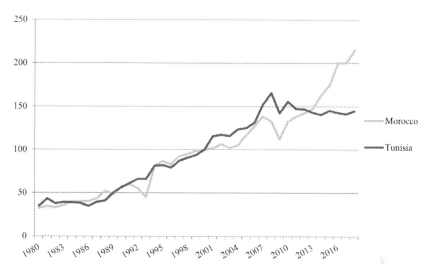

Figure A.4 Export volume index (2000 = 100), 1980–2018.
Source: World Bank (2020)

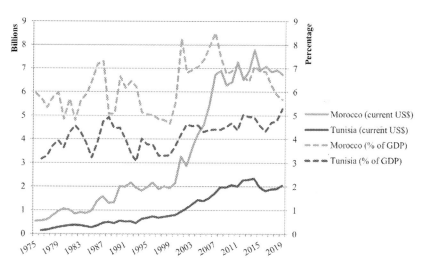

Figure A.5 Personal remittances received, 1975–2019.
Source: World Bank (2020)

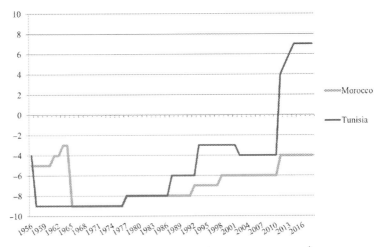

Figure A.6 Changes in political systems, 1956–2018 *.
Source: PolityV Project (Marshall and Gurr 2020)

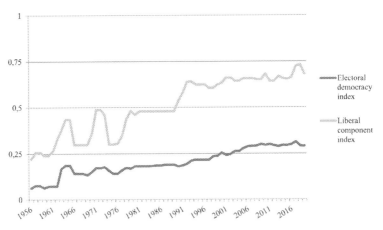

Figure A.7 Changes in electoral and liberal components of democracy, Morocco, 1956–2019 †.
Source: V-Dem Project (Coppedge 2020)

---

* Polity2 scores range from -10 to +10. The 21-point scale covers a spectrum of political regimes spanning from institutionalized autocracies through mixed regimes to consolidated democracies. It can also be converted into three regime categories as 'autocracies' (-10 to -6), 'hybrid' regimes (-5 to +5) and 'democracies' (+6 to +10).

† The liberal component index of V-Dem captures the extent to which the protection of individual and minority rights is achieved by constitutionally protected civil liberties, strong rule of law, an independent judiciary and effective checks and balances. The electoral democracy index of V-Dem captures the extent to which rulers are made responsive to citizens through electoral competition, political and civil society organizations, clean and regular elections, freedom of expression and independent media. One can interpret scores of 0 as 'closed autocratic', 0.25 as 'autocratic', 0.5 as 'ambivalent', 0.75 as 'minimally democratic' and 1 as 'democratic'.

Appendices

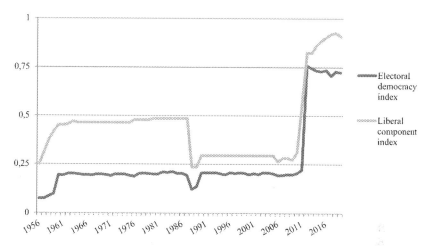

Figure A.8 Changes in electoral and liberal components of democracy, Tunisia, 1956–2019[*].
Source: V-Dem Project (Coppedge 2020)

---

[*] ibid.

Appendix 3 Moroccan Immigration Policy Changes, 1900–2020

The following tables systematically retrace changes in Moroccan immigration policy between 1900 and 2020, distinguishing five areas: broader socio-political developments relevant to immigration (Table A.2); main legal and informal immigration policy changes (Table A.3); main institutional changes on immigration (Table A.4); international and diplomatic activities on immigration (Table A.5); and national as well as international civil society work on immigration (Table A.6).

Table A.2. *Key socio-political developments and events related to immigration in Morocco*

Year	Measure
1912	Fes Treaty: Establishment of French and Spanish protectorates on Moroccan territory.
1956	Independence from France (2 February) and Spain (7 March), Mohammed V continues to head the Moroccan monarchy.
1961	Hassan II becomes King (3 March) after the death of his father, Mohammed V (26 February).
1965–1970	State of emergency in Morocco.
1984	Morocco leaves the African Union after it recognizes the Sahrawi Arab Democratic Republic (SADR).
1987	Morocco applies for membership in the EU (rejected for geographical reasons).
1990	Creation of the Consultative Council on Human Rights (CCDH).
1999	Mohammed VI becomes King (30 July) after the death of his father Hassan II (23 July).
1999	Mohammed VI introduces his new concept of authority, based on the protection of rights and liberties to consolidate the rule of law in Morocco, triggering widespread hope.
2000	Publication of the *Berber Manifesto* that claims the recognition of Tamazight language, culture and identity.
2001	Start of pro-active Africa policy by King Mohammed VI with a series of royal visits.

Table A.2. (*cont.*)

Year	Measure
2003	Creation of the Equity and Reconciliation Commission (IER) to indemnize victims of the regime of Hassan II.
2003	Terrorist attacks in Casablanca (16 May) – forty-five people are killed, including twelve suicide bombers, leading to 5,000 arrests across the country.
2004	In January, a progressive reform of the family code (Mudawana) is enacted.
2005	Ceuta and Melilla incidents (28 August, 28 September, 5 October) – around 1,400 migrants try to climb over the fences surrounding the two Spanish enclaves in northern Morocco, and at least twelve migrants are shot dead by border guards.
2011	The 20 February movement leads to protests across Morocco. A new constitution is elaborated and enacted in July 2011.
2011	Creation of the National Council on Human Rights (CNDH) under the direction of Driss el Yazami, former director of the Council for the Moroccan Community Abroad (CCME).
Since 2016	In October, beginning of popular protests in the Rif, led by the Hirak movement.
Since 2017	Morocco officially requests to join the Economic Community of Western African States (ECOWAS).
2017	In January, Morocco officially reintegrates into the African Union after thirty-three years.
2017	In October, creation of a Delegate Ministry of African Affairs within the MoFA.
2020	With COVID-19 reaching Morocco, the country enters into a lockdown on 20 March, including a travel ban. Restrictions are progressively lifted starting from 20 May. However, the country remains in a health emergency state, and new restrictions are enacted as a response to rising infections in September 2020.

Table A.3. *Morocco's main legal and informal policy changes on immigration*

Year	Measure
1915[1]	Transfer of French immigration law to Moroccan territory. Criteria according to which people are not allowed entry or can be expelled from the Moroccan territory are set out.
1931[2]	Introduction of work permits as well as sanctions for irregular entry and work.
1934[3]	The work permit is conditioned to the labour market situation. Sanctions for employers or carriers of irregular migrants are introduced, and penalties for irregular migrants increased.
1940[4]	People considered a risk to national security or subject to expulsion can be assigned a specific residence and the execution of labour for the common good.
1941–1951[5]	Penalties for irregular entry and stay (fines and imprisonment sentences) are increased three times.
1955[6]	Ratification of 1951 *Geneva Refugee Convention* by France.
1957[7]	Morocco confirms its ratification of the 951 *Geneva Refugee Convention*. Nonetheless, there is no functioning national refugee determination procedure in Morocco by the end of 2020.
1963–1964[8]	Bilateral Agreements with Algeria, Tunisia and Senegal to reciprocally facilitate entry and stay of nationals of these countries and equal treatment for socio-economic rights. These agreements have not been consistently implemented.
1970s	Bilateral partnerships between Morocco and francophone African countries set up quotas and publicly funded scholarships for African students wishing to study in Morocco.
1993[9]	Ratification of the *UN International Convention on the Protection of the Rights of All Migrant Workers and Members of Their Families*; it entered into force in July 2003.
2003[10]	Creation of the Labour Code unifying existing labour regulations. Articles 516–521 consolidate the work permit requirement and employer sanctions.
2003[11]	Law 02-03 unifies regulations on entry and stay of foreigners in Morocco and introduces high fines and prison sentences for irregular entry and exit of the territory and support of irregular migrants. In parallel, a *National Strategy to Fight Illegal Migration* is elaborated.
2005[12]	Introduction of exemptions from the labour market test for foreigners married to a Moroccan, for refugees, high-skilled workers and investors.
2007	Launch of the *National Strategy to Fight Against Human Trafficking*.
2010[13]	Internal hospital regulations guarantee healthcare access to foreigners irrespective of their legal status.
2011[14]	Adoption of Morocco's new constitution. Article 30 guarantees the right to asylum.
2012[15]	Syrian children are allowed to register in Moroccan public and private schools.
Since 2013	Elaboration of a law to introduce penalties for racial (and potentially other types of) discrimination. It has not been discussed in Parliament by the end of 2020.

Table A.3. (cont.)

Year	Measure
2013[16]	Children of 'Sub-Saharan' and Sahelian migrants are allowed to register in Moroccan public schools regardless of their legal status. This is later expanded to include all foreign children.
2013[17]	Setting out of criteria for the exceptional regularization campaign of irregular migrants between January and December 2014.
Since 2014	Elaboration of draft Law 95-14 (later draft Law 72-17) to replace Law 02-03 on immigration. It has not been discussed in Parliament by the end of 2020.
Since 2014	Elaboration of draft Law 26-14 (later draft Law 66-17) to establish a Moroccan asylum office and national refugee determination procedure. It has not been discussed in Parliament by the end of 2020.
2014	Adoption of the *National Strategy of Immigration and Asylum* (SNIA).
2014	Informal regularization of migrant associations and Moroccan migration advocacy CSOs.
2015[18]	Elaboration of a healthcare insurance for regularized migrants and refugees similar to the healthcare assistance for poor Moroccans (RAMED). However, the program has not been effectively implemented by the end of 2020.
2015[19]	Creation of an accelerated residence permit procedure for foreign investors and rare competencies.
2016[20]	Law 19-12 regulates the working and employment conditions of domestic workers (both Moroccans and foreigners).
2016[21]	Law 27-14 specifies the identification, protection and punishments related to human trafficking. Victims of human trafficking are not granted a residence permit beyond the end of the legal process.
2016	Second regularization campaign between December 2016 and December 2017.
2016[22]	Regularized migrants are exempted from the labour market test (called 'ANAPEC procedure') and thus granted eased access to the Moroccan labour market.
2017	Regularized migrants renewing their residence permits will now receive a three-year permit instead of a one-year permit.
2018	On 28 March, the CNDH announces that non-accompanied minors and foreigners with a secondary school education can benefit from regularization.
2018	Since mid-2018, renewals of residence permits become more difficult, with more and more documents being requested by Moroccan authorities.
2019	In October, on request of regional authorities, Moroccan bus companies requires 'Africans' to show valid residence permits to board long-distance busses, an incident that triggers large-scale civil society outrage and is condemned by the CNDH, as well as Moroccan parliamentarians.
2020	Explicit exclusion of migrants from the governments' Coronavirus Pandemic Fund set up in March for vulnerable people and informal workers despite lobbying by CSOs and the CNDH.
2020	In May, UNHCR signs a Cooperation Agreement with the National Council of the Order of Physicians (CNOM) to improve refugees' healthcare access.

Table A.4. *National institutional changes related to immigration in Morocco*

Year	Measure
1957[23]	Morocco creates a Bureau of Refugees and Stateless People (BRA) within the Ministry of Foreign Affairs in charge of granting refugee status. In practice, the BRA has not really been functional until 2013.
1986	Creation of the Moroccan Agency for International Cooperation (AMCI) under the Ministry of Foreign Affairs to organize and promote student migration to Morocco.
2003[24]	Law 02-03 creates a new Directorate of Migration and Border Surveillance within the Ministry of Interior, as well as a Migration Observatory.
2005	The BRA officially closes.
2013	Reopening of the BRA in September, which is now evaluating refugee claims together with UNHCR.
2013	In October, the Ministry for Moroccans Living Abroad is renamed Ministry for Moroccans Living Abroad and Migration Affairs (MCMREAM). Also, two new departments are created to implement the regularization campaign and to coordinate the new migration policy: the Directorate of Migration Affairs and the Directorate of International Cooperation.
2013[25]	In September, creation of an inter-ministerial commission to implement the new migration agenda.
2014	Launch of the National Appeals Commission for regularization in June, led by the CNDH but with representatives of Moroccan ministries, civil society and migrant organizations.
2015	Article 247 of the 2015 Finance Law allows foreign residents in Morocco to profit from public subventions on housing.
2015	The services of the Entraide Nationale, Morocco's public social relief institution created in 1957, are opened to migrants regardless of legal status.
2015	The Moroccan labour market agency ANAPEC opens its job search services to regularized migrants.
2016[26]	Law 27-14 creates a National Commission to coordinate the anti-human trafficking policy. It is launched in May 2019, with members from ministries and civil society.
2016	Elaboration of the *National Strategic Plan on Migrant Health* (PSNSM) 2016–2021 to improve migrants' access to healthcare services in Morocco.
2017	Downgrading of the MCMREAM to a Delegate Ministry and integration in the Ministry of Foreign Affairs in the course of the new government formation in April 2017.
2017–2018	Between March 2017 and December 2018, the BRA stopped assessing refugee status applications.
2019	In the course of the new government formation in October, the Delegate Ministry's mandate over immigration affairs is removed. The MCMREAM is reduced again to the MCMRE, returning to the pre-2013 situation. Immigration is now part of the Ministry of Foreign Affairs, African Cooperation and Moroccans Residing Abroad.

Table A.5. *International activities and diplomatic developments around immigration in Morocco*

Year	Measure
1965	UNHCR opens an honorary representation in Morocco.
2001	IOM starts to work in Morocco.
2004	IOM starts organizing Assisted Voluntary Returns of Western and Central African migrants from Morocco.
2004	UNHCR starts to send international staff to Morocco without Moroccan authorities' approval.
2005[27]	In February, a Cooperation Agreement is signed between Morocco and IOM that allows them to open a bureau (in 2007).
2006	Morocco hosts the first Euro-African Conference on Migration and Development in Rabat, hereby launching the Rabat Process.
2006	The Swiss Development Cooperation Agency (SDC) starts to work on migration issues in Morocco, mainly supporting Caritas in their humanitarian work and, after 2011, also GADEM in their advocacy work. In 2013, the funding schemes in Morocco are officialized through a cooperation agreement between Switzerland and Morocco.
2006	Creation of a UN inter-agency thematic group on migration (GMT) to coordinate the work of UN agencies on migration in Morocco.
2007[28]	In July, a Headquarters Agreement is signed between Morocco and UNHCR to grant them the right to conduct refugee status determination procedures in Morocco.
2013	In June, Morocco and the EU sign a joint declaration for a Mobility Partnership. Negotiations start in January 2015, but apart from project funding, there has been no tangible outcome.
2013	Morocco launches the African Alliance for Migration and Development at the UN General Assembly in New York in October to promote itself as a regional model for responsible and solidary migration management.
2014	The EU SHAKARA project (2014–2017) is launched to foster migration and development planning in Morocco.
2014	The MCMREAM and the Swiss Development Cooperation Agency (SDC) start a technical committee to coordinate funding activities on migration.
2015	The German Development Cooperation GIZ launches several multi-million projects on immigration, asylum and integration policy in Morocco.
2016	The UN and the MCMREAM launch the Joint Support Program for the Implementation of the SNIA (2017–2021), involving eight UN agencies.
2017	After rejoining the African Union, Morocco is put in charge of coordinating and driving the migration dossier at the African Union.
2018	In January, Mohammed VI presents his African Migration Agenda by Morocco at the African Union.
2018	On 30 August, Morocco's MoI, MoFA, MCMREAM and CNDH organize a meeting with African ambassadors to justify the mediatized forced displacement of migrants to the south and interior of Morocco.
2018	Morocco presides over the Global Forum of Migration and Development (GFMD) in 2018 and hosts the UN International Migration Conference in December, leading to the signature of the *UN Global Compact for Safe, Orderly and Regular Migration*.

Table A.5. (cont.)

Year	Measure
2018	In December, Morocco and the African Union sign a Headquarter Agreement to host the African Migration Observatory in Rabat. On 18 December 2020, the headquarter of the observatory is inaugurated.
2019	In May, the report by the UN Special Rapporteur on contemporary forms of racism, racial discrimination, xenophobia and related intolerance condemns discrimination and violence against Western and Central African migrants in Morocco.
2020	Morocco leads two regional diplomatic efforts on the implementation of the Marrakesh Compact: In March, Morocco develops a Roadmap for the Western Mediterranean within the 5+5 dialogue; in December, Morocco hosts the First African Regional Forum on the Marrakesh Compact.

Table A.6. *Civil society developments on immigration in Morocco*

Year	Measure
1961	Creation of the Association of Senegalese Nationals Residing in Morocco (ARSEREM).
1981	Creation of the Confederation of African pupils, students and interns in Morocco (CESAM).
1994	Creation of the Moroccan Association for Studies and Research on Migrations (AMERM), also working on immigration from the early 2000s.
1995	Caritas starts to work with Western and Central African migrants in Rabat.
2000	The Moroccan Association of Human Rights (AMDH, created in 1979) starts to work on irregular migration, first of Moroccans, then also of Western and Central Africans.
2001	Creation of the association of Friends and Families of Victims of Clandestine Migration (AFVIC).
2002	Creation of the International Mutual Aid Committee (CEI) at the Evangelical Church in Rabat to provide humanitarian aid to migrants. In parallel, house churches start to play an important role in providing support for irregular migrants.
2003	Caritas and the French association La Cimade are founding members of the first Plateforme Migrants (PFM), active until 2006.
2004	The Moroccan Organization of Human Rights (OMDH, created in 1988) starts to work on immigration.
2005	Caritas opens the Migrant Reception Centre (CAM) in Rabat. In 2008, a second reception centre is opened in Casablanca, the JRS, and in 2011 a third one in Tangier, the TAM.
2005	The Foundation Orient-Occident (FOO, created in 1994) starts to work on migration.
2005	Creation of the Council of Sub-Saharan migrants in Morocco (CMSM).
2006	Creation of Collective of Migrant Workers in Morocco (CTMM), legalized by the Moroccan state in June 2014.
2006	Creation of the Anti-Racist Group for the Defense of Foreigners and Migrants (GADEM), legalized by the Moroccan state in December 2013.
2007	OMDH and UNHCR create a centre for legal assistance for refugees and asylum seekers in Rabat and Oujda. The centre in Rabat is closed in 2013.
2007	The Moroccan Association for the Support and Promotion of Small Enterprises (AMAPPE) starts to work on refugee labour market integration together with UNHCR.
2010	Creation of the African Cultural Centre of Morocco (CCAM) in Rabat.
2010	Organization of the first edition of the yearly cultural Festival Migrant'scène in Rabat by the GADEM and DABATEAR. It echoes the French festival Migrant'scène organized by the NGO La Cimade since 2006.
2011	Creation of the Collective of Sub-Saharan communities in Morocco (CCSM), legalized by the Moroccan state in May 2015.
2012	Creation of the Democratic Organization of Immigrant Labour (ODTI), the first migrant union in Morocco. In 2014, a specific sub-section for Filipino workers is created within the ODTI.
2012	Creation of the National Migrant Protection Platform (PNPM), reuniting different Moroccan and international CSOs working on migration, amongst which are Caritas, Droit et Justice, FOO, Médecins du Monde Belgique, and OMDH.

Table A.6. (*cont.*)

Year	Measure
2012	In December, organization of the first edition of the yearly Migrant Week (La Semaine des Migrants) by the ODTI. Starting in 2015, the Migrant Week is organized by the MCMREAM.
2013	The Association Law and Justice (Droit et Justice) starts offering refugees legal assistance.
Since 2014	Creation of numerous migrant associations and pro-immigrant civil society organizations. By 2016, the MCMREAM lists 27 CSOs specialized in migration and sixty-four generalist CSOs who have expanded their work to include migrants.
2016	Creation of the Civil Council for the Fight Against All Forms of Discrimination, a collective of fourteen Moroccan civil society organizations.
2017	Three main Moroccan labour unions, the UMT, the UGTM and the CDT, decide to create migrant sections.
2017	Creation of the Civil Council to Fight Against all Forms of Discrimination by a group of CSOs, including GADEM and ALECMA.
2018	UNHCR launches a project together with AMAPPE and ANAPEC to foster the insertion of refugees into the labour market and their entrepreneurship. By 2020, 400 refugees benefitted from the project, and 173 refugee-led projects were financed.
2018	In June, the Platform of Sub-Saharan Associations and Communities in Morocco (ASCOMS) is created, with initially seventeen members.
2018	In mid-2018, police violence against migrants, internal displacements and expulsions increase again, leading to large-scale civil society protests. In September, nine civil society associations launch the 'coups et blessures' campaign to monitor violence against migrants in the months leading up to the Marrakesh Compact.
2018	In November, the ninth edition of the yearly Festival Migrant'scène is forbidden at the last minute by local authorities in Tangiers without written justification.
2019	A civil society collective of six associations launches the SAVE project for the identification and support of victims of human trafficking.
2020	Civil society mobilizes to extend the state support program of the Coronavirus Emergency Fund to vulnerable migrants and to deliver financial and emergency support to migrants in need.

Appendix 4 Tunisian Immigration Policy Changes, 1900–2020

The following tables systematically retrace changes in Tunisian immigration policy between 1900 and 2020, distinguishing five areas: broader socio-political developments relevant to immigration (Table A.7); main legal and informal immigration policy changes (Table A.8); main institutional changes on immigration (Table A.9); international and diplomatic activities on immigration (Table A.10); and national as well as international civil society work on immigration (Table A.11).

Table A.7. *Key socio-political developments and events related to immigration in Tunisia*

Year	Measure
1881	Tunisia becomes a French protectorate.
1956	Treaties of Bardo and La Marsa: Independence from France (20 March). Habib Bourguiba is nominated Prime Minister, then becomes President in 1957.
1957	On 25 July, a new Constitution is passed. The Beylical Monarchy is abolished, and the Republic is proclaimed.
1987	In October, Zine el-Abidine Ben Ali is nominated Prime Minister. In November, he deposes Bourguiba for health reasons and becomes President.
2008	Strikes and protests around the mining basin of Gafsa in the first half of the year are crushed by the state. They are often seen as a prelude to the 2011 revolution.
2010	On 17 December, Mohamed Bouazizi's self-immolation in Sidi Bouzid triggers the Tunisian 'Jasmin Revolution'.
2011	After weeks of protest and the repositioning of the army on the side of the protestors, President Ben Ali is toppled on 14 January 2011. The democratization process starts.
2011[1]	A new law on associations facilitates the creation of NGOs in Tunisia and the opening of offices for international organizations and associations.
2011	In October, the moderate, Islamist Ennahdha Party wins Tunisia's first free elections.

247

Table A.7. (*cont.*)

Year	Measure
2013	In February, the leftist opposition politician Chokri Belaïd is assassinated, triggering a political crisis that leads to the government's demission. In July, another leftist opposition politician, Mohamed Brahmi, is assassinated, reinforcing the political crisis in Tunisia.
2014[2]	On 26 January, the new Constitution is adopted by the Constituent Assembly. Article 26 guarantees a constitutional right to political asylum and protection from extradition.
2014	In October and November, parliamentary and presidential elections are held, with the secularist Nidaa Tounes Party winning a plurality. Beji Caid Essebsi is elected President, replacing Interim President Moncef Marzouki.
2015	In March, twenty-three people are killed during a terrorist attack at the Bardo Museum close to Tunis; in June, thirty-eight people are killed at the beach in Port al-Kantaoui; in November, twelve people are killed in an attack on the Presidential Guard in Tunis. A state of emergency is declared in November 2015 and is repeatedly extended until the end of 2020.
2015	The 2015 Nobel Peace Prize is awarded to the Tunisian National Dialogue Quartet (the UGTT, the UTICA, the LTDH and the Tunisian Order of Lawyers) formed in 2013 when the democratic transition has been endangered by political assassinations and social unrest.
2017–2018	Renewed protests in Tunis and the Southern, interior regions call for economic justice and mobilize against the 'reconciliation law' that provides an amnesty for corruption charges under the old regime.
2019	Presidential and parliamentary elections are held in Tunisia between July and October, respectively. Independent conservative candidate Kais Saied wins the presidency, and the fragmentation of the political party landscape is reinforced in the Parliament.
Since 2020	In February, after months of negotiations, a coalition under Ettakatol politician Elyes Fakhfakh is sworn in but resigns in July already. A technocratic government is installed in September 2020. This instable situation is the prelude to the political crisis that unfolds starting in July 2021, when President Saied dismisses the government and freezes the Parliament, and later on moves to draft a new constitution that would install a hyper-presidential system.
2020	With COVID-19 reaching Tunisia, the country enters into a lockdown on 22 March, including a travel ban, with restrictions being progressively lifted starting from 4 May. In October, new restrictions are introduced in response to growing infection numbers.

Table A.8. *Tunisia's main legal and informal policy changes on immigration*

Year	Measure
1898[3]	Introduction of immigration controls: Foreigners have to declare and justify their residence in Tunisia, but no measures are taken to restrict immigration.
1930[4]	Introduction of work permits, including a preference for national workers, a limitation of work permits to highly qualified workers and sanctions for irregular employment.
1953[5]	Introduction of administrative taxes to be paid by employers for every new or renewed work contract of a foreign employee, as well as for the visas of the workers' family.
1954[6]	Ratification of 1951 *Geneva Refugee Convention* by France.
1957[7]	Bourguiba asks UNHCR to support the Tunisian government in dealing with Algerian refugees and hereby recognizes that it is bound by the *Geneva Refugee Convention*.
1960s	Bilateral and multilateral co-operation agreements with francophone African countries set up quotas for the training and education of students and professionals.
1963–1973[8]	Bilateral Agreements with Algeria, Tunisia and Libya to reciprocally facilitate entry and stay of nationals of these countries and equal treatment for socio-economic rights. In practice, these agreements are not consistently implemented.
1966[9]	The labour code requires all foreigners to have a work contract signed by the employer and the administration and sets out sanctions for employers and irregular workers.
1968[10]	Law 68-7 sets out the criteria for entry and stay of foreigners in Tunisia and lays down the sanctions for irregular entry and stay, for falsification of documents, as well as for the help of irregular migrants' entry, exit or stay in Tunisia.
1975[11]	Law 75-40 lays down access rules for passports and travel documents for Tunisians, as well as for travel documents for foreigners. It also sanctions irregular entry and exit.
1993[12]	The Investment Code allows fully exporting firms to recruit management personnel from abroad – up to four people per firm. Beyond this number, the firm has to conform to a recruitment and 'Tunisification' program by the Ministry of Labour.
1994[13]	A Labour Code revision increases the penalties for irregular employment, both for the employer and the employee.
1994[14]	Introduction of a 10-dinar-per-week fine for irregular stay through a decree by the Ministry of Finance, allowed for in the 1968 law.
2004[15]	Law 2004-06 introduces strict sanctions for irregular immigration, emigration and support for irregular migrants. It punishes family members and those protected by professional secret (lawyers, doctors) if they do not denounce acts of irregular entry or exit.
Since 2011	Elaboration of a draft law establishing a Tunisian asylum office and national refugee determination procedure.
Since 2012	Elaboration of a *National Migration Strategy* (first draft in 2013, second draft in November 2015, third draft in August 2017) comprising five axes,

Table A.8. (cont.)

Year	Measure
	the last one covering immigration. In 2020, the strategy is redrafted for the fourth time.
2012	Tunisia unilaterally decides to apply the 1963 Establishment Convention and allows Algerians to work in Tunisia without a work permit. This decision is made official in an October 2015 agreement between Algeria and Tunisia that abolished work permits in both countries starting from 2016.
2013[16]	The penalty for irregular stay is increased from 10 to 20 dinars per week.
2013	After the closure of the Choucha camp in summer 2013, the Minister of Social Affairs promises residence permits to the remaining refugees and migrants – the promise is not fulfilled due to the refusal of the Ministry of Interior.
2014	Libyan schools are created with the approval of the Tunisian Ministry of Education. Also, Libyan children are allowed to enter Tunisian public schools.
2014–2016	A Contingency Plan is elaborated by the Tunisian authorities together with UNHCR to prepare for an eventual new asylum crisis at the Libyan border. The preference for an urban approach in hosting incoming refugees in 2014 is changed back in 2016 to a preference for a camp approach.
2014–2015[17]	Foreigners are required to pay a 30-dinar tax upon exit from Tunisia. In reaction to public and diplomatic protest, Tunisia removes this requirement in March 2015 for Maghreb nationals (Morocco, Algeria, Libya, Mauritania), Tunisians living abroad, political refugees, diplomatic personnel and those expelled with the assistance of IOM, UNHCR or their home country. In August 2015, the solidarity tax is removed entirely.
2016[18]	Law 2016-61 sets out the protection mechanisms and penalties to prevent and fight human trafficking. It does not, however, grant a residence permit to victims of trafficking beyond the time of the legal proceedings.
2016[19]	Revision of the Investment Law expands the rights of firms to recruit foreigners in highly skilled positions regardless of the opposability of national workers.
2016[20]	Libyans are now allowed to buy property in Tunisia without the authorization of the governor. In reaction to public protest, this possibility is restricted two months later to property above 200 million dinars.
2017[21]	A maximum of 3,000-dinar penalty for irregular stay is introduced (equivalent to 150 weeks in irregularity), as well as exemptions for victims of trafficking, refugees and partners of Tunisians. The exemption is later expanded to students and trainees.
2017	In June 2017, the thirty-five people remaining in the Choucha camp (closed since 2013) are evicted by the Ministry of Defense. They are transferred to a Sport and Youth Centre in La Marsa close to Tunis, where they are still in 2020, (unsuccessfully) claiming their recognition as refugees and resettlement outside Tunisia.
2018[22]	Law 2018-50 penalizes racial discrimination by a prison sentence of one month to one year and a fine of up to 1,000 dinars, and creates a National Commission to Fight Discrimination.

Table A.8. (*cont.*)

Year	Measure
2019	In May, an administrative decision by the MoSA allows refugees registered with UNHCR that have contracts authorized by the Ministry of Labour or that are self-employed to access Tunisian social services via the CNSS. In June 2020, a refugee is for the first time part of the CNSS.
2019–2020	In spring 2019, the Contingency Plan is updated once more to deal with increasing arrivals from Libya, and in January 2020, a site is identified in the region of Bir El Fatnassiya to set up a camp should refugee arrivals cross the threshold of 300 per day.
2020	In April, the Ministries of Interior, Social Affairs and Human Rights announces COVID-19 related measures for migrants, including the delaying of rents, the prolongation of visas and the access of migrants to state support programs.
2020	In December, a Memorandum of Understanding between UNHCR and the Tunisian government is signed to include vulnerable refugees and asylum seekers in state assistance services offered by the Tunisian Union for Social Solidarity (UTSS).

Table A.9. *National institutional changes related to immigration in Tunisia*

Year	Measure
1991	The Tunisian Red Crescent (founded in 1956), Tunisia's public social relief institution, is charged to receive asylum requests and transmit them to UNHCR.
2012[23]	Creation of the State Secretariat for Migration and Tunisians Abroad (SEMTE) within the Ministry of Social Affairs to coordinate all policies on migration, led by a State Secretary and the General Directorate on International Cooperation on Migration (DGCIM).
2012	Creation of an inter-ministerial Commission on Migration, operational until 2014.
2014	In January, with the new government, the State Secretary for Migration and Tunisians Abroad (SEMTE) disappears at the governmental level; the DGCIM continues to work at the operational level.
2014[24]	Creation of the National Migration Observatory (ONM), de facto operational since 2015.
2015	In February, re-creation of the State Secretary within the Ministry of Social Affairs, this time responsible for two dossiers – Social Integration and Migration.
2016	In January, the post of State Secretary for Social Integration and Migration is dissolved again; the DGCIM continues to work at the operational level.
2016	In August, the post of State Secretary for Migration and Tunisians Abroad is recreated, this time under the umbrella of the Ministry of Foreign Affairs.
2017	In February, creation of a National Commission in charge of fighting human trafficking.
2017	In September, with the new government, the post of State Secretary for Migration and Tunisians Abroad is moved back to the Ministry of Social Affairs.
2018	In November, a government reshuffling leads to the upgrading of the migration dossier to a Ministry in Charge of Emigration and Tunisians Abroad attached to the head of government.
2019	In October, ONM and INS launch the Tunisia-HIMS survey of Tunisia's immigrant and emigrant populations, rolled out in 2020–2021. This survey is part of the EU-funded Households International Migration Surveys in the Mediterranean (HIMS) project.
2020	In February, the migration dossier disappears again from the newly formed government (which resigns in July). In September, the new government recreates the SEMTE once more as a State Secretary attached to the Ministry of Foreign Affairs.
2020	On 21 July, the Council of Ministers approves a decree creating the National Commission for the Fight against Racial Discrimination in charge of implementing the 2018 law.

Table A.10. *International activities and diplomatic developments around immigration in Tunisia*

Year	Measure
1963	UNHCR opens an honorary representation in Tunisia, which is operational from the early 1990s until 2011.
2000[25]	In September, a Cooperation Agreement between Tunisia and IOM is signed (ratified in April 2001), leading to the opening of an IOM office in Tunis in March 2001.
2003	Relocation of the African Development Bank (AfDB) from Ivory Coast to Tunisia due to the political crisis in Ivory Coast. The AfDB moves back to Abidjan in 2014.
2011	In February, UNHCR opens the Choucha refugee camp in the southeast of Tunisia.
2011[26]	Headquarters Agreement between Tunisia and UNHCR to grant them the right to conduct refugee status determination procedures in Tunisia.
2012	ICMPD launches its ETMA project (2012–2014) on migration, later continuing work with the MoI on border management (2015–2017) and local migration governance (MC2CM project, 2015–2018).
2013	In June, UNHCR closes the Choucha refugee camp in the southeast of Tunisia.
2013	ILO launches a regional project on labour migration (IRAM project, 2013–2017) involving the UGTT and the UTICA. In 2017, the FAIR project took over this work.
2013	Launch of IOM project 'Mainstreaming migration into development planning' (2013–2017), which includes focused cooperation with the MoH.
2014	The Swiss Development Cooperation Agency (SDC) and the EU launch a coordination group for all international organizations and European development funding agencies working on migration in Tunisia. They elaborate a common 6-point advocacy agenda.
2014	In March, Tunisia and the EU sign a joint declaration for a Mobility Partnership. Negotiations start in October 2016, but apart from project funding, there has been no outcome.
2015	UNHCR launches a project to work towards the enactment of Tunisia's asylum law (2015–2018).
2015	ICMPD launches the Mediterranean City-to-City Migration Project (MC2CM) to bring together city-level civil servants to share and implement best practices on migrant integration at the local level. The project's second phase ends in 2020.
2016	The EU LEMMA project (2016–2019) is launched to support the mobility partnership and assist Tunisian institutions in their migration strategy.
2017	The FES launches the regional PROMIG project (2017–2020) to support the Network of Unions on Mediterranean and Sub-Saharan Migration (RSMMS) in

Table A.10. (cont.)

Year	Measure
	its work on rights-based migration policies across Western, Central and Northern Africa, as well as Europe.
2018	ProGreS Migration Tunisie (2018–2021) is implemented by ICMPD to operationalize the migration strategy, foster local migrant integration, mobilize the diaspora and develop better migrant reinsertion programs.
2020	In June, the Centre for Development Information and Education (CIES) and the Tunisian Union of Social Solidarity (UTSS) launch their first training course on 'Socio-economic inclusion of migrants' for Tunisian municipalities and CSOs, funded by ICMPD and ILO as part of the I-Migr project.

Table A.11. *Civil society developments on immigration in Tunisia*

Year	Measure
1993	Creation of the Association of African Students and Interns in Tunisia (AESAT), under control of the Ministry of Higher Education.
2007–2014	Tunisia's main labour union, the UGTT, establishes a network of unions between Europe and Western, Central and Northern Africa. The Network of Unions on Mediterranean and Sub-Saharan Migration (RSMMS) is created in 2009 and effectively launched in 2014.
2011	The INGO Euromed Rights opens a regional Maghreb bureau in Tunis, acting as coordinator of civil society on migration issues and monitoring EU–Tunisia relations.
2011	The Tunisian Forum for Economic and Social Rights (FTDES) is officially created in 2011 and starts to work on migrants' rights and migrants disappeared in the Mediterranean Sea.
2011	Creation of the Tunisian Council for Refugees and Migrants (CTRM), an association of Tunisian lawyers, which is again dissolved in 2015.
2011	Creation of the Tunisian Association for the Support of Minorities (ATSM), whose work also includes immigrants.
2012	Opening of the House of Rights and Migrations (Maison des Droits et des Migrations) in Tunis by Terre d'Asile Tunisie (TAT), the Tunisian branch of France Terre d'Asile.
2012	Creation of the Association for the Defense of Black Tunisians' rights (ADAM), active until 2014.
2013	Creation of M'nemty, an association of Black Tunisians fighting against racial discrimination.
2014	Creation of the Association of the Syrian Community/Colony in Tunisia.
2014	In 2014, the Association of Active Ivoirians in Tunisia (ASSIVAT) is created. Two other associations were later created to represent the Ivoirian community: the Association of Ivoirians in Tunisia (AIT) in 2018 and the Union of Ivorians in Tunisia (UIT) in 2020.
2015	The INGO Médecins du Monde Belgique (MdM-B) starts to work in Tunisia on migrant's health.
2015	Tunisia's main labour union, the UGTT, starts to cooperate with irregular migrant workers through an ILO project.
2015	The Tunis-based Arab Institute of Human Rights (IADH) starts working with UNHCR on refugee rights.
2015	The INGO Adventist Development and Relief Agency (ADRA) launches a project on the integration of refugees in the labour market in cooperation with UNHCR.
2016	The Media and Human Rights Observatory starts working on Libyan migrants access to healthcare.
2016	Creation of the Association of Sub-Saharan Workers in Tunisia (ASTT).
2016	The INGO Lawyers without Borders starts to work on victims of human trafficking together with FTDES.
2016	Launch of EU-funded project of TAT and a Tunisian NGO, Beity, for the defense of migrants rights, legal assistance and support for migrants, including the creation of a legal clinic.

Table A.11. (cont.)

Year	Measure
2016	Launch of EU-funded project of FTDES and Lawyers without Borders on legal support for victims of human trafficking (2016–2018).
2016	In September, TAT creates a second Maison du Droit et des Migrations in Sfax.
2016	Creation of Afrique Intelligence in Sfax and the Union of African Leaders (ULA) in Tunis to bring together high-skilled African migrants.
2016	In December, AESAT launches the Facebook campaign 'I don't want to die in Tunisia because I am Black' after the attack of three students in Tunis.
2016	In June, the Tunisian Council for Refugees (CTR) is created as an NGO to work together with UNHCR on the protection of refugees and asylum seekers. It has several offices across the Tunisian territory and, since mid-2019, has taken over the registration of asylum seekers and management of reception centres from the Red Crescent.
2017	In May, organization of the cultural Festival Jaou in Tunis with the topic Tunisia: Migrant Nation, covering both historical and current immigration and emigration.
2017	The INGO Mercycorps (present in Tunisia since 2011) starts working on immigration in Tunisia, Mali and Niger.
2019	Minority Rights Group (MRG) launches the project 'For the Consolidation of the Capacity of Tunisian Civil Society in the Fight Against all Forms of Discrimination', focusing on racial and sexual discrimination. A network of nine Anti-Discrimination Points (PAD) is created across the territory, through which Tunisian CSOs monitor discriminations. In 2020–2021, a follow-up project is implemented focusing on racial discrimination.
2020	In March, the Cellule Solidarité Africaine Covid-19 Tunisie is created to raise funds for migrants in distress due to COVID-19. In April, sixty-one associations and twenty-three deputies call upon the government to provide more systematic protection of migrants in times of COVID-19, including an exceptional regularization.
2020	On 6 June, in the context of the Black Lives Matter protests in the United States, thirty-one Tunisian associations organize a large-scale anti-racism protest in Tunis. In November, the association 'Loi 50' is created in reference to Law 50 on racial discrimination passed in 2018 to combat all forms of racial discrimination.
2020	In July, in an unprecedented decision, the administrative tribunal of Tunis requests the liberation of twenty-two migrants unlawfully detailed in the Ouardiya centre. The case has been brought to the court in June by FTDES, Lawyers without Borders, TAT and the World Organization Against Torture (OMCT).
2020	On 2 December, the UGTT decides to accept foreign workers as members.
2020	On 18 December, on the occasion of the International Migrant Day, the FTDES, ATFD, EuroMed, TAT, LTDH and IADH call upon Tunisia's President and government to move forward with the asylum law and protection of migrants.

Notes

Chapter 1

1 I first introduced the idea of issue-specific and regime-specific immigration policy processes in Natter (2018b).
2 I introduced the concept of Morocco as a 'liberal monarchy' in Natter (2021b).
3 All official bulletins since 1956 are available online at the homepages of the Moroccan General Secretariat of the Government (www.sgg.gov.ma/Legislation/BulletinsOfficiels.aspx) and the Tunisian Ministry of Higher Education and Research (www.cnudst.rnrt.tn/wwwisis/jort.06/form.htm).

Chapter 2

1 Chapter 2 updates and expands the categorization of immigration policy theories I first introduced in Natter (2018b) and provides the starting point for theory-building in this book.

Chapter 3

1 France24, *Manifestations en Tunisie: "La révolution continue"*, 14 January 2018; Jeune Afrique, *Qui sont les militants de « Fech Nestanew », qui mobilise contre la vie chère en Tunisie ?*, 11 January 2018.
2 Nawaat, *Frontière tuniso-libyenne: le mur de la discorde*, 12 July 2015.
3 Yabiladi, *Maroc: 3000 domestiques philippines « exploitées et maltraitées »*, 6 December 2012.
4 Infomigrants, *Coronavirus : au Maroc, des dizaines de migrants sub-sahariens arrêtés et confinés de force*, 29 June 2020.
5 Investir en Tunisia, *Les deux tiers du peuple libyen vivent en Tunisie, affirme Mehdi Jomâa*, 22 November 2014.
6 Le Point, *Les Libyens en Tunisie: "chez eux" pour combien de temps ?*, 2 March 2015.
7 RFI, *Frontière tuniso-libyenne: Tunis hausse le ton à l'égard des étrangers*, 3 August 2014.

8 Yabiladi, *Nasser Bourita et Amira El Fadil inaugurent le siège de l'Observatoire africain des migrations à Rabat*, 18 December 2020.
9 Facebook, *Cellule Solidarité Africaine Covid19 Tunisie*.
10 FTDES, *Communiqué de presse: Les mesures du gouvernement sont encourageantes, mail il faut des décisions plus fortes pour protéger les migrants.es et les réfugiés.ées contre le Covid-19*, 10 April 2020.
11 EuroMedRights, *Communiqué de presse : Maroc, Migrant.e.s et réfugié.e.s sont aussi vulnérables face au Covid-19*, 30 March 2020; GADEM, *Communiqué de presse : Protection contre le Covid-19: tou-te-s égaux-ales?*, 30 March 2020; and GADEM, *Communiqué de presse: Pour un moratoire sur l'application des dispositions de la loi n° 02-03 relatives au séjour des étranger-e-s au Maroc pour raison humanitaire durant toute la période de l'état d'urgence sanitaire!*, 23 April 2020.
12 Infomigrants, *Coronavirus: au Maroc, des dizaines de migrants sub-sahariens arrêtés et confinés de force*, 29 June 2020; Yabiladi, *Maroc: Après le confinement, la chasse aux migrants reprend*, 9 October 2020.
13 Yabiladi, *Maroc : L'Ordre des médecins se joint au HCR pour l'accès des migrants aux soins*, 20 May 2020; 2M, *Protection des réfugiés : Le HCR se félicite de la qualité de la coopération avec le Maroc*, 6 October 2020.
14 Yabiladi, *#SolidaritéCovid : Un collectif d'associations marocaines pour venir en aide aux migrants*, 15 April 2020.

Chapter 4

1 This section partly draws on arguments and empirical material I published in a more extensive form in Natter (2014b).
2 Le Matin, *La lutte contre l'émigration clandestine: une priorité nationale*, 20 December 2003.
3 France24, *Morocco uses migrants to press Spain over W.Sahara: analysts*, 18 May 2020; APNews, *Spain, Morocco square off after 8,000 migrants arrive by sea*, 18 May 2020.
4 MoroccoWorldNews, *Dear Maroc Hebdo, African Immigrants are not a Danger to Morocco*, 3 November 2012.
5 Yabiladi, *Assabah relaye les propos d'une Marocaine qualifiant les Subsahariens de «cafards»*, 29 November 2019.
6 Afrik.com, *Les Noirs victimes de racisme au Maroc: Un sujet encore tabou*, 27 May 2005; SeneNews, *Interview du prof. Chouki El Hamel « les attitudes racistes sont enracinées dans la culture marocaine »*, 11 September 2014.
7 GISTI, *Non-governmental euro-african manifest on migrations, fundamental rights and freedom of movement*, 3 July 2006.
8 L'Economiste, *Une presse déchaînée*, 20 December 2005.
9 This section builds upon an argument I first introduced in Natter (2021b) and provides an expanded analysis of the empirical material underpinning it.
10 MoroccoWorldNews, *IOM Ready to Support Morocco in Implementing its Migration Policy*, 13 February 2017.
11 TelQuel, *En Afrique, le « soft power » à la marocaine*, 9 September 2016.

Notes to pages 95–121

12 ATMF Press Release, *1er Mai 2012: lancement de la campagne de régularisation des sans papiers(e) au Maroc*, 3 May 2012.
13 Yabiladi, *Les Subsahariens au Maroc réclament leurs droits*, 11 November 2011.
14 TelQuel, *L'irresponsabilité des responsables de la politique migratoire*, 14 February 2015.
15 TelQuel, *Les Subsahariens n'auront plus besoin de passer par l'Anapec pour travailler au Maroc*, 20 September 2016.
16 This section party draws on empirical material I used in Natter (2021a), where I develop the concept of ad-hocratic immigration governance.
17 Yabiladi, *Depuis mars, blocage des cartes de séjour pour les réfugiés au Maroc*, 28 December 2017; TelQuel, *Les réfugiés peuvent à nouveau obtenir des titres de séjour au Maroc*, 12 December 2018.
18 Infomigrants, *Maroc : la crainte de l'expulsion pour des migrants incapables de renouveler leur titre de séjour*, 10 July 2020; Yabiladi, *Maroc : Des ONG dénoncent le durcissement des conditions de renouvellement des titres de séjour*, 21 July 2020.
19 TelQuel, *Une première: un juge enquête sur la détention de migrants*, 27 February 2015.
20 TelQuel, *Immigration: le double discours. Racisme, affrontements, meurtres ... La regularisation ne suffit pas. Une politique d'integration s'impose*, 12-18 September 2014.
21 Yabiladi, *Le Maroc laisse libre cours à une répression mal contrôlée contre les migrants subsahariens*, 25 October 2018.
22 Yabiladi, *Tanger : Le festival Migrant'scène interdit par les autorités locales*, 9 November 2018.
23 Yabiladi, *Maroc : Après le confinement, la chasse aux migrants reprend*, 9 October 2020.

Chapter 5

1 This section partly draws on empirical material I used in Natter (2021b) and expands its analysis.
2 LeDesk, *En plein désert, des réfugiés syriens ballotés entre le Maroc et l'Algérie dans le dénuement le plus total*, 23 April 2017.
3 TelQuel, *Mohammed VI met fin au calvaire des familles syriennes bloquées près de Figuig*, 20 June 2017.
4 Yabiladi, *Le Maroc laisse libre cours à une répression mal contrôlée contre les migrants subsahariens*, 25 October 2018.
5 Yabiladi, *Depuis mars, blocage des cartes de séjour pour les réfugiés au Maroc*, 28 December 2017.
6 Yabiladi, *Discrimination des Subsahariens au Maroc : Une députée PPS interpelle le ministre des Transports*, 2 November 2019; Yabiladi, *Maroc : Titre de séjour obligatoire pour acheter un ticket d'autocar pour les Subsahariens*, 29 Octobre 2019.
7 Yabiladi, *Migrants subsahariens: De Fès au Parlement, la vague de racisme déferle*, 25 May 2017.

8 Yabiladi, *Racisme : Le PJD fait barrage à la question écrite de son élu à Tiznit*, 4 June 2019; Yabiladi, *Les élus de Tiznit sonnent la charge contre les migrants subsahariens*, 3 June 2019.
9 Yabiladi, *Politique migratoire au Maroc: Défis et évolutions récentes*, 27 December 2016.
10 This section partly draws on empirical material I used in Natter (2021b) and expands its analysis.
11 TV5MONDE, *Rencontre des migrants avec Anis Birou, ministre chargé de la question migratoire*, 20 December 2013.
12 Yabiladi, *Le «soft power migratoire» du Maroc a besoin d'une société civile forte et crédible [Tribune]*, 6 December 2018.
13 Yabiladi, *Migration: Le Gadem lance la campagne d'alerte «Coûts Et Blessures»*, 22 September 2018; Yabiladi, *Maroc : Amnesty International dénonce la répression des migrants subsahariens*, 9 September 2018.
14 L'Economiste, *Enquête L'Economiste-Sunergia. Migrants subsahariens: Des résultats surprenants!*, 21 March 2018.
15 Club de l'Economiste, *Interview with Driss el Yazami*, 21 November 2014.
16 Medias24, *Tué à Tanger, Charles Ndour était un migrant sénégalais en situation régulière*, 1 September 2014; Yabiladi, *Affrontements entre migrants subsahariens et population d'un quartier de Casablanca*, 25 November 2017; Yabiladi, *Maroc : Les agressions des migrants dans le nord vont crescendo selon l'AMDH*, 4 June 2019.
17 Dakaractu, *Libération des Sénégalais qui avaient saccagé l'ambassade de leur pays*, 4 July 2013.
18 Yabiladi, *Migration : Le Maroc s'explique devant le corps diplomatique africain*, 31 August 2018.
19 Yabiladi, *Maroc: Après le confinement, la chasse aux migrants reprend*, 9 October 2020.
20 La Nouvelle Tribune, *RAM recrute en Afrique sub-saharienne*, 2 February 2014.
21 HuffPostMaghreb, *Abdou Souleye Diop, nouvel associé gérant de Mazars*, 6 February 2017.
22 UNHCR, *Communiqué de presse : Employabilité et insertion économique des réfugiés au Maroc: le Ministère Délégué chargé des Marocains Résidant à l'Etranger et des Affaires de la Migration, la CGEM, et le HCR signent un partenariat*, 18 May 2018.5.
23 Emission2M, *Dans les coulisses de l'univers des salariés étrangers*, 9 March 2015.
24 GADEM, *Note informative sur le procès de cinq réfugiés*, July 2009.
25 Le Courriel de L'Atlas, *Maroc: Les magistrats créent leur association indépendante*, 29 August 2011.
26 TelQuel, *Une première: un juge enquête sur la détention de migrants*, 27 February 2015.

Chapter 6

1 AfricanManager, *Des organisations lancent un appel urgent à Saïed*, 17 December 2020.
2 This section partly draws on empirical material I used in Natter (2021b), where I discuss domestic politics around immigration an emigration throughout the 2011 revolution.

3 Citoyens à la Une. *La minorité noire tunisienne*, 13 December 2011.
4 HuffPostMaghreb, *Tunisie: A la rencontre des habitants de Gosba, le « village des noirs »*, 13 February 2015; EnBref, *Médenine: un bus pour les blancs, un autre pour les noirs*, 19 April 2016.
5 Jeune Afrique, *Etre noire en Tunisie*, 12 July 2004; Jeune Afrique, *Le racisme au Maghreb*, 23 August 2004.
6 Investir en Tunisia, *Les deux tiers du peuple libyen vivent en Tunisie, affirme Mehdi Jomâa*, 22 November 2014.
7 JeuneAfrique, *Escalade militaire en Libye : la Tunisie se prépare à un nouvel afflux de réfugiés*, 10 January 2020.
8 RFI, *Frontière tuniso-libyenne: Tunis hausse le ton à l'égard des étrangers*, 3 August 2014.
9 Le Temps, *Forza Tounes contre l'accès des libyens à la propriété en Tunisie*, 31 December 2016.
10 This section partly draws on empirical material I used in Natter (2021a), where I develop the concept of ad-hocratic immigration governance.
11 InfoMigrants, *UNHCR and Tunisia sign accord to improve refugee assistance*, 7 December 2020.
12 Nawaat, *Levée du visa pour 7 pays par le ministère des Affaires Etrangères: d'étranges decisions*, 27 April 2015.
13 France24, *La Tunisie adopte une loi contre les discriminations raciales, « la première dans le monde arabe »*, 10 October 2018.
14 Euromed Rights, *Communiqué de presse: TUNISIE: La nécessité d'une loi contre le racisme et les discriminations*, 21 March 2016.
15 HuffPostMaghreb, *Kitoko Saby, une tunisienne noire. Une "sous-citoyenne" pour les racistes*, 5 October 2016; Baya.tn, *Discrimination raciale: Mehdi Ben Gharbia présente ses excuses à Sabrine NGOY*, 8 October 2016.
16 HuffPostMaghreb, *Manifestation contre le racisme devant le Théâtre Municipal après l'agression de trois Congolais*, 25 December 2016; Nawaat, *Pour Chris, Jemima et Sarah, le racisme peut tuer*, 27 December 2016.
17 HuffPostMaghreb, *Tunisie: Youssef Chahed appelle à accélérer l'adoption d'une loi contre le racisme*, 26 December 2016.
18 Jeune Afrique, *Loi contre le racisme: « tournant historique » en Tunisie, mais où en sont l'Algérie et le Maroc?*, 11 October 2018.
19 France24, *La Tunisie adopte une loi contre les discriminations raciales, « la première dans le monde arabe »*, 10 October 2018.
20 HuffPostMaghreb, *La loi contre les discriminations raciales: Un pas en avant mais c'est insuffisant, alertent ces ONG*, 11 June 2018.
21 ArabReformInitiative, *Facing up to Racism in Tunisia: Interview with Khawla Ksiksi*, 8 June 2020.
22 Minority Rights International, *The "Black Spring" taking Tunisia*, 29 July 2020; Terre d'Asile Tunisie, *Black Lives Matter protests are boosting Tunisia's anti-racist movement*, 11 August 2020.
23 BBCNewsAfrica, *The black Arabs fighting against racial discrimination*, 27 June 2020.

Chapter 7

1 Inkyfada, *La lutte contre le racisme s'invite à l'Assemblée*, 13 April 2018.
2 All details of the vote can be accessed at https://majles.marsad.tn/2014/fr/lois/5a6e09964f24d07616046849/votes.
3 InfoMigrants, *En Tunisie, des centres d'accueil saturés face à l'afflux de migrants*, 27 August 2019; JeuneAfrique, *Escalade militaire en Libye : la Tunisie se prépare à un nouvel afflux de réfugiés*, 10 January 2020.
4 This section offers an expanded analysis of some of the empirical material I used in Natter (2021c).
5 Businessnews, *Slim Khalbous: L'Afrique occupe une place particulière dans le système universitaire tunisien*, 22 August 2017.
6 InfoMigrants, *L'inextricable demande d'asile des migrants de La Marsa, "prisonniers" en Tunisie*, 2 July 2019; EspaceManager, *Tunisie: Appel à la régularisation des migrants et à la libération des détenus d'El Ouardia*, 20 April 2020.
7 HuffPostMaghreb, *L'UGTT s'engage dans la lutte contre l'exploitation des travailleurs étrangers en Tunisie*, 14 February 2019.
8 AfrikYes, *Tunisie: L'UGTT ouvre ses portes aux travailleurs subsahariens, une première dans le monde arabe*, 2 December 2020.
9 Businessnews, *Le ministre de l'Enseignement: Les élèves libyens auront accès aux écoles publiques tunisiennes*, 8 August 2014.
10 I introduced this argument in Natter (2021c), where I also discuss strange such shifting alliances with regards to emigration policies.
11 HuffPostMaghreb, *La Tunisie s'engage à faire la lumière sur un incident impliquant un diplomate sénégalais et un policier*, 9 July 2015.
12 HuffPostMaghreb, *L'Instance de lutte contre le trafic d'êtres humains dévoile le nombre et la nature des cas reçus*, 6 February 2018.
13 EspaceManager, *Tunisie: Appel à la régularisation des migrants et à la libération des détenus d'El Ouardia,* 20 April 2020.
14 Infomigrants, *La justice tunisienne ordonne la libération de migrants en détention*, 17 July 2020.

Chapter 8

1 HRW, *Algérie: Mettre fin aux expulsions sommaires*, 9 December 2016; JeuneAfrique, *Algérie: des Maliens expulsés accusent les autorités de mauvais traitements*, 12 December 2016.

Appendix 3

1 Dahir of 8 December 1915, In: B.O. n°161 of 13 December 1915.
2 Dahir of 20 October 1931, In: B.O. n°993 of 6 November 1931.
3 Dahir of 15 November 1934, In: B.O. n°1152 of 23 November 1934.
4 Dahir of 2 January 1940, In: B.O. n°1421 of 19 January 1940.

Notes to pages 240–248

5 Dahir of 16 May 1941, Dahir of 1 May 1950, Dahir of 21 February 1951, respectively In: B.O. n°1491 of 23 May 1941, B.O. n°1967 of 7 July 1950, B.O. n°2006 of 6 April 1951.
6 Dahir of 8 August, In: B.O. n°2237 of 9 September 1955.
7 Dahir 1-57-271 of 26 August 1957 and Dahir 2-57-1256 of 29 August 1957, In: B.O. n°2341 of 6 September 1957.
8 Establishment Convention with Algeria (15 March 1963), Senegal (27 March 1964) and Tunisia (9 December 1964).
9 Dahir 4-93-5 of 14 June 1993; Dahir 1-93-517 of 2 August 2011, In: B.O. n°6018 of 2 February 2012.
10 Dahir 1-03-194 of 11 September 2003, In: B.O. n°5210 of 6 May 2004
11 Dahir 1-03-196 of 11 November 2003, In: B.O. n°5162 of 20 November 2003.
12 Circular n°1391-05 of the Ministry of employment and professional formation of 25 November 2005.
13 Circular n°456-11 of the Ministry of Health of 6 July 2010, In: BO n°5926 of 17 March 2011.
14 Dahir 1-11-91 of 29 July 2011, In: B.O. n°5964bis of 30 July 2011.
15 Note n°2-4676 by the Ministry of Education of 11 December 2012.
16 Circular n°13-487 of 9 October 2013 and Circular n°5-2014 of 21 January 2014 by the Ministry of National Education.
17 Circular n°8303 of 16 December 2013 by the Ministry of Interior and the Ministry for the Community of Moroccans Residing Abroad and Migration Affairs.
18 Partnership Convention of 26 October 2015 between the Ministry for the Community of Moroccans Residing Abroad and Migration Affairs, the Ministry of Health, the Ministry of Interior and the Ministry of Finance.
19 ANAPEC, *Note conjointe (Intérieur-Emploi-Industrie-DGSN-ANAPEC-AMDI) relative à la mise en place d'une procédure spécifique d'octroi de titre de séjour pour les investisseurs étrangers et compétences rares*, September 2015.
20 Dahir 1-16-121 of 10 August 2016, In: B.O. n°6493 of 22 August 2016.
21 Dahir 1-16-127 of 25 August 2016, In: B.O. n°6526 of 15 December 2016.
22 This circular by the Ministry of Employment could not be identified or found. Interviewees all attest its existence and it is acted upon by relevant administrations, but no one had seen it on paper.
23 Dahir 1-57-271 of 26 August 1957 and Dahir 2-57-1256 of 29 August 1957, In: B.O. n°2341 of 6 September 1957.
24 Dahir 1-03-196 of 11 November 2003, In: B.O. n°5162 of 20 November 2003.
25 Dahir 2-13-731 of 30 September 2013.
26 Dahir 1-16-127 of 25 August 2016, In: B.O. n°6526 of 15 December 2016.
27 Dahir 1-06-116 of 22 February 2005, In: B.O. n°5536 of 21 June 2007.
28 Dahir 1-08-90 of 20 October 2008, In: B.O. n°5692 of 18 December 2008.

Appendix 4

1 Decree-law 88 of 24 September 2011, In: J.O.R.T. n°74 of 30 September 2011.
2 Constitution promulgated on 27 January 2014, In: J.O.R.T. Special Edition of 20 April 2015.

3 Decree of 13 April 1898, In: Coleda (1953).
4 Decree of 20 February 1930, In: Coleda (1953).
5 Decree of 2 July 1953, In: Coleda (1953).
6 Decree of 2 June 1955, In: J.O.R.T n°47 of 14 June 1955.
7 Communication of 24 October 1957 by the Permanent Representative of Tunisia at the UN to the UN Secretary General.
8 Establishment Agreements with Algeria (26 July 1963), with Tunisia (9 December 1964) and Libya (6 June 1973).
9 Law 66-27 of 30 April 1966, In: J.O.R.T n°22 of 17-24 May 1966.
10 Law 68-7 of 8 March 1968, In: J.O.R.T n°11 of 8-12 March 1968.
11 Law 75-40 of 14 May 1975, In: J.O.R.T n°34 of 20 May 1975.
12 Law 93-120 of 27 December 1993, In: J.O.R.T n°99 of 28 December 1993.
13 Law 94-29 of 21 February 1994, In: J.O.R.T n°15 of 22 February 1994.
14 Decree 94-815 of 11 April 1994, In: J.O.R.T n°30 of 19 April 1994.
15 Law 2004-06 of 3 February 2004, In: J.O.R.T n°11 of 6 February 2004.
16 Decree 2013-930 of 1 February 2013, In: J.O.R.T. n°14 of 15 February 2013.
17 Law 2014-54 of 19 August 2014, In: J.O.R.T. n°68 of 22 August 2014; Law 2015-4 of 16 March 2015, In: J.O.R.T. n°22/23 of 20-4 March 2015; Law 2015-30 of 18 August 2015, In: J.O.R.T. n°67 of 21 August 2015.
18 Law 2016-61 of 3 August 2016, In J.O.R.T. n°66 of 12 August 2016.
19 Law 2016-71 of 30 September 2016, In: J.O.R.T. n°82 of 7 October 2016.
20 Note n°27-2016 of 31 October 2016 and note n°28-2016 of 26 December 2016 by the Ministry of State Property and Land Affairs.
21 Decree 2017-1061 of 26 September 2017, In: J.O.R.T. n°79 of 3 October 2017.
22 Law 2018-50 of 23 October 2018, In: J.O.R.T. n°86 of 26 October 2018.
23 Decree 2012-634 of 8 June 2012, In: J.O.R.T. n°49 of 22 June 2012.
24 Decree 2014-1930 of 30 April 2014, In: J.O.R.T. n°45 of 6 June 2014.
25 Law 2001-37 of 18 April 2001, In J.O.R.T. n°32 of 20 April 2001.
26 Decree-law 2011-92 of 29 September 2011, In: J.O.R.T. n°75 of 4 October 2011.

References

Aarts, Paul, and Francesco Cavatorta. 2013. *Civil Society in Syria and Iran: Activism in Authoritarian Contexts*. Boulder, CO: Lynne Rienner.
Abbassi, Driss. 2009. *Quand la Tunisie s'invente: entre Orient et Occident, des imaginaires politiques*. Paris, France: Editions Autrement.
Abdel Aziz, Teymour. 2013. "Supporting Access to Finance for Micro, Small & Medium Enterprises with Partial Credit Guarantees: The Moroccan Experience." In *MENA Knowledge and Learning Quick Notes Series n.94*. Washington, DC: World Bank.
Abdelaaty, Lamis E. 2021. *Discrimination and Delegation: Explaining State Responses to Refugees*. Oxford: Oxford University Press.
Abdelmoumni, Fouad. 2013. "Le Maroc et le Printemps arabe." *Pouvoirs* 145 (2):123–40.
Abdul Hamid, Maha. 2013. "Black Tunisians Historically Marginalized." Beirut, Lebanon: Assafir Al-Arabi. https://assafirarabi.com/en/3461/2013/06/19/black-tunisians-historically-marginalized/
Abizadeh, Arash. 2008. "Democratic Theory and Border Coercion: No Right to Unilaterally Control Your Own Borders." *Political Theory* 36(1):37–65.
Acharya, Amitav. 2014. "Global International Relations (IR) and Regional Worlds: A New Agenda for International Studies★." *International Studies Quarterly* 58(4):647–59.
Acosta Arcarazo, Diego, and Luisa F. Freier. 2015. "Turning the Immigration Policy Paradox Upside Down? Populist Liberalism and Discursive Gaps in South America." *International Migration Review* 49(3):659–96.
Adam, Ilke, Florian Trauner, Leonie Jegen, and Christof Roos. 2020. "West African Interests in (EU) Migration Policy: Balancing Domestic Priorities with External Incentives." *Journal of Ethnic and Migration Studies* 46(15):3101–18.
Adamson, Fiona B. 2019. "Sending States and the Making of Intra-diasporic Politics: Turkey and Its Diaspora(s)." *International Migration Review* 53(1):210–36.
Adamson, Fiona B., Triadafilos Triadafilopoulos, and Aristide R. Zolberg. 2011. "The Limits of the Liberal State: Migration, Identity and Belonging in Europe." *Journal of Ethnic and Migration Studies* 37(6):843–59.
Adamson, Fiona B., and Gerasimos Tsourapas. 2019. "Migration Diplomacy in World Politics." *International Studies Perspectives* 20(2):113–28.
———. 2020. "The Migration State in the Global South: Nationalizing, Developmental, and Neoliberal Models of Migration Management." *International Migration Review* 54(3):853–82.

266   References

AfDB. 2011. "Impact du conflit en Libye sur l'économie Tunisienne: Une évaluation préliminaire." In *Note analytique trimestrielle pour l'Afrique du Nord*. Tunis, Tunisia: African Development Bank.

Afrobarometer. 2015a. "Afrobarometer Round 6 – Summary of Results for Morocco." www.afrobarometer.org/wp-content/uploads/2022/02/mor_r6_sor.pdf

2015b. "Afrobarometer Round 6 – Summary of Results for Tunisia." https://www.afrobarometer.org/wp-content/uploads/2022/02/tun_r6_sor_en.pdf

2018a. "Afrobarometer Round 7 – Summary of Results for Morocco." https://www.afrobarometer.org/wp-content/uploads/2022/02/ab_r7_dispatchno285_migration_au_maroc.pdf

2018b. "Afrobarometer Round 7 – Summary of Results for Tunisia." https://www.afrobarometer.org/wp-content/uploads/migrated/files/publications/Summary%20of%20results/tun_r7_sor_eng.pdf

AI. 2020. "Les droits humains au Moyen-Orient et en Afrique du Nort. Rétrospective 2019." Amnesty International.

Alemán, José, and Dwayne Woods. 2014. "No Way Out: Travel Restrictions and Authoritarian Regimes." *Migration and Development*. 3(2):285–305.

Aleya-Sghaier, Amira. 2012. "The Tunisian Revolution: The Revolution of Dignity." *The Journal of the Middle East and Africa* 3(1):18–45.

Alioua, Mehdi. 2009. "Le 'passage au politique' des transmigrants subsahariens au Maroc: Imaginaire migratoire, réorganisation collective et mobilisation politique en situation de migration transnationale." Pp. 279–303 in *Le Maghreb à l'épreuve des migrations subsahariennes*, edited by Ali Bensaâd. Paris, France: Karthala.

Alioua, Mehdi, Jean-Noel Ferrié, and Helmut Reifeld. 2018. "La nouvelle politique migratoire marocaine." Rabat, Morocco: Konrad Adenauer Stiftung.

Allal, Amin, and Karine Bennafla. 2011. "Les mouvements protestataires de Gafsa (Tunisie) et Sidi Ifni (Maroc) de 2005 à 2009." *Revue Tiers Monde* 5:27–45.

Allal, Amin, and Vincent Geisser. 2011. "La Tunisie de l'après-Ben Ali." *Cultures & Conflits* 83:118–25.

Alonso, Sonia, and Saro Claro da Fonseca. 2011. "Immigration, Left and Right." *Party Politics* 18(6):865–84.

AlShehabi, Omar Hesham. 2021. "Policing Labour in Empire: The Modern Origins of the Kafala Sponsorship System in the Gulf Arab States." *British Journal of Middle Eastern Studies* 48(2):291–310.

Álvarez Velasco, Soledad. 2020. "From Ecuador to Elsewhere: The (Re)Configuration of a Transit Country." *Migration and Society* 3(1):34.

AMERM. 2008. *L'immigration subsaharienne au Maroc – Analyse socio-économique*. Rabat, Morocco: Association marocaine d'Etudes et de Recherche en Migrations.

2009. *Le tissu associatif et le traitement de la question migratoire au Maroc*. Rabat, Morocco: Association marocaine d'Etudes et de Recherche en Migrations.

Anderson, Joseph Trawicki. 2021. "Managing Labour Migration in Malaysia: Foreign Workers and the Challenges of 'Control' beyond Liberal Democracies." *Third World Quarterly* 42(1):86–104.

Anderson, Lisa. 1986. *The State and Social Transformation in Tunisia and Libya, 1830–1980*. Princeton, NJ: Princeton University Press.

1987. "The State in the Middle East and North Africa." *Comparative Politics* 20 (1):1–18.
Appiah-Nyamekye Sanny, Josephine, and Mohammed Abderebbi. 2019. "L'emploi pèse lourd dans les attitudes relatives à l'immigration/émigration au Maroc." In *Dépêche d'Afrobaromètre No. 285*. Afrobarometer.
Arrighi, Jean-Thomas, and Rainer Bauböck. 2017. "A Multilevel Puzzle: Migrants' Voting Rights in National and Local Elections." *European Journal of Political Research* 56(3):619–39.
Art, David. 2016. "Archivists and Adventurers: Research Strategies for Authoritarian Regimes of the Past and Present." *Social Science Quarterly* 97 (4):974–90.
Austin, Gareth. 2007. "Reciprocal Comparison and African History: Tackling Conceptual Eurocentrism in the Study of Africa's Economic Past." *African Studies Review* 50(3):1–28.
Avon, Dominique, and Youssef Aschi. 2014. "La Constitution tunisienne et l'enjeu de la liberté individuelle : un exemple d'accommodement au forceps." *Raison publique*.
Ayubi, Nazih N. 1995. *Over-Stating the Arab State: Politics and Society in the Middle East*. London: I. B. Tauris.
B.O. 2003a. "Law 02-03 relative to the entry and stay of foreigners in Morocco, and to irregular emigration and immigration." edited by Bulletin Officiel No. 5162: 1295–1302.
   2003b. "Official Bulletin: Deliberations in Parliament – Introduction of law 02.03 related to the entry and stay of foreigners in Morocco, and to irregular emigration and immigration." Pp. 1239–68, edited by Chambre des Représentants. Rabat, Morocco: Royaume du Maroc.
Badoual, Rita Aouad. 2003. "« Esclavage » et situation des « Noirs » au Maroc dans la première moitié du XXe siècle." Pp. 337–59 in *Les relations transsahariennes à l'époque contemporaine*, edited by Laurence Marfaing and Steffen Wippel. Paris, France: Karthala.
Bahmad, Jamal. 2015. "From Slavery to the Screen : Sub-Saharan Migrants in Moroccan History and Cinema." Pp. 151–57 in *Migrants au Maroc: Cosmopolitisme, présence d'étrangers et transformations sociales*, edited by Nadia Khrouz and Nazarena Lanza. Rabat, Morocco: Konrad-Adenauer-Stiftung.
Bailleul, Adeline. 2015. "Réfugiés syriens au Maroc: L'exil pour survivre." in *Huffington Post – Maroc*.
Bakewell, Oliver. 2015. "Moving from War to Peace in the Zambia-Angola Borderlands." Pp. 194–217 in *Mobility Makes States: Migration and Power in Africa*, edited by Darshan Vigneswaran and Joel Quirk. Philadelphia: University of Pennsylvania Press.
Bakewell, Oliver, and Gunvor Jónsson. 2013. "Theory and the Study of Migration in Africa." *Journal of Intercultural Studies* 34(5):477–85.
Bale, Tim. 2008. "Politics Matters: A Conclusion." *Journal of European Public Policy* 15(3):453–64.
Bamba, Mamadou. 2015. "Mobilité des Musulmans ivoiriens au Maroc : entre formation islamique et tourisme religieux." Pp. 72–78 in *Migrants au Maroc:*

Cosmopolitisme, présence d'étrangers et transformations sociales, edited by Nadia Khrouz and Nazarena Lanza. Rabat, Morocco: Konrad-Adenauer-Stiftung.

Barre, Abdelaziz. 2003. "Les relations entre le Maroc et les pays d'Afrique subsaharienne." in *Les relations transsahariennes à l'époque contemporaine*, edited by Laurence Marfaing and Steffen Wippel. Paris, France: Karthala.

——— 2012. "Les nouveau axes de la diplomatie marocaine." Pp. 41–58 in *Le Maghreb et son Sud : vers des liens renouvelés*, edited by Mansouria Mokhefi and Alain Antil. Paris, France: CNRS Editions.

Bartels, Inke. 2015. "Reconfiguration of Tunisian Migration Politics after the 'Arab Spring' – The Role of Young Civil Society Movements." Pp. 62–79 in *Youth, Revolt, Recognition – The Young Generation during and after the "Arab Spring"*, edited by Isabel Schäfer. Berlin, DE: Mediterranean Institute Berlin.

Bastien, Joëlle. 2009. "Goal Ambiguity and Informal Discretion in the Implementation of Public Policies: The Case of Spanish Immigration Policy." *International Review of Administrative Sciences* 75(4):665–85.

Bayart, Jean-Francois. 1996. "L'historicité de l'Etat importé." *Cahiers du CERI – Centre d'études et de recherches internationales* 1–44.

——— 2009. *The State in Africa: The Politics of the Belly*. Cambridge, UK: Polity.

Bayat, Asef. 2010. *Life as Politics: How Ordinary People Change the Middle East*. Amsterdam, the Netherlands: Amsterdam University Press.

Beau, Nicolas, and Jean-Pierre Tuquoi. 2011. *Notre Ami Ben Ali: L'envers du miracle tunisien*. Paris, France: La Découverte.

Becker, Howard S. 1963. *Outsiders: Studies in the Sociology of Deviance*. New York, NJ: The Free Press.

——— 1968. "Social Observation and Social Case Studies." Pp. 232–38 in *International Encyclopedia of the Social Sciences*, edited by David L. Sills, Robert King Merton, and Immanuel Maurice Wallerstein. New York: Macmillan.

Bel Hadj Zekri, Abderazak. 2009. "Migration et société civile en Tunisie." in *CARIM Notes d'analyse et de synthèse 14*. Florence, Italy: European University Institute (EUI).

Belguendouz, Abdelkrim. 2003. *Le Maroc non africain, gendarme de l'Europe? Alerte au projet de loi n° 02-03 relative à l'entrée et au séjour des étrangers au Maroc, à l'émigration et l'immigration irrégulière*. Salé, Morocco: Imprimerie Beni Snassen.

——— 2009. "Le Maroc et la migration irrégulière, une analyse sociopolitique." Florence Italy: Robert Schuman Center for Advanced Studies, European University Institute.

Bellin, Eva. 1994. "Civil Society: Effective Tool of Analysis for Middle East Politics?" *PS: Political Science and Politics* 27(3):509–10.

——— 1995. "Civil Society in Formation: Tunisia." Pp. 120–47 in *Civil Society in the Middle East*, edited by R. Augustus. Norton. New York: Brill.

Ben-Layashi, Samir, and Bruce Maddy-Weitzman. 2010. "Myth, History and Realpolitik: Morocco and its Jewish Community." *Journal of Modern Jewish Studies* 9(1):89–106.

Ben Achour, Olfa. 2015. "De la velléité à la volonté : l'émigration des Juifs de Tunisie de 1943 à 1967, un phènomène complexe." in *History*. Toulouse, France: Toulouse 2, Université de Tunis I.

References

Ben Achour, Souhayma. 2019. "Les libertés individuelles des étrangères et des étrangers en Tunisie: Les métèques de la République." Tunis, Tunisia: Association Tunisienne de Défense des Libertés Individuelles (ATDLI), Heinrich Böll Stiftung.

Ben Ahmed, Mustapha. 2011. "Le rôle des syndicats maghrébins dans la gestion de la migration subsaharienne." Pp. 63–70 in *Le Maghreb et les migrations subsahariennes – Le role des associations et des syndicats*, edited by Rafael Bustos, Olivia Orozco, Lothar Witte, and Ralf Melzer. Tunis, Tunisia: Fondation Friedrich Ebert (FES).

Ben Jemia, Monia. 2006. "Immigration et droit." in *Aspects juridiques des migrations dans l'espace Euro-maghrébin*. Tunis, Tunisia: Faculté des sciences juridiques, politiques et sociales.

2009. "La répression des migrations clandestines en Tunisie." Pp. 267–78 in *Le Maghreb à l'épreuve des migrations subsahariennes*, edited by Ali Bensaâd. Paris, France: Karthala.

Ben Jemia, Monia, and Souhayma Ben Achour. 2014. "Plaidoyer pour une réforme des lois relatives aux migrants, aux étrangers et à la nationalité en Tunisie." Sousse, Tunisia: CeTuMA; EuroMed Rights.

Ben Sedrine, Saïd. 2018. "Défis à relever pour un accueil décent de la migration subsaharienne en Tunisie." Tunis, Tunisia: Friedrich Ebert Stiftung (FES).

Benjelloun, Sara. 2018a. "Mise en œuvre et enjeux diplomatiques de la nouvelle politique migratoire." Pp. 77–121 in *La nouvelle politique migratoire marocaine*, edited by Mehdi Alioua, Jean-Noel Ferrié, and Helmut Reifeld. Rabat, Morocco: Konrad Adenauer Stiftung.

2018b. "Nouvelle politique migratoire et opérations de régularisation." Pp. 35–75 in *La nouvelle politique migratoire marocaine*, edited by Mehdi Alioua, Jean-Noel Ferrié, and Helmut Reifeld. Rabat, Morocco: Konrad Adenauer Stiftung.

Bensaâd, Ali. 2002. "La grande migration africaine à travers le Sahara." *Méditerranée* 99(3–4):41–52.

2005. "Les migrations transsahariennes, une mondialisation par la marge." Pp. 13–36 in *Marges et mondialisation : Les migrations transsahariennes*, edited by Ali Bensaâd. Paris, France: Maghreb-Mashrek.

2015. "L'immigration subsaharienne au Maghreb. Le Maroc entre dans le deuxième âge." Pp. 241–56 in *Migrations en Méditerranée : Permanences et mutations à l'heure des révolutions et des crises*, edited by Camille Schmoll, Helene Thiollet, and Catherine Wihtol de Wenden. Paris, France: CNRS Editions.

Bensadoun, Mickael. 2007. "The (Re)Fashioning of Moroccan National Identity." Pp. 13–35 in *The Maghrib in the New Century: Identity, Religion and Politics*, edited by Bruce Maddy-Weitzman and Daniel Zisenwine. Gainesville: University Press of Florida.

Berriane, Johara. 2015. "Pilgrimage, Spiritual Tourism and the Shaping of Transnational 'Imagined Communities': The Case of the Tidjani Ziyara to Fez." *International Journal of Religious Tourism and Pilgrimage* 3(2):1–10.

Berriane, Mohamed, Hein de Haas, and Katharina Natter. 2015. "Revisiting Moroccan Migrations." *The Journal of North African Studies* 20(4):503–21.

2021. "Social Transformations and Migrations in Morocco." in *International Migration Institute Working Paper 171*. Amsterdam, the Netherlands.

Betts, Alexander. 2021. "Refugees And Patronage: A Political History Of Uganda's 'Progressive' Refugee Policies." *African Affairs* 120(479):243–76.

Bhambra, Gurminder K. 2014. *Connected Sociologies*. London, UK: Bloomsbury Academic.

Bhambra, Gurminder K., Yolande Bouka, Randolph B. Persaud, Olivia U. Rutazibwa, Vineet Thakur, Duncan Bell, Karen Smith, Toni Haastrup, and Seifudein Adem. 2020. "Why Is Mainstream International Relations Blind to Racism? Ignoring the Central Role of Race and Colonialism in World Affairs Precludes an Accurate Understanding of the Modern State System." *Foreign Policy*, 3 July.

Bierschenk, Thomas, and Jean-Pierre Olivier de Sardan (Eds.). 2015. *States at Work: Dynamics of African Bureaucracies*. Leiden, the Netherlands: Brill.

Blair, Christopher, Guy Grossman, and Jeremy M. Weinstein. 2020. "Forced Displacement and Asylum Policy in the Developing World." Stanford/ETH Zürich: Immigration Policy Lab.

Blair, Harry. 1997. "Donors, Democratisation and Civil Society: Relating Theory to Practice." Pp. 23–42 in *Too Close for Comfort? NGOs, States and Donors*, edited by David Hulme and Michael Edwards. London, UK: Macmillan.

Boesen, Elisabeth, and Laurence Marfaing (Eds.). 2007. *Les Nouveaux Urbains dans l'espace Sahara-Sahel: Un cosmopolitisme par le bas*. Paris, France: Karthala-ZMO.

Bonjour, Saskia. 2011. "The Power and Morals of Policy Makers: Reassessing the Control Gap Debate." *International Migration Review* 45(1):89–122.

Boswell, Christina. 2003. "The 'external dimension' of EU Immigration and Asylum Policy." *International Affairs* 79(3):619–38.

2007a. "Migration Control in Europe after 9/11: Explaining the Absence of Securitization." *JCMS-Journal of Common Market Studies* 45(3):589–610.

2007b. "Theorizing Migration Policy: Is There a Third Way?" *International Migration Review* 41(1):75–100.

Boubakri, Amor. 2007. "L'adhésion de la Tunisie aux instruments internationaux relatifs aux réfugiés." *Etudes Internationales* 105:93–118.

Boubakri, Hassen. 2004. "Transit Migration between Tunisia, Libya and Sub-Saharan Africa: Study Based on Greater Tunis." in *Regional Conference on "Migrants in Transit Countries: Sharing Responsibility for Management and Protection"*. Istanbul, Turkey.

2009. "L'administration des migrations irrégulières par l'Etat tunisien : dispositifs règlementaires et relations avec l'Europe." Pp. 285–309 in *La politique européenne d'immigration*, edited by Abdelkhaleq Berramdane and Jean Rossetto. Paris, France: Editions Karthala.

2011. "Extraits des interviews avec un visiteur de prison et deux réfugiés ivoiriens en Tunisie." Pp. 35–40 in *Le Maghreb et les migrations subsahariennes – Le role des associations et des syndicats*, edited by Rafael Bustos, Olivia Orozco, Lothar Witte, and Ralf Melzer. Tunis, Tunisia: Fondation Friedrich Ebert (FES).

2013. "Revolution and International Migration in Tunisia." Florence, Italy: European University Institute, Robert Schuman Centre for Advanced Studies, Migration Policy Center (MPC).

2015. "Migration et asile en Tunisie depuis 2011: vers de nouvelles figures migratoires?" *Revue Européenne des Migrations Internationales* 31(3–4):17–39.

Boubakri, Hassen, and Sylvie Mazzella. 2005. "La Tunisie entre transit et immigration : politiques migratoires et conditions d'accueil des migrants africains à Tunis." *Autrepart* 4(36):149–65.

Boubakri, Hassen, and Swanie Potot. 2012. "De l'élan citoyen à la mise en place d'une politique migratoire en Tunisie. L'accueil des réfugiés de Libye en 2011." *Migrations Société* 24(143):121–38.

Boukhars, Anouar. 2011. *Politics in Morocco – Executive Monarchy and Enlightened Authoritarianism*. New York: Routledge.

Boukhssass, Mohammed Karim. 2020. "Irregular Migrants and Coronavirus: A Double Suffering." Rabat, Morocco: Moroccan Institute for Policy Analysis (MIPA).

Brachet, Julien, Armelle Choplin, and Olivier Pliez. 2011. "Le Sahara entre espace de circulation et frontière migratoire de l'Europe." *Hérodote* 142(3):163–82.

Brand, Laurie A. 2002. "States and Their Expatriates: Explaining the Development of Tunisian and Moroccan Emigration-Related Institutions." San Diego, CA: The Center for Comparative Immigration Studies (CCIS).

2006. *Citizens Abroad – Emigration and the State in the Middle East and North Africa*. Cambridge, UK: Cambridge University Press.

2014. "Arab Uprisings and the Changing Frontiers of Transnational Citizenship: Voting from Abroad in Political Transitions." *Political Geography* 41:54–63.

Bredeloup, Sylvie, and Olivier Pliez. 2005. "Migrations entre les deux rives du Sahara." *Autrepart* 36(4):3–20.

Breunig, Christian, Xun Cao, and Adam Luedtke. 2012. "Global Migration and Political Regime Type: A Democratic Disadvantage." *British Journal of Political Science* 42:825–54.

Brobbey, Collins Adu-Bempah. 2018. "Democratization and Legitimization of Xenophobia in Ghana." Pp. 69–79 in *The Political Economy of Xenophobia in Africa*, edited by Adeoye O. Akinola. Cham, Switzerland: Springer International Publishing.

Brooker, Paul. 2014. *Non-Democratic Regimes: Theory, Government, and Politics*. Basingstoke, UK: Palgrave Macmillan.

Brubaker, Rogers. 1992. *Citizenship and Nationhood in France and Germany*. Cambridge, MA: Harvard University Press.

Brumberg, Daniel. 2002. "Democratization in the Arab World? The Trap of Liberalized Autocracy." *Journal of Democracy* 13(4):56–68.

Bueno de Mesquita, Bruce, Alastair Smith, Randolph M. Siverson, and James D. Morrow. 2003. *The Logic of Political Survival*. Cambridge, MA: MIT Press.

Bustos, Rafael, Olivia Orozco, Lothar Witte, and Ralf Melzer. 2011. "Le Maghreb et les migrations subsahariennes – Le role des associations et des syndicats." Tunis, Tunisia: FES.

Calavita, Kitty. 1992. *Inside the State: The Bracero Program, Immigration and the INS*. New York: Routledge.
Camau, Michel, and Vincent Geisser. 2003. *Le syndrome autoritaire: Politique en Tunisie de Bourguiba à Ben Ali*. Paris, France: Presses de SciencesPo.
Carens, Joseph. 2013. *The Ethics of Immigration*. Oxford, UK: Oxford University Press.
CARIM. 2003. "Refugee Population in Tunisia, 1993–2002." in *Demographic & Economic Module* edited by Consortium for Applied Research on International Migration (CARIM). Florence, Italy.
――― 2010. "Foreign Students in Tunisia, 1996–2009." in *Demographic & Economic Module* edited by Consortium for Applied Research on International Migration (CARIM). Florence, Italy.
Carruthers, Susan L. 2005. "Between Camps: Eastern Bloc 'Escapees' and Cold War Borderlands." *American Quarterly* 57(3):991–42.
Cassani, Andrea, and Luca Tomini. 2020. "Reversing Regimes and Concepts: From Democratization to Autocratization." *European Political Science* 19(2):272–87.
Cassarini, Camille. 2020. "L'immigration subsaharienne en Tunisie: De la reconnaissance d'un fait social à la création d'un enjeu gestionnaire." *Migrations Société* 179(1):43–57.
Cassarino, Jean-Pierre. 2007. "Informalising Readmission Agreements in the EU Neighbourhood." *The International Spectator* 42(2):179–96.
――― 2014. "Channelled Policy Transfers: EU-Tunisia Interactions on Migration Matters." *European Journal of Migration and Law* 16:97–123.
Castells, Manuel. 1975. "Immigrant Workers and Class Struggles in Advanced Capitalism: The Western European Experience." *Politics and Society* 5(1):33–66.
Castles, Stephen. 2004. "The Factors that Make and Unmake Migration Policies." *International Migration Review* 38(3):852–84.
Castles, Stephen, Hein de Haas, and Mark J. Miller. 2014. *The Age of Migration: International Population Movements in the Modern World*. Basingstoke, UK: Palgrave Macmillan.
Castles, Stephen, and Godula Kosack. 1985. *Immigrant Workers and Class Structure in Western Europe*. New York: Oxford University Press.
Cavatorta, Francesco (Ed.). 2012. *Civil Society Activism under Authoritarian Rule – A Comparative Perspective*. London, UK: Routledge.
Cavatorta, Francesco, and Emanuela Dalmasso. 2009. "Liberal Outcomes through Undemocratic Means: The Reform of the Code de statut personnel in Morocco." *Journal of Modern African Studies* 47(4):487–506.
Charmaz, Kathy. 2014. *Constructing Grounded Theory : A Practical Guide through Qualitative Analysis*. London, UK: SAGE Publications.
Cherti, Myriam, and Michael Collyer. 2015. "Immigration and Pensée d'Etat: Moroccan Migration Policy Changes as Transformation of 'Geopolitical Culture'." *Journal of North African Studies* 20(4):590–604.
Choate, Mark I. 2010. "Tunisia, Contested: Italian Nationalism, French Imperial Rule, and Migration in the Mediterranean Basin." *California Italian Studies* 1(1):1–20.

Chung, Erin A. 2010. "Workers or Residents? Diverging Patterns of Immigrant Incorporation in Korea and Japan." *Pacific Affairs* 83(4):675–96.

Cimade, and AFVIC-PFM. 2004. "Gourougou, Bel Younes, Oujda : la situation alarmante des migrants subsahariens en transit au Maroc et les conséquences des politiques de l'UE." Paris, France: La Cimade-SSI.

CMSM, and GADEM. 2012. "Recrudescence de la répression envers les migrants au Maroc – Une violence qu'on croyait révolue." Conseil des migrants subsahariens au Maroc (CMSM); Groupe antiraciste d'accompagnement et de défense des étrangers et migrants (GADEM).

CNDH. 2013. "Etrangers et droits de l'homme au Maroc: Pour une politique d'asile et d'immigration radicalement nouvelle (résumé exécutif)." Rabat, Morocco: Conseil National des Droits de l'Homme.

2014. "Opération exceptionnelle de régularisation: Commission nationale de suivi et de recours."

2015. "Migration : La Commission nationale de recours adopte de nouvelles mesures permettant de régulariser 92% des étrangers ayant déposé des demandes de régularisation." Rabat, Morocco: Conseil national des droits de l'Homme.

Cohen, Michael D., James G. March and Johan P. Olsen. 1972. "A Garbage Can Model of Organizational Choice." *Administrative Science Quarterly* 17 (1):1–25.

Cole, Phillip. 2000. *Philosophies of Exclusion: Liberal Political Theory and Immigration*. Edinburgh, Scotland: Edinburgh University Press.

2012. "Taking Moral Equality Seriously: Egalitarianism and Immigration Controls." *Journal of International Political Theory* 8(1–2):121–34.

Coleda, Michel. 1953. "La main d'oeuvre étrangère en Tunisie." *Bulletin Economique et Social de la Tunisie* 81:58–66.

Collyer, Michael. 2006. "States of Insecurity: Consequences of Saharan Transit Migration." in Working Paper No. 31. Oxford, UK: Centre on Migration, Policy and Society (COMPAS), University of Oxford.

Comaroff, Jean, and John L. Comaroff. 2012. "Theory from the South: Or, How Euro-America is Evolving Toward Africa." *Anthropological Forum* 22(2):113–31.

Connell, Raewyn. 2007. *Southern Theory: The Global Dynamics of Knowledge in Social Science*. Cambridge, UK: Polity Press.

2018. "Decolonizing Sociology." *Contemporary Sociology* 47(4):399–407.

Coppedge, Michael, John Gerring, Carl Henrik Knutsen, Staffan I. Lindberg, Jan Teorell, David Altman, Michael Bernhard, M. Steven Fish, Adam Glynn, Allen Hicken, Anna Luhrmann, Kyle L. Marquardt, Kelly McMann, Pamela Paxton, Daniel Pemstein, Brigitte Seim, Rachel Sigman, Svend-Erik Skaaning, Jeffrey Staton, Steven Wilson, Agnes Cornell, Nazifa Alizada, Lisa Gastaldi, Haakon Gjerløw, Garry Hindle, Nina Ilchenko, Laura Maxwell, Valeriya Mechkova, Juraj Medzihorsky, Johannes von Römer, Aksel Sundström, Eitan Tzelgov, Yi-ting Wang, Tore Wig, and Daniel Ziblatt. 2020. "V-Dem Country–Year Dataset v10," edited by Varieties of Democracy (V-Dem) Project.

Cornelius, Wayne A., Takeyuki Tsuda, Philip L. Martin and James F. Hollifield (Eds.). 2004. *Controlling Immigration: A Global Perspective*. Stanford, CA: Stanford University Press.

Coyault, Bernard. 2015. "Les « églises de maison » congolaises de Rabat : la participation du secteur (religieux) informel à la pluralisation religieuse au Maroc." Pp. 55–64 in *Migrants au Maroc: Cosmopolitisme, présence d'étrangers et transformations sociales*, edited by Nadia Khrouz and Nazarena Lanza. Rabat, Morocco: Konrad-Adenauer-Stiftung.

Cubertafond, Bernard. 2001. *La vie politique au Maroc*. Paris, France: L'Harmattan.

Cuttitta, Paolo. 2020. "Non-governmental/Civil Society Organisations and the European Union-externalisation of Migration Management in Tunisia and Egypt." *Population, Space and Place* 26(7):e2329.

Czaika, Mathias, and Hein de Haas. 2013. "The Effectiveness of Immigration Policies." *Population and Development Review* 39(3):487–508.

Czaika, Mathias, Hein de Haas, and Maria Villares-Varela. 2018. "The Global Evolution of Travel Visa Regimes." *Population and Development Review* 3 (3):589–622.

Dahl, Adam. 2018. *Empire of the People: Settler Colonialism and the Foundations of Modern Democratic Thought*. Lawrence, KA: University Press of Kansas.

de Haas, Hein. 2003. *Migration and Development in Southern Morocco: The Disparate Socio-Economic Impact of Out-Migration on the Todgha Oasis Valley*. Amsterdam, The Netherlands: University of Amsterdam Press.

2007a. "Between Courting and Controlling: The Moroccan State and 'its' Emigrants." in Working Paper No. 54. Oxford, UK: Centre on Migration, Policy and Society (COMPAS), University of Oxford.

2007b. "Morocco's Migration Experience: A Transitional Perspective." *International Migration* 45(4):39–70.

2007c. "The Myth of Invasion: Irregular Migration from West Africa to the Maghreb and the European Union." Oxford, UK: International Migration Institute, University of Oxford.

2014a. "Chapitre 2: Un siècle de migrations marocaines : Transformations, transitions et perspectives d'avenir." Pp. 61–91 in *Marocains de l'Extérieur 2013*, edited by Mohamed Berriane. Rabat, Morocco: Fondation Hassan II pour les Marocains Résidant à l'Etranger & OIM.

2014b. "Morocco: Setting the Stage for Becoming a Migration Transition Country?". Washington, DC: Migration Policy Institute (MPI).

de Haas, Hein, Katharina Natter, and Simona Vezzoli. 2018. "Growing Restrictiveness or Changing Selection? The Nature and Evolution of Migration Policies." *International Migration Review* 52(2):314–67.

de Haas, Hein, and Simona Vezzoli. 2011. "Leaving Matters: The Nature, Evolution and Effects of Emigration Policies." Oxford, UK: International Migration Institute, University of Oxford.

Deane, Shelley. 2013. "Transforming Tunisia: The Role of Civil Society in Tunisia's Transition." London, UK: International Alert.

DEMIG. 2015. "DEMIG C2C, version 1.2, Full Internal Edition." edited by University of Oxford International Migration Institute (IMI). Oxford, UK.

Diallo, Alimou. 2016. "Démarcher auprès de la bureaucratie locale pour un titre de séjour au Maroc: Sociologie historique des démarches administratives" in *Doctoral Seminar, École de gouvernance et d'économie (EGE)*. Rabat, Morocco.

References

Dinas, Elias, Vasiliki Fouka, and Alain Schläpfer. 2021. "Family History and Attitudes toward Out-Groups: Evidence from the European Refugee Crisis." *The Journal of Politics* 83(2):647–61.

Dini, Sabine, and Caterina Giusa. 2020. *Externalising Migration Governance Through Civil Society. Tunisia as a Case Study*. London, UK: Palgrave Macmillan.

Djebali, Taoufik. 2005. "Ethnicity and Power in North Africa: Tunisia, Algeria and Morocco." in *Race and Nation: Ethnic Systems in the Modern World*, edited by Paul Spickard. New York: Routledge.

El Hamel, Chouki. 2012. *Black Morocco: A History of Slavery, Race, and Islam*. Cambridge, UK: Cambridge University Press.

El Qadim, Nora. 2010. "La politique migratoire européenne vue du Maroc : Contraintes et opportunités." *Politique Européenne* 31:91–118.

———. 2015. *Le gouvernement asymétrique des migrations : Maroc-Union Européenne*. Paris, France: Dalloz.

Ellermann, Antje. 2013. "When Can Liberal States Avoid Unwanted Immigration? Self-Limited Sovereignty and Guest Worker Recruitment in Switzerland and Germany." *World Politics* 65(3):491–538.

Entman, Robert M. 1993. "Framing: Toward Clarification of a Fractured Paradigm." *Journal of Communication* 43(4):51–58.

Escribà-Folch, Abel, and Joseph Wright. 2015. *Foreign Pressure and the Politics of Autocratic Survival*. Oxford, UK: Oxford University Press.

Eule, Tobias. 2014. *Inside Immigration Law: Migration Management and Policy Application in Germany*. Farnham, UK: Ashgate.

Fargues, Philippe. 2013. EU Neighbourhood Migration Report 2013. Florence, Italy: Migration Policy Centre (MPC), European University Institute (EUI).

Fargues, Philippe, and Christine Fandrich. 2012. "Migration after the Arab Spring." in *Migration Policy Center (MPC) Research Report 9*. Florence, Italy: European University Institute (EUI).

Feenstra, Robert C., Robert Inklaar, and Marcel P. Timmer. 2015. "The Next Generation of the Penn World Table." *American Economic Review* 105 (10):3150–82.

Feliu Martínez, Laura. 2009. "Les migrations en transit au Maroc. Attitudes et comportement de la société civile face au phénomène" *L'Année du Maghreb* 5:343–62.

Ferrié, Jean-Noel, and Mehdi Alioua. 2018. "Politiques migratoires et sérénité de l'action publique." Pp. 19–34 in *La nouvelle politique migratoire marocaine*, edited by Mehdi Alioua, Jean-Noel Ferrié, and Helmut Reifeld. Rabat, Morocco: Konrad Adenauer Stiftung.

Fiddian-Qasmiyeh, Elena. 2020. "Recentering the South in Studies of Migration." *Migration and Society* 3:1–18.

FIDH/GADEM. 2015. "Maroc. Entre rafles et régularisation: Bilan d'une politique migratoire indécise." Paris, France: Fédération internationale des ligues des droits de l'Homme (FIDH)/Le Groupe antiraciste d'accompagnement et de défense des étrangers et migrants (GADEM).

Filomeno, Felipe A., and Thomas J. Vicino. 2020. "The Evolution of Authoritarianism and Restrictionism in Brazilian Immigration Policy: Jair Bolsonaro in Historical Perspective." *Bulletin of Latin American Research*.

Findlay, Allan M. 1980. "Patterns and Processes of Tunisian Migration." in Department of Geography. Durham, UK: Durham University.
FitzGerald, David Scott. 2006. "Inside the Sending State: The Politics of Mexican Emigration Control." *International Migration Review* 40(2):259–93.
FitzGerald, David Scott, and David Cook-Martín. 2014. *Culling the Masses: The Democratic Origins of Racist Immigration Policy in the Americas*. Cambridge, MA: Harvard University Press.
FitzGerald, David Scott, and Asher Hirsch. 2022. "Norm-busting: Rightist Challenges in US and Australian Immigration and Refugee Policies." *Third World Quarterly* 43(7):1587–1606.
Florio, Erminia. 2019. "The Legacy of Historical Emigration: Evidence from Italian Municipalities." Tor Vergata University, CEIS.
Freeman, Gary P. 1995. "Modes of Immigration Politics in Liberal-Democratic States." *International Migration Review* 29(4):881–902.
Freier, Luisa F. 2013. "Open Doors (for Almost all): Visa Policies and Ethnic Selectivity in Ecuador." in London School of Economics (LSE) Working Paper 188. London, UK.
FRONTEX. 2011. "FRAN Quarterly, Issue 1, January–March 2011." Warsaw, Poland: FRONTEX.
Frowd, Philippe M. 2020. "Producing the 'transit' Migration State: International Security Intervention in Niger." *Third World Quarterly* 41(2):340–58.
FTDES, and Migreurop. 2020. "Politiques du non-accueil en Tunisie: Des acteurs humanitaires au service des politiques sécuritaires européennes." Tunis, Tunisia: Forum Tunisien pour les Droits Economiques et Sociaux & Migreurop.
GADEM. 2010. "Note à l'intention du Comité de lutte contre les discriminations raciales." Groupe antiraciste d'accompagnement et de défense des étrangers et migrants (GADEM).
2018. "Couts et blessures. Rapport sur les opérations des forces de l'ordre menées dans le nord du Maroc entre juillet et septembre 2018: Éléments factuels et analyse." Rabat, Maroc: Groupe antiraciste d'accompagnement et de défense des étrangers et migrants (GADEM).
GADEM, and Anafé. 2017. "Privés de liberté en « zone de transit » – Des aéroports français aux aéroports marocains." Groupe antiraciste d'accompagnement et de défense des étrangers migrants; Association nationale d'assistance aux frontières pour les étrangers.
Gamlen, Alan. 2008. "The Emigration State and the Modern Geopolitical Imagination." *Political Geography* 27(8):840–56.
Garcés-Mascareñas, Blanca. 2012. *Labour Migration in Malaysia and Spain: Markets, Citizenship and Rights*. Amsterdam, The Netherlands: Amsterdam University Press.
Garelli, Glenda, Federica Sossi, and Martina Tazzioli. 2015. "Migrants in Tunisia: Detained and Deported." Storiemigranti.
Garelli, Glenda, and Martina Tazzioli. 2017. *Tunisia as a Revolutionized Space of Migration*. New York: Palgrave Macmillan.
Gazzotti, Lorena. 2021a. *Immigration Nation. Aid, Control and Border Politics in Morocco*. Cambridge, UK: Cambridge University Press.
2021b. "(Un)making Illegality: Border Control, Racialized Bodies and Differential Regimes of Illegality in Morocco." *The Sociological Review*.

Gazzotti, Lorena, Melissa Mouthaan, and Katharina Natter. 2022. *Embracing Complexity in 'Southern' Migration Governance, Territory, Politics, Governance.* (online first).

Geddes, Andrew. 2003. *The Politics of Migration and Immigration in Europe.* London: Sage.

Geisser, Vincent. 2019. "Tunisie, des migrants subsahariens toujours exclus du rêve démocratique." *Migrations Société* 177(3):3–18.

George, Alexander L., and Andrew Bennett. 2005. *Case Studies and Theory Development in the Social Sciences.* Cambridge, MA: MIT Press.

Gisselquist, Rachel M., and Finn Tarp. 2019. "Migration Governance and Policy in the Global South: Introduction and Overview." *International Migration* 57 (4):247–53.

Giusa, Caterina. 2018. "« On a fait la révolution pour être libres. Libres de partir »: Les départs des harragas de la Tunisie en révolution." *Mouvements* 93:99–106.

Givens, Terri, and Adam Luedtke. 2005. "European Immigration Policies in Comparative Perspective: Issue Salience, Partisanship and Immigrant Rights." *Comparative European Politics* 3:1–22.

Glasius, Marlies, Meta de Lange, Jos Bartman, Emanuela Dalmasso, Aofei Lv, Adele Del Sordi, Marcus Michaelsen, and Kris Ruijgrok. 2018. *Research, Ethics and Risk in the Authoritarian Field.* London, UK: Palgrave Macmillan.

Gobe, Éric, and Larbi Chouikha. 2014. "La Tunisie politique en 2013 : de la bipolarisation idéologique au « consensus constitutionnel » ?" *L'Année du Maghreb* 11:301–22.

Golash-Boza, Tanya Maria. 2012. *Immigration Nation: Raids, Detentions, and Deportations in Post-9/11 America.* Abingdon, UK: Routledge.

Goldschmidt, Elie. 2004. "Etudiants et migrants congolais au Maroc: politiques d'accueil et strategies migratoires." Pp. 149–71 in *Les relations transsahariennes à l'époque contemporaine,* edited by Steffen Wippel and Laurence Marfaing. Paris, France: Karthala.

Gränzer, Siegelinde. 1999. "Changing Discourse: Transnational Advocacy Networks in Tunisia and Morocco." Pp. 109–33 in *The Power of Human Rights – International Norms and Domestic Change,* edited by Thomas Risse, Stephen C. Ropp, and Kathryn Sikkink. Cambridge, UK: Cambridge University Press.

Greenhill, Kelly M. 2010. *Weapons of Mass Migration: Forced Displacement, Coercion, and Foreign Policy.* Ithaca, NY: Cornell University Press.

2016. "Open Arms Behind Barred Doors: Fear, Hypocrisy and Policy Schizophrenia in the European Migration Crisis." *European Law Journal* 22(3):317–32.

Grindle, Merilee S., and John W. Thomas. 1991. *Public Choices and Policy Change – The Political Economy of Reform in Developing Countries.* Baltimore, MD: Johns Hopkins University Press.

Guild, Elspeth, Kees Groenendijk, and Sergio Carrera. 2009. *Illiberal Liberal States: Immigration, Citizenship and Integration in the EU.* London, UK: Routledge.

Guiraudon, Virginie, and Gallya Lahav. 2000. "A Reappraisal of the State Sovereignty Debate: The Case of Migration Control." *Comparative Political Studies* 33(2):163–95.

Gurowitz, Amy. 1999. "Mobilizing International Norms: Domestic Actors, Immigrants, and the Japanese State." *World Politics* 51(3):413–45.

Hagelund, Anniken. 2020. "After the Refugee Crisis: Public Discourse and Policy Change in Denmark, Norway and Sweden." *Comparative Migration Studies* 8(1):13.
Hall, Peter. 1997. "The Role of Interests, Institutions, and Ideas in the Comparative Political Economy of the Industrialized Nations " Pp. 174–207 in *Comparative Politics: Rationality, Culture, and Structure*, edited by Mark I. Lichbach and Alan S. Zuckerman. Cambridge, UK: Cambridge University Press.
      2006. "Systematic Process Analysis: When and How to Use It." *European Management Review* 3:24–31.
Hall, Peter A., and Rosemary C.R. Taylor. 1996. "Political Science and the Three New Institutionalisms." *Political Studies* 44(5):936–57.
Hamlin, Rebecca. 2014. *Let Me Be a Refugee: Administrative Justice and the Politics of Asylum in the United States, Canada, and Australia*. Oxford, UK: Oxford University Press.
Hammar, Thomas (Ed.). 1985. *European Immigration Policy: A Comparative Study*. Cambridge, Uk: Cambridge University Press.
Hampshire, James. 2013. "Immigration and the Liberal State." Pp. 1–15 in *The Politics of Immigration*, edited by James Hampshire. Cambridge, UK: Polity Press.
Hannoum, Abdelmajid. 2020. *Living Tangier. Migration, Race, and Illegality in a Moroccan City*. Philadelphia, PA: Penn Press.
Hansen, Randall. 2002. "Globalization, Embedded Realism, and Path Dependence. The Other Immigrants to Europe." *Comparative Political Studies* 35(3):259–83.
Harbeson, John W., Donald Rothchild, and Naomi Chazan (Eds.). 1994. *Civil Society and the State in Africa*. Boulder, CO: Lynne Rienner.
Hart, David M. 2000. "Tribalism: The Backbone of the Moroccan Nation." Pp. 7–22 in *Tribe and Society in Rural Morocco*, edited by David M. Hart. London, UK: Frank Cass Publishers.
Hartigan, Kevin. 1992. "Matching Humanitarian Norms with Cold, Hard Interests: The Making of Refugee Policies in Mexico and Honduras, 1980–89." *International Organization* 46(3):709–30.
Hassani-Idrissi, Mostafa. 2015. "Manuels d'histoire et identité nationale au Maroc." *Revue internationale d'éducation de Sèvres* 69:53–64.
Hassenteufel, Patrick. 2008. *Sociologie politique: L'action publique*. Paris, France: Armand Colin.
Haug, Sebastian, Jacqueline Braveboy-Wagner, and Günther Maihold. 2021. "The 'Global South' in the Study of World Politics: Examining a Meta Category." *Third World Quarterly* 42(9):1923–44.
Haugen, Heidi O. 2015. "Destination China: The Country Adjusts to its New Migration Reality." in *Migration Information Source*. Washington, DC: Migration Policy Institute.
Haus, Leah. 1999. "Labor Unions and Immigration Policy in France." *International Migration Review* 33(3):683–716.
HCP. 2009. "Les résidents étrangers au Maroc." Rabat, Morocco: Haut Commissariat au Plan (HCP).

2015. "Note sur les premiers résultats du Recensement Général de la Population et de l'Habitat 2014." Rabat, Morocco: Haut Commissariat au Plan (HCP).

2020. "Résultats de l'Enquête Nationale sur la Migration Internationale 2018–2019." Rabat, Morocco: Haut Commissariat au Plan (HCP).

Henninger, Jakob, and Friederike Römer. 2021. "Choose Your Battles. How Civil Society Organisations Choose Context-Specific Goals and Activities to Fight for Immigrant Welfare Rights in Malaysia and Argentina." *Social Policy & Administration*:1–17.

Herbst, Jeffrey. 2000. *States and Power in Africa: Comparative Lessons in Authority and Control*. Princeton, NJ: Princeton University Press.

Hertog, Steffen. 2013. "State and Private Sector in the GCC after the Arab Uprisings." *Journal of Arabian Studies* 3(2):174–95.

Hibou, Béatrice. 2005. "The 'Privatization' of the State: North Africa in Comparative Perspective." Pp. 71–95 in *The Dynamics of States: The Formation and Crises of State Domination*, edited by Klaus Schlichte. Aldershot, UK: Ashgate.

2006. *La force de l'obéissance: Economie politique de la répression en Tunisie*. Paris, France: La Découverte.

2010. "Tunisia: Discipline and reform – I." in *Sociétés politiques comparées*. Paris, France: FASOPO.

2015a. "La formation asymétrique de l'État en Tunisie. Les territoires de l'injustice." Pp. 99–149 in *L'État d'injustice au Maghreb. Maroc et Tunisie*, edited by Irene Bono, Béatrice Hibou, Hamza Meddeb, and Mohamed Tozy. Paris, France: Editions Karthala.

2015b. "Le bassin minier de Gafsa en déshérence : Gouverner le mécontentement social en Tunisie." Pp. 301–77 in *L'État d'injustice au Maghreb. Maroc et Tunisie*, edited by Irene Bono, Béatrice Hibou, Hamza Meddeb, and Mohamed Tozy. Paris, France: CERI.

Hibou, Béatrice, and Mohamed Tozy. 2015. "Une lecture wébérienne de la trajectoire de l'Etat au Maroc." *Sociétés politiques comparées – Revue européenne d'analyse des sociétés politiques* 37:1–22.

Hicken, Allen. 2011. "Clientelism." *Annual Review of Political Science* 14(1):289–310.

Hinnebusch, Raymond. 2015. "Change and Continuity after the Arab Uprising: The Consequences of State Formation in Arab North African States." *British Journal of Middle Eastern Studies* 42(1):12–30.

Hobson, John M. 2012. *The Eurocentric Conception of World Politics: Western International Theory, 1760–2010*. Cambridge, UK: Cambridge University Press.

Hollifield, James F. 1992a. *Immigrants, Markets, and States: The Political Economy of Postwar Europe*. Cambridge, MA: Harvard University Press.

1992b. "Migration and International Relations: Cooperation and Control in the European Community." *International Migration Review* 23(2):568–95.

2004. "The Emerging Migration State." *International Migration Review* 38(3):885–912.

HRW. 2014. "Abused and Expelled: Ill-Treatment of Sub-Saharan African Migrants in Morocco." Human Rights Watch (HRW).

Hujo, Katja, and Nicola Piper. 2007. "South–South Migration: Challenges for Development and Social Policy." *Development* 50(4):19–25.

Huysmans, Jef. 2009. *The Politics of Insecurity. Fear, Migration and Asylum in the EU*. New York: Routledge.

IACE. 2016. "Rapport National sur l'Emploi 2016." Tunis, Tunisia: Institut Arabe des Chefs d'Entreprise (IACE).

ILO. 2018. "Women and Men in the Informal Economy: A Statistical Picture (third edition)." Geneva, Switzerland: International Labor Organization (ILO).

Infantino, Federica. 2010. "La frontière au guichet. Politiques et pratiques des visas Schengen aux Consulat et à l'Ambassade d'Italie au Maroc." *Champ pénal / Penal field, nouvelle revue internationale de criminologie* VII.

2011. "Les mondes des étudiants subsahariens au Maroc." Pp. 101–19 in *D'une Afrique à l'Autre: Migrations subsahariennes au Maroc*, edited by Michel Peraldi. Rabat, Morocco: Editions Karthala.

INS. 2015. "Recensement général de la Population et l'Habitat 2014." Tunis, Tunisia: Institut National de la Statistique (INS).

IOM. 2012. "Humanitarian Response to the Libyan Crisis in 2011." Geneva, Switzerland: International Organization for Migration.

2013. "Etude exploratoire sur la traite des personnes en Tunisie." Tunis, Tunisia: International Organization for Migration.

Iskander, Natasha. 2010. *Creative State – Forty Years of Migration and Development Policy in Morocco and Mexico*. Ithaca, NY: ILR Press.

J.O.R.T. 2004. "Official Bulletin: Deliberations in Parliament – Draft Law Relating to the Revision and Completion of Law No. 40 of 1975 dated May 14, 1975 Concerning Passports." Pp. 786–802, edited by Chambre des Représentants. Tunis, Tunisia: Republic of Tunisia.

J/TIP. 2017. "Trafficking in Persons Report – June 2017." Washington, DC: Office to Monitor and Combat Trafficking in Persons, U.S. Department of State.

Jackson, Robert H., and Carl G. Rosberg. 1982. "Why Africa's Weak States Persist: The Empirical and the Juridical in Statehood." *World Politics* 35(1):1–24.

Jaulin, Thibaut, and Björn Nilsson. 2015. "Voter ici et là-bas : les Tunisiens à l'étranger depuis 2011." *Revue Européenne des Migrations Internationales* 31(3&4):41–71.

Jones, Charles O. 1970. *An Introduction to the Study of Public Policy*. Belmont, CA: Duxbury Press.

Joppke, Christian. 1998. "Why Liberal States Accept Unwanted Immigration." *World Politics* 50(2):266–93.

Joseph Mbembe, Achille. 2016. "Decolonizing the University: New Directions." *Arts and Humanities in Higher Education* 15(1):29–45.

Just, Aida. 2019. "Political Regimes and Immigrant Party Preferences." *Comparative Political Studies* 52(5):651–86.

Karadağ, Sibel. 2019. "Extraterritoriality of European Borders to Turkey: An Implementation Perspective of Counteractive Strategies." *Comparative Migration Studies* 7(1):12.

References

Karibi, Khadija. 2015. "Migrants subsahariens à Rabat, une entrée spatiale : l'épreuve des espaces publics." Pp. 165–71 in *Migrants au Maroc: Cosmopolitisme, présence d'étrangers et transformations sociales*, edited by Nadia Khrouz and Nazarena Lanza. Rabat, Morocco: Konrad-Adenauer-Stiftung.

Kaur, Amarjit. 2014. "Managing Labour Migration in Malaysia: Guest Worker Programs and the Regularisation of Irregular Labour Migrants as a Policy Instrument." *Asian Studies Review* 38(3):345–66.

Keck, Margaret E., and Kathryn Sikkink. 1998. *Activists Beyond Borders: Advocacy Networks in International Politics*. Ithaca, NY: Cornell University Press.

Kemp, Adriana, and Nelly Kfir. 2016. "Mobilizing Migrant Workers' Rights in "Nonimmigration" Countries: The Politics of Resonance and Migrants' Rights Activism in Israel and Singapore." *Law & Society Review* 50(1):82–116.

Khrouz, Nadia. 2011. "La situation des migrants subsahariens au Maghreb du point de vue des associations maghrébines." Pp. 43–52 in *Le Maghreb et les migrations subsahariennes – Le role des associations et des syndicats*, edited by Rafael Bustos, Olivia Orozco, Lothar Witte, and Ralf Melzer. Tunis, Tunisia: Fondation Friedrich Ebert (FES).

2016. "La pratique du droit des étrangers au Maroc : essai de praxéologie juridique et politique." in Department of Political Sciences. France: Université Grenoble Alpes.

2019. *L'étranger au Maroc: Droit et pratiques*. Paris, France: L'Harmattan.

Kimball, Ann. 2007. "The Transit State: A Comparative Analysis of Mexican and Moroccan Immigration Policies." San Diego, CA: The Center for Comparative Immigration Studies (CCIS).

King, Stephen J. 2003. *Liberalization against Democracy: The Local Politics of Economic Reform in Tunisia*. Bloomington: Indiana University Press.

Kingdon, John W. 2003. *Agendas, Alternatives, and Public Policies*. New York: Longman.

Klotz, Audie. 2012. "South Africa as an Immigration State." *Politikon* 39(2):189–208.

2013. *Migration and National Identity in South Africa, 1860–2010*. Cambridge: Cambridge University Press

Koch, Natalie. 2013. "Introduction – Field Methods in "Closed Contexts": Undertaking Research in Authoritarian States and Places." *Area* 45(4):390–39.

Kommers, Donald P. 2012. "Constitutions and National Identity." *The Review of Politics* 74(1):127–33.

Krasner, Stephen. 1978. *Defending the National Interest: Raw Materials Investments and US. Foreign Policy*. Princeton, NJ: Princeton University Press.

Laacher, Smain. 2007. *Le peuple des clandestins*. Paris: Calmann-Lévy.

Labidi, Lassaad, Lotfi Bennour, and Ali Jaidi. 2017. "L'emploi formet et informel des travailleurs immigrés en Tunisie: Cartographie et profils socio-économiques." Tunis, Tunisia: Observatoire National de la Migration (ONM) & Bureau International du Travail (BIT) & Haut Commissariat des Droits de l'Homme (HCDH).

Lacroix, Thomas. 2004. "Contrôle et instrumentalisation de la société civile maghrébine: le cas du Maroc et de la Tunisie." *L'année du Maghreb* I:100–15.

Lacroix, Thomas, Peggy Levitt, and Ilka Vari-Lavoisier. 2016. "Social Remittances and the Changing Transnational Political Landscape." *Comparative Migration Studies* 4(16):1–5.

Lahlou, Mehdi. 2011. "Le Maghreb dans son environnement régional et international : Un schéma migratoire reconfiguré, dans les faits et dans l'approche politique." Paris, France: Ifri-Programme Migrations, identités, citoyenneté.

Lanza, Nazarena. 2011. "Liens et échanges entre le Maroc et l'Afrique subsaharienne: Eléments pour une perspective historique." Pp. 21–35 in *D'une Afrique à l'autre. Migrations subsahariennes au Maroc*, edited by Michel Peraldi. Paris, France: Karthala.

Laouali, Souley Mahamadou, and Jean-Baptiste Meyer. 2012. "Le Maroc, pays d'accueil d'étudiants étrangers." *Hommes et migrations* 1300:114–23.

Larsén, Magdalena Frennhoff. 2007. "Trade Negotiations between the EU and South Africa: A Three-level Game." *Journal of Common Market Studies* 45(4):857–81.

Laube, Lena. 2019. "The Relational Dimension of Externalizing Border Control: Selective Visa Policies in Migration and Border Diplomacy." *Comparative Migration Studies* 7(29):1–22.

Leca, Jean. 2012. "L'état entre politics, policies et polity ou peut-on sortir du triangle des Bermudes ?" *Gouvernement et action publique* 1(1):59–82.

Lemaire, Léa. 2019. "The European Dispositif of Border Control in Malta. Migrants' Experiences of a Securitized Borderland." *Journal of Borderlands Studies* 34(5):171–732.

Levantino, Antonina. 2015. "Mobilité qualifiée et étudiante au Sud et au Nord de la Méditerranée." Pp. 323–42 in *Migrations en Méditerranée : Permanences et mutations à l'heure des révolutions et des crises*, edited by Camille Schmoll, Helene Thiollet, and Catherine Wihtol de Wenden. Paris, France: CNRS Editions.

Levitt, Peggy. 1998. "Social Remittances: Migration Driven Local-Level Forms of Cultural Diffusion." *International Migration Review* 32(4):926–48.

Lewis, David. 2002. "Civil Society in African Contexts: Reflections on the Usefulness of a Concept." *Development and Change* 33(4):569–86.

2013. "Civil Society and the Authoritarian State: Cooperation, Contestation and Discourse." *Journal of Civil Society* 9(3):325–40.

Lipsky, Michael. 1980. *Street-Level Bureaucracy: Dilemmas of the Individual in Public Services*. New York: Russell Sage Foundation.

Liu, Hong, and Els Van Dongen. 2016. "China's Diaspora Policies as a New Mode of Transnational Governance." *Journal of Contemporary China* 25(102):805–21.

Lori, Noora. 2019. *Offshore Citizens: Permanent Temporary Status in the Gulf*. Cambridge, UK: Cambridge University Press.

Maerz, Seraphine F., Amanda B. Edgell, Matthew C. Wilson, Sebastian Hellmeier, and Staffan I. Lindberg. 2021. "A Framework for

References

Understanding Regime Transformation: Introducing the ERT Dataset." in V-Dem Working Paper No.113. Gothenburg, Sweden.

Manby, Bronwen. 2018. *Citizenship in Africa. The Law of Belonging.* Oxford, UK: Hart Publishing.

Marino, Stefania, Judith Roosblad, and Rinus Penninx (Eds.). 2017. *Trade Unions and Migrant Workers: New Contexts and Challenges in Europe.* Cheltenham, UK: Edward Elgar Publishing.

Marshall, Monty G., and Ted Robert Gurr. 2020. "Polity5: Political Regime Characteristics and Transitions, 1800–2018. Dataset Users' Manual." Center for Systemic Peace.

Marzouki, Nadia. 2016. "La transition tunisienne: du compromis démocratique à la réconciliation forcée." *Pouvoirs* 156(1):83–94.

MAS. 2013. "Stratégie Nationale de Migration (SNM)." edited by Secrétariat d'Etat aux Migrations et aux Tunisiens à l'Etranger (SEMTE). Tunis, Tunisia: Ministère des Affaires Sociales.

——— 2015. "Stratégie Nationale Migratoire (SNM)." edited by Secrétariat d'Etat chargé de la Migration et de l'Intégration Sociale (SEMIS). Tunis, Tunisia: Ministère des Affaires Sociales.

——— 2017. "Stratégie Nationale Migratoire (SNM)." edited by Secrétariat d'Etat Chargé de l'Immigration et des Tunisiens à l'Etranger (SEITE). Tunis, Tunisia: Ministère des Affaires Sociales.

Masbah, Mohammed. 2017. "A New Generation of Protests in Morocco? How Hirak al-Rif Endures." Arab Reform Initiative (ARI).

Massey, Douglas S. 1999. "International Migration at the Dawn of the 21st Century: The Role of the State." *Population and Development Review* 25 (2):303–22.

Mayblin, Lucy, and Joe Turner. 2020. *Migration Studies and Colonialism.* Hoboken, NJ: John Wiley & Sons.

Mazepus, Honorata, Wouter Veenendaal, Anthea McCarthy-Jones, and Juan Manuel Trak Vásquez. 2016. "A Comparative Study of Legitimation Strategies in Hybrid Regimes." *Policy Studies* 37(4):350–69.

Mazzella, Sylvie (Ed.). 2009. *La mondialisation étudiante: le Maghreb entre Nord et Sud.* Paris, France: Karthala.

Mbolela, Emmanuel. 2011. "La situation des migrants subsahariens au Maroc vécue et racontée par un migrant congolais." Pp. 23–33 in *Le Maghreb et les migrations subsahariennes – Le role des associations et des syndicats*, edited by Rafael Bustos, Olivia Orozco, Lothar Witte, and Ralf Melzer. Tunis, Tunisia: Fondation Friedrich Ebert (FES).

MCMREAM. 2014. "Stratégie Nationale d'Immigration et d'Asile (SNIA)." edited by Ministère Chargé des Marocains Résidents à l'Etrangers et des Affaires de la Migration. Rabat, Morocco: Royaume du Maroc.

——— 2016. "Politique Nationale d'Immigration et d'Asile 2013–2016." edited by Ministère Chargé des Marocains Résidant à l'Étranger et des Affaires de la Migration. Rabat, Morocco: Royaume du Maroc.

——— 2018. "Politique Nationale d'Immigration et d'Asile: Rapport 2018." edited by Chargé des Marocains Résidant à l'Étranger et des Affaires de la Migration Ministère Délégué auprès du Ministre des Affaires Etrangères et de la Coopération Internationale. Rabat, Morocco: Royaume du Maroc.

Meddeb, Hamza. 2012. "Courir ou mourir. Course à el khobza et domination au quotidien dans la Tunisie de Ben Ali." in *Centre d'Etudes et de Recherches Internationales (CERI)*. Paris, France: Institut d'Etudes Politiques de Paris.

Menin, Laura. 2016. "'Anti-black racism': Debating Racial Prejudices and the Legacies of Slavery in Morocco." in *Shadows of Slavery in West Africa and Beyond Working Paper Series*.

Merolla, Daniela. 2017. "Beyond 'two Africas' in African and Berber Literary Studies." Pp. 215–34 in *The Face of Africa*, edited by Wouter van Beek, Jos Damen, and Dick Foeken. Leiden, the Netherlands: Leiden University, African Studies Centre Leiden.

Meyers, Eytan. 2000. "Theories of International Immigration Policy – A Comparative Analysis." *International Migration Review* 34(4):1245–82.

Migdal, Joel S. 2001. "The State-in-society Approach" in *State in Society – Studying How States and Societies Transform and Constitute One Another*. New York: Cambridge University Press.

Migdal, Joel S., and Klaus Schlichte. 2005. "Rethinking the State." Pp. 1–40 in *The Dynamics of States: The Formation and Crises of State Domination*, edited by Klaus Schlichte. Aldershot, UK: Ashgate.

Migreurop. 2006. "Guerre aux migrants – Le Livre Noir de Ceuta et Melilla." Paris, France: Migreurop.

Miller, David. 2016. *Strangers in Our Midst: The Political Philosophy of Immigration*. Cambridge, MA: Harvard University Press.

Miller, Michael K., and Margaret E. Peters. 2014. "Migration Policy and Autocratic Power." in *Annual Meeting of the American Political Science Association*. Washington, DC.

'2020. "Restraining the Huddled Masses: Migration Policy and Autocratic Survival." *British Journal for Political Science* 50(2):403–33.

Milner, James H.S. 2006. "The Politics of Asylum in Africa: The Cases of Kenya, Tanzania and Guinea." in Department of International Development. Oxford, United Kingdom: University of Oxford.

2009. *Refugees, the State and the Politics of Asylum in Africa*. New York: Palgrave Macmillan.

Mirilovic, Nikola. 2010. "The Politics of Immigration: Dictatorship, Development and Defense." *Comparative Politics* 42(3):273–92.

2015. "Regime Type, International Migration, and the Politics of Dual Citizenship Toleration." *International Political Science Review* 36(5):510–25.

Mitchell, Christopher. 1989. "International Migration, International Relations and Foreign Policy." *International Migration Review* 23(3):681–708.

(Ed.). 1992. *Western Hemisphere Immigration and United States Foreign Policy*. University Park: Penn State University Press.

MoE. 2013. "Circulaire n° 13-487 du 9 octobre 2013 concernant l'intégration des élèves étrangers issus des pays du Sahel et subsahariens dans le système scolaire marocain." edited by Ministère de l'Education Nationale. Rabat, Morocco.

Moghadam, Amin. 2018. "Politics of Citizenship and Migration in a Post-revolutionary Iran" in The Politics of Migration Policies: Towards an Empirically Grounded, Comparative Political Theory of Migration Politics, workshop held on 17–18 December 2018. Paris, France.

Mohamed, Mohamed Hassan. 2010. "Africanists and Africans of the Maghrib: Casualties of Analogy." *The Journal of North African Studies* 15(3):349–74.

MoI. 2020. "Working Session between the Ministers of Interior and Social Affairs and the Minister to the Head of Government in charge of Human Rights and the Relationship with Constitutional Bodies and Civil Society on the Situation of Foreigners Residing in Tunisia, 7 April 2020." Tunisia, Tunis: Ministry of Interior.

MoI, and MCMREAM. 2013. "Circulaire régissant l'opération exceptionnelle de régularisation de la situation de séjour des étrangers." Rabat, Morocco.

Mongia, Radhika. 2018. *Indian Migration and Empire. A Colonial Genealogy of the Modern State*. Durham, NC: Duke University Press.

Monjib, Maâti. 2011. "The 'Democratization' Process in Morocco: Progress, Obstacles, and the Impact of the Islamist-Secularist Divide." Saban Center for Middle East Policy, Brookings Institution.

Mosler, Hannes B., and Luicy Pedroza. 2016. "An Unexpected Pioneer in Asia: The Enfranchisement of Foreign Residents in South Korea." *Ethnopolitics* 15 (2):187–210.

Mouley, Sami. 2016. "Étude qualitative d'évaluation de l'impact socioéconomique et des besoins des Libyens en Tunisie." Tunis, Tunisia: International Organization for Migration (IOM) & Organisation National de la Migration (ONM).

Mourji, Fouzi, Jean-Noel Ferrié, Saadia Radi, and Mehdi Alioua. 2016. "Les migrants subsahariens au Maroc : Enjeux d'une migration de résidence." Rabat, Morocco: Konrad-Adenauer-Stiftung e.V.

Moustafa, Tamir, and Tom Ginsburg. 2008. "Introduction: The Functions of Courts in Authoritarian Politics." in *Rule by Law: The Politics of Courts in Authoritarian Regimes*, edited by Tom Ginsburg and Tamir Moustafa. Cambridge, UK: Cambridge University Press.

Mouthaan, Melissa. 2019. "Unpacking Domestic Preferences in the Policy-'receiving' State: the EU's Migration Cooperation with Senegal and Ghana." *Comparative Migration Studies* 7(1):35.

Mrad Dali, Inès. 2009. "Identités multiples et multitudes d'histoires : les « Noirs tunisiens » de 1846 à aujourd'hui." Paris, France: EHESS.

———. 2015. "Les mobilisations des « Noirs tunisiens » au lendemain de la révolte de 2011." *Politique africaine* 140:61–81.

MSF. 2005. "Violence et immigration: Rapport sur l'immigration d'origine sub-saharienne en situation irrégulière au Maroc." Médecins sans Frontières.

———. 2013. "Violence, Vulnerability and Migration: Trapped at the Gates of Europe – A Report on the Situation of Sub-Saharan Migrants in an Irregular Situation in Morocco." Médecins sans Frontières.

Murphy, Emma. 2013. "The Tunisian Elections of October 2011: A Democratic Consensus." *The Journal of North African Studies* 18(2):231–47.

———. 2014. "The Foreign Policy of Tunisia." Pp. 233–57 in *The Foreign Policies of Middle East States*, edited by Raymond Hinnebusch and Anoushiravan Ehteshami. Boulder, CO: Lynne Rienner Publishers.

MVI. 2001. "Discours de SM le Roi Mohammed VI à Ajdir Izayane (province de Khénifra) le 17 octobre 2001." Moroccan King Mohammed VI.

2016. "Discours de SM le Roi à la nation à l'occasion du 63ème anniversaire de la Révolution du Roi et du Peuple of 20 August 2016." Moroccan King Mohammed VI.

2018. "SM le Roi adresse un message au 30è sommet de l'Union africaine (UA) le 29 Janvier 2018." Moroccan King Mohammed VI.

Mzali, Hassen. 1997. "Marché du travail, migrations internes et internationales en Tunisie." *Revue Région et Développement* 6:151–83.

Nasraoui, Mustapha. 2016. "La situation socio-économique des travailleurs subsahariens en Tunisie." Tunis, Tunisia: Division de la Migration et de la Coopération Internationale, Union Générale des Travailleurs Tunisiens (UGTT) & Maison du droit et des migrations, Terre d'Asile Tunisie (TAT).

Nassar, Jessy, and Nora Stel. 2019. "Lebanon's Response to the Syrian Refugee Crisis – Institutional Ambiguity as a Governance Strategy,." *Political Geography* 70:44–54.

Natter, Katharina. 2014a. "Fifty Years of Maghreb Emigration: How States Shaped Algerian, Moroccan and Tunisian Emigration." Oxford, UK: International Migration Institute, University of Oxford.

2014b. "The Formation of Morocco's Policy Towards Irregular Migration (2000–2007): Political Rationale and Policy Processes." *International Migration* 52(5):15–28.

2015a. "Almost Home? Morocco's Incomplete Migration Reforms." in *World Politics Review*.

2015b. "Revolution and Political Transition in Tunisia: A Migration Game Changer." in *Migration Information Source*. Washington, DC: Migration Policy Institute.

2018a. "Autocratic Immigration Policymaking: The Illiberal Paradox Hypothesis." in IMIn Working Paper 147 Amsterdam, The Netherlands: International Migration Institute Network (IMIn).

2018b. "Rethinking Immigration Policy Theory Beyond 'Western Liberal Democracies'." *Comparative Migration Studies* 6(4):1–21.

2021a. "Ad-hocratic Immigration Governance: How States Secure Their Power over Immigration through Intentional Ambiguity." *Territory, Politics, Governance*.

2021b. "Crafting a 'liberal monarchy': Regime Consolidation and Immigration Policy Reform in Morocco." *Journal of North African Studies* 26(5):850–74.

2021c. "Tunisia's Migration Politics Throughout the 2011 Revolution: Revisiting the Democratisation – Migrant Rights Nexus." *Third World Quarterly*.

Natter, Katharina, and Hélène Thiollet. 2022. "Migration Politics Across the World." *Third World Quarterly* 43(7): 1515–1665.

Naujoks, Daniel. 2013. *Migration, Citizenship and Development – Diasporic Membership Policies and Overseas Indians in the United States*. Oxford, UK: Oxford University Press.

2018. "Immigration and Refugee Governance in India." in The Politics of Migration Policies: Towards an Empirically Grounded, Comparative Political Theory of Migration Politics, workshop held on 17–18 December 2018. Paris, France.

Nawyn, Stephanie J. 2016. "Migration in the Global South: Exploring New Theoretical Territory." *International Journal of Sociology* 46(2):81–84.

Norman, Kelsey P. 2016a. "Between Europe and Africa: Morocco as a Country of Immigration." *The Journal of the Middle East and Africa* 7(4):421–39.

2016b. "Migration to MENA Host States: Examining Engagement Practices in Egypt, Morocco & Turkey." in *APSA 2016 Annual Meeting*.

2019. "Inclusion, Exclusion or Indifference? Redefining Migrant and Refugee Host State Engagement Options in Mediterranean 'Transit' Countries." *Journal of Ethnic and Migration Studies* 45(1):42–60.

2020a. "Migration Diplomacy and Policy Liberalization in Morocco and Turkey." *International Migration Review*.

2020b. *Reluctant Reception: Refugees, Migration and Governance in the Middle East and North Africa*. Cambridge, UK: Cambridge University Press.

Olson, Mancur Jr. 1965. *The Logic of Collective Action: Public Goods and the Theory of Groups*. New York, NJ: Schocken Books.

ONM. 2020. "Data Portal: Tunisiens résidant à l'Etranger." Tunis, Tunisia: Ministry of Social Affairs: Observatoire National de la Migration (ONM).

OTE/DIRP. 2012. "Répartition de la communauté tunisienne à l'étranger 2012." Tunis, Tunisia: Office des Tunisien a l'Etranger (OTE), Direction de l'Information et des Relations Publiques (DIRP).

Owen, Roger. 2004. *State, Power and Politics in the Making of the Modern Middle East*. London, UK: Routledge.

Palier, Bruno, and Yves Surel. 2005. "Les « trois I » et l'analyse de l'État en action." *Revue française de science politique* 1(55):7–32.

Paoletti, Emanuela. 2011. "Migration and Foreign Policy: The Case of Libya." *Journal of North African Studies* 16(2):215–31.

Parliament. 2014. "214th session of oral questions of the Moroccan Parliament, 2 December 2014." Rabat, Morocco: Chambre des Représentants.

Patterson, Lee Ann. 1997. "Agricultural Policy Reform in the European Community: A Three-level Game Analysis." *International Organization* 51(1):135–65.

Perkins, Kenneth J. 2004. *A History of Modern Tunisia*. Cambridge, UK: Cambridge University Press.

Perlmutter, Ted. 1996. "Bringing Parties Back in: Comments on 'Modes of Immigration Politics in Liberal Democratic Societies'." *International Migration Review* 30(1):375–88.

Perrin, Delphine. 2009. "Immigration et création juridique au Maghreb: La fragmentation des mondes et des droits." Pp. 245–65 in *Le Maghreb à l'épreuve des migrations subsahariennes*, edited by Ali Bensaâd. Paris, France: Karthala.

Peters, Margaret E. 2017. *Trading Barriers: Immigration and the Remaking of Globalization*. Princeton, NJ: Princeton University Press.

Pierson, Paul. 2000. "Increasing Returns, Path Dependence, and the Study of Politics." *The American Political Science Review* 94(2):251–67.

Pierson, Paul, and Theda Skocpol. 2002. "Historical Institutionalism in Contemporary Political Science." Pp. 693–721 in *Political Science: The State of the Discipline*, edited by Ira Katznelson and Helen V. Milner. New York: W.W. Norton & Company.

Piper, Nicola. 2006. "Migrant Worker Activism in Singapore and Malaysia: Freedom of Association and the Role of the State." *Asian and Pacific Migration Journal* 15(3):359–80.

Planes-Boissac, Véronique. 2012a. "Asylum and Migration in the Maghreb – Country Fact Sheet: Morocco." Copenhagen, Denmark: Euro-Mediterranean Human Rights Network (EMHRN).

    2012b. "Asylum and Migration in the Maghreb – Country Fact Sheet: Tunisia." Copenhagen, Denmark: Euro-Mediterranean Human Rights Network (EMHRN).

PNPM. 2014. "L'opération de régularisation à mi-parcours." Rabat, Morocco: Plateforme Nationale Protection Migrants (PNPM).

Pomeranz, Kenneth. 2000. *The Great Divergence: China, Europe, and the Making of the Modern World Economy*. Princeton, NJ: Princeton University Press.

Portes, Alejandro, and John Walton. 1981. *Labor, Class, and the International System*. New York: Academic Press.

Pouessel, Stéphanie. 2012a. "Les marges renaissantes : Amazigh, juif, Noir. Ce que la révolution a changé dans ce "petit pays homogène par excellence" qu'est la Tunisie." *L'Année du Maghreb* 8:143–60.

    (Ed.). 2012b. *Noirs au Maghreb: Enjeux identitaires*. Tunis, Tunisia: IRMC – Karthala.

    2016. "Le national à distance. Circulation de normes et réécriture du politique de la Tunisie." *L'année du Maghreb* 14(1):169–86.

Putnam, Robert D. 1988. "Diplomacy and Domestic Politics: The Logic of Two-Level Games." *International Organization* 42(3):427–60.

Ramadan, Adam. 2008. "The Guests' Guests: Palestinian Refugees, Lebanese Civilians, and the War of 2006." *Antipode* 40(4):658–77.

R. C. 2013. "Communiqué du 9 Septembre: SM le Roi préside à Casablanca une séance de travail consacrée à l'examen des divers volets relatifs à la problématique de l'immigration au Maroc." Rabat, Morocco: Royal Cabinet.

Redissi, Hamadi. 2007. "Etat fort, société civile faible en Tunisie." *Maghreb-Machrek* 192:89–117.

Regragui, Ismaïl. 2013. *La diplomatie publique marocaine: Une stratégie de marque religieuse?* Paris, France: L'Harmattan.

Reslow, Natasja. 2013. "Partnering for Mobility? Three-level Games in EU External Migration Policy." in Department of Political Science. Maastricht, the Netherlands: Maastricht University.

    2019. "Transformation or Continuity? EU External Migration Policy in the Aftermath of the Migration Crisis." Pp. 95–115 in *Constitutionalising the External Dimensions of EU Migration Policies in Times of Crisis* edited by Sergio Carrera, Juan Santos Vara, and Tineke Strik. Cheltenham, UK: Edward Elgar Publishing.

Reslow, Natasja, and Maarten Vink. 2015. "Three-Level Games in EU External Migration Policy: Negotiating Mobility Partnerships in West Africa." *Journal of Common Market Studies* 53(4):857–74.

Risse, Thomas, Stephen C. Ropp, and Kathryn Sikkink (Eds.). 1999. *The Power of Human Rights: International Norms and Domestic Change*. Cambridge, UK: Cambridge University Press.

Roman, Emanuela, and Ferruccio Pastore. 2018. "Analysing Migration Policy Frames of Tunisian Civil Society Organizations: How Do They Evaluate EU Migration Policies?" in *MEDRESET Working Paper No. 14*.

Roniger, Luis. 2004. "Political Clientelism, Democracy, and Market Economy." *Comparative Politics*:353–75.
Rosenblum, Marc R. 2004a. "The Intermestic Politics of Immigration Policy: Lessons from the Bracero Program." Pp. 139–82 in *Political Power and Social Theory*, edited by E. Davis Diane. Bingley, UK: Emerald Group Publishing Limited.
  2004b. "Moving Beyond the Policy of No Policy: Emigration from Mexico and Central America." *Latin American Politics and Society* 46(4):91–125.
Rosenblum, Marc R., and Idean Salehyan. 2004. "Norms and Interests in US Asylum Enforcement." *Journal of Peace Research* 41(6):677–97.
Rousselet, Lélia. 2015. "La 'stratégie africaine' du Maroc: un nouveau rôle pour la politique étrangère marocaine?" in *Political Science*. Paris, France: SciencesPo.
Ruhs, Martin. 2011. "Openness, Skills and Rights: An Empirical Analysis of Labour Immigration Programmes in 46 High- and Middle-Income Countries " in COMPAS Working Paper Series. Oxford, UK: COMPAS, University of Oxford.
  2013. "The Rights of Migrant Workers Reframing the Debate." Pp. 1–12 in *The Price of Rights – Regulating International Labor Migration*. Princeton, NJ: Princeton University Press.
Russell, Sharon S. 1989. "Politics and Ideology in Migration Policy Formulation: The Case of Kuwait." *International Migration Review* 23(1):24–47.
Sadiq, Kamal. 2005. "When States Prefer Non-Citizens over Citizens: Conflict over Illegal Immigration into Malaysia." *International Studies Quarterly* 49 (1):101–22.
Sadiq, Kamal, and Gerasimos Tsourapas. 2021. "The Postcolonial Migration State." *European Journal of International Relations* 27(3):884–912.
Sahraoui, Nina. 2015. "Acquiring 'voice' through 'exit': How Moroccan Emigrants Became a Driving Force of Political and Socio-economic Change." *Journal of North African Studies* 20(4):522–39.
Salamé, Ghassan. 2002. *The Foundations of the Arab State*. Oxon, UK: Routledge.
Sanyal, Romola. 2018. "Managing through ad hoc Measures: Syrian Refugees and the Politics of Waiting in Lebanon." *Political Geography* 66:67–75.
Sassen, Saskia. 1996. "Beyond Sovereignty: Immigration Policy-Making Today." *Social Justice* 23(3):9–20.
Sater, James N. 2002. "The Dynamics of State and Civil Society in Morocco." *Journal of North African Studies* 7(3):101–18.
Sayad, Abdelmalek. 1999. "Immigration et pensée d'Etat." *Actes de la recherche en sciences sociales* 129:5–14.
Scaglioni, Marta. 2017. "'I Wish I Did Not Understand Arabic!' Living as a Black Migrant in Contemporary Tunisia." in *Shadows of Slavery in West Africa and Beyond Working Paper Series*.
Schäfer, Isabel. 2017. "Les partis politiques tunisiens: Fragmentés, autocentrés et à la recherche d'un profil." in *Programme régional dialogue politique sud Mediterranée*. Berlin, Germany: Konrad-Adenauer-Stiftung e. V.
Schultz, Caroline. 2020. "Ambiguous Goals, Uneven Implementation – How Immigration Offices Shape Internal Immigration Control in Germany." *Comparative Migration Studies* 8(10):1–18.

Sciortino, Guiseppe. 2004. "Between Phantoms and Necessary Evils. Some Critical Points in the Study of Irregular Migrations to Western Europe." *IMIS-Beiträge* 24:17–44.

Seawright, Jason, and John Gerring. 2008. "Case Selection Techniques in Case Study Research: A Menu of Qualitative and Quantitative Options." *Political Research Quarterly* 61(2):294–308.

Seeley, Nicholas. 2010. "The Politics of Aid to Iraqi Refugees in Jordan." in Middle East Report 256. Richmond, VA: Middle East Research and Information Project (MERIP).

Sefrioui, Houcine. 1973. *La condition des étrangers au Maroc.* Casablanca, Morocco: Dar El Kitab.

Seklani, Mahmoud. 1974. "La population de la Tunisie." Paris, France: Comité International de Coordination des Recherches Nationales de Démographie (CICRED).

Shih, Victor. 2015. "Research in Authoritarian Regimes: Transparency Tradeoffs and Solutions." Pp. 20–22 in *Newsletter of the American Political Science Association Organized Section for Qualitative and Multi-Method Research.* American Political Science Association 13.

Shin, Adrian J. 2017. "Tyrants and Migrants: Authoritarian Immigration Policy." *Comparative Political Studies* 50(1):14–40.

Sidi Hida, Bouchra. 2015. "Migration au Maroc et faits du « printemps arabe » : cas des Syriens." Pp. 111–18 in *Migrants au Maroc: Cosmopolitisme, présence d'étrangers et transformations sociales*, edited by Nadia Khrouz and Nazarena Lanza. Rabat, Morocco: Konrad-Adenauer-Stiftung.

Skleparis, Dimitris. 2016. "(In)securitization and Illiberal Practices on the Fringe of the EU." *European Security* 25(1):92–111.

Skocpol, Theda. 1985. "Bringing the State Back In: Strategies and Analysis in Current Research." Pp. 3–37 in *Bringing the State Back In*, edited by Peter B. Evans, Dietrich Rueschemeyer, and Theda Skocpol. New York: Cambridge University Press.

Slagter, Jonathan. 2019. "An 'Informal' Turn in the European Union's Migrant Returns Policy towards Sub-Saharan Africa." in *Migration Information Source.* Washington, DC: Migration Policy Institute. www.migrationpolicy.org/article/eu-migrant-returns-policy-towards-sub-saharan-africa

Solomon, Peter H. 2007. "Courts and Judges in Authoritarian Regimes." *World Politics* 60(1):122–45.

Song, Sarah. 2019. *Immigration and Democracy.* Oxford, UK: Oxford University Press.

Soysal, Yasemin N. 1994. *Limits of Citizenship: Migrants and Postnational Membership in Europe.* Chicago, IL: University of Chicago Press.

Stel, Nora. 2020. *Hybrid Political Order and the Politics of Uncertainty: Refugee Governance in Lebanon.* Abingdon, UK: Routledge.

2021. "Uncertainty, Exhaustion, and Abandonment beyond South/North Divides: Governing Forced Migration through Strategic Ambiguity." *Political Geography* 88:102391.

Stepan, Alfred. 1981. *The State and Society: Peru in Comparative Perspective.* Princeton, NJ: Princeton University Press.

References

Stock, I., A. Üstübici, and S.U. Schultz. 2019. "Externalization at Work: Responses to Migration Policies from the Global South." *Comparative Migration Studies* 7(48):1–9.

Taing, Jean-Pierre 2015. "Les migrations chinoises au Maroc : les commerçants séjourneurs de Casablanca." Pp. 45–51 in *Migrants au Maroc: Cosmopolitisme, présence d'étrangers et transformations sociales*, edited by Nadia Khrouz and Nazarena Lanza. Rabat, Morocco: Konrad-Adenauer-Stiftung.

Tansey, Oisin. 2007. "Process Tracing and Elite Interviewing: A Case for Non-probability Sampling." *PS: Political Science and Politics* 40(4):765–72.

Tarrow, Sidney. 2010. "The Strategy of Paired Comparison: Toward a Theory of Practice." *Comparative Political Studies* 43(2):230–59.

TAT. 2016. "Portraits de migrants – Description de l'immigration en Tunisie par les migrants accompagnés à la permanence d'accueil de TAT de janvier 2014 à mars 2016." Tunis, Tunisia: Terre d'Asile Tunisie.

——— 2018. "Attentes et satisfaction des étudiants subsahariens en Tunisie: Des portes qui s'ouvrent, des opportunités à saisir." Tunis, Tunisia: Terre d'Asile Tunisie.

Taylor, Charles. 1998. "The Dynamics of Democratic Exclusion." *Journal of Democracy* 9(4):143–56.

Teitelbaum, Michael S. 1984. "Immigration, Refugees, and Foreign Policy." *International Organization* 38(3):429–50.

Therrien, Catherine, and Chloé Pellegrini. 2015. "French Migrants in Morocco: From a Desire for Elsewhereness to an Ambivalent Reality." *Journal of North African Studies* 20(4):605–21.

Thiollet, Helene. 2019. "Immigrants, Markets, Brokers, and States: The Politics of Illiberal Migration Governance in the Arab Gulf." in International Migration Institute Working Paper 155. Amsterdam, NL: International Migration Institute, University of Amsterdam.

Thiollet, Hélène. 2011. "Migration as Diplomacy: Labour Migrants, Refugees, and Arab Regional Politics in the Oil-Rich Countries." *International Labor and Working-Class History* 79:103–21.

——— 2015. "Migration et (contre)révolution dans le Golfe: Politiques migratoires et politiques de l'emploi en Arabie saoudite." *Revue Européenne des Migrations Internationales* 31(3):121–43.

——— 2016. "Managing Migrant Labour in the Gulf: Transnational Dynamics of Migration Politics since the 1930s." in IMI Working Paper 131. Oxford, UK: International Migration Institute.

——— 2021. "Migrants and Monarchs: Regime Survival, State Transformation and Migration Politics in Saudi Arabia." *Third World Quarterly*:1–21.

Tilly, Charles. 1975. "Reflections on the History of European State-Making." Pp. 3–83 in *The Formation of National States in Western Europe*, edited by Charles Tilly. Princeton, NJ: Princeton University Press.

——— 1992. *Coercion, Capital and European States, A.D. 990–1992*. Cambridge, MA: Blackwell Publishing.

Timmermans, Stefan, and Iddo Tavory. 2012. "Theory Construction in Qualitative Research: From Grounded Theory to Abductive Analysis." *Sociological Theory* 30(3):167–86.

Toğral Koca, Burcu. 2016. "Syrian Refugees in Turkey: From 'guests' to 'enemies'?" *New Perspectives on Turkey* 54:55–75.

Torpey, John. 1997. "Coming and Going: On the State Monopolization of the Legitimate 'Means of Movement'." *Sociological Theory* 16(3):239–59.

Touhami, Habib. n.d. "Migrations interieures: Evolution, axe et effets demographiques."

Trimberger, Ellen. 1978. *Revolution from Above: Military Bureaucrats and Development in Japan, Turkey, Egypt, and Peru.* New Brunswick, NJ: Transaction Books.

Tsourapas, Gerasimos. 2017. "Migration Diplomacy in the Global South: Cooperation, Coercion and Issue Linkage in Gaddafi's Libya." *Third World Quarterly* 38(10):2367–85.

⸻ 2018. "Authoritarian Emigration States: Soft Power and Cross-Border Mobility in the Middle East." *International Political Science Review* 39 (3):400–16.

⸻ 2019a. *The Politics of Migration in Modern Egypt: Strategies for Regime Survival in. Autocracies.* Cambridge: Cambridge University Press.

⸻ 2019b. "The Syrian Refugee Crisis and Foreign Policy Decision-Making in Jordan, Lebanon, and Turkey." *Journal of Global Security Studies* 4 (4):464–81.

⸻ 2020. "Global Autocracies: Strategies of Transnational Repression, Legitimation, and Co-Optation in World Politics." *International Studies Review* 23(3):616–44.

Tyszler, Elsa. 2015. "Ceuta & Melilla, centres de tri à ciel ouvert aux portes de l'Afrique – Rapport conjoint Migreurop-GADEM." Migreurop/Le Groupe antiraciste d'accompagnement et de défense des étrangers et migrants (GADEM).

Umpierrez de Reguero, Sebastián A., Inci Öykü Yener-Roderburg, and Vivian Cartagena. 2021. "Political Regimes and External Voting Rights: A Cross-National Comparison." *Frontiers in Political Science* 3(10):1–15.

UN-HRC. 2019. "Report of the Special Rapporteur on Contemporary Forms of Racism, Racial Discrimination, Xenophobia and Related Intolerance. Visit to Morocco." New York: United Nations, Human Rights Council.

UNDESA. 2019. "International Migration 2019." New York: United Nations, Department of Economic and Social Affairs, Population Division.

UNHCR. 2000. "Chapter 2: Decolonisation in Africa." in *The State of The World's Refugees 2000: Fifty Years of Humanitarian Action,* edited by UNHCR.

⸻ 2013. "Leaving Libya – A review of UNHCR's emergency operation in Tunisia and Egypt, 2011–2012." Geneva, Switzerland: Policy Development and Evaluation Service, UNHCR.

⸻ 2015. "Operational Update – Morocco, October/December 2015."

⸻ 2020a. "Factsheet – Morocco, September 2020." Rabat, Morocco: UNHCR.

⸻ 2020b. "Factsheet – Tunisia, September 2020." Tunis, Tunisia: UNHCR.

⸻ 2021. "Global Trends. Forced Displacement in 2020." Geneva, Switzerland: United Nations High Commissioner for Refugees.

Üstübici, Aysen. 2015. "Dynamics in Emigration and Immigration Policies of Morocco: A Double Engagement." *Migration and Development* 4(2):238–55.

References

2016. "Political Activism between Journey and Settlement: Irregular Migrant Mobilisation in Morocco." *Geopolitics* 21(2):303–24.

2018. *The Governance of International Migration: Irregular Migrants' Access to Right to Stay in Turkey and Morocco*. Amsterdam, NL: Amsterdam University Press.

V-Dem. 2021. "Autocratization Turns Viral. Democracy Report 2021." Gothenburg, Sweden: University of Gothenburg, Varieties of Democracy Institute.

Vairel, Frédéric. 2004. "Le Maroc des années de plomb : équité et réconciliation?" *Politique africaine* 96(4):181–95.

2013. "Protesting in Authoritarian Situations: Egypt and Morocco in Comparative Perspective" in *Social Movements, Mobilization, and Contestation in the Middle East and North Africa*, edited by J. Beinin and F. Vairel. Redwood City, CA: Stanford University Press.

Valluy, Jérôme. 2007. "Le HCR au Maroc : acteur de la politique européenne d'externalisation de l'asile." *L'Année du Maghreb* III:547–75.

Van Dongen, Els. 2018. "Notes for a Comparative Research Agenda: Four Key Points from Chinese Migration Policies" in The Politics of Migration Policies: Towards an Empirically Grounded, Comparative Political Theory of Migration Politics, workshop held on 17–18 December 2018. Paris, France.

Vermeren, Pierre. 2002. *Le Maroc en transition*. Paris, France: La Découverte.

2011. *Le Maroc de Mohammed VI: La transition inachevée*. Paris, France: La Découverte.

Vezzoli, Simona, and Marie-Laurence Flahaux. 2017. "How Do Post-Colonial Ties and Migration Regimes Shape Travel visa Requirements? The Case of Caribbean Nationals." *Journal of Ethnic and Migration Studies* 43(7):1141–63.

Vignati, Davide. 2009. "Role, Influence and Use of the Media in Policy-Making Process for Migration Issues in Sending and Transit Countries in the Mediterranean." Geneva, Switzerland: Graduate Institute for International Studies of Geneva.

Vigneswaran, Darshan. 2018. "The Complex Sources of Immigration Control." in The Politics of Migration Policies: Towards an Empirically Grounded, Comparative Political Theory of Migration Policies, workshop held on 17–18 December 2018. Paris, France.

2020. "Migrant Protection Regimes: Beyond Advocacy and towards Exit in Thailand." *Review of International Studies* 46(5):652–71.

Vigneswaran, Darshan, and Joel Quirk (Eds.). 2015. *Mobility Makes States: Migration and Power in Africa*. Philadelphia: University of Pennsylvania Press.

Wallerstein, Immanuel. 1974. *The Modern World-System*. New York: Academic Press.

Waltz, Susan E. 1995. *Human Rights and Reform: Changing the Face of North African Politics*. Berkeley: University of California Press.

Waterbury, John. 1970. *The Commander of the Faithful: The Moroccan Political Elite*. New York: Columbia University Press.

Weber, Max. 1922. "Kapitel IX. Herrschaftssoziologie." in *Wirtschaft und Gesellschaft. Zweiter Teil.*
Weiner, Myron. 1985. "On International Migration and International Relations." *Population and Development Review* 11(3):441–55.
Weyel, Silja. 2015. "Labour Market Integration of sub-Saharan Migrants in Morocco: The Case of Call-centres." Pp. 88–95 in *Migrants au Maroc: Cosmopolitisme, présence d'étrangers et transformations sociales*, edited by Nadia Khrouz and Nazarena Lanza. Rabat, Morocco: Konrad-Adenauer-Stiftung.
Weyland, Kurt. 2009. "The Diffusion of Revolution: '1848' in Europe and Latin America." *International Organization* 63(3):391–423.
  2012. "The Arab Spring: Why the Surprising Similarities with the Revolutionary Wave of 1848?" *Perspectives on Politics* 10(4):917–34.
Whitaker, Beth Elise. 2005. "Citizens and Foreigners: Democratization and the Politics of Exclusion in Africa." *African Studies Review* 48(1):109–26.
Willis, Michael J. 2002. "Political Parties in the Maghrib: The Illusion of Significance?" *The Journal of North African Studies* 7(2):1–22.
  2012. *Politics and Power in the Maghreb. Algeria, Tunisia and Morocco from Independence to the Arab Spring.* London, UK: Hurst & Company.
World Bank. 2020. "World Development Indicators." Washington, DC: World Bank.
Wunderlich, Daniel. 2010. "Differentiation and Policy Convergence against Long Odds: Lessons from Implementing EU Migration Policy in Morocco." *Mediterranean Politics* 15(2):249–72.
Wyrtzen, Jonathan. 2014. "Colonial Legacies, National Identity, and Challenges for Multiculturalism in the Contemporary Maghreb." Pp. 17–34 in *Multiculturalism and Democracy in North Africa: Aftermath of the Arab Spring*, edited by Moha Ennaji. New York: Routledge.
Yardımcı-Geyikçi, Şebnem, and Özlem Tür. 2018. "Rethinking the Tunisian Miracle: A Party Politics View." *Democratization* 25(5):787–803.
Yerkes, Sarah. 2017. "Democracy Derailed?" Washington, DC: Carnegie Endowment for International Peace.
  2020. "Tunisia: General Overview of the Country." Washington, DC: Carnegie Endowment for International Peace.
Young, Crawford. 1994. *The African Colonial State in Comparative Perspective.* New Haven, CT: Yale University Press.
Youssef, Maro. 2018. "A Murky State-Civil Society Relationship in Tunisia." Open Democracy.
Zartman, William I. 1988. "Opposition as a Support of the State." Pp. 61–87 in *Beyond Coercion: The Durability of the Arab State*, edited by Adeed Dawisha and William I. Zartman. London, UK: Croom Helm.
Zeleza, Paul Tiyambe. 2006. "The Inventions of African Identities and Languages: The Discursive and Developmental Implications." Pp. 14–26 in *Selected Proceedings of the 36th Annual Conference on African Linguistics*, edited by Olaoba F. Arasanyin and Michael A. Pemberton. Somerville, MA: Cascadilla Proceedings Project.
Zemni, Sami. 2016. "From Revolution to Tunisianité: Who is the Tunisian People? Creating Hegemony through Compromise." *Middle East Law and Governance* 8(2–3):131–50.

Zhou, Yang-Yang, and Guy Grossman. 2021. "When Refugee Exposure Increases Incumbent Support Through Development: Evidence from Uganda." OSF Preprints.

Zolberg, Aristide R. 1978. "International Migration Policies in a Changing World System." Pp. 241–86 in *Human Migration: Patterns and Policies*, edited by William H. McNeill and Ruth S. Adams. London, UK: Indiana University Press.

　2006. *A Nation by Design – Immigration Policy in the Fashioning of America*. Cambridge, MA: Harvard University Press.

Index

20 February movement, Morocco, 47, 54

Abdelhamid, Maha, 151
'abid (slave), 86, 204
ad-hocratic immigration governance
    as deliberate strategy, 31, 203
    in Morocco, 75–76, 99, 102–5, 107, 109
    in Tunisia, 77, 158–59
Adventist Development and Relief Agency (ADRA), Tunisia, 157
Afghan refugees in Iran, 34
African Commission, CGEM, Morocco, 135
African Alliance for Migration and Development, 76
African Development Bank (AfDB), 68, 142, 151, 165, 211
African embassies
    in Morocco, 133–34
    in Tunisia, 190
African Migration Agenda (Mohammed VI), 76
African Migration Observatory (AU), 76, 94
African state, the, 20
African Union (AU), 11, 55, 76, 94, 127, 139, 202
Afrique Intelligence, Tunisia, 180
Afrobarometer, 129, 152, 171
Agadir Charter, 53
agenda-setting, policy cycle model, 218–19
Al-Amal Bank, 62
Alaouite dynasty, Morocco, 44
Algeria
    Algerian refugees in Tunisia, 33, 67, 141
    Algerian workers in Tunisia, 158
    migrant expulsions from Morocco, 82
    Morocco, tensions with, 11, 54, 82–83, 93, 112, 202
Alioua, Mehdi, 96
Amazigh culture, 44, 47, 52–54, 56, 206
ambivalence, policy of (Norman), 30, 104, 202

amicales, 62
Amiri, Khalil, 148
Amiyeto, Marcel, 128
Amnesty International (AI)
    in Morocco, 48, 88, 109, 127
    in Tunisia, 50, 179
ANAPEC procedure, Morocco, 75, 100, 119, 129
Angola, 42
Anti-Discrimination Points (PAD), Tunisia, 162
Anti-Racist Defence and Support Group of Foreigners and Migrants (GADEM), Morocco
    advocacy strategies, 127
    in civil society market, 123
    on differential treatment of migrants, 102
    financial support scheme for migrants, 78
    founding of, 87, 96, 109
    Geneva Committee, report to, 98
    legalization of, 75
    Migrant'scène festival, cancellation, 106
    Moroccan state, relationship with, 111, 114–15, 124–25
appendix to the state, markets as, 28
Arab Institute for Human Rights (IADH), 50, 179, 185, 194
Arab Institute of CEOs, 193
Arab Spring, 18, 92
Arab state, the, 20
Argentina, 26, 37
Article 26, Tunisian constitution, 146, 170
Article 30, Moroccan constitution, 95
Assabah, 85
Association for the Defence of Black Tunisians' rights (ADAM), 151, 180–81
Association Light on Irregular Emigration in the Maghreb (ALECMA), Morocco, 78, 95
Association of African Students and Trainees in Tunisia (AESAT)

Index

advocacy for migrant protection, 147, 182
Ben Ali regime, relationship with, 178
business interests, relations with, 193
Libyan refugees, response to, 72, 180
racism, condemnation of, 161, 169
state institutions, relations with, 184
student numbers in Tunisia, 159
Association of Maghreb Workers in France (ATMF), 96, 128
Association of Sub-Saharan Workers in Tunisia (ASTT), 180, 183
Association of Tunisian Magistrates (AMT), 194
asylum law
  in Morocco, 99, 103, 117, 211
  in Tunisia, 3, 73, 147–50, 163–64, 181, 187, 191
asylum seekers
  in Morocco, 66, 89
  in Tunisia, 141–42, 178, 182
Authority to fight against human trafficking, Tunisia, 194
autocracies
  centralization and coherence under, 210
  civil society in, 26–27, 138
  decision-making under, 40–41, 117, 218
  divide-and-rule strategies, 45, 47, 53, 167, 206
  economic actors in, 28
  immigration policymaking in, 138–39
  institutional ambiguity in, 30
  international norms, adherence to, 39
  legal actors in, 32
  public opinion, role in, 27
Ayari, Yassine, 170

Bangladesh, 33
Bardo, Treaty of, 48
Basri, Driss, 47, 84
Baz, Ali el, 96
Ben Ali, President Zine El Abidine
  civil society under, 26, 144, 178–79, 214
  immigration policies of, 71, 142–44, 146, 167, 196
  institutional legacy, 175
  IOs, surveillance of, 189, 217
  judiciary under, 194
  law against human trafficking, 159
  modernization agenda, 205
  opposition, silencing of, 207
  political agendas of, 44
  presidency of, 2, 50–51
  select migrant groups, protection of, 151–52
  Tunisians abroad, voting rights, 63
Ben Gharbia, Mehdi, 161
Ben Youssef, Salah, 56
Benhima, Driss, 135
Berber Dahir, 1930, Morocco, 53
Berber Manifesto, 2000, Morocco, 54
Bir El Fatnassiya camp, Tunisia, 173
Birou, Anis, 93, 112
Black Lives Matter, 162
Black minorities
  as 'undeserving' population, 5
  in Morocco, 55, 86, 120, 130
  in Tunisia, 56–57, 150–51, 160–63, 182, 207
  institutionalized racism, 201
  slavery, legacy of, 86, 204
blackmailing strategy, migration as, 37, 143
boomerang effect (Keck and Sikkink), 26, 187
Botswana, 158
Bouayach, Amina, 89
Bouazizi, Mohammed, 51
Bourguiba, President Habib, 44, 49–50, 56–57, 140–41, 205, 207
Bracero program, United States, 29
British colonial policies, 32
British empire, 34
Bureau of Emigration and Foreign Labour Force, Tunisia, 157
Bureau of Refugees and Stateless People (BRA), Morocco, 75, 81, 89, 104, 109–10, 117
bureaucratic politics
  approaches to immigration policymaking, 25, 28, 40, 111, 209–12, 227
  arbitrariness of, 82, 100
  centre-periphery dynamics, 120
  colonial legacy, 204, 219
  commonalities in modern states, 8–9, 24, 221, 225
  in Morocco, 116, 138
  in Tunisia, 168, 184, 197
Burkina Faso, 57, 158
bus companies (Moroccan), 'African' residence permits, 120

Cameroon, 66
Caribbean states, 34
Caritas, 77, 86, 123, 147, 165, 178, 180
Casablanca
  airport waiting zone detentions 2015, 105
  terrorist attacks 2003, 84
Cavalieri, Jean-Paul, 119

Index

Cellule Solidarité Africaine Covid-19 Tunisie, 77
Central African Republic, 158
Centre for Legal and Judicial Studies (CEJJ), Tunisia, 149, 165, 191
centre-periphery dynamics, in Morocco, 119–20
Ceuta, 83, 87–88, 109
Chahed, Youssef, 161, 184
children
   refugee and migrant children in Morocco, 75, 90, 104
   refugee children in Tunisia, 186
China, 34
Chinese migration to Morocco, 66
Choucha refugee camp, Tunisia, 145–46, 150, 173–74, 180, 213
Christian minorities
   in Morocco, 70, 130
   in Tunisia, 70
CIMADE, 86, 109
Civil Council for the Fight Against All Forms of Discrimination, Morocco, 123
civil servants
   Moroccan, 29, 45, 84, 112, 119–20, 132, 210
   personal motivation, importance of, 211
   Tunisian, 145, 167, 172, 174, 184, 197
Civil Society Organizations (CSOs)
   advocacy strategies, 126–28, 185–87
   civil society market, Morocco, 122–24
   CNDH, relationship with, Morocco, 114
   cooperation in Tunisia, 182
   democratization, impact of, Tunisia, 177–84, 196
   fragmentation in Tunisia, 181–82
   influence in Morocco, 75, 78, 214–15
   influence in Tunisia, 73, 77, 144, 157, 165, 214–15
   influence on state actors, 26
   IOs, relationship with, Tunisia, 187
   liberalization, impact of, Morocco, 122
   mobilization in Morocco, 86–87
   mobilization in Tunisia, 179–81
   Moroccan monarchy, reciprocal dependency, 114–15
   state-civil society dynamics, Morocco, 124–28
   state-civil society dynamics, Tunisia, 184–88
   weakness under Ben Ali, Tunisia, 178–79
claims-makers, 42
client politics, in democracies, 4, 25, 28
clientism
   in autocracies, 28
   in Tunisia, 49
Clinique Hijra, Morocco, 137
Club des Juges, Morocco, 137
Cold War refugees, 35
Collective of Migrant Workers in Morocco (CTMM), 128
Collective of Sub-Saharan Communities in Morocco (CCSM), 95
colonization
   in Morocco, 45, 53, 64, 70, 79–82, 107
   in Tunisia, 48–49, 64, 70, 140
   legacies of, 34, 40, 203–5
Committee for the Respect of Liberties and Human Rights (CRDHT), Tunisia, 161
Committee on Political Affairs and External Relations, Tunisia, 168
Committee on Public Legislation and Public Administration, Tunisia, 168
Confederation of African Pupils, Students and Interns in Morocco (CESAM), 81
Congo-Brazzaville, 158
Congolese refugees and irregular migrants, Morocco, 89, 102
Congolese students, attacks on, Tunisia, 161
Congress for the Republic (CPR), Tunisia, 51
constitution
   Moroccan 2011, 47, 95, 110, 137, 206
   Tunisian 2014, 56, 160
Constitutional Democratic Youth (JCD), Tunisia, 178
Consultative Council on Human Rights (CCDH), Morocco, 46, 95, 113
controlled case comparisons, in theory-building, 12
Convention of the Protection of the Rights of All Migrant Workers and Members of Their Families (UN), 39, 95, 97, 107, 186
co-optation, strategy of, Morocco, 34, 45–46, 206–7
Coronavirus Pandemic Fund, Morocco, 77
Côte d'Ivoire, 64, 67–68, 81, 89, 94, 133, 141, 193
Coulibaly, Ali, 94
Council for Morocco's Community Abroad (CCME), 42, 62, 89, 128
Council of Congolese Refugees and Asylum Seekers (ARCOM), Morocco, 87
Council of Sub-Saharan Migrants in Morocco (CMSM), 75, 87, 91, 95, 115
coups et blessures campaign (hits and wounds), GADEM, Morocco, 127

Index

COVID-19, 52, 77–78, 106, 164, 177, 195
crisis, as window of opportunity, 42–43
Crispi, Francesco, 64
Cuba, 37

dawla, concept of, 20
decision-making, in policy cycle model, 218–19
Delegate Ministry of African Affairs (Morocco), 55
Democratic Bloc, Tunisia, 170
Democratic Confederation of Labour (CDT), Morocco, 129
Democratic Constitutional Rally (RDC), Tunisia, 49
Democratic Organization of Immigrant Labour (ODTI), Morocco, 112, 114–15, 124–25, 128
Democratic Organization of Labour (ODT), Morocco, 128
Democratic Republic of Congo (DRC), 64, 89, 158
democratization, in shaping immigration politics, 163, 196–97
demonstration effect, 37, 96–97, 208
dependency theories, on immigration policymaking, 35, 226
depoliticization of immigration, in Tunisia, 10–11, 34, 148, 152–53, 170–71, 196, 207
dhimmi, 70
Diop, Abdou Souleye, 135
Directorate for Migration Affairs, Morocco, 75, 99
Directorate of Borders and Foreigners, Tunisia, 157, 167, 185
Directorate of Migrations and Border Surveillance (DMST), Morocco, 70, 82, 117
Doctors of the World Belgium (MdM-B), 157, 181, 184–86
Doctors Without Borders (MSF), 98, 102
domestic politics
  approaches to immigration policymaking, 25–28, 110, 212–15, 223, 226
  in Tunisia, post-revolution, 145–46, 150–52
Droit et Justice, Morocco, 137

economic actors
  immigration policies, role in, 213, 215
  in Morocco, 131
  in Tunisia, 158, 188, 192–93
Economic Community of West African States (ECOWAS), 55

Ecuador, 27, 36–37
education, access to
  in Morocco, 71, 75, 89–91, 99, 104
  in Tunisia, 153, 186
Egypt, 30, 36
El Gosba, segregated school buses, 151
elites
  in Morocco, 45–46
  in Tunisia, 49, 57, 170–71
embedded liberalism hypothesis (Hollifield), 38
employment, access to
  in Morocco, 62, 66, 71, 82, 91, 99–100, 135–36
  in Tunisia, 142, 157, 190, 193
Ennahdha Party, Tunisia, 51–52, 169–70
Entraide Nationale (EN), Morocco, 75, 102, 110, 118
entrepreneurs
  African, in Tunisia, 193
  European, in Morocco, 66
Equity and Reconciliation Commission, Morocco, 47, 88
ethnicity, in politics, 20
Ettakatol Party, Tunisia, 51
Euro-African Conference on Migration and Development, 2006, Morocco, 87–88
Euromed Rights, Tunisia, 161, 181–82, 184–85
European Union (EU)
  migration externalization efforts, 4, 35, 83, 97, 124, 143, 166
  Morocco, relations with, 94, 97, 106, 109–10, 133
  Tunisia, relations with, 146–47, 166, 182, 187–88, 197
executive power
  in Morocco, 99
  role in immigration policy, 40, 209–10
exemption regimes, 202–3
expulsion of migrants
  from Morocco, 71, 82, 90–91, 99, 105, 108, 134
  from Tunisia, 174
external agenda setting
  immigration policy, role in, 215–16
  Moroccan and Tunisian response to, 190–92, 197, 216–17
  Tunisian human trafficking law, role in, 159–60

family code (mudawana); Morocco), 47, 137
Figuig refugee crisis, Morocco, 2017, 112, 202
Filipino houseworkers, 66, 102, 128

football, racial violence, Tunisia, 169
For a policy of regularization of irregular migrants in the context of Morocco's constitutional reform (ODTI), 128
foreign policy interests, role in immigration policymaking, 35–38, 220, 223
Foreigners and human rights in Morocco: For a radically new immigration and asylum policy (CNDH), 95, 98
Foreigners Bureaus (MoI), Morocco, 112
Foundation Hassan II, Morocco, 62
France
  French citizens in Morocco, 66
  French citizens in Tunisia, 68
  immigration law, legacy of in Morocco, 79–81
  immigration policies, 32
  Moroccan migrants in, 60
  Tunisia, relations with, 165
French Development Cooperation (AFD), 189
French Federation of Tunisians for a Citizenship of Both Shores (FTCR), 180
Friends and Families of Victims of Clandestine Migration (AFVIC), Morocco, 86, 115

Gaddafi regime, fall of, 68, 154
Gafsa, strikes, 50
General Confederation of Enterprises in Morocco (CGEM), 135
General Directorate for International Cooperation on Migration (DGCIM), Tunisia, 147, 149, 172, 191
General Directorate for National Security (DGSN), Morocco, 125
General Directorate for Planning and Follow-up (DGPS), Tunisia, 172
General Union of Moroccan Workers (UGTM), 129, 158
General Union of Tunisian Workers (UGTT), 51, 179–84, 190, 195
generic policy processes, in immigration policymaking, 8, 40–43, 224
Geneva
  Geneva Refugee Convention, 81, 95, 141, 149
  UN Convention, evaluation committee, 97–98
geopolitical rebordering, 93, 103, 107, 202
German Development Agency (GIZ), 123, 132
Germany
  emigration and immigration history, 35
  immigration and asylum policies, 32
  Tunisian migrants in, 60
Ghali, Brahim, 83
Global Compact for Safe, Orderly and Regular Migration (UN), 76, 127
Global Forum on Migration and Development, 76
Global North
  autocratic tendencies in, 6
  liberal norms in, 38
Global North and Global South as binary categories, 21
Global South
  institutionalist approaches to, 31
  international relations approaches to, 35
  migration politics, theory-building on, 23–24
  national identity and state formation narratives, 33
  scholarship on, 6–7
globalization theory approaches to immigration policymaking, 23, 25, 38–40, 107
good cop/bad cop dynamics, King and administration, Morocco, 112–13, 209
Gourougou forest, Morocco,, 105
Greece, 35
Green March, Morocco, 1975, 54
group-based exemptions
  Morocco, 102, 104, 136, 203
  Tunisia, 142, 158–59, 182, 192, 196
Guinea, 66, 81
Gulf States
  illiberal migration governance in, 40
  Kafala system, 34
  Tunisian workers in, 160

Hassan II, King of Morocco, 46–47, 53, 81
Health and Social Affairs Commission on students from Western and Central Africa, Tunisia, 185
healthcare, access to
  COVID-19 in Morocco, 78
  health insurance in Morocco, 75
  irregular migrants in Morocco, 71, 91
  regularization, impact of in Morocco, 99–100
  in Tunisia, 73, 154–55
  UNHCR, role in Morocco, 89
Heart of Tunisia Party, 52
hegemonic stability approaches to immigration policymaking, 35
Hirak movement, Morocco, 48

Index

historical-culturalist approaches to immigration policymaking, 22, 25, 32–35, 40, 107, 204
hits and wounds (coups et blessures) campaign, GADEM, Morocco, 127
Houphouët-Boigny, Felix, 141
housing, access to
  in Morocco, 79, 120
  in Tunisia, 155
hukou registration system, China, 34
human trafficking
  law against, Morocco, 39, 99, 103–4
  law against, Tunisia, 39, 74, 159–60, 163, 189, 194
  Tunisian policy on, 143
Husainid dynasty, Morocco, 48

I don't want to die in Tunisia because I'm Black, social media campaign, 161
illiberal paradox, 9–10, 138, 221, 226
immigration policies
  ambiguity in, 30–31, 41–42
  bureaucratic politics, role in, 25, 28, 40, 111, 209–12, 227
  definition of, 22
  democratization, role in, 163, 196–97
  domestic politics, role in, 25–28, 110, 212–15, 223
  economic actors, role in, 213, 215
  exemption regimes and informality, 202–3
  incoherence by design, 177, 197
  informality of, 156–58, 210
  symbolic nature of, 198–99
  theoretical approaches to, 20–22, 25–28, 226–27
immigration regime, 22
implementation, policy cycle model, 218–19
incoherence by design, 177, 197
Independent Superior Commission for Elections (ISIE), Tunisia, 145
India, 33–34
informal labour market
  in Morocco, 135–36
  role in immigration policies, 215, 225
institutions
  institutional dynamics in modern nation states, 40
  institutional identities, 167, 175–77, 211
  institutionalist approaches to immigration policymaking, 22, 28–32, 107, 138, 166–67
Interministerial Delegation for Human Rights (DIDH), Morocco, 76, 103, 110, 118

internal displacements, Morocco, 105, 113, 134, 137
International Association of Refugee Law Judges (IARLJ), 194
International Centre for Migration Policy Development (ICMPD), 166, 190
International Human Rights Federation (FIDH), 88, 179
International Labour Organization (ILO), 158, 181, 183, 190
International Migrants Day, 75, 150
International Mutual Aid Committee (CEI), Morocco, 86
international norms
  immigration policymaking, role in, 38–40, 217–18, 226
  in CSO lobbying strategy, Tunisia, 186
  Moroccan liberalization, role in, 97–99, 107
  Tunisian human trafficking law, role in, 159–60
  UNHCR Headquarters Agreement, Morocco, 88–90
International Organization for Migration (IOM)
  COVID-19, response to, 77
  irregular stay penalties, advocacy on, 157–58
  Libyan refugees, support for, 68, 72, 173
  in Morocco, 88, 109, 132
  Red Crescent, competition with, 182
  in Tunisia, 144, 165, 189
  voluntary return program, 132, 188
International Organizations (IOs)
  in Morocco, 88, 131–33
  in Tunisia, 166, 173, 181, 188–92
international relations approaches to immigration policymaking, 23, 25, 35–38, 40, 107, 215–18
interviews, in research project, 13–16
IRAM project (ILO), 183
Iran, 33
Iraqi refugees in Jordan, 200
irregular emigration, from Morocco and Tunisia, 60
irregular migrants
  bus company segregation, Morocco, 120
  healthcare, access to in Morocco, 91
  integration of, in Morocco, 101–2
  IOs in Morocco, humanitarian support, 133
  regularization, demands for in Morocco, 95
  restrictions on, in Morocco, 70–71, 82–84

302   Index

irregular migrants (cont.)
   in Tunisia, 71, 157–59, 178–79, 182
   violence against, in Morocco, 105–8
irregular stay penalties, Tunisia
   advocacy on, 73, 158, 184, 186
   doubling of, 148
   exemptions from, 41, 157, 182, 212
   informal reform of, 163, 203
   introduction of, 142
   MoF, responsibility for, 174
   racialization of, 201
   student exemptions, 176–77, 180
irregular workers
   in Morocco, 102, 136
   in Tunisia, 151
Islamism
   in Algeria, 53
   in Morocco, 46, 206
   in Tunisia, 50–51
issue-specific policy processes in immigration policy, 8–9, 225
Istiqlal party, Morocco, 45–46
Italy
   emigration and immigration history, 35
   Italian population in Tunisia, 64, 68
   Moroccan migrants in, 60
   politicization of immigration, 36
   Tunisia, relations with, 143, 165
   Tunisian migrants in, 60, 63

Japan, 41, 164
Jarray, Fethi, 186
Jaziri, Houcine, 42, 145, 148, 150, 169
Jendoubi, Kamel, 42, 145, 184
Jewish minorities, in Tunisia, 56, 64, 70
Jomâa, Mehdi, 68, 153
Jordan, 31, 36, 200
jurisprudence on immigration, Tunisia, 194
Justice and Development Party (PJD), Morocco, 47, 85, 121, 206

Kafala system, 34
Karoui, Nabil, 52
Kenya, 57
kinship, in politics, 20
Ksiksi, Jamila Debbech, 169
Ksiksi, Khawla, 161
Kuwait, 29

Labour Code, Tunisian, 71, 192–93
Labour Day march, Rabat, 95
labour market test, Morocco, 75, 81, 100–1, 104, 203
Lacy-Swing, William, 93

Lahbib, Kamel, 89
laissez-faire
   Morocco's migrant policies, 139
   purposive, in immigration policies, 22
   Tunisia's Libyan policy, 153–55, 199
Lampedusa, 159
Lando, Lorena, 160
Latin America, 196
Laws, France
   Law 2003-1119, 84
Laws, Morocco
   Law 02-03, 70, 82–84
   Law 26-14, 103
   Law 27-14, 76, 103
   Law 66-17, 103
   Law 72-17, 103
   Law 95-14, 103
Laws, Tunisia
   Law 2003-99, 143
   Law 2004-06, 71, 74, 142–43, 168, 182
   Law 2011-88, 179
   Law 2016-61, 74, 160
   Law 2018-50, 74, 161
   Law 68-7, 70
   Law 75-40, 70
Lawyers without Borders (ASF), Tunisia, 194–95
Lebanon, 31
legal actors
   in autocracies, 32
   in Morocco, 131, 136–37, 210
   in Tunisia, 188, 193–95, 197
   migrants' rights, role in, 210
legalistic explanations to immigration policymaking, 107
legitimation strategies
   as driver of immigration policies, 30, 198
   CNDH report as, Morocco, 98
   Moroccan liberalization as, 30, 92, 94, 107
   selectorate, support by, 212
   Tunisian democratization as, 30, 147, 166, 189, 192, 197
liberalism, as global norm, 38–40
Liberia, 81
Libya
   civil war, 73
   Libyan children in Tunisia, 186
   Libyan immigration in Tunisia, 10, 145, 148, 166, 173, 199
   political crisis, 68–69
   Tunisian migrants in, 60
Lijan al-Ahya (neighbourhood committees, Tunisia), 50

Index

M'nemty (My Dream), Tunisia, 151, 162, 180
Maghreb Social Forum, 89
makhzen, bilad al (lands of sovereignty), 44–45, 126
Malaysia, 28, 164
Mali, 64, 67, 133
Maltese labourers, in Tunisia, 64
Maroc Hebdo, 85
Marxist approaches to the state, 25, 35
Marzouki, Moncef, 184–85
Mauritania, 54, 81–82, 193
May, Raouf el, 161
Médecins du Monde Belgique (MdM-B), 157, 181, 184–86
Media and Human Rights Observatory, Tunisia, 155
Mediterranean Sea, migrant crossings, 147, 159, 178, 180
Melilla, Morocco, 87–88, 105, 109
Members of Parliament (MPs), Tunisia
　CSOs relationship with, 185
　depoliticization of immigration, role in, 166, 169
　returned exiles, role of, 145–46, 169–70
Mexico, 36–37, 42
Mhenni, Hadi, 143
migrant associations
　in Morocco, 86–87, 104, 114–15, 122, 124, 127–28, 160, 214
　in Tunisia, 178, 203
migrant categorization, 101–2, 200–1
Migrant Platform (PFM), Morocco, 87
migrant unions, in Morocco, 128–29
Migrant Week (Semaine des Migrants), Morocco, 126, 128
migrant workers
　in Morocco, 128–29
　in Tunisia, 179–80, 183–84, 186, 192–93
Migrant'scène festival, Morocco, 106
migration diplomacy, 36–38, 76
migration externalization, 4, 23, 35, 83, 124, 143, 166
migration regime, 22
migration working group, EU-Tunisia, 191
Migreurop, 86, 109
Ministry for Moroccans Residing Abroad (MRE), 62, 117
Ministry in Charge of Moroccans Residing Abroad and Migration Affairs (MCMREAM)
　asylum law, role in, 103
　budget limitations, 100–1
　CGEM, partnership with, 135
　civil society market, role in, 123
　coordinating role, 119
　creation of, 75–76
　CSOs, partial cooperation with, 124–27
　Directorate for Migration Affairs, creation of, 99
　downgrading of, 76
　funding of, 102, 202
　future of, 139
　institutional power of, 110, 117–19
　IOs, relationship with, 132–33
　migrant children in schools, policy on, 104
　political irrelevance, 121
　regularization, civil society role in, 115
Ministry of Education (MoE), Morocco, 75
Ministry of Employment and Professional Training (MoEPF), Tunisia, 157, 174, 193
Ministry of Finance (MoF), Tunisia, 41, 71, 157, 159, 174, 176, 184
Ministry of Foreign Affairs (MoFA), Morocco
　BRA, incorporation of, 81, 110
　MCMREAM, integration of, 76, 101, 119, 121
　MoI, turf wars with, 117–18
　UNHCR Headquarters Agreement, 89
Ministry of Foreign Affairs (MoFA), Tunisia
　EU, relationship with, 187
　MoI, conflict with, 174–75
　MoSA, turf wars with, 172, 175
　under Ben Ali, 189
　UNHCR Headquarters Agreement, 142
　visa requirements, 158
Ministry of Health (MoH), Morocco, 75, 102, 118–19, 124, 132
Ministry of Health (MoH), Tunisia, 176, 184, 189
Ministry of Higher Education (MoHE), Tunisia, 153, 174, 177–78, 184, 193
Ministry of Justice (MoJ), Morocco, 118
Ministry of Justice (MoJ), Tunisia, 149, 159–60, 165, 174, 191, 194
Ministry of Labour (MoL), Morocco, 91
Ministry of Social Affairs (MoSA), Tunisia, 72, 172, 175
Ministry of the Interior (MoI), Morocco
　as bad cop, 112
　draft law 26-14, rewriting of, 103
　Entraide Nationale, conflict with, 118
　immigration control as power, 29, 84
　institutional identity, 139
　MCMREAM, sidelining of, 119
　ministerial turf wars, 29, 117–18

304   Index

Ministry of the Interior (MoI), Morocco (cont.)
  monopoly on immigration control, 109–10
  regularization campaigns, 74–75, 112
  security operations, 137
  voluntary return program, 132
Ministry of the Interior (MoI), Tunisia
  asylum law, reluctance over, 150
  CSOs, relationship with, 179, 185
  hermetic isolation of, 176
  immigration, control over, 142, 144, 165, 167–68, 196
  informal regularization mechanisms, 157
  inter-institutional relations, 174–77
  IOs, surveillance of, 189
  Libyan refugees, depoliticization in Tunisia, 154
  security approach, 73, 176–77
  veto power of, 197
  visa reform, resistance to, 158
mirror effect, 35, 96, 130, 160, 167, 169, 207–8
Mobility Partnership, EU-Tunisia/Morocco, 91, 147, 182
Mobutu Sese Seku, 81
Mohammed V, King of Morocco, 45
Mohammed VI, King of Morocco
  Africa policy, 31, 54–55, 76, 94, 107, 110, 131, 139, 206, 209
  Basri, Driss, dismissal of, 84
  civil society, reciprocal dependency, 115
  as Commander of the Faithful, 206
  as defender of women's rights, 138
  depolarization of immigration, role in, 121–22, 129
  as economic actor, 131, 136
  Equity and Reconciliation Commission, 47, 88
  Figuig refugee crisis, 112, 202
  as good cop, 112–13
  as liberal monarch, 11, 38, 47, 92–94, 98, 106, 111
  liberalization of immigration policy, role in, 2, 41, 74, 209–10
  on migrant rights in Europe, 97
  modernization agenda, 31, 107
  Moroccan bureaucracy, relationship with, 116
  UN evaluation report, response to, 97–98
  Yazami, Driss el, appointment to CNDH, 95
Moroccan Agency for International Cooperation (AMCI), 81

Moroccan Association for the Support and Promotion of Small Enterprises (AMAPPE), 89
Moroccan Association of Human Rights (AMDH), 46, 86–87, 98, 125, 127
Moroccan Association of Studies and Research on Migration (AMERM), 84
Moroccan Labour Union (UMT), 129
Moroccan Organization of Human Rights (OMDH), 46, 87, 89, 114, 124, 127
Moroccan security services, 112, 124, 127
Moroccans Residing Abroad (MRE), 62
Morocco
  ad-hocratic immigration governance, 102–5
  Africa policy, 11, 33, 88, 93–94, 106, 134, 216
  Algeria, tensions with, 11, 54, 82–83, 93, 112, 202
  Asian migrants in, 66
  authoritarian consolidation and controlled liberalization, 11, 45–48
  civil society dynamics, 26, 122–31
  colonial legacy, 34, 44–45, 53, 64, 70, 79–82, 107
  constitution 2011, 47, 95, 110, 137, 206
  COVID-19, response to, 77–78
  diaspora, 61–62, 86, 96–97
  economic actors in, 28, 134–36
  economy, 131, 135–36
  as emigration country, 35, 58–62, 93, 96–97, 107
  European migrants in, 64, 66, 71, 102
  European Union, relations with, 83–84, 88, 94, 215–16
  foreign policy, 107
  imigration policy origins, 79–82
  as immigration country, 63–66
  immigration as national undertaking, 120–22
  immigration policy in, 70–71, 106
  institutional dynamics, 90–91, 103, 115–20, 211–12
  IOs, role of, 131–33
  international reputation, 88
  legal actors, role of, 32, 131, 136–37, 210
  liberalization of immigration policy, 74–76
  liberalization, drivers of, 92–99
  liberalization, future of, 139
  monarchy, power of, 45–46, 53
  national identity, 53–55, 130, 205–6
  national security, immigration control as, 84–85
  pluralism, state reaction to claims of, 206–7

Index

policy incoherence in, 118–19
public opinion on migrants, 27, 41, 129–31
state formation dynamics, 44–48, 79
symbolic politics, liberalization as, 99–100
three-level games, in domestic and foreign policy, 36–37, 88, 92
Western and Central African migrants in, 64–66, 70
Mosbah, Saadia, 162
mudawana (family code), Morocco, 47, 137

National Agency for Employment and Independent Work (ANETI), Tunisia, 190
National Agency for the Promotion of Employment and Independent Work (ANAPEC), Morocco
labour market test, 75, 100, 119, 129
SNIA, role in implementation, 110
National Appeals Commission, Morocco, 113
National Commission to Fight Discrimination, Tunisia, 161
National Constituent Assembly (NCA), Tunisia, 56, 146, 160
National Council for Tunisians Abroad, 63
National Council of the Order of Physicians (CNOM), Morocco, 78
National Council on Human Rights (CNDH), Morocco
asylum law, role in, 95
bus company segregation, response to, 120
churches, public construction of, 131
COVID-19, response to, 77–78
CSOs, relationship with, 124–27
IOs, relationship with, 132
liberalization of immigration policy, role in, 74, 98, 110–11
long-term impact of, 139
monarchy, relationship with, 113–14
regularization process, role in, 112
Yazami, Driss el, influence of, 42, 96
National Day Against Racial Discrimination, Tunisia, 161
National Dialogue Quartet, Tunisia, 51, 182
national identity
conceptions of, 205–6
immigration policymaking, role in, 32–33, 225–28
Moroccan, 53–55, 130, 205–6
Tunisian, 55–57, 151–52, 205
National Migration Observatory (ONM), Tunisia, 63, 172, 175, 184
National Migration Strategy (SNM), Tunisia, 72–73, 148–49, 165, 172, 175, 184, 191–92
National Social Security Fund (CNSS), Tunisia, 157
National Strategy on Immigration and Asylum (SNIA), Morocco
creation of, 75
CSOs, role in, 126
dysfunctional implementation of, 110, 118–20
IOs, role in, 132–33
private sector, role in, 135
National Union of Popular Forces (UNFP), Morocco, 46
neighbourhood committees (Lijan al-Ahya, Tunisia), 50
Neo-Destour party, Tunisia, 49
neopatrimonialism
dynamics of, 20
in Morocco, 46
in Tunisia, 44–50
Network of Unions on Mediterranean and Sub-Saharan Migration (RSMMS), 183
neutral diplomacy, Tunisian, 57
Ngoy, Sabrine, 161
Nidaa Tounes Party, Tunisia, 51
Niger, 31
Nigeria, 64, 89
North America, migration policies, 22, 35
Nouicer, Radhouane, 42, 146

Office for Professional Training and Employment (OFPE), Tunisia, 62
Office for Professional Training and Work Promotion (OFPPT), Morocco, 91
Office for Tunisians Abroad (OTE), 63, 175
Oil Crisis, 1973, 60
Orient-Occident Foundation (FOO), Morocco, 89
Ouardiya detention centre, Tunisia, 142, 194–95

Pakistan, 33
Palestinian refugees
in Lebanon, 31, 200
in Tunisia, 67, 141, 216
party politics
immigration policymaking, role in, 25, 27, 215

party politics (cont.)
  in Morocco, 121–22
  in Tunisia, 166, 168, 170–71
patronage, systems of, 28
Perrault, Gilles, 46
Personal Status Code, Tunisia, 49
Philippines, 36
Platform of Sub-Saharan Associations and Communities in Morocco (ASCOMS), 123
police violence
  in Morocco, 71, 91, 93, 96, 105, 108, 134
  in Tunisia, 50
policy cycle, model of, 218–19
Polisario, 54, 83
political economy approaches to immigration policymaking, 22, 25–28, 40, 107, 139, 166, 226
political entrepreneurs, 42
political remittances, ambiguity of, Tunisia, 169
political sociology approaches to immigration policymaking, 7, 24, 28, 32, 224, 228
politicization of immigration
  migrant categorization, role in, 200–1
  regime strategies, role in, 198–200
  symbolic nature of, 201–2
politics of uncertainty, 31, 202
pragmatic neutrality (Tunisia's Libyan policy), 153–54
private schools, Libyan, in Tunisia, 153
private sector
  in Morocco, 131, 134–36
  in Tunisia, 57, 188, 192–93
private universities, 64, 67
public opinion
  autocracies, role in, 27
  in liberal democracies, 10, 222
  in Morocco, 27, 213
  in Tunisia, 27, 192

Rabat
  African embassies in, 133
  Labour Day march, 2012, 95
  Rabat Process, 88
  refugee sit-in, legal response to, 136
Rachidi, Hicham, 124
racism
  in Morocco, 55, 82, 85–86, 96, 131
  in Tunisia, 57, 150–51, 156, 160–63, 169–70, 180, 182, 185, 205, 213, 215
  institutionalized, 201
  law against, Tunisia, 74, 186
  slavery, legacy of, 86, 204

Red Crescent, 72, 77, 142, 173, 178, 182, 185
refugees
  in Morocco, 66, 89, 119
  in Tunisia, 67, 68, 141–42
  regularization of, Morocco, 104
regime effect
  boundaries of, 138, 196, 208, 224, 226–27
  in domestic politics, 212
  executive actors, role of, 31
  in immigration politics, 4–7
  international norms, influence of, 39
  international politics, role of, 215
  legal actors, role of, 31
  in modern nation states, 40
  in Morocco, 138, 210, 218
  in policy cycle model, 218–19
  in political economy and institutional dynamics, 24, 166
  in Tunisia, 196
regime-specific policy processes, in immigration policy, 9
registration of refugees, Morocco, 89
regularization campaigns, 2014 and 2017 in Morocco
  civil society, role in, 115
  legal situation of refugees, 104
  limited effects of, 100
  local regularization commissions, 112–13
  MoI security operations, 137
  post-campaign state violence, 105
  as progressive showcase, 74–75, 92–94, 201–2
  results of, 99
regularization mechanisms in Tunisia, 157, 163–64
remittances, economic impact of, 62–63
rent
  geopolitical or diplomatic, 37, 215
  rentierism, dynamics of, 20
research methodology, 15–16
residence permits
  in Morocco, 41, 100, 105, 119–20
  in Tunisia, 156–58, 160, 164, 168, 174, 176, 186
Rights and Liberties Commission of the Parliament, Tunisia, 185
Romdhani, Messaoud, 161
Royal Air Maroc (RAM), 135
royal cards (legal papers), Morocco, 99–100
Royal Institute for Amazigh Culture (IRCAM), Morocco, 54

Index

Sahrawi Arab Democratic Republic (SADR), 54–55
Sahrawi refugees, 89
Saied, President Kais, 52
Salafist assasinations, 2013, Tunisia, 51
Saudi Arabia, 27, 29
school buses, segregation, Tunisia, 151
securitarian approach to immigration
  in Morocco, 106, 109, 111, 122, 126, 139
  in Tunisia, 144, 148, 163, 178
Seddiki, Abdeslam, 100, 136
selectorate, 212
Senegal
  embassy, Tunisia, 190
  embassy sit-in, Morocco, 134
  Senegalese in Morocco, 64, 67, 81–82, 133–34
  Tunisia, bilateral agreements with, 141
  Tunisinan businesses in, 193
Senghor, Léopold Sédar, 141
siba, bilad al (lands of dissidence), 44
Sierra Leone, 64, 81, 89
silent disobedience, Tunisian-EU relations, 192
Singapore, 32
slavery and the slave trade, legacies of, 48, 55, 64, 86, 203–4, 219
small or medium enterprises (SMEs), in Morocco, 135
social services, access to
  in Morocco, 41, 75
  in Tunisia, 157
social theory, 20, 228
South Africa, 33–34
South Korea, 36–37, 41, 164, 196
sovereignty, as driver of immigration policies, 8, 30, 36, 198, 220
Spain
  Moroccan migrants in, 60
  Moroccan relations with, 37, 83
state
  concept of, 20
  fragmentation of policymaking in, 40–41
  immigration policymaking, role in, 28–32
  Marxist approaches to, 25
  permanent reinvention of, 204
  political economy approaches to, 25
state formation
  as ongoing process, 203–4
  in Morocco, 44–48, 79, 119
  in Tunisia, 44, 48–52, 167–68, 197
  mirror and demonstration effects, 207–8
  Moroccan liberalization, role in, 107
  national identity, conceptions of, 205–6

pluralism, claims for, 206–7
slavery and colonization, legacies of, 204–5
State Secretariat for Migration and Tunisians Abroad (SEMTE)
  bureaucratic reshuffling, role in, 172, 175
  civil society, relations with, 184
  coordinating role, 174
  creation of, 63, 72, 145, 147
  inter-ministerial cooperation, 165
  international actors, relations with, 189
  lack of resources, 202
  MoFA, relationship with, 188
  National Migration Strategy (SNM), 72–73, 148–49, 165, 172, 175, 184, 191–92
strange bedfellows, CSOs and IOs, 187
student immigration
  in Morocco, 64, 81
  in Tunisia, 67, 157, 159, 174, 176–78, 180, 186, 193
sub-Saharan African migrants
  ANAPEC procedure, exemption from, Morocco, 100
  discrimination against in Morocco, 82, 85, 121, 201, 204
  discrimination against in Tunisia, 150–52, 160–62, 190, 201, 204
  education, access to in Morocco, 104
  as irregular workers in Morocco, 180
  irregular stay penalties in Tunisia, 201
  politicization of in Morocco, 2, 221
  regularization in Morocco, 92, 96
  residence permits, access to in Morocco, 102
Sufi pilgrims, in Morocco, 64
Swiss Development Cooperation Agency (SDC), 88, 123, 191
symbolic politics, Moroccan liberalization as, 99–100, 107
Syrian refugees
  in Jordan and Lebanon, 31
  in Morocco, 66, 102, 104, 112, 202
  in Tunisia, 68
  in Turkey, 200

Taboubi, Noureddine, 184
Tamazight language, 53
Tampere Conclusions 1999, 83
Tangiers, Morocco
  migrant arrests and expulsions, 105–6
  migrant demonstrations, 134
Terre d'Asile Tunisie (TAT)
  advocacy for migrant protection, 72, 147
  COVID-19, response to, 77

Terre d'Asile Tunisie (TAT) (cont.)
  exemptions, negotiation of, 157–58
  irregular migrants, support for, 181
  joint civil society agenda, 182
  Libyan refugees, support for, 155
  Ouardiya detention centre, legal case, 194–95
  social media campaigns, 161
  state institutions, relations with, 184–85
  unionization of migrant workers, 183
Thailand, 28–29
theory-building in immigration policymaking
  bureaucratic politics approaches to, 25, 28, 40, 111, 209–12, 227
  controlled case comparisons, 12
  dependency theories, 35, 226
  domestic politics approaches, 25–28, 110, 212–15, 223
  foreign policy approaches, 35–38, 220, 223
  generic policy processes, 8, 40–43, 224
  globalization theory approaches, 23, 25, 38–40, 107
  hegemonic stability approaches, 35
  historical-culturalist approaches, 22, 25, 32–35, 40, 107, 204
  institutionalist approaches, 22, 28–32, 107, 138, 166–67
  international relations approaches, 23, 25, 35–38, 40, 107, 215–18
  issue specific immigration policy processes, 8–9, 225
  policy cycle model, 218–19
  political economy approaches, 22, 25–28, 40, 107, 139, 166, 226
  political sociology approaches, 7, 24, 28, 32, 224, 228
  regime specific policy processes, 9
  typology of immigration policy processes, 7–10, 224–27
  world systems approaches, 35, 226
three-level games
  as flexible foreign policy tool, 36–37
  European, African and domestic interests, 212, 216, 220, 225
  Moroccan, 36–37, 88, 92, 98, 106, 188, 198
  Tunisian, 166, 190
Tindouf refugee camp, Algeria, 89
Tiznit, Morocco, 121
Tlemçani, Abderrahman, 106
transit migration
  in migration studies, 20
  in Morocco, 84–85, 106, 216
  in Tunisia, 73
transnational advocacy networks, trade unions, 26
travel visas, as migration policy tool, 31
Troika governments, Tunisia, 51
Tunisia
  Africa policy, 57, 190
  Algerian refugees in, 33
  colonial legacy, 34, 140
  COVID-19, response to, 77
  democratic institutions in, 31, 168–69
  democratization, impact of, 10–11, 26, 162–63, 166–67
  depoliticization of immigration, 10–11, 34, 148, 152–53, 170–71, 196, 207
  diaspora, 62–63
  domestic politics, 150–52
  economic actors in, 28, 192–93
  economy of, 52, 158
  as emigration country, 35, 58–63
  EU, relations with, 143, 182, 187–88
  as Europe's border guard, 168
  European migrants in, 64, 68
  European Union, relations with, 215–16
  external agenda setting, response to, 189–92, 197
  foreign policy, 57, 140–41, 166
  government volatility, 171–73
  as immigration country, 63–64, 67–69
  institutional dynamics, 173–77
  legal actors in, 32, 197, 210
  Libyan refugees in, 10, 68–69, 72–73, 145, 153–56, 166, 173
  national identity, 55–57, 151–52, 205
  as "off shore state", 57
  political instability, 51–52
  political party landscape, 166, 168, 170–71
  power, diffusion of, 209–10
  public opinion on migration, 27
  refugee policy, 141–42
  state formation dynamics, 44, 48–52, 166–67
  three-level games, domestic and foreign policy as, 36–37, 166, 190, 220
  Western and Central African migrants in, 67–68, 150–52, 159–60, 182
Tunisian Association for the Support of Minorities (ATSM), 151, 180
Tunisian Association of Democratic Women (ATFD), 179, 195
Tunisian Constitutional Court, 195

Index

Tunisian Council for Refugees (CTR), 178, 181–82
Tunisian Forum for Economic and Social Rights (FTDES), 72, 77, 147, 161, 165, 179–80, 195
Tunisian League for Human Rights (LTDH), 51, 179, 184, 195
Tunisian Union of Industry, Trade and Crafts (UTICA), 51, 184, 190
Tunisians First policy, 11, 150–52, 163, 185
Tunisians Residing Abroad (TRE), 62, 169, 186
turf wars, bureaucratic
  in modern states, 225
  in Morocco, 29, 117–18, 211
  in Tunisia, 165, 172–73
  migration regime, role in, 22
Turkey, 30, 36–37, 200, 208, 226
two-level game, 36
typology of immigration policy processes, 7–10, 224–27

Ukraine, 36
Ummah, Islamic fraternity, 34
UN Human Rights Council, 127
UN International Migration Conference, Marrakesh 2018, 76
UNHCR
  CGEM partnership, Morocco, 135
  Choucha refugee camp, Tunisia, 145, 173, 180
  Headquarters Agreement, Morocco 2007, 88–90
  Headquarters Agreement, Tunisia 2011, 146
  IADH, cooperation with, Tunisia, 194
  in Morocco, 78, 90, 109, 119, 132–33, 136
  in Tunisia, 72, 141–42, 144, 153–54, 157, 165, 181–82, 189
  Libyan refugees in Tunisia, resettlement of, 68
  OMDH, cooperation with, Morocco, 137
  registration of asylum seekers, Morocco, 66
Union of African Leaders (ULA), Tunisia, 180
Union of Industry, Trade and Crafts (UTICA), Tunisia, 57, 193
Union Socialiste des Forces Populaires (USFP), Morocco, 85

unions, labour
  in Morocco, 128–29
  in Tunisia, 180–84
  transnational advocacy networks, role in, 26
United States, 37
U.S. State Department watch list, 159–60, 191

violence against migrants
  CSO denunciations of, Morocco, 122, 126–27
  legal response to, Morocco, 136
  in Morocco, 71, 76, 91, 99, 105–8, 113, 127
  in Tunisia, 169, 190
voluntary return program (IOM), 132, 188

war on terror, 50, 143
Welcome and Orientation Centres, Tunisia, 142
Western and Central Africa
  immigration policies in, 35
  migrants in Morocco, 71, 85–86
  migrants in Tunisia, 150–52, 159–60, 182, 184
Western liberal democracies
  civil society in, 26
  disproportionate attention to, in migration studies, 20, 23–24
  diversity and fragmentation of interests and actors, 210
  immigration policy theories on, 24
  immigration policymaking in, 5–7, 20, 22, 25
  legal actors in, 32
  regime effect, 6
  undeserving populations, oppression of, 5
Western Sahara, 33, 37, 54–55, 82–83, 89, 92, 107
Western state, the, 20
women's rights
  in Morocco, 47
  in Tunisia, 49
work permits
  in Morocco, 79, 91, 104, 136
  in Tunisia, 68, 157
World Health Organization (WHO), 72
World Organization Against Torture (OMCT), 195
World Refugee Day, 112

world systems approaches to immigration policymaking, 35, 226

Yazami, Driss el
as central figure in reform, 110, 208
CNDH, appointment to, 95
on construction of churches, 131
on migrant expulsions, 134
migrant unions, support for, 128
personality of, 42
as progressive opinion leader, 89
as refugee in France, 96
Years of Lead, Morocco, 46–47
Yemen, 66
Youssoufi, Abderrahmane, 46

Zaire, 64, 81
Zambia, 42
Zaouia, Khalil, 174
Zimbabwe, 158

Printed in the United States
by Baker & Taylor Publisher Services